PRACTICING COGNITIVE BEHAVIORAL THERAPY
With
Children and Adolescents

David J. Palmiter, Jr., PhD, ABPP, is professor, Department of Psychology and Counseling at Marywood University, Scranton, Pennsylvania, and a private practitioner. He is a board-certified clinical psychologist with over 25 years of experience working with children, adults, and families. He is a fellow of the American Psychological Association (APA), American Academy of Clinical Psychology, and the Pennsylvania Psychological Association, for whom he is a past president. Dr. Palmiter is the author of more than 30 publications in peer-reviewed journals, professional newsletters, and invited book chapters, including such publications as *Professional Psychology: Research and Practice, Teaching of Psychology, American Journal of Orthopsychiatry, Psychological Reports,* and *The Pennsylvania Psychologist.* He was also a regular contributor to the APA Division 42 newsletter, *The Independent Practitioner,* where he wrote quarterly columns on practice with children, Internet applications, and social media. Additionally, he authored *Working Parents, Thriving Families: 10 Strategies That Make a Difference* (2011), an award-winning book on how parents can promote resilience in their children. Dr. Palmiter has given over 300 presentations at national professional conferences and regional continuing-education workshops. He has worked extensively with local and national media on parenting, including NPR, *U.S. News & World Report, USA Today, The Wall Street Journal,* and *kidsinthehouse.com.* Dr. Palmiter maintains a blog, hecticparents.com, as well as an active Twitter presence, @helpingparents. His primary website is helpingfamilies.com.

PRACTICING COGNITIVE BEHAVIORAL THERAPY
With
Children and Adolescents

A Guide for Students and Early Career Professionals

David J. Palmiter, Jr., PhD, ABPP

SPRINGER PUBLISHING COMPANY

NEW YORK

Springer Publishing Company, LLC
11 West 42nd Street
New York, NY 10036
www.springerpub.com

Acquisitions Editor: Nancy S. Hale
Composition: Westchester Publishing Services

ISBN: 978-0-8261-3118-8
e-book ISBN: 978-0-8261-3119-5

16 17 18 19 20 / 6 5 4 3 2

The author and the publisher of this Work have made every effort to use sources believed to be reliable to provide information that is accurate and compatible with the standards generally accepted at the time of publication. The author and publisher shall not be liable for any special, consequential, or exemplary damages resulting, in whole or in part, from the readers' use of, or reliance on, the information contained in this book. The publisher has no responsibility for the persistence or accuracy of URLs for external or third-party Internet websites referred to in this publication and does not guarantee that any content on such websites is, or will remain, accurate or appropriate.

Library of Congress Cataloging-in-Publication Data

Names: Palmiter, David J., Jr., author.
Title: Practicing cognitive behavioral therapy with children and adolescents : a guide for students and early career professionals / David J. Palmiter, Jr.
Description: New York, NY : Springer Publishing Company, LLC, [2016] | Includes bibliographical references.
Identifiers: LCCN 2016005621 | ISBN 9780826131188 (hard copy : alk. paper) | ISBN 9780826131195 (e-book)
Subjects: | MESH: Cognitive Therapy—methods | Child | Adolescent | Counseling—methods | Professional-Family Relations
Classification: LCC RJ505.C63 | NLM WS 350.2 | DDC 618.92/891425—dc23 LC record available at http://lccn.loc.gov/2016005621

Special discounts on bulk quantities of our books are available to corporations, professional associations, pharmaceutical companies, health care organizations, and other qualifying groups. If you are interested in a custom book, including chapters from more than one of our titles, we can provide that service as well.

For details, please contact:
Special Sales Department, Springer Publishing Company, LLC
11 West 42nd Street, 15th Floor, New York, NY 10036-8002
Phone: 877-687-7476 or 212-431-4370; Fax: 212-941-7842
E-mail: sales@springerpub.com

Printed in the United States of America by McNaughton & Gunn.

*This book is dedicated to my supervisees, past, present, and future.
To me, as you bumble and tumble and strive and screech and find the art
and healer within you, you are beauteous beauties who gift me
more than I gift you. Thank you for allowing me to travel with you
for a brief time and for helping me to find the art and teacher within me.*

CONTENTS

Foreword by Edward J. O'Brien   xi
Preface   xvii

1 Introduction   *1*
  Remarks for Trainees and Early Career MHPs   *1*
  Conventions in This Volume   *4*
  Parent-Lunatics   *6*
  Positive Ethics   *8*
  Multiculturalism   *9*

Section I: Establishing the Foundation

2 The Initial Evaluation   *19*
  The Framework of the Evaluation   *19*
  The Preinterview Work   *21*
  The Office   *21*
  The Initial Interview   *22*
  Individual Interview With the Kid   *31*
  Work in Between Sessions   *32*
  Evaluating Suicidal Ideation   *32*

3 Feedback and Treatment Planning   *39*
  Feedback Session   *39*
  Treatment Planning   *46*
  Types of Treatment Contracts   *52*

4 Techniques for Facilitating Adherence and
  Responding to Resistance   *57*
  Facilitating Adherence   *57*
  Responding to Resistance   *66*

Section II: Engaging the Youth

5 Externalizing the Problem   *79*
  Explanation   *81*
  Additional Commentary   *90*
  Intervention Tracking Log   *92*

6   Behavioral Activation and Sleep Hygiene   *95*
    The Modular Treatment Approach   *95*
    Behavioral Activation   *96*
    Sleep Hygiene   *105*

7   Physiological Calming and Mindfulness   *111*
    Physiological Calming   *111*
    Measuring Relaxation   *118*
    Mindfulness Strategies   *121*

8   Coping/Happy Thoughts, Gratitude, and
Crisis = Pain + Opportunity   *127*
    Beginning Sessions   *127*
    Coping Thoughts   *128*
    Gratitude   *133*
    Crisis = Pain + Opportunity   *138*

Section III: Engaging the Parent(s)

9   Parent Integration and Special Time   *147*
    Timing of the Parent Session   *147*
    Preparing the Kid for the Parent Session   *148*
    The Parent Consultation   *152*
    Funeral Exercise   *159*
    Additional Parent Sessions   *162*

10   Thought Testing and the Serenity Prayer   *167*
    Thought Testing   *167*
    Serenity Prayer   *176*

11   Problem Solving   *183*
    Problem Solving in a Family Session   *183*
    Problem Solving in an Individual Session   *191*

12   Establishing and Growing Strengths and Acts of Kindness   *199*
    Establishing a Foundation   *199*
    Strengths Development Plan   *201*
    Teaching About WAIT   *206*
    Acts of Kindness   *207*

13   Defiant Kids   *213*
    Setting a Context   *213*
    Parent Work With Kids Age 12 and Under   *215*
    Parent Work With Kids Age 13 and Older   *223*
    Punishment   *228*

Section IV: Final Phase and Termination

14 Using Exposures   *235*
        Engaging the Kid   *235*
        Engaging the Parent   *240*
        Exposure Nuances   *241*
        Sessions Going Forward   *243*
        Nuances With Other Populations   *247*

15 Termination and Booster Sessions   *251*
        Context   *251*
        Introducing Termination to a Kid   *252*
        Introducing Termination to the Parents First   *257*
        Introducing Termination to Parents Second   *259*
        The Last Session Prior to Starting Booster Sessions   *260*
        Booster Sessions   *261*

Section V: Surprising Events and Special Circumstances

16 Surprising Events With Kids   *271*

17 Surprising Events With Parents   *287*
        A Pattern of Interfering Transference   *298*

18 Should You or Should You Not?   *301*

Appendices

A   *Intake Forms   315*
B   *Family Psychiatric History Forms   323*
C   *Developmental History Form   327*
D   *Interpersonal Inventory   343*
E   *Sentence Completion Tasks   345*
F   *Individual Interview With the Youth   351*
G   *Lethality Evaluation Form   355*
H   *Treatment Plan Form   357*
I   *Intervention Tracking Log   359*
J   *Recommended Resources   361*

Index   363

FOREWORD

One of the best students I ever taught (I will call her Robyn) went on to a doctoral training program in clinical psychology a number of years ago. This student was very smart in both academic and practical intelligence, showed great self-awareness of her own strengths and weaknesses, had a strong ethical compass, and was very dedicated to developing her professional abilities. A year after she started her doctoral program, I was happy that she agreed to come back to my class and talk about life in her doctoral program and about her experience in treating her first client. This first client had many social anxieties and some depressive symptoms; Robyn described what seemed like very appropriate cognitive behavioral strategies with this client that were delivered in the context of a positive humanistic relationship. The client got much better during therapy, which was a very encouraging experience for Robyn. However, Robyn ended her presentation to my class on a less upbeat note as she told the class that she didn't know what it was she had done that was helpful for the client and she was worried because she wasn't sure if her next client would replicate her initial client success or turn out to be a horrible failure and prove that Robyn had chosen the wrong career. I believe that I now have a solution for her!

David J. Palmiter's book, *Practicing Cognitive Behavioral Therapy With Children and Adolescents*: *A Guide for Students and Early Career Professionals,* will not eliminate the universal experience of new therapists feeling like imposters, but it will go a long way toward providing a conceptual and practical framework that the therapist in training and early career mental health professional can use to anchor the early stages of learning how to work with children and adolescents. Although this book is focused on students in practicum training and those new to child and adolescent clinical work, I believe it will also be a great resource for many practicing child clinical psychologists. Palmiter has clearly put in his 10,000 hours of preparation in coming to write this book and has accumulated a wonderful mix of clinical acumen that he combines with a careful and deep awareness of evidence-based practice issues. Dr. Palmiter's clinical work with children and adolescents puts him in the category of what Skovholt and Jennings (2004) called "Master Therapists." As mental health clinicians we often hear of each other's work, and some individual clinicians "rise to the top" in terms of their work, achieving exceptional successes with their clients. Over the years I have heard many stories of Dr. Palmiter's work that describe children being brought back to a successful life path after having suffered from seemingly impossible mental health problems. Palmiter's book illustrates one of the characteristics of "Master Therapists" in the depth and passion of his seeking and integrating sources of knowledge to offer help to his clients. His book integrates the core of the cognitive behavioral model with insights derived from psychodynamic, positive psychology; philosophical writings; and spiritual writings. In this book, Reik's (1948) "listening with the third ear" meets B. F. Skinner's token economy (Skinner, Jordan, Wagner, & Hall, 1972).

This book is simultaneously both very conceptual and very practical. I have taught graduate-level cognitive behavioral therapy (CBT) courses for more decades than I choose to recall, and Palmiter's book includes the entire pantheon of evidence-based CBT treatments (e.g., relaxation training, cognitive reframing, exposure therapy, mindfulness, token economies, and behavioral contracting). He also integrates cutting-edge work in positive psychology into the conceptual model for this work (e.g., gratitude lists and visits, identification of and building on character strengths). This wide-ranging conceptual work is matched, point by point, with practical examples and narratives that vivify how therapists can enact these interventions in work with a wide variety of child and adolescent presenting symptoms. It is these practical elements that will be of most help (and perhaps will be the most challenging as well, as they model a very high standard of care) to clinicians in training. This book will not replace a good introductory course in CBT. However, students with a strong introductory knowledge of CBT will find this book to be a great complement to such an introduction as the trainee learns to implement these evidence-based therapies in practicum experiences with clients.

An essential starting point in the Palmiter approach is illustrated in the carpenter's axiom: "Measure Twice: Cut Once." So much in the world of psychotherapy, at least as practiced in public mental health programs and in settings that are constricted by insurance policies that limit the quality of care, involves a "fly by the seat of your pants" approach. Clients are screened, determined to be eligible for care, and then the therapy begins. In contrast, Palmiter's work involves a careful case formulation that is based on an in-depth analysis of the child or adolescent client, his or her family, and school settings (and other relevant settings) in which the client lives. School records are accumulated, previous mental health treatments and diagnoses of both the child and her or his parents are examined, medical issues are considered, rating scales describing the behavior of the child client are completed, and diagnostic interviews and at least screening-level mental health assessments are completed by the parents. Out of this extensive set of client and family information comes a diagnostic case formulation, an individualized understanding of the sources of the client's problems and strengths, and the development of treatment plans and goals that will guide at least the initial stages of the treatment (subject to revision, depending on how well the treatment progresses based on these initial formulations). Palmiter's work here is consistent with best practices in medicine where many elaborate tests might be ordered to correctly diagnosis a patient's cancer before determining appropriate surgery, chemotherapy, and/or radiation therapy. Much of the magic in the outcomes Palmiter and his student therapists achieve follows from the careful diagnostic and case formulation work that is the focus of the first few weeks of the therapy.

This work is presented in a very human and personal manner. Palmiter shows how CBT always relies on the development of a thoughtful, positive, empathic, and genuine relationship with clients. Some who are not well trained in CBT caricature this approach as a collection of therapeutic interventions applied in an impersonal or mechanical manner. Anyone well trained in CBT knows that from the outset people like Aaron Beck insisted that relationship issues (in the form of the Rogerian triad, for example) are a crucial part of cognitive therapy (e.g., Beck, Rush, Shaw, & Emery, 1979). In addition, those with experience in CBT know that there is nothing so important in building a positive relationship with clients as when the therapist presents specific strategies that begin to help them overcome the problems that brought them into treatment.

Palmiter's approach is in keeping with the most current best practices in CBT in that it is module focused rather than manual focused (e.g., Barlow et al., 2011). Fifteen years ago, evidence-based therapy in CBT was somewhat equated with manual-focused therapy. Many dozens of treatment manuals (hundreds of which exist today) were developed for disorder after disorder on the assumption that most clients come into therapy with *either* anxiety *or* depression. Clinicians often complained that these manuals made little sense, as it was much more common for clients to be polysymp-tomatic when they entered treatment—more likely to be suffering from *both* anxiety *and* depression (e.g., Brown, Campbell, Lehman, Grisham, & Mancill, 2001). Barlow and Palmiter have taken the point of view that the clinician can achieve the best out-comes by flexibly applying a set of modules that have been shown to be effective for the particular symptoms being uniquely experienced by each client (e.g., behavioral activation for depression, exposure for anxiety). I can't think of an evidence-based therapy approach that has been widely validated in the past 30 years that is not inte-grated into Palmiter's book.

An important feature in this book is that each treatment module comes with tai-lored self-monitoring forms that provide a way to promote change and continuously evaluate progress. It is up to the clinician to link the treatment modules to a concep-tualization of the client's underlying problems and determine how and when these modules should be deployed. For example, Palmiter describes the value of deploying behavior therapy techniques early in therapy to decrease acting-out problems and then later deploying more cognitive strategies to deal with the client's depression. Perhaps if the initial behavioral interventions are successful in reducing acting-out behavior, the depressive symptoms may also go away, or at least be decreased (there is nothing more depressing than the "attention" that acting-out teenagers get from "the system").

Some clinicians in training (and clinical trainers) may question the specificity of Palmiter's intervention examples. However, these examples are presented in a very creative and clear manner, with the intervention wording presented in verbatim detail and then clearly annotated as to the rationale for each element of the interven-tion. I generally agree with the rationale for this training approach where clinicians should first overlearn basic skills of client engagement, reframing, problem solving, and so forth, and then later on evolve their own individualized intervention styles. Overlearning these basic skills as a core of one's practice (when these skills are based on a strong evidence-based foundation) will serve the student well when fac-ing new and unexpected challenges or during times of high levels of work stress. The child clinical psychologist who masters the methods in this book will be well served in dealing with a very wide variety of clinical problems, particularly those involving internalizing disorders such as anxiety and depression. This book is also clear in describing the limits of the methods presented (e.g., "simple" posttraumatic stress can be treated with these methods, "complex trauma" symptoms require additional work that is beyond the scope of this book).

This book is based on an in-depth understanding of our current thinking about taking an *evidence-based practice* approach. Evidence-based practice is an oft-repeated mantra in today's world of training and practice in clinical psychology, and yet I often find that students and professionals in the field have no in-depth understanding of what actually constitutes such practice. I once was part of a clinical qualifying exam where a student explained that his interpersonal approach to a client's problem was evidence based because he found a case study article where someone had once used this approach with a client carrying the same diagnosis as the student's client (ignoring meta-analyses of the many dozens of successful clinical trial outcome studies using a CBT approach with the same client problems). The American Psychological Association has evolved, along with the field of medicine more generally, in understanding the complexities of what defines evidence-based practice (or what we used to call *empirically validated therapies*; APA Presidential Task Force on Evidence-Based Practice, 2006). Palmiter's approach is consistent with the best current thinking about evidence-based treatment. Where the evidence is overwhelming (e.g., utilizing exposure treatments for most anxiety symptoms, cognitive reframing for emotional disorders more generally), it would be rather poor practice to not at least consider employing modules derived from this clinical "toolbox." And yet, the complexity of the clients we treat requires a *great deal* of flexibility in determining which of these tools best fit our idiographic case formulation of the individual client. An evidence-based outlook also informs us that we can sometimes do the best for our clients by recognizing that they are low on a scale of readiness for change. Rather than burning ourselves out as we attempt to achieve treatment goals that the client is not ready to work on, Palmiter wisely follows the clinical maxim that in successful therapy the therapist should not be working harder than the client.

Not only does this book mirror and expand upon the best CBT writings, but Palmiter's writing brings in a considerable amount of evidence-based material from the best empirically supported work in the broader field of psychotherapy, as described in books such as *Bergin and Garfield's Handbook of Psychotherapy and Behavior Change* (Lambert, 2013). Palmiter has read widely in the psychotherapy literature and integrates many insights into this book from diverse points of view such as humanistic, psychodynamic, and interpersonal approaches.

This is a magical book (not only in its liberal citation of magic tricks that Dr. Palmiter uses to help engage even the most resistant child and adolescent clients). It is full of humor, appropriate self-disclosure (and a discussion of guidelines to define what is appropriate vs. inappropriate self-disclosure), and humanity. For example, Palmiter describes himself as a "parent-lunatic" filled with all the worries that parenting brings in today's overscheduled and complicated world of online social networking and cyberbullying. Awareness of his own issues as a parent helps him normalize the intense anxieties that parents bring into therapy for their children.

In addition to clearly presenting a cornucopia of clinical skills, this book provides a glimpse into the intense dedication and humane concern for client well-being that is the core of the best clinical work.

Edward J. O'Brien, PhD
Director of Clinical Training, PsyD Program
Marywood University
Scranton, PA

REFERENCES

APA Presidential Task Force on Evidence-Based Practice. (2006). Evidence-based practice in psychology. *American Psychologist, 61*(4), 271–285. doi:10.1037/0003-066X.61.4.271

Barlow, D. H., Farchione, T. J., Fairholme, C. P., Ellard, K. K., Boisseau, C. L., Allen, L. B., & Ehrenreigh-May, J. (2011). *Unified protocol for transdiagnostic treatment of emotional disorders. Therapist guide.* New York, NY: Oxford University Press.

Beck, A. T., Rush, A. J., Shaw, B. F., & Emery, G. (1979). *Cognitive therapy of depression.* New York, NY: Guilford Press.

Brown, T. A., Campbell, L. A., Lehman, C. L., Grisham, J. R., & Mancill, R. B. (2001). Current and lifetime comorbidity of the DSM-IV anxiety and mood disorders in a large clinical sample. *Journal of Abnormal Psychology, 110*(4), 585–599.

Lambert, M. J. (2013). *Bergin and Garfield's handbook of psychotherapy and behavior change* (6th ed.). New York, NY: Wiley.

Reik, T. (1948). *Listening with the third ear: The inner experience of a psychoanalyst.* New York, NY: Farrar, Straus, & Giroux.

Skovholt, T. M., & Jennings, L. (2004). *Master therapists: Exploring expertise in therapy and counseling.* Boston, MA: Pearson Education.

Skinner, B. F., Jordan, P., Wagner, B. R., & Hall, E. (1972). *Token economy: Behaviorism applied.* Carlsbad, CA: McGraw-Hill Films, CRM Productions.

PREFACE

Were I to use one word to describe why I wrote this book, I would use "frustrations." You kindly and whimsically ask, "Why Dr. Palmiter, of what frustrations do you speak?" I reply that they number thusly:

1. Despite completing bountiful doses of relevant coursework before seeing real child or teen clients for the first time, most therapist-trainees have zero clue what to actually say or do when offering evaluations and treatment to children, teens, and parents. This creates terrible anxiety. And it has been this way ever since Freud started analyzing Anna's dreams! It's like some sort of cruel hazing that all psychotherapy trainees are made to endure. It really doesn't have to be this way. And as I can't find a single book that addresses this concern by offering step-by-step instructions, I've written this one.

2. Despite wonderful and flourishing developments in the field of positive psychology, and bountiful evidence having been generated regarding what promotes resilience and happiness in children, teens, and families, there doesn't appear to be a single book available that helps clinicians to offer positive psychology interventions to children and teens. There are plenty of parenting books that help parents to promote happiness and resilience in their kids; I know, I've written one. But there are no volumes that I can find that help therapist-trainees integrate positive psychology into cognitive behavioral therapy. So, imagine a parent said this to a therapist: "I really appreciate that you've done this cognitive behavioral therapy with my kid to heal his depression. It's been wonderful! Thank you! Now, because you rock so much, I need to ask, do you have any therapy you can offer to him to promote his happiness?" If that trainee looked on her bookshelf or on Amazon for help, she'd end up sucking air.

3. Despite earning graduate degrees in how to do psychotherapy, and despite years of doing clinical work with youth, the number 1 (with a bullet) question that clinicians ask me at workshops regarding child and adolescent clinical work is (paraphrasing), "What can I do about these pain-in-the-ass parents?" The number 1a question is, "How can I help, and not strangle, resistant kids?" Think about the unique problem we have as mental health professionals (MHPs) serving youth and their parents. If a mom takes her kid to a pediatrician for a wellness check, she is unlikely to say, "Ah, you can examine her, but

not with a stethoscope!" Or, if a dad needs to have his son's cavity treated, it's unlikely he'll say to his dentist, "Nah, you can't use a drill, but you can use a flower. I'm really looking for a dentist who does flower drilling with kids." Is there another class of clinicians who deals with as much resistance as MHPs? And my experience at workshops suggests that many experienced MHPs, never mind trainees, are left wondering how to respond effectively. Try searching for a book that offers help. It's like looking for a unicorn that speaks Greek.

4. One of the earlier subtitles for this book was "OMG, What Would I Do if My Client____?!" That title didn't get past my sage acquisitions editor at Springer Publishing Company, Nancy S. Hale. But that wording addresses another common source of freaking out among trainees: how to respond when parents or kids do surprising things, as they so often do, beguiling and mysterious beings that they are. I can't find any texts that cover this topic. So, I wanted to address that because I'm really not into the whole hazing/rite-of-passage/sadomasochistic/let's-let-them-freak-out-so-we-can-be-their-rescuer-and-show-how-wise-we-are supervision model.

5. I've been doing clinical supervision for more years than I care to admit. (This is probably the same reason I can't yet allow myself to put the AARP magazines that are delivered to me in my waiting room. Notice, I say "delivered to me" and not "my" magazines.) Grizzled vet that I am, there are two frustrations that I commonly experience when doing supervision that I'm hoping this book will alleviate for me and others of my kind. First, I feel bad as students struggle to write down example phrasing I offer to them regarding what they can say to parents, children, and teens. If you're a supervisor, or your first supervision experiences are now in your rearview mirror, you know what I mean. It seems necessary but not right. So, I just want to provide specific language that folks can adopt or adapt and by doing so (hopefully) reduce the amount of panicky transcription that goes on in supervision meetings. Second, I want to spend time in supervision going over case material. That's where the big-time learning takes place. With this book available, students can read the relevant didactic material between supervisions and (hopefully) create more time for specific case reviews.

6. The evidence suggests that most kids experience some kind of a mental health problem by the time they reach adulthood. However, only about a quarter to a third of them get any professional help for it. And among those that get help, most suffer for years first; when they finally go for help, they often don't get the kind of care that a steely-eyed behavioral scientist would consider to be state of the art. While there are plenty of books and treatment manuals that cover evidence-based interventions for youth, I've found none that are as specifically prescriptive as I think is most helpful to those MHPs who want to improve their evidence-based game.

Frustrations aside, I'm writing this book for two other reasons, the second of which is my top motivation.

1. I wish to contribute to the small but growing evidence base indicating that using magic in clinical work with youth can be a wonderful way to facilitate an alliance, respond to resistance, and make clinical teaching points more approachable. In using magic when doing clinical work with youth, I feel like someone panning for gold who has found a mostly undiscovered and bountiful stream. I just keep finding more and more uses for it. So I'd like to share some of these insights.

2. I'm a meaning junkie. And I take great meaning from helping MHPs in their missions to understand, heal, and advance the mental health of children, teens, and their families. Such MHPs do the work of angels, and I so very much enjoy being a support. Most contemporary authors don't make much money. But if we're lucky and have well understood our readers' needs, we make lots of meaning.

So, ready to go? Okay, let's get after it!

CHAPTER 1

Introduction

This chapter is the most eclectic in this volume. Here I (a) make some opening remarks for mental health professionals (MHPs) and trainees who are new to doing cognitive behavioral therapy (CBT) and positive psychology (PP) treatments with kids suffering from an internalizing disorder, (b) describe a few conventions in this volume, (c) review a concept I call "parental lunacy," and (d) make some overview comments regarding positive ethics and multiculturalism.

REMARKS FOR TRAINEES AND EARLY CAREER MHPs

Even a thief takes 10 years to learn his trade.
—Japanese proverb

This book is designed to be helpful to anyone who endeavors to apply CBT and PP interventions with kids, no matter the clinician's or the trainee's level of experience. These interventions are very effective in treating internalizing disorders. In this volume, I take you to the point of first contact through termination and booster sessions, offering specific steps and language to use all along the way. I also cover the common challenges that come up when doing this sort of clinical work as well as what MHPs can do to proactively reduce the odds that those challenges occur.

However, before I get to all that I want to address trainees, and those who are still finding their clinical legs, and talk about a common phenomenology among those new to working clinically with kids: self-doubt and insecurity.

I have an acute memory of three points in my training: my first class, my first practicum client, and the first time I did on-call work by myself. These memories are acute because, in each instance, I was terrified.

My first class was within the PhD program in clinical psychology at George Washington University (GWU). The faculty there, throughout the interview process, noted that they tended to get over 300 applications for eight openings each year. I don't know if they said this to comfort us (i.e., "If you're one of the more than 292 yuck-a-bucks we reject, don't take it personally"), to imply that what they were offering was special ("People really, really like us"), or just because they had to say something as we were nervously eating our doughnuts. But they said it a lot, or so it seemed at the time. So, when I got in, and later sat there waiting for my first class to begin, several thoughts went through my mind: "I've perpetrated a massive fraud." "These other seven people are *a lot* smarter than you, so watch what you say." "What would the faculty think if they found out that this was the *only* doctoral program I got into?" "What happens if I can't cut it?" Any of this sound familiar?

My first client was at the counseling center at GWU, at the start of my second year in the program. Of course, completing four undergraduate years of psychology and one year of graduate training left me with exactly NONE of the information I needed to be a therapist, or at least that's how it felt at the time. Sure, I had survived a year of graduate-level classes, but now my fraudulent status would surely become impossible to hide. I so well remember my first-ever supervision session, which occurred before my first-ever intake. I went in prepared to take copious notes on what I should say or do with my first-ever client. However, and despite my pleas, my supervisor kept repeating various versions of "Just go do the interview and then we'll talk about it later." I flashed to the image of a sadistic father throwing his child into the middle of a cold lake and maniacally laughing as he trumpeted, "Swim, you little s**t!" What I didn't say—for fear of having her realize how incompetent I was—was "I HAVE NO CLUE HOW TO DO THE INTERVIEW!" But, she was insistent. So I left the supervision anxiously resolved to do my best. However, my anxiety reached a completely new (and previously unknown to me) height when I saw the S-word on the form. That's right: "suicidal." "OMG," I thought, "now I'm actually going to end up killing somebody!" I then proceeded to break the world's record for "most-amount-of-research-done-on-how-to-conduct-a-suicide-evaluation-within-a-24-hour-period." I put the key points of my learning on yellow sticky pads that I positioned around the office in places I could see but the client could not (again trying to avoid being found out to be a fraud).

I did my first on-call work during my postdoctoral year. (How completely foreign it felt to not have any more hoops to jump through. I remember thinking, "Who am I if not a circus pony jumping through the next hoop for his masters in order to earn my feed bag for the day?") I was working full-time in a community mental health center in Norwich, New York, and I had to take my share of on-call. You would think that my 4 years of practicum, across six to eight sites, and my full-time year of internship would leave me relaxed about such a duty. It didn't. Again, I had imposter thoughts and fears about killing someone.

Why do I share these vignettes with you? Because I bet you can relate. This isn't because I imagine that you and I are uniquely neurotic. This is because my 20-plus years of training others have taught me that these kinds of thoughts and fears are normative among trainees. They just aren't always openly acknowledged and discussed. So I've written this book to help you along in your desire to work effectively and meaningfully with children, teens, and their families. I'm going to provide you with *very specific* instructions on how to do what when, as well as how to think about, and respond to, situations when the fecal matter hits the fan. I will also explain the underlying principles for the specific steps as I go.

I'd like to make one other point about the efficacy of this work. When I attended GWU in the late 1980s, the training was exclusively psychodynamic. I don't know how much the doubt we trainees were experiencing about the efficacy of the therapeutic enterprise was secondary to GWU's training model (i.e., the benefit typically takes more time to accrue in insight-oriented treatments), or perhaps just about all trainees wonder about this, but we all were very fretful about this question: "Does this s**t *really* work?" Of course, we all were too chicken to ask our supervisors, probably for fear of exposing our imposter status. However, I find contemporary trainees wonder the same thing about efficacy. Yes, everyone is exposed to the treatment outcome literature in lecture courses, and the accounts there are impressive, and you can find such references in the References and Bibliography section at the end of this chapter. But the question lingers. So, let me address that before we start: This s**t not only works, it usually works amazingly well! As a man, I'll never give birth to a child, but I've given rebirth to more people than I can begin to remember. I'll give you a quick example.

I was at a large Super Bowl party last year that probably had 200 adults and kids in attendance. As I was walking to the food table, a man and a woman stopped me. The woman said something like, "Dr. Palmiter, we wanted to just stop you and thank you for all you did for our son. He is so different now. The transformation is amazing"—the mom started to choke up—"He's just the boy we always knew he could be and we are just so grateful." The dad was misty-eyed and just nodded. She added, "So, thank you." I told them how touched I was, hugged them, and went on my way. But what was notable about that moment is that I didn't remember who they were. I didn't even recognize their faces. This isn't because I'm brain-damaged, despite what my teen children sometimes assert. My unfamiliarity with them occurred because outcomes like theirs happen so often that it's impossible to keep track of them all. People say things like, "Thank you for giving us our child back," and "Why isn't this stuff taught on maternity units in hospitals?" Just last week, a parent texted me, "You saved my daughter's life. I'm forever in your debt." The problem is not, "Does this stuff work?" The problem is, sometimes, "How do I process the large abundance of back-to-back, day-in-and-day-out meaning?"

In my informal surveys of kid MHPs, this is a common experience. There's nothing special about me. I'm the guy who got into only one doctoral program (and one doctoral internship). But I do have a God-given aptitude for this work, and I work very hard at learning and refining my craft. So, if you likewise have an aptitude for clinical work, and you likewise are willing to get after it, you'll also get to the highly rewarding place of wondering how to handle all of the meaning that comes your way. In this volume, it is my plan to give you many of the specific tools and techniques you'll need to get there.

By the way, for me, it took 2 years after I was licensed to feel like I had found my stride. If you count my undergraduate years, that's 12 years total. This brings to mind the proverb I used to open this chapter. So, if you're in doubt about your adequacy, and if you're in doubt about the efficacy of the kid clinical enterprise, and if you're frustrated by how slow your practical skill set seems to grow, and if you feel like academic classes aren't leaving you prepared to meet with other humans to do clinical work, *JOIN THE CLUB* . . . but, I'm here to tell you that it's glorious on the other side and worth every little bit of sacrifice and suffering you are now engaging in.

CONVENTIONS IN THIS VOLUME

Creativity is allowing yourself to make mistakes. Art is knowing which ones to keep.
—*Scott Adams*

The primary sections in this book are (a) laying the foundation for the interventions, (b) the clinical interventions for kids and parents, and (c) how to think about and respond to surprising events. The first section is all about establishing a good foundation for doing interventions, something that is too often missing in clinical work with youth. The second section regards the nuts-and-bolts of delivering healing. The third section covers evidence-based strategies for facilitating adherence and responding to resistance and surprising events. There are also a number of unique features of this volume:

► This volume integrates interventions from the PP literature with traditional CBT. Traditional clinical psychology asks the question: "How do we reduce or eliminate this pain?" PP asks the question: "How do we promote joy and meaning?" In my read of the extant literature regarding kids, the same factors that promote resilience in kids are the same ones that promote happiness and meaning. Actually, I wrote a book for parents on how to promote resilience in kids, deploying what I believe to be the top 10 strategies suggested by the extant science (i.e., *Working Parents, Thriving Families: 10 Strategies That Make a Difference*). In this book, I'm reviewing what MHPs can do to promote the same.

   We MHPs need to know how to heal pain as well as how to promote joy and meaning in kids, teens, and their families. Certainly, our clients who are in pain want both. However, the CBT literature is far more developed than the PP literature, across the age spectrum; fortunately, the resilience literature on kids allows for sage clinical extrapolations. Regardless of the state of the science, in the References and Bibliography section at the end of each chapter you will find the references that support the recommendations for each chapter.

► Beginning with Chapter 2, you will find specific wording on how to proceed clinically. I offer these scripts only because I have found that having samples of specific words to use comforts trainees. With each script I will include the rationale for why I say what I say. Please understand that I'm not looking to train a small army of MHPs to say things the same way I do; that would be weird and unproductive. Moreover, I fully expect that even those who quote these scripts verbatim will morph them into words that fit their own styles over time. These scripts simply offer a place to start.

▶ Whenever I use the words "kid," "kids," or "youth" I mean both children and teens. When I mean to speak about one of those subgroups I'll indicate such.

▶ Many of the interventions in this volume could be easily adapted for group treatments, both with kid groups and with parent groups.

▶ I'm going to vary chapters regarding whether the kid client is a male or a female. Aiden is the male and his parents are Tanisha and Bill. Monica is the female and her parents are Paula and Roberto. This is merely a writing convention.

▶ All volumes have important material that goes uncovered. For example, in the evaluation chapters I won't be presenting material on how to reach diagnostic closure (e.g., here's how the data look when rendering a diagnosis of generalized anxiety disorder) or how to do a lethality evaluation. Moreover, I will discuss multicultural issues only a little bit beyond this first chapter. There are only so many pages available, unfortunately.

I number among a small group of MHPs that are learning that magic can be a wonderful tool to use in kid clinical work. Hence, each chapter, starting with the next one, will include a sidebar instruction on how to use a magic trick with a kid client. I use magic for the following purposes:

• To enhance the alliance with kids. As I'll review in the evaluation chapter, most kids are either neutral or opposed to seeing an MHP. I've seen so many instances when sharing a few moments of magic causes a kid to relax and enjoy being in the consulting room. Moreover, I'll sometimes say to a kid as he's leaving, "Remind me next time and I'll show you my magic water bottle that won't pour water out unless I want it to."

• To weaken resistance-facilitating moods. Magic helps anxious kids to relax, angry kids to be amused, and depressed kids to smile. Magic is magical in this way.

• To teach kids a new prosocial skill. As I cover in Chapter 12, becoming good at something that others enjoy is a major resilience-promoting factor. As most kids enjoy a good magic trick, teaching a kid to do magic can promote self-esteem. Moreover, to be successful, magic tricks call for effective patter, which requires interpersonal engagement. It may be tough to incentivize a kid to learn things like nonverbal social skills when that kid has little or no interest in such. But, if that kid gets interested in magic and sees that such behaviors are essential to success in that hobby, such a kid can become motivated to do things like make eye contact. For example, an MHP can first arrange for a kid to do a magic trick for his mom on his own and then do it again, after he has been coached on how to deploy effective patter; the mom's feedback, and the kid's experience, both reinforce the value of the prosocial verbal and nonverbal cuing.

• To help to teach a kid a CBT principle, such as the value of shifting one's focus to positive memories (e.g., see Sidebar 8.1 in Chapter 8).

I continue to be delighted by the ways that other MHPs use magic in their practices, as can be witnessed by reviewing the references in the References and Bibliography section at the end of this chapter. For these reasons, each chapter has at least one sidebar at the end where I will teach you a magic trick that you can try with your kid clients.

Try some of these magic tricks with kids and I think you'll like what happens. And you might even decide to teach a supervisor, if she treats you well, a trick or two!

PARENT-LUNATICS

When I was a kid my parents moved a lot, but I always found them.
—Rodney Dangerfield

This is an excerpt from my aforementioned parenting book that reviews what I mean when I refer to parents as lunatics.

> I worked with parents and their children in a clinical setting for about 10 years before I had my first of 3.0 children (were I to count our Portuguese Water Dog I'd say 3.5 . . . though my wife says 4.0 as she counts both me and the dog). Until I had my first child, it seemed to me that the parents with whom I was working would, from time to time, temporarily lose their minds. This temporary insanity would occur in the context of us having established a good working relationship. The parents seemed to realize that I cared about them and their child. They also seemed to view me as competent and appeared invested in our shared goals for healing their child. Yet, despite all of this, they would occasionally distort something I said and become angry or hurt. They recovered quickly enough, usually by the next session, but this temporary "insanity" confused and troubled me. I usually didn't see it coming and had no clue what was causing it. Then I became a father and it became instantly clear: The average parent loves his child so much it makes him crazy.
>
> My wife and I suffered from infertility for 3 years before our first child, a girl, was conceived. When she was born it was like crawling out of hell and into Eden; we were instantly healed and indescribably elated. During the 9 months of pregnancy, my wife and I were obsessive in how much we studied, prepared, hoped, and worried; during the latter part of the pregnancy I would calm myself, and imagine what she would be like, by listening to the Elton John song "Blessed."

My eldest ended up being delivered by emergency C-section, which was maddening in itself. After she was delivered, I accompanied her and the nurse to the neonatal unit. As the nurse was prepping, I was allowed a few moments alone with my new baby. I offered her my little finger, which she began to suck on as the song "Blessed" played over the intercom (a gift from the Master Lover). In that moment I felt so much love that it hurt, and I found it difficult to breathe. While I had had experiences of intense love before, I had never experienced anything like this. Other loves in my life felt like some combination of exciting, gentle, and soothing waves I could either float or swim in as I chose. This love felt too powerful and big for me physically and mentally, like a huge and powerful wave that knocked me knees-over-elbows and carried me where it would. I still cannot describe or write about this experience without tears.

Later in the week, when my wife and I were readying for the discharge, we were filled with peace and patience. We also realized, and understood, that the discharge nurse had to review a number of things with us that were obvious: "Yes, when our daughter is crying we should consider feeding her, as that may mean she is hungry. Good health tip. Thank you."

"Make sure to change her diaper routinely."

"Yes, a good hygiene strategy. We appreciate that." And it went on like that for about 20 to 30 minutes. No problem because, as I said, we were in Eden.

Then, in the evening of our first night home, we found blood discharge in our baby's diaper. The madness that descended upon us was intense. Here we were, 3 years trying to have a baby, and there was something seriously wrong with her. It took me about 45 minutes to get the on-call pediatrician on the phone—45 minutes that felt like 2 days. After hearing the problem, the pediatrician immediately tried to be reassuring. He adopted a soft tone and said exactly this: "Dave, your daughter has just been born. She is still going through a lot of hormonal changes. Blood discharge from the vagina is common and not to be worried about."

My first-ever bout of parental lunacy—and I've since had hundreds of them—was to respond: "Well, if it's so blankety-blank common, how come that blankety-blank nurse at that blankety-blank hospital didn't mention this on that long list of blankety-blank obvious blankety-blank guidelines that she gave us!" Except I wasn't saying "blankety-blank."

Sensing that the real emergency was a psychiatric one, he tried to calm me with a joke: "Dave; relax, man. Just think of it as her first period." At that point I lost consciousness.

Three years later, while driving to the hospital to deliver our third child, my wife brought up the pediatrician's comment and I got red hot about it all over again. Yes siree. Becoming a dad helped me to understand why my parent-clients sometimes act like lunatics; and, should I forget, I need only monitor myself for a week or two.

When working with parents, we MHPs would all do well to remember this lunacy. This is part of the reason why kindness, empathy, and an artful delivery of science-based evaluation and intervention procedures are essential skills for any effective kid MHP.

POSITIVE ETHICS

A quiet conscience makes one strong!
—Anne Frank

This volume approaches kid clinical work from the vantage point of positive ethics. Knapp and VandeCreek have represented this perspective: "Ethics could also be viewed as a way to help psychologists fulfill their highest potential as psychologists. It could mean relying on an underlying philosophical system to help psychologists think through complex ethical dilemmas. Ethics should focus not only on how a few psychologists harm patients but also on how all psychologists can do better at helping them. This view of ethics is called positive or active ethics" (2006, p. 10). Thus, positive ethics is less about avoiding screwups and more about maximizing missions. Kid clinicians operating predominantly from a perspective of not stepping on land mines can be filled with anxiety, stress, and self-doubt. Kid clinicians operating predominantly from a perspective of maximizing understanding, healing, and happiness can be filled with a sense of purpose, flow, and self-efficacy. Both perspectives are important. It's just a question of which one is the engine and which one is the caboose.

The ethical principles that are the foundation of positive ethics are those listed in the American Psychological Association *Ethical Principles of Psychologists and Code of Conduct*: beneficence and nonmaleficence, fidelity and responsibility, integrity, justice, and respect for people's rights and dignity (American Psychological Association, 2002). If you think about it for a moment, these principles are pretty inspirational. Put in lay terms, we kid clinicians want (a) to do clinical work that promotes healing and happiness and avoids causing or accentuating pain and suffering; (b) to promote and deserve trusting relationships with families and the villages that surround them; (c) to passionately and steadfastly pursue the truth, as that is what best promotes understanding and excellence in service delivery; (d) to be fair and honest with ourselves and the families and systems with which we work; and (e) to respect that every kid and family is on their own unique path; hence, our job is not to try to get kids and families to switch to our path but to understand their path so that we can tailor our science and art in a way that maximizes their good outcomes. In this volume it is my aspiration to offer organizing schemas and methodologies that adhere closely to these ethical principles. You'll ultimately be the judge regarding how well or how poorly I do that.

MULTICULTURALISM

The only way to understand another culture is to assume the frame of reference
of that culture.
—Carl Rogers

Coming to understand how our differences from others affect us, and how to work effectively with that knowledge, is an essential meta-skill for MHPs. However, many multicultural trainings I've attended seemed to inspire defensiveness and needlessly complicate learning for people who are power up in our culture (e.g., white heterosexual Christian men). What follows are excerpts from an article I wrote for *The Pennsylvania Psychologist* during my year as that organization's president:

> In my last column I proposed this definition of positive multiculturalism (Palmiter, 2012, pp. 8–9):
>
> > *To explore and understand our cultural differences and to learn how an understanding of such can enrich our professional missions. This process endorses the concept that all humans are impacted by cultural differences in a manner that traverses a wide continuum of reactions, some of which are conscious and some of which are unconscious, some of which are adaptive and some of which are not. In considering these issues positive multiculturalism eschews the promotion of shame and embraces the promotion of enrichment.*
>
> . . . As someone who works regularly with youth, I note two relevant trends in the literature:
>
> - There is a consistent trend for undertreatment of minority youth, even when controlling for the financial resources of the family (e.g., Burns, Phillips, Wagner, Barth, Kolko, Campbell, & Landsverk, 2004; Cuffe, Waller, Cuccaro, Pumariega, & Garrison, 1995; Kataoka, Zhang, & Wells, 2002; Leslie, Weckerly, Landsverk, Hough, Hurlburt, & Wood, 2003; Zewelanji, Evans, & Barbour, 2005).
>
> - Minority youth are treated differently than Caucasian youth when interacting both with traditional mental health systems (e.g., Kilgus, Pumariega, & Cuffe, 1995; Zito, Safer, dosReis, & Riddle, 1998) and systems serving youth at large (e.g., Zewelanji et al., 2005).
>
> Similar trends exist among adult minority populations as well (e.g., Fortuna, Alegria, & Gao, 2010). Indeed, the October 2012 edition of the *American Psychologist* has a special section on "Ethnic Disparities in Mental Health Care."

I don't believe this occurs because the mental health community is racist or evil. While I can't argue why it does happen, I believe a major contributing factor is the way we discuss, or don't discuss, race. I have five related vignettes from my own journey.

#1: My wife of 22 years, Lia, is African American and I'm an Irish guy. Early in our marriage we entered a church in the southern suburbs in Chicago (this was during a time when *National Geographic* could create a map of neighborhoods in Chicago based on ethnicity). Lia was the only person of color there. I remember a palpable and strong feeling of being unwelcome. I had never had this feeling before in my life, and I certainly wasn't expecting to feel it then. If someone had challenged, "Well, what did anyone say or do to make you feel unwelcome?" I would have had to do a "hummida, hummida, hummida," as I couldn't say. (It harkened me back to many of the diversity trainings I had had through the years when I thought the presenter, usually a person of color, was overreacting to a concern under review.)

#2: I previously worked at a large outpatient medical facility in NW Indiana. The clientele and the clinical team were diverse. On the day that the O. J. Simpson verdict was due to be delivered, clinicians were gathered in the physicians' lunchroom. This was the only time that the African American and Caucasian clinicians were segregated by those designations. When the verdict came in, the African American clinicians were bombastically jubilant while the Caucasian clinicians were somberly silent. Though this phenomenon was nearly as in our faces as the verdict itself, no one talked about it.

#3: A few years ago I needed to get rehab for an injury. As Lia had been to that same facility months earlier, she asked me to mention her to some of the clinicians there. The clinician who did my intake remembered Lia and was joyful in recounting their interactions. This clinician then called over a colleague and cheerfully said, "This is Lia's husband!" The second clinician didn't know whom she was talking about. So, the first clinician started rattling off a bunch of Lia's characteristics (but not her race), which wasn't helping the second clinician. I thought to myself, "Say she's Black. Y'all don't get a lot of Black folks in here and that'd do it." I speculated that the clinician who remembered Lia was worried that bringing up race could somehow make her look racist. So, finally, I, with a neutral tone, said "Lia is Black." This had two immediate effects: The second clinician remembered her and both clinicians became visibly uncomfortable.

#4: At a diversity training event I attended a few years ago, only a few attendees actively engaged in dialogue with the presenter, even though the presenter was striving for an interactive training. Afterwards I was discussing this with a colleague. This psychologist is a gentle soul who doesn't have a discernable aggressive or rude bone in her body. But she said, "I was afraid to speak some of my doubts out loud about the material out of fear that I'd unknowingly commit a microaggression."

#5: For years I asked graduate students and workshop attendees to do a simple exercise. I asked them to take out a piece of paper and number it from one to six. I told them that I would name a variety of demographic characteristics and then have them write a "yes" if they would alter their clinical methods based upon that characteristic and a "no" if they would not. I then called out characteristics like this: 1. race, 2. sex, 3. sexual orientation, 4. age, 5. psychological mindedness, and 6. psychiatric condition. I found that about 40% or more would say that they would not alter a case approach based on the first three while 80% or more would on the final three. My speculation is that folks feared that if they said they altered how they approached clinical work based on the first three that they could be deemed as suffering from an "ism."

I believe that the dynamics I just reviewed are facilitated by the difficulty we have thinking and talking about diversity. As I wrote in my last column, we seem slow to acknowledge how others' differences (e.g., skin color, sex, sexual orientation, religion) impact us. We fear that this human condition (i.e., to be impacted by differences) could make us, or could be used to label us as, racist, sexist, ageist, homophobic, and so on. The harmful ripples from this paralysis in open discussion are many (e.g., the sorts of unfortunate outcomes I reviewed at the top of this article).

I would propose three immediate action steps. First, take Harvard University's Race Implicit Association Test, which is located at implicit.harvard.edu. This is one resource to help us to consider our humanity as we interact with people who are different from us. Second, I would propose considering whether there could be value in asking clients who are different from us, or who have some salient minority status in their community, two questions. First, "(Client's name), I'm (salient characteristic), you're (salient characteristic). What's that like for you?" Second, "You're (salient minority characteristic), living in (location). What's that like for you?" These questions communicate at least two things: We get how important these matters can be and it's not dangerous to talk about them. Third, when we come together to share our perspectives on our differences, let's assume that all of us are good-hearted, well-intended people who only want to discover how each other's differences may enrich us. So, let's be slow to use words like "racist," "sexist," and "microaggression" just like the positive ethics people ask us to be slow to use words like "unethical." Such a kind and respectful approach can't be the wrong thing to do. Right?

We all do well to think of multicultural awareness and training as a lifelong journey that never ends. After I've offered an all-day workshop on this topic to engaged and interested participants, I've been left with the feeling that we've merely completed one lap on what truly is an endless course. So, in this brief segment you and I have only taken one or two steps together. But I hope that you are, or have become, interested in learning more. For those interested, I would close with two additional recommendations. First, learn more about the science behind implicit bias and how it affects us all. My favorite book on this topic is *Everyday Bias* by Howard Ross (2014). Second, embrace this calling by Dr. Martin Luther King, Jr:

> Whatever career you may choose for yourself—doctor, lawyer, teacher—let me propose an avocation to be pursued along with it. Become a dedicated fighter for civil rights. Make it a central part of your life. It will make you a better doctor, a better lawyer, a better teacher. It will enrich your spirit as nothing else possibly can. It will give you that rare sense of nobility that can only spring from love and selflessly helping your fellow man. Make a career of humanity. Commit yourself to the noble struggle for human rights. You will make a greater person of yourself, a greater nation of your country, and a finer world to live in.
>
> —Martin Luther King, Jr., April 18, 1959

Okay, ready to get after it? Well, just turn the page and saddle up!

REFERENCES AND BIBLIOGRAPHY

Albano, A. M., & Kendall, P. C. (2002). Cognitive behavioural therapy for children and adolescents with anxiety disorders: Clinical research advances. *International Review of Psychiatry, 14*(2), 129–134.

American Psychological Association. (2002). *Ethical principles of psychologists and code of conduct.* Retrieved from http://www.apa.org/ethics/code2002.html

Arnberg, A., & Öst, L. G. (2014). CBT for children with depressive symptoms: A meta-analysis. *Cognitive Behaviour Therapy, 43*(4), 275–288.

Ayres, I., & Siegelman, P. (1995). Race and gender discrimination in bargaining for a new car. *The American Economic Review, 85*(3), 304–321.

Barrett, P. M., Duffy, A. L., Dadds, M. R., & Rapee, R. M. (2001). Cognitive-behavioral treatment of anxiety disorders in children: Long-term (6-year) follow-up. *Journal of Consulting and Clinical Psychology, 69*(1), 135–141.

Brent, D. A. (1997). *Cognitive therapy treatment manual for depressed and suicidal youth* (STAR Center Publications). Pittsburgh, PA: University of Pittsburgh Health System Services for Teens at Risk.

Brent, D. A., Kolko, D. J., Birmaher, B., Baugher, M., Bridge, J., Roth, C., & Holder, D. (1998). Predictors of treatment efficacy in a clinical trial of three psychosocial treatments for adolescent depression. *Journal of the American Academy of Child & Adolescent Psychiatry, 37*(9), 906–914.

Burns, B. J., Phillips, S. D., Wagner, H. R., Barth, R. P., Kolko, D. J., Campbell, Y., & Landsverk, J. (2004). Mental health need and access to mental health services by youths involved with child welfare: A national survey. *Journal of the American Academy of Child & Adolescent Psychiatry, 43*(8), 960–970.

Cartwright-Hatton, S., Roberts, C., Chitsabesan, P., Fothergill, C., & Harrington, R. (2004). Systematic review of the efficacy of cognitive behaviour therapies for childhood and adolescent anxiety disorders. *British Journal of Clinical Psychology, 43*(4), 421–436.

Chu, B. C., & Harrison, T. L. (2007). Disorder-specific effects of CBT for anxious and depressed youth: A meta-analysis of candidate mediators of change. *Clinical Child and Family Psychology Review, 10*(4), 352–372.

Cohen, J. A., Deblinger, E., Mannarino, A. P., & Steer, R. A. (2004). A multisite, randomized controlled trial for children with sexual abuse–related PTSD symptoms. *Journal of the American Academy of Child & Adolescent Psychiatry, 43*(4), 393–402.

Copperfield, D. (1985). *Project Magic.* Retrieved from www.projectmagic.org

Cuffe, S. P., Waller, J. L., Cuccaro, M. L., Pumariega, A. J., & Garrison, C. Z. (1995). Race and gender differences in the treatment of psychiatric disorders in young adolescents. *Journal of the American Academy of Child & Adolescent Psychiatry, 34*(11), 1536–1543.

Deblinger, E., Mannarino, A. P., Cohen, J. A., Runyon, M. K., & Steer, R. A. (2011). Trauma-focused cognitive behavioral therapy for children: Impact of the trauma narrative and treatment length. *Depression and Anxiety, 28*(1), 67–75.

Fortuna, L., Alegria, M., & Gao, S. (2010). Retention in depression treatment among ethnic and racial minority groups in the United States. *Depression and Anxiety, 27*(5), 485–494.

Gaynor, S. T., Weersing, V. R., Kolko, D. J., Birmaher, B., Heo, J., & Brent, D. A. (2003). The prevalence and impact of large sudden improvements during adolescent therapy for depression: A comparison across cognitive-behavioral, family, and supportive therapy. *Journal of Consulting and Clinical Psychology, 71*(2), 386.

Gladwell, M. (2007). *Blink: The power of thinking without thinking.* New York, NY: Back Bay Books.

Hart, R., & Walton, M. (2010). Magic as a therapeutic intervention to promote coping in hospitalized pediatric patients. *Continuing Nursing Education, 36*(1), 11–16.

Hofmann, S. G., Asnaani, A., Vonk, I. J., Sawyer, A. T., & Fang, A. (2012). The efficacy of cognitive behavioral therapy: A review of meta-analyses. *Cognitive Therapy and Research, 36*(5), 427–440.

In-Albon, T., & Schneider, S. (2006). Psychotherapy of childhood anxiety disorders: A meta-analysis. *Psychotherapy and Psychosomatics, 76*(1), 15–24.

Ishikawa, S. I., Okajima, I., Matsuoka, H., & Sakano, Y. (2007). Cognitive behavioural therapy for anxiety disorders in children and adolescents: A meta-analysis. *Child and Adolescent Mental Health, 12*(4), 164–172.

Kataoka, S. H., Zhang, L., & Wells, K. B. (2002). Unmet need for mental health care among U.S. children: Variation by ethnicity and insurance status. *American Journal of Psychiatry, 159*(9), 1548–1555.

Kilgus, M. D., Pumariega, A. J., & Cuffe, S. P. (1995). Influence of race on diagnosis in adolescent psychiatric inpatients. *Journal of the American Academy of Child & Adolescent Psychiatry, 34*(1), 67–72.

Kilmer, R. P., Cowen, E. L., Wyman, P. A., Work, W. C., & Magnus, K. B. (1998). Differences in stressors experienced by urban African American, White, and Hispanic children. *Journal of Community Psychology, 26*(5), 415–428.

Knapp, S. J., & VandeCreek, L. D. (2006). *Practical ethics for psychologists: A positive approach.* Washington, DC: American Psychological Association.

Kowalik, J., Weller, J., Venter, J., & Drachman, D. (2011). Cognitive behavioral therapy for the treatment of pediatric posttraumatic stress disorder: A review and meta-analysis. *Journal of Behavior Therapy and Experimental Psychiatry, 42*(3), 405–413.

Kwong, E., & Cullen, N. (2007). *Teaching magic tricks to patients as an adjunct to their rehabilitation program.* Annual Scientific Meeting. Toronto, Canada: Canadian Association of Physical Medicine and Rehabilitation.

Leach, M. J. (2005). Rapport: A key to treatment success. *Complementary Therapies in Clinical Practice, 11*(4), 262–265.

Leslie, L. K., Weckerly, J., Landsverk, J., Hough, R. L., Hurlburt, M. S., & Wood, P. A. (2003). Racial/ethnic differences in the use of psychotropic medication in high-risk children and adolescents. *Journal of the American Academy of Child & Adolescent Psychiatry, 42*(12), 1433–1442.

Levin, D. M. (2006). Magic arts counseling: The tricks of illusion as intervention. *Georgia School Counselor Association Journal, 13,* 14–23.

Lyons, M., & Menolotto, A. M. (1990). Use of magic in psychiatric occupational therapy: Rationale, results, and recommendations. *Australian Occupational Therapy Journal, 37*(2), 79–83.

Mandell, D. S., Listerud, J., Levy, S. E., & Pinto-Martin, J. A. (2002). Race differences in the age at diagnosis among Medicaid-eligible children with autism. *Journal of the American Academy of Child & Adolescent Psychiatry, 41*(12), 1447–1453.

Monga, S., Rosenbloom, B. N., Tanha, A., Owens, M., & Young, A. (2015). Comparison of child–parent and parent-only cognitive-behavioral therapy programs for anxious children aged 5 to 7 years: Short- and long-term outcomes. *Journal of the American Academy of Child & Adolescent Psychiatry, 54*(2), 138–146.

Moscowitz, J. (1973). The sorcerer's apprentice or the use of magic in child psychotherapy. *International Journal of Psychotherapy, 2,* 138–162.

Norton, M. I., & Sommers, S. R. (2011). Whites see racism as a zero-sum game that they are now losing. *Perspectives on Psychological Science, 6*(3), 215–218.

Oetzel, K. B., & Scherer, D. G. (2003). Therapeutic engagement with adolescents in psychotherapy. *Psychotherapy: Theory, Research, Practice, Training, 40*(3), 215–225.

Olatunji, B. O., Cisler, J. M., & Deacon, B. J. (2010). Efficacy of cognitive behavioral therapy for anxiety disorders: A review of meta-analytic findings. *Psychiatric Clinics of North America, 33*(3), 557–577.

Ougrin, D., Tranah, T., Stahl, D., Moran, P., & Asarnow, J. R. (2015). Therapeutic interventions for suicide attempts and self-harm in adolescents: Systematic review and meta-analysis. *Journal of the American Academy of Child & Adolescent Psychiatry, 54*(2), 97–107.

Palmiter, D. (2013, March). Help us increase kids' access to mental health care. *The Pennsylvania Psychologist, 73,* 2, 5.

Palmiter, D. J. (2004). A national survey of the assessment practices of child clinicians. *American Journal of Orthopsychiatry, 74,* 122–128.

Palmiter, D. J. (2011). *Working parents, thriving families: 10 strategies that make a difference.* North Branch, MN: Sunrise River Press.

Palmiter, D. J. (2012). Positive multiculturalism. *The Pennsylvania Psychologist, 72, 2, 7.*

Pincus, D. B., May, J. E., Whitton, S. W., Mattis, S. G., & Barlow, D. H. (2010). Cognitive-behavioral treatment of panic disorder in adolescence. *Journal of Clinical Child & Adolescent Psychology, 39*(5), 638–649.

Ross, H. J. (2014). *Everyday bias: Identifying and navigating unconscious judgments in our daily lives.* New York, NY: Rowman & Littlefield.

Shavers, V. L., Fagan, P., Jones, D., Klein, W. M., Boyington, J., Moten, C., & Rorie, E. (2012). The state of research on racial/ethnic discrimination in the receipt of health care. *American Journal of Public Health, 102*(5), 953–966.

Sofronoff, K., Attwood, T., & Hinton, S. (2005). A randomised controlled trial of a CBT intervention for anxiety in children with Asperger syndrome. *Journal of Child Psychology and Psychiatry, 46*(11), 1152–1160.

Spencer, K. (2012). Hocus focus: Evaluating the benefits of magic tricks with special populations. *Journal of the International Association of Special Education, 13*(1), 87–99.

Stark, K., & Kendall, P. C. (1996). *Treating depressed children: Therapist manual for "taking action."* Ardmore, PA: Workbook Publishing.

Stehouwer, R. S. (1983). Using magic to establish rapport and improve motivation in psychotherapy with children: Theory, issues, and technique. *Psychotherapy in Private Practice, 1,* 85–94.

Townsend, E., Walker, D. M., Sargeant, S., Vostanis, P., Hawton, K., Stocker, O., & Sithole, J. (2010). Systematic review and meta-analysis of interventions relevant for young offenders with mood disorders, anxiety disorders, or self-harm. *Journal of Adolescence, 33*(1), 9–20.

Vagnoli, L., Caprilli, S., Robiglio, A., & Messeri, A. (2005). Clown doctors as a treatment for preoperative anxiety in children: A randomized prospective study. *Pediatrics, 116,* e563–e567.

Watson, H. J., & Rees, C. S. (2008). Meta-analysis of randomized, controlled treatment trials for pediatric obsessive-compulsive disorder. *Journal of Child Psychology and Psychiatry, 49*(5), 489–498.

Weinstein, S. M., Henry, D. B., Katz, A. C., Peters, A. T., & West, A. E. (2014). Treatment moderators of child- and-family-focused cognitive-behavioral therapy for pediatric bipolar disorder. *Journal of the American Academy of Child & Adolescent Psychiatry, 54*(2), 116–125.

Weisz, J. R., Weiss, B., Han, S. S., Granger, D. A., & Morton, T. (1995). Effects of psychotherapy with children and adolescents revisited: A meta-analysis of treatment outcome studies. *Psychological Bulletin, 117*(3), 450.

Zewelanji, S., Evans, S. W., & Barbour, K. (2005). The significance of culture: Understanding barriers to care and the diagnosis of ADHD in African-American youth. *Emotional and Behavior Disorders in Youth, 5,* 61–67.

Zito, J. M., Safer, D. J., dosReis, S., & Riddle, M. A. (1998). Racial disparity in psychotropic medications prescribed for youths with Medicaid insurance in Maryland. *Journal of the American Academy of Child & Adolescent Psychiatry, 37*(2), 179–184.

SECTION I

Establishing the Foundation

CHAPTER 2

The Initial Evaluation

The first step to wisdom is getting things by their right name.
—*Chinese proverb*

This is one of the most important chapters in this book, as the quality of the evaluation determines how effective the treatment plan and interventions will be.

THE FRAMEWORK OF THE EVALUATION

The field of child clinical psychology hasn't done a good job establishing a standard of care for outpatient mental health evaluations. My research and clinical experience both indicate that child clinicians vary widely in how they conduct outpatient mental health evaluations. This is a problem for our field. Therefore, one of the projects I invested in was cochairing a statewide task force that endeavored to address, among other concerns, this issue. This was a collaborative effort of the Pennsylvania Psychological Association (PPA) and the Pennsylvania Chapter of the American Academy of Pediatrics. The work began in the summer of 2011 and ended in the summer of 2013, though data analysis continues as I write this work. What follows are the evaluation standards that we developed and which were endorsed by each organization. Each of these standards represents a blending of empirical science and practical clinical concerns (i.e., a cost–benefit analysis). These standards are written for a context of a pediatrician making an outpatient referral to a mental health professional (MHP), so standards 1 and 7 would not be germane in other outpatient referral scenarios (e.g., self-referral) and were published in *The Pennsylvania Psychologist*, which is the bulletin of PPA.

1. Let the pediatric practice know that the evaluation is underway (i.e., not the findings but just that the process is underway). This could occur at one of two points in time: (a) at the point that the initial evaluation appointment for the case is scheduled (assuming an oral release to do so has been granted during

the phone call) or (b) after the family comes in for the initial evaluation appointment and signs a release of information to the pediatrician.

2. Complete a family interview with the child and at least one adult who lives with the child; ideally, all parental figures would take part.

3. Complete an individual interview with the child.

4. Obtain parent, teacher, and child behavior rating scales, assuming that all involved possess sufficient reading skills and parents are willing to cooperate.

5. Screen caregivers the child lives with for mental health problems.

6. When they exist, the psychologist will endeavor to review the following:

   a. The child's school records (i.e., report cards, state achievement testing, special education records, and discipline records)

   b. Previous mental health evaluation and treatment

   c. Medical records that could be relevant to the presenting concerns

   d. Forensic records

   e. Records from children and youth services

   f. Other records that could be relevant to an evaluation of the presenting concerns

7. Within 2 weeks of finishing the evaluation, and assuming sufficient written releases have been executed, send a written summary to the pediatrician that includes at least the following elements:

   a. Sources of information for the evaluation

   b. Diagnostic impression

   c. Recommendations for either further evaluation or for treating the problem(s) that have been diagnosed

   d. Case disposition (i.e., what the family has agreed to do regarding the recommendations)

In my own survey research of a little over 300 mental health professionals (MHPs), the majority reported *not* doing things like using rating scales, screening a parent for psychopathology, and reviewing school records. It is beyond the scope of this book to review the details of the underlying science, though the References and Bibliography section of this chapter includes the relevant citations. But I assert that each of these elements is very important and should always be included unless there is a strong clinical reason to do otherwise (e.g., obtaining a certain record could cause a harmful delay). In the rest of this chapter, I review how to implement this framework with a family.

THE PREINTERVIEW WORK

I would argue that the clinical work starts at the point of the first phone call by a parent. If an MHP conceives of the work starting at the point of the first clinical interview, that MHP may have more no-shows and cancellations than MHPs who view the work starting at the first phone call.

It's important to remember the phenomenology of the parent calling up an MHP for the first time. These folks are fraught with ambivalence: "My kid will think there's something seriously wrong with him if I take him to a shrink!" "I'm such a failure that I can't handle this on my own!" "I don't want to be told what a horrible parent I am." "OMG, how expensive is this going to be?!" And so forth. For this reason I try to make sure I have 15 minutes available for the first call. It often will not take that long, but it is a tax on our budding relationship if a parent needs 15 minutes and I have only 5.

In this initial call I get a statement of the concern(s) the parent has about her child, offer empathy, find out what the family parenting composition is (e.g., is this a divorced family?), review the goals and methods of the evaluation, review the default three-session framework that I cover in this chapter, share my fees, cover who I would like to have come to the first appointment (i.e., usually all adults involved in parenting unless I'm told that certain adults can't behave functionally if they are in the same room together—please see Chapter 17 for more on this subject), and endorse that doing an evaluation seems like a good idea given the concerns that were expressed. I also direct the parent to intake forms on my website for her to download, complete, and bring to the first appointment (see Appendix A). (Please keep in mind that the regulations in your state may require a different language and that relevant federal and state regulations are always evolving.)

I try to keep the intake forms I use to a minimum. For example, I don't ask families to fill out behavior rating scales in advance. While I understand that doing so could be helpful, I find that I'm more likely to get an accurate report on rating scales if I first establish an alliance with all the players in the first interview. No matter how you proceed, I believe it is very important to review your primary goals and methods in this phone call and to repeat such in your intake forms, as well as other important policies and procedures.

THE OFFICE

I've experienced numerous instances of clients examining every little detail of my office and reaching either good or bad conclusions about me based on their observations. I speculate that people do not engage in the same degree of scrutiny with their accountants or chiropractors. But, when you're considering sharing your innermost demons and worries, especially regarding your "baby," you tend to notice a lot more about your prospective confidant. These are the elements that I've found to be important for the office:

▶ A consulting room that is soundproof. If loud conversations can be overheard in the waiting area that is a significant burden to overcome.

▶ Reading material for men, women, teens, and kids; something for young kids to play with is also a plus (e.g., I have a train set). For example, I once had a dad emphatically note that the clinic I was directing at the time was the very first place he had been to that had anything for a man to read in the waiting room.

▶ A well-sanitized bathroom.

▶ An aura of organized peace and physical comfort. I don't think you have to be a peaceful or organized person to facilitate a strong alliance as a kid MHP, but I think it's advisable to create a peaceful and organized space.

▶ Zero evidence that anyone can accidentally or intentionally learn about another client (e.g., through computer screens or charts left lying about).

If your space is lacking one of these elements, I would prioritize fixing that. (I have pictures of my space on my website to serve as a model.)

THE INITIAL INTERVIEW

Anyone who hopes to learn the noble game of chess from books will soon discover that only the openings and endgames admit of an exhaustive systematic presentation and that the infinite variety of moves which develop after the opening defy any such description. This gap in instruction can only be filled by a diligent study of games fought out by masters.
—Sigmund Freud

When the family first arrives (i.e., the youth of concern and the parents we've agreed would come), I introduce myself and ask them to take a seat in the waiting room. I then ask for my intake forms and share the fee agreement to be signed (I also review fees in the initial call). I then take the forms into my office and review them. I prepare the pages I will take notes on with the following headers: Chief Complaints, Strengths, Psychosocial Stress, Family History, Personal History, Psychiatric History, Family Psychiatric History, Family Substance Use, Kid Substance Use, and Medical and Developmental History. Once everything is completed I ask the family to come in and make themselves comfortable in my consulting area. I then follow this script (for each section of script I share in this volume, you will find a rationale section that follows immediately after):

Before we begin I'd like to take a moment to make sure we are on the same page and to address any questions or concerns you might have. This is an evaluation. That usually means that I have two things I'm trying to accomplish: First, I'm going to try to figure out what is causing the problems that have brought you to me. Second, I'm going to try to develop a plan for fixing those problems (a). *Sometimes a plan for fixing the problems involves ongoing work with me, but other times it doesn't, because other things might seem like they'd be more helpful* (b). *There are a number of methods I use to try to reach those two goals* (c). *I will obviously interview you about the problems. But then I will need to go into other areas of your life, both from right now and from the past. Some of the questions I ask might not seem like they're connected to why you are here, but I ask them so that I can do a thorough job for you* (d). *Before the evaluation is finished there will also be adult time to talk alone* (looking at the parents) *as well as time for you and I, Aiden, to talk alone too* (looking at the kid). *I mention this at the start because I find that families are very different in terms of what they discuss in front of each other. So, just because I ask a question today doesn't mean that today is the best time to answer it. If you would rather wait until you are alone with me, just say so and I'll respect that* (e). *There will also be some rating forms I'll ask you to complete and some records I will need to obtain, which I'll review at the end of our appointment today. You'll return those materials to me before our next appointment, which I'll reserve primarily for giving you feedback on the two goals I just mentioned. Finally, everything that you tell me stays in this office. I don't take the records anywhere or discuss what you tell me with others. The only exceptions are the ones that I've reviewed in the intake forms. For instance, if you tell me something that indicates that someone is in danger or a minor is being abused or neglected, I'm required to take steps to ensure safety. But these exceptions are not common in my practice. Do you have any questions* (f)? *Okay, I'd like to begin by asking your son some questions. I'm not even interested in facts as much as I am how your son here looks at things. For this reason, it would be very helpful to me if you wouldn't contribute, even nonverbally. Then when he and I are finished, I'll ask you for your thoughts about what we discussed* (g). (Addressing the youth) *What do you like to be called? . . . Aiden, what brings you in?*

Explanation

a. Research makes it clear that coming to an agreement about goals and methods is essential to forming an alliance, in this instance an evaluation alliance. We are explicitly promising to do two things (only): generate a diagnostic formulation and offer recommendations for interventions. This part is the goal language.

b. One of the moms I served early in my career taught me this lesson. In the feedback session, when I recommended that she take her son to another MHP who was better equipped to handle her son's problems, she justifiably complained: "Wow. If I knew we wouldn't be able to keep seeing you I wouldn't have told you so many deeply personal things!" Over the years I've found that many families equate a promise to do an evaluation with a promise to do treatment, or a willingness to do an evaluation with a willingness to do ongoing treatment. We need to be clear on this point. Ironically, I've found that this ends up being a comfort to those parents who are very ambivalent about coming in; they don't want to feel like they are signing up for a bigger dose of involvement until they form a relationship and learn more about what the kid mental health enterprise consists of.

c.   This is the methods language.

d.   Parents who are more psychologically minded don't need to hear the language in this part of the introduction. They get it. However, less psychologically minded parents might be put off by questions that they do not judge to be directly pertinent to their kid's wellness unless we prepare them (e.g., questions about their marriage).

e.   Again, a justifiably angry mom taught me to incorporate this language. At the end of the evaluation I asked what the process had been like for her. She replied, "Good, except that I was upset that you asked if I had any financial stress. I really didn't think that was an appropriate thing to discuss in front of a 10-year-old!" It's easy for us to forget how power down our clients can feel in our office. Therefore, I try to empower families to let me know if a given topic is best covered at another time. If a kid subsequently tells me that he prefers to wait until we are alone, I'll ask at the next appointment, which is slated to be the individual interview. If an adult indicates this, I'll leave time at the end of the family interview and ask the kid to sit in the waiting room so we can discuss the matter(s).

f.   I find it's only the more assertive people who can say if they have a question or concern about the process, so I'm looking for nonverbal expressions. If I see anything suggesting that the person may have a question or concern, I'll follow up by saying: *Y'know this is a very unusual experience for many people to have. Also, I'm sharing a ton of information quickly. Therefore, it wouldn't be surprising if you had a question or a concern.* (Directing myself to the person I've noticed had a nonverbal response): *How about you, Tanisha, any questions or concerns about the process?*

g.   This is an important structure for the evaluation. How many kids want to be there? If a kid wants to be there, this is usually either because he's lonely or is very psychologically minded. For the rest, they are either neutral or opposed: coat zipped up, arms crossed, cap down over face, and sitting as low in the couch as gravity will allow. Few things can fuel this resistance more than having the parents begin with a litany of concerns, which for many kids sounds pretty critical. So, I start with the kid. Moreover, when the reasonable side of their kid is accessed, many parents start feeling some relief and hope. So, this is a significant alliance-building strategy.

I imagine that many of you are wondering, "Okay, but what if the kid won't cooperate?" In Chapter 4 I review a protocol for the most resistant kids. For now, I'll cover how to proceed if the kid is cooperative, which is most of the time, in my experience.

It's a basic psychosocial interviewing technique to let the interviewee run the interview as long as (a) needed information is being offered and (b) the person isn't perseverating at length on a given point. I take over the interview when the kid is done or he is stuck on some aspect that isn't useful. The kid may start talking about the family of origin, or her friends, or where he wants to go to college. That's okay, as long as it's information I need. I just flip through my pages and fill in the information at the appropriate spots. I find most kids don't take much time with their initial statement. However, I'm interested in the kid stating (a) what problems he thinks he has; (b) any additional problems his parents may think he has, even if he disagrees; (c) an overview of school functioning; (d) an overview of social functioning; and (e) the kid's thoughts about anything that stands out in the intake paperwork (e.g., there has been a divorce, the kid is taking a stimulant medication). Once this is done, and it usually is finished in 15 to 20 minutes, I'll say: *Aiden, I'm going to ask your parents some of these same questions now. You can say things if you'd like. I mean, don't interrupt us. But, if there's a pause and you'd like to say something, feel free. And I'll have more questions for you later.* I then turn to the parents and say: *So, what brings you in?* For younger children who are challenged by sitting still I'll say: *Aiden, this is how it's going to go. I'm going to ask your parents some questions. Then we are going to talk about what's good about you. When we are done doing that I have some toys you can play with here in the office. So, I just need you to sit there and listen for a few minutes, then you can play.* When it comes time for the kid to play, I'll just ask that he not take out more than three kinds of toys at once so that the clean up doesn't take more than a few moments.

As was the case with their child, the parents run the interview until I need to take over. Then I do so in the following order (I've listed some sample questions in each section).

Chief Complaints

In this section I'm looking to ask those questions that determine what diagnoses, if any, are applicable. I feel free to consult whatever diagnostic system I'm using (*International Classification of Diseases* or *Diagnostic and Statistical Manual of Mental Disorders*) as I do the interview in order to make sure that I've covered my bases. In addition to current symptoms, I want to know about onset date(s) and course. In a written psychosocial report, the data that supports a given diagnostic impression is usually articulated here. Four quick guidelines: (a) I think it's very important to avoid clinical sounding terms when other language is equally useful. For example, I wouldn't ask, "Does Aiden here ever show any disordered eating?" but would ask things like: *How many healthy meals a day does Aiden eat?* (b) I try to avoid asking for a diagnostic impression and focus on getting raw data. For example, I wouldn't ask, "Is Aiden depressed?" but would ask: *In a typical week, for what percentage of that week does Aiden seem sad?* Numbers are good, even if they are rough estimates. (c) Regarding teens, I don't ask them if they are sexually active or use substances in front of their parents, as that is an invitation to lie, and when they lie to me it starts an unhelpful dynamic. I usually wait for my individual interview with the teen to ask these questions. However, if the family brings up these concerns then I'll ask about what they've stated; I also feel free to ask parents if they have any concerns. (d) I try to avoid jargon whenever possible (e.g., avoiding words like "psychiatric" and "bipolar"). I also use *how come* instead of "why" as it's less confrontational, and I almost always ask for guesses when people say "I don't know."

Strengths

As I reviewed in Chapter 1, the large majority of parents who are actively engaged in parenting are crazy people. Thus, reviewing a kid's strengths is very helpful for relaxing both parents and kids. Of course, these data also provide essential information for understanding a kid and for tailoring interventions. How I do this is to say to the parents: *Okay, we've talked about the problems, so now I'd like to have the two of you tell me what is good about Aiden. And, by that I mean what's good about his personality and what things is he good at?*

It's interesting to see how parents respond to this question. Some parents can't wait to tell me about their kid's strengths and do so with gusto (my clinical experience is that those who do end up having a better prognosis). Others struggle, or can't help but add "buts" to what they say. (I wish I knew who it was who first said, "nothing before 'but' matters.") Such parents may need more direct questioning and redirection. Once the parents are done I'll turn to the kid and ask a few questions: *Was there anything you heard that you disagree with? Was there anything you heard that surprised you? What would you like to add?* The answers to these questions tell me a lot about how praise is manifested in the family as well as how much family members know about what each other values.

Once I have my final list of strengths, I'll read it back to the kid and state: *So, you have way more strengths than problems. So, Aiden, this is sort of like going to the dentist. Most of the teeth are fine and healthy, but you may have a few spots that need help.* In these few moments I find that the alliance tends to be strengthened for everyone in the room; the only exception I sometimes find is that stepparents who are angry at the kid may squirm.

Psychosocial Stress

If parents are merely asked about what stress they experience, they will rephrase the question in their minds to "What stress are we experiencing that could be causing Aiden's symptoms?" However, this is not what we want, as that would be to share their diagnostic formulation. We want the raw data. So I'll ask it this way: *All families have stress. That's just part of being alive. What stress do you guys experience, either as individuals or as a family, even if it's typical stuff?* Some of the areas I always want to know about are financial stress, job-related stress, stress of raising kids, medical stresses, and stresses with extended family. (Stress within the parents' relationship is covered in the following section.) Pertaining to vocations (which may be as a stay-at-home parent), I'll ask for a satisfaction rating (1–10); find out how many hours are worked, including at home; and try to determine what degree of stress it might be causing the person. While these are some common stresses I ask about, I feel free to ask about other areas depending on what is presenting. Experienced MHPs learn that confusion is a beacon for where to inquire further; if I'm unsure about something, I ask.

Family History

My goal here is to have an appreciation for what life in this household feels like. To that end, the questions I ask across families are rarely identical. However, I usually start this section, as it is a natural segue from the stress section, with the marriage. I start by asking: *How many years have you guys been married?* Then: *I'll remind you that you may want to defer answering certain questions until we are alone, but I'll just continue on unless you tell me to stop. On a scale from 1 to 10, with 10 being the most satisfied, how satisfied are you in your marriage?* The goal here is to get a quick sense for the health of the marriage and, in instances where there are problems, what the headlines are; not the full text, just the headlines. Some other things I'll commonly ask: *How often do the two of you* (looking at the parents) *spend time together having adult fun, either by yourselves or with other adults, no kids? How about the family? How often do all of you do something fun together whether it's at home or outside of the home? What rituals do you guys have as a family that you enjoy, be they daily, weekly, or seasonal? How do you guys discipline? Do you practice any religion* (getting some details if the answer is affirmative)*?* If relevant: *Do you have any concerns about your other kid/kids* (briefly sampling relationships with them, school success, and social success)*? What challenges do you face with monitoring your kids at home or outside of the home? What are your relationships like with extended family? How often do you folks watch TV or surf the Internet for fun?* And so forth. At some point I'll *feel* like I know what it's like *to live in their house* and so will move on. (There is also a developmental history form I pass out that reviews some of this content. This form is Appendix C.)

In instances when families are divorced, questions about how the adults get along, romantic attachments of each parent and how these attachments get along with the kids, visitation schedules, and headlines regarding tensions between the adults are all relevant. Throughout the interview, if we start getting into content that I believe is inappropriate for their kid to hear, I'll suspend the questioning and wait until I'm alone with them to proceed. My tolerance for this is also informed by my sense for what the kids get regular exposure to anyway.

In instances when the family identifies with a minority group (e.g., racial, religious), it's *very* important to ask them what that's like for them. For example: *What's it like for you folks to be Hispanic and living in a primarily Caucasian part of the world?* Or: *Are there any stresses you folks experience as a function of being a same-sex couple?* This can also be a good place to ask what it's like for the family to be working with you if you are racially different. As a follow up: *So, given these stresses you're experiencing, what's it like for you to be working with a* (your race) *clinician?* I find that this is one of the three most challenging areas for new clinicians to learn because of the anxiety it can provoke. The other two are dealing with sexualized transference and discussing fees. I've often quipped to my supervisees that the ideal training case would be a client who is racially different, expresses a sexual attraction, and complains about the fee!

Personal History

This is the section for learning about a kid's academic, extracurricular, and social lives. Regarding academics, I want to know about current grades; effort exerted on academics (e.g., *Aiden, if 100% is your best effort on homework, including studying for tests, where would you say you're at?*); how the kid gets along with teachers; if there is any history for special education interventions; and detentions, suspensions, and expulsions and the history for each of these over the years. As I'll usually be able to review report cards, I don't worry too much about possibly missing something important.

Regarding the kid's extracurricular life, I'm interested in knowing what clubs, sports, or activities the kid has engaged in, how successful he's been, how much he enjoys them, and the parents' attitudes about them. A top resilience-promoting factor is a kid (a) knowing his strengths and (b) manifesting them in the world in ways that matter (see Chapter 12). So extracurricular activities offer an important opportunity to manifest strengths.

Regarding the kid's social life, I want to know how many good friends the kid has as well as friendly acquaintances. Many kids ask, "What do you mean by 'good friend'?" So I answer: *Someone you could tell anything to.* Topics of interest include time spent with friends inside and outside of school, how often the kid gets invited to parties, any problems with teasing or bullying, and if there are any concerns regarding social networking drama. I usually save questions about romantic interests for the individual interview with the kid.

Psychiatric History

The question is simply: *Has Aiden ever been seen by an MHP before?* If the answer is "yes," I want to know the timeline, whether a diagnostic impression was shared, and goals and methods of the therapy. It's interesting to me that I've never once had a parent be able to review the diagnostic impression, goals for the work, and methods that were used to try to reach the goals. In all fairness, they may have been told, but it didn't stick. My theory is that those parents who can answer these questions stay with that provider.

Family Psychiatric History

I ask: *Has any blood relative on either side of the family been in counseling as far as you know?* If "yes," I say: *I don't need details, but just in a word or two, for what?* I then follow up with: *Are there any other family members who might have had a need for counseling that they didn't pursue?* If the initial answer is "no," then I ask that same last question. If an adult (other than one who is adopted or grew up without contact) tells me that no family member has ever had a need for counseling, I'm learning a lot about how the adult might be viewing contact with me. (This section is also augmented by one of the forms I ask the parents to take home, as you'll note later in this chapter, and which you can find in Appendix B.)

Family Substance Use History

Again, we would *not* ask for a diagnostic formulation by asking things like, "Does anyone have a problem with alcohol?" Instead, we ask: *I know it can vary, Bob, but in a typical week, how many days might you have something alcoholic to drink?* Followed up by (unless the person claims no weekly usage): *I know it can vary, but what is the typical amount that you'll drink?* If we suspect a problem is present—which can also be signaled by rising tension in the room—we can ask more (e.g., *Have you or anyone else ever had a concern about your drinking? Ever found yourself wishing to cut down on drinking? Had any DUIs over the years, even if it was just due to bad luck? How often have you been eligible for a DUI but dodged a bullet?*). An alternative way to ask this question initially, if you have reason to suspect substance use is an issue, would be to say: *Bill, you're working one and a half jobs, taking care of a sick parent, and raising three kids. That's a TON of stress. Sometimes when people are under that much stress they might use alcohol to feel better. How about you?* (The latter is an example of a principle to employ in clinical work. If a truthful answer to a question could cause narcissistic injury, it's usually a good idea to set an empathic context.) These questions are asked of each adult. I also ask similar questions regarding recreational drug use.

Kid Substance Use

As I mentioned previously, I'll usually save these questions for the individual interview. But here I can ask about anything the family has raised or just ask the parents a few directed questions like: *Do you have any concern that Aiden here might be drinking or using drugs?* If "yes," then I'll find out what the parents know and/or fear.

Medical and Developmental History

I just ask for high points here: *Does Aiden have a significant medical history or has he experienced any important developmental delays?* This gives me a chance to interview the family about any significant issues. Otherwise I rely on the developmental history form I give them (see Appendix C).

Concluding the Interview

Once I have about 5 or 10 minutes to go I start wrapping up. I begin by stating: *Based on what you've told me, I'd like to put together some forms for you to take home and fill out. Give me just a few moments here to do that.* There are a few categories of forms that I give out.

▶ For every parent involved I want to use (a) an omnibus rating scale, (b) scales that target areas of concern, (c) a screen for parental psychopathology, and (d) a family psychiatric history form (see Appendix B). I will ask the parent who seems most in the know (usually the mom) to fill out a developmental history form (see Appendix C).

▶ For every kid, assuming she has at least fifth-grade reading level, I ask for (a) an omnibus rating scale, (b) scales that target areas of concern, (c) an interpersonal inventory, (d) a sentence completion task (the latter two forms are Appendix D and Appendix E, respectively), and (e) a measure assessing strengths.

▶ I will have asked how many teachers the kid currently has. Then, for every teacher I ask for (a) an omnibus rating form and, if it's relevant, (b) a rating scale on a specific area of concern.

It is beyond the scope of this volume to list and review evaluation tools available for kids. However, I've listed some resources in Appendix J.

Once I have the packets put together, I'll turn to the parents and say: *Mom, here's your set, and Dad, here's yours. It would be helpful to me if you would fill these out without consulting with each other, even after you've finished. I find that if there are any differences across your forms, it's most helpful to me if you discuss them first in front of me. These forms all regard Aiden, except for the top form* (which is the screen for parental psychopathology). *Fill the top form out regarding yourself as it'll give me a good read on what toll stress is taking on you.* As parental psychopathology is the top moderator in the child psychotherapy outcome research, I started making this request a long time ago. At first, I was worried that parents might consider me intrusive. But that has not been my experience—though a small minority may complete the form without endorsing any symptoms. To the kid I say: *Aiden, these are your forms. The only people who should see them are you and me. That is why I am putting them in this manila envelope for you. It would be most helpful if you could bring these back with you to our next appointment. Oh, and don't worry about getting things right or wrong as this isn't about that. And you'll find that sometimes you'll go back and forth between let's say a "3" and a "4," but don't overthink it—just go with your first feeling. Finally, be sure to not skip any items and to fill out items on the back page also.* I then give the teacher forms to the parent, stating: *These are forms for Aiden's teachers to complete. Schools vary regarding how to best coordinate this request. If you're unsure, you could always just ask the principal. Oh, and it's up to you if you mention me. If you don't care to, you can always just say that you've found these forms are a way for you to get more detailed information on how Aiden is doing, and ask if they would mind filling them out.* (In Chapter 4 I review how to respond to situations where the parents don't want to have the teachers complete ratings.)

I next list what records I want the parents to get for me, sending me things I can keep for myself. These usually include all end-of-the-year report cards, all state achievement testing, records from previous mental health contacts, any discipline records that might exist (e.g., detentions), and any other relevant records (e.g., legal). I suggest that we not mail off releases but that they go to the person or agency of concern and either wait while the records are copied for them or get a date by which they'll be mailed to me.

I tell parents that we can schedule the individual interview with their kid right now but that I'll wait to schedule the feedback session until I receive everything back. I then say: *I know the really important questions you have I won't be able to address until the feedback session, but do any of you have any more immediate questions or concerns before we stop?* I then also sometimes (depending on time) ask each person, starting with the kid: *Is this what you expected today, better or worse?* It's rare to hear "worse," but if I do I'd make time to discuss that. We then schedule the individual interview. After that I'll turn to the kid and ask: *Do you like magic?* In my experience that's like asking someone, "Do you like puppies?" If I get a neutral or positive answer (which is typical), I'll light my wallet on fire, following it up by stating that we can do some magic together at the next appointment if he likes (you can purchase a fire wallet at www.penguinmagic.com, but the one I use I purchased at www.theatremagic.com).

INDIVIDUAL INTERVIEW WITH THE KID

This interview has three goals: (a) to further enhance the alliance, (b) to rule out internalizing problems, and (c) to see if the kid's perspective on anything important is different without his parents in the room.

I begin as follows: *Aiden, before we start it's important that you understand a rule that I have about things you tell me. I don't know if we'll ever be alone again. But, if we are, this rule always goes even if I don't mention it again. That rule is that I don't tell anyone what you tell me without your permission. The only exception is if you tell me something that means that you or someone else is in danger. Otherwise, if you tell me something I'd like to be able to tell your parents, I wouldn't do so unless you said it was okay, no matter how much I want to tell them. Did you know that was a rule?* I find about half of kids answer "no," making this even more important to say.

I next ask how he felt about the first interview: *Did you like it, not like it, or in between?* If I get a positive or negative response I'll ask for the reason(s). I'll also ask what conversation occurred between him and his parents about it afterward.

I then begin, using the form you'll find in Appendix F titled "Individual Interview With the Youth." In the first interview I ask the front-door question about depression, anxiety, and so forth. These interview questions come at the same issues we covered in the family interview, but from the back door. Front-door questions ask about symptoms. Back-door questions get at the same content less directly. For example, an angry child once said the animal he'd choose to be would be a leech, so he could crawl across the room, attach himself to my face, and suck the blood out of me. A suicidal teen once said he'd like to meet Kurt Cobain so he could find out if their interest in suicide was similar, while an anxious girl once said she wanted to be a cheetah because they escape danger the fastest. A single answer usually doesn't carry that much weight, but over the course of the interview themes often emerge. You'll also notice that sex, drugs, and rock-n-roll type questions are covered in this interview at the end.

For children and younger teens, I also try to leave time for them to do at least a drawing of their family and to make up a pretend story about the picture. If time allows, I'll also ask for them to do a drawing about anything, as long as they can make up a pretend story about it. For the drawing medium I give the choice between paper and pencil/crayon or drawing software on my computer (I use KidPix, but there are many other viable choices).

I'll also ask if the kid would like to see a magic trick and learn how to do it. As I reviewed in Chapter 1, I don't do this to help with my clinical formulations. I do it because it is fun, takes only a few moments, and facilitates the alliance. The first trick I show and teach kids is in Sidebar 2.1, at the end of this chapter.

WORK IN BETWEEN SESSIONS

One of the most important components of the evaluation phase is the time I spend on my own going over my notes, records, and rating scales. A complex array of data presents itself for analysis. The task is to answer this question: What theory of this child and family explain most, or even all, of these data?

As a practical matter, I tell my families that the sooner they get back to me rating scales and records, the sooner we can meet for feedback; sometimes I need to help a parent to strategize, but I usually leave it to them to work through obstacles. Once I have everything, I'll call the family and set the feedback session, planning for when I will invest the 2 to 3 hours I'll need to put everything together. When I was new to kid clinical work, I'd spend at least double that time. Of course, for those of you who report to a supervisor, you'll need even more time to write your draft psychosocial report and meet with your supervisor. I know this seems like a lot, and it is, but being thorough, in a cost-effective way, pays many dividends later.

EVALUATING SUICIDAL IDEATION

It is beyond the scope of this volume to give comprehensive coverage to lethality evaluations. However, please see Appendix G for an interview form that contains the relevant content to collect so that you can make an informed decision about how to proceed, in consultation with a supervisor or colleague. Also, in the References and Bibliography section of this chapter I include a brief article I wrote for *The Pennsylvania Psychologist* that describes how to use this form.

SIDEBAR 2.1

The four fire engines. This is the first magic trick I ever remember learning as a kid. Prepare by separating out the four aces in a standard deck of cards. Then, put any other three cards behind the last ace, positioning them so that only the four aces are viewable. This is the pattern:

Showing the four aces: *Aiden, each of these aces is a fire truck, and the rest of the deck here is a city. Go ahead and look to see that there are no other fire trucks in the city. Okay, so let's put the city facedown and put the four fire trucks on top* (make sure you don't flash the three cards that are behind the last ace). *In the city a fire alarm rings, so the first truck goes out into the city to put it out* (you then put the top card, which is not an ace, somewhere into the deck). *While that truck is out, another fire alarm goes off somewhere else in the city so that truck has to go out to put that one out. You put that one back into the city like I did the first time. OMG, then a THIRD alarm goes off so the third truck has to go out* (repeat with the kid putting the third card back into the deck), *leaving only one fire truck in the station. Fortunately, no other fire alarms go off and the three trucks finish their job. So, you knock three times on the top to bring the three fire trucks home.* Then, turn over the four aces.

If I have time and the kid is interested I'll show him how to do the trick. Assuming the kid expresses an interest, I'll tell him that he has to agree to three rules before I show him any magic tricks:

1. He has to agree to practice it before showing it to anyone (I sometimes encourage the kid to show it to me first at the next appointment, practicing in between).

2. He agrees to show the trick only one time to each person.

3. He has to agree to not tell anyone how to do it. I'll say to him: *Here's a good way to not offend anyone who wants to know how to do it. Ask me right now how to do that trick.* (The kid asks.) *Can you keep a secret?* (The kid says "yes.") *Well, so can I* (followed by a big smile).

REFERENCES AND BIBLIOGRAPHY

Achenbach, T. M. (2005). Advancing assessment of children and adolescents: Commentary on evidence-based assessment of children and adolescent disorders. *Journal of Clinical Child & Adolescent Psychology, 34*(3), 541–547.

Achenbach, T. M. (2006). As others see us: Clinical and research implications of cross-informant correlations for psychopathology. *Current Directions in Psychological Science, 15*(2), 94–98.

Achenbach, T. M., McConaughy, S. H., & Howell, C. T. (1987). Child/adolescent behavioral and emotional problems: Implications of cross-informant correlations for situational specificity. *Psychological Bulletin, 101*(2), 213–232.

Ackerman, S. J., Benjamin, L. S., Beutler, L. E., Gelso, C. J., Goldfried, M. R., Hill, C., & Rainer, J. (2001). Empirically supported therapy relationships: Conclusions and recommendations for the Division 29 Task Force. *Psychotherapy Theory Research & Practice, 38*(4), 495–497.

Ackerman, S. J., & Hilsenroth, M. J. (2003). A review of therapist characteristics and techniques positively impacting the therapeutic alliance. *Clinical Psychology Review, 23*(1), 1–33.

Ahn, C. M., Ebesutani, C., & Kamphaus, R. (2014). A psychometric analysis and standardization of the Behavior Assessment System for Children-2, Self-Report of Personality, Child Version among a Korean sample. *School Psychology Quarterly, 29*(2), 198–212.

Althoff, R. R., Ayer, L. A., Rettew, D. C., & Hudziak, J. J. (2010). Assessment of dysregulated children using the Child Behavior Checklist: A receiver operating characteristic curve analysis. *Psychological Assessment, 22*(3), 609–617.

Anderson, S. K., & Handelsman, M. M. (2013). A positive and proactive approach to the ethics of the first interview. *Journal of Contemporary Psychotherapy, 43*(1), 3–11. doi:10.1007/s10879 -012-9219-3

Baldwin, S. A., Wampold, B. E., & Imel, Z. E. (2007). Untangling the alliance-outcome correlation: Exploring the relative importance of therapist and patient variability in the alliance. *Journal of Consulting and Clinical Psychology, 75*(6), 842–852.

Bedi, R. P. (2006). Concept mapping the client's perspective on counseling alliance formation. *Journal of Counseling Psychology, 53*(1), 26–35.

Bedi, R. P., & Richards, M. (2011). What a man wants: The male perspective on therapeutic alliance formation. *Psychotherapy, 48*(4), 381–390.

Bigham, K., Daley, D. M., Hastings, R. P., & Jones, R. P. (2013). Association between parent reports of attention deficit hyperactivity disorder behaviours and child impulsivity in children with severe intellectual disability. *Journal of Intellectual Disability Research, 57*(2), 191–197.

Bordin, E. S. (1979). The generalizability of the psychoanalytic concept of the working alliance. *Psychotherapy: Theory, Research & Practice, 16*(3), 252–260.

Burstein, M., Stanger, C., & Dumenci, L. (2012). Relations between parent psychopathology, family functioning, and adolescent problems in substance-abusing families: Disaggregating the effects of parent gender. *Child Psychiatry and Human Development, 43*(4), 631–647.

Cheng, M. S. (2007). New approaches for creating the therapeutic alliance: Solution-focused interviewing, motivational interviewing, and the medication interest model. *Psychiatric Clinics of North America, 30*(2), 157–166.

Dowdy, E., Chin, J. K., Twyford, J. M., & Dever, B. V. (2011). A factor analytic investigation of the BASC-2 Behavioral and Emotional Screening System Parent Form: Psychometric properties, practical implications, and future directions. *Journal of School Psychology, 49*(3), 265–280.

Dowdy, E., Twyford, J. M., Chin, J. K., DiStefano, C. A., Kamphaus, R. W., & Mays, K. L. (2011). Factor structure of the BASC-2 Behavioral and Emotional Screening System Student Form. *Psychological Assessment, 23*(2), 379–387.

Dumas, J. E., & Albin, J. B. (1986). Parent training outcome: Does active parental involvement matter? *Behaviour Research and Therapy, 24*(2), 227–230.

Elliott, S. N., & Busse, R. T. (1993). Behavior rating scales: Issues of use and development. *School Psychology Review, 22*(2), 313–321.

Fong, M. L., & Cox, B. G. (1983). Trust as an underlying dynamic in the counseling process: How clients test trust. *Personnel & Guidance Journal, 62*(3), 163.

Frick, P. J., Barry, C. T., & Kamphaus, R. W. (2010). *Clinical assessment of child and adolescent personality and behavior.* New York, NY: Springer.

Friedlander, M. L., Escudero, V., Heatherington, L., & Diamond, G. M. (2011). Alliance in couple and family therapy. *Psychotherapy, 48*(1), 25–33.

Gunlicks, M. L., & Weissman, M. M. (2008). Change in child psychopathology with improvement in parental depression: A systematic review. *Journal of the American Academy of Child & Adolescent Psychiatry, 47*(4), 379–389.

Herzhoff, K., Tackett, J. L., & Martel, M. M. (2013). A dispositional trait framework elucidates differences between interview and questionnaire measurement of childhood attention problems. *Psychological Assessment, 25*(4), 1079–1090.

Javo, C., Rønning, J. A., Handegård, B. H., & Rudmin, F. W. (2009). Cross-informant correlations on social competence and behavioral problems in Sami and Norwegian preadolescents. *European Child & Adolescent Psychiatry, 18*(3), 154–163.

Jones, K. D. (2010). The unstructured clinical interview. *Journal of Counseling & Development, 88*(2), 220–226.

Karver, M. S., Handelsman, J. B., Fields, S., & Bickman, L. (2005). Meta-analysis of therapeutic relationship variables in youth and family therapy: The evidence for different relationship variables in the child and adolescent treatment literature. *Clinical Psychology Review, 26*, 50–65.

Kaslow, N. J., Deering, C. G., & Racusin, G. R. (1994). Depressed children and their families. *Clinical Psychology Review, 14*(1), 39–59.

Knobloch-Fedders, L. M., Pinsof, W. M., & Mann, B. J. (2004). The formation of the therapeutic alliance in couple therapy. *Family Process, 43*(4), 425–442.

Kosterman, R., Hawkins, J. D., Mason, W. A., Herrenkohl, T. I., Lengua, L. J., & McCauley, E. (2010). Assessment of behavior problems in childhood and adolescence as predictors of early adult depression. *Journal of Psychopathology & Behavioral Assessment, 32*(1), 118–127.

Laskey, B. J., & Cartwright-Hatton, S. (2009). Parental discipline behaviours and beliefs about their child: Associations with child internalizing and mediation relationships. *Child: Care, Health, and Development, 35*(5), 717–727.

MacFarlane, P., Anderson, T., & McClintock, A. S. (2015). The early formation of the working alliance from the client's perspective: A qualitative study. *Psychotherapy, 52*(3), 363–372.

McClintock, A. S., Anderson, T., & Petrarca, A. (2015). Treatment expectations, alliance, session positivity, and outcome: An investigation of a three-path mediation model. *Journal of Clinical Psychology, 71*(1), 41–49.

Myers, C. L. (2013). Comparing results from the Clinical Assessment of Behavior and Child Behavior Checklist with referred preschoolers. *Psychology in the Schools, 50*(1), 1–12.

Ormhaug, S. M., Jensen, T. K., Wentzel-Larsen, T., & Shirk, S. R. (2014). The therapeutic alliance in treatment of traumatized youths: Relation to outcome in a randomized clinical trial. *Journal of Consulting and Clinical Psychology, 82*(1), 52–64.

Palmiter, D. (2013, March). Help us increase kids' access to mental health care. *The Pennsylvania Psychologist, 73*(2), 5.

Palmiter, D. J. (2004). A survey of the assessment practices of child and adolescent clinicians. *American Journal of Orthopsychiatry, 74*(2), 122–128.

Palmiter, D. J. (2008). Child clinician's corner: Sample content for an individual interview with a child or teen. *The Independent Practitioner, 28*, 149–151.

Palmiter, D. J. (2011, June). Assessing teenagers for suicidal ideation. *The Pennsylvania Psychologist, 71*(6), 13–14.

Pandolfi, V., Magyar, C. I., & Dill, C. A. (2009). Confirmatory factor analysis of the Child Behavior Checklist 1.5-5 in a sample of children with autism spectrum disorders. *Journal of Autism & Developmental Disorders, 39*(7), 986–995.

Patterson, C. L., Anderson, T., & Wei, C. (2014). Clients' pretreatment role expectations, the therapeutic alliance, and clinical outcomes in outpatient therapy. *Journal of Clinical Psychology, 70*(7), 673–680.

Price, M., Higa-McMillan, C., Ebesutani, C., Okamura, K., Nakamura, B. J., Chorpita, B. F., & Weisz, J. (2013). Symptom differentiation of anxiety and depression across youth development and clinic-referred/nonreferred samples: An examination of competing factor structures of the Child Behavior Checklist DSM-oriented scales. *Development & Psychopathology, 25*(4), 1005–1015.

Råbu, M., Halvorsen, M. S., & Haavind, H. (2011). Early relationship struggles: A case study of alliance formation and reparation. *Counseling & Psychotherapy Research, 11*(1), 23–33.

Rescorla, L. A., Achenbach, T. M., Ginzburg, S., Ivanova, M., Dumenci, L., Almqvist, F., . . . Verhulst, F. (2007). Consistency of teacher-reported problems for students in 21 countries. *School Psychology Review, 36*(1), 91–110.

Rescorla, L., Achenbach, T., Ivanova, M. Y., Dumenci, L., Almqvist, F., Bilenberg, N., & Leung, P. (2007). Behavioral and emotional problems reported by parents of children ages 6 to 16 in 31 societies. *Journal of Emotional & Behavioral Disorders, 15*(3), 130–142.

Roussos, A., Karantanos, G., Richardson, C., Hartman, C., Karajiannis, D., Kyprianos, S., . . . Zoubou, V. (1999). Achenbach's Child Behavior Checklist and Teachers' Report Form in a normative sample of Greek children 6–12 years old. *European Child & Adolescent Psychiatry, 8*(3), 165.

Sander, J. B., & McCarty, C. A. (2005). Youth depression in the family context: Familial risk factors and models of treatment. *Clinical Child and Family Psychology Review, 8*(3), 203–219.

Schmidt, F., Chomycz, S., Houlding, C., Kruse, A., & Franks, J. (2014). The association between therapeutic alliance and treatment outcomes in a group triple P intervention. *Journal of Child & Family Studies, 23*(8), 1337–1350.

Shirk, S. R., Karver, M. S., & Brown, R. (2011). The alliance in child and adolescent psychotherapy. *Psychotherapy, 48*(1), 17–24.

Stanger, C., & Lewis, M. (1993). Agreement among parents, teachers, and children on internalizing and externalizing behavior problems. *Journal of Clinical Child Psychology, 22*(1), 107.

Stockings, E., Degenhardt, L., Lee, Y. Y., Mihalopoulos, C., Liu, A., Hobbs, M., & Patton, G. (2015). Symptom screening scales for detecting major depressive disorder in children and adolescents: A systematic review and meta-analysis of reliability, validity, and diagnostic utility. *Journal of Affective Disorders, 174*, 447–463.

Taber, B. J., Leibert, T. W., & Agaskar, V. R. (2011). Relationships among client–therapist personality congruence, working alliance, and therapeutic outcome. *Psychotherapy, 48*(4), 376–380.

Tyron, G. S., & Winorgrad, G. (2011). Goal consensus and collaboration. *Psychotherapy, 48*(1), 50–57.

Van Meter, A., Youngstrom, E., Youngstrom, J. K., Ollendick, T., Demeter, C., & Findling, R. L. (2014). Clinical decision making about child and adolescent anxiety disorders using the Achenbach System of Empirically Based Assessment. *Journal of Clinical Child & Adolescent Psychology, 43*(4), 552–565.

CHAPTER 3

Feedback and Treatment Planning

FEEDBACK SESSION

Feedback is the breakfast of champions.
—Ken Blanchard

My clinical experience and the research are in harmony: We parent-lunatics *love* good feedback. My style is to begin with the parent(s) alone, leaving the kid in the waiting room and telling the kid that I'll bring her in at the end. (For younger children, I may offer some play materials, though most come equipped with entertainment.) I start with the parents alone, as I want to be able to speak plainly, in adult language, without concern for how a kid might misinterpret something I've said.

Here is an outline of the feedback session:

1. Review of my lingering questions

2. An explanation of how measurement is used to help diagnose

3. A review of the specific diagnostic formulation and how I arrived at it

4. A review of the etiology and prevalence research regarding the diagnosis or diagnoses in question

5. A pause for parent questions and comments

6. A review of the recommendations without consideration—within reason—of resources

7. Sometimes: a review of the next most likely possibility if the current formulation is incorrect

8. A pause for parent questions and comments

9. Inviting the kid to join the interview

   a. A review of the kid's strengths

   b. A summary of the problem areas

   c. A summary of the recommendations

10. Ask if anyone has any lingering questions or comments. Ask if the family wants to schedule the next appointment or if they prefer to go home and reflect first.

1. Once the parents come into the consulting room I usually have some follow-up questions I need to ask. They will endorse items on rating scales that I don't understand, there will be information in the records that needs clarification, or I need to learn things in order to reach closure on a differential diagnosis or a recommendation. I have these questions written down in advance and say something like this before I begin: *I have a few follow-up questions for you before I get to feedback. Because I have a lot that I want to do today, I'm going to ask for your permission to interrupt you once I've gotten what I need for any given question.* (I find that parents assent to this readily.)

2. After these final questions have been addressed I'm ready to give the feedback:

Okay, I'm ready to give you some feedback. I'd like to do this in two parts. First, I'll share a diagnostic formulation, and second, I will share my recommendations. If you have questions as I go, I'd ask you to wait until I've finished sharing my diagnostic impression, at which point I'll pause for questions and comments before I get to the recommendations. I have some writing material on the table in front of you in case you'd like to write down questions as I go (a). Once Monica joins us I'll review her considerable strengths. For now though I'm going to jump right in with a model for understanding the problems that concern you (b).

3. *In clinical psychology we know that most kids experience most problems some of the time. What kid isn't sad some of the time? Or worried? Or inattentive? In order to avoid making a mountain out of a molehill, we look for a given problem to be present to an unusual degree for kids of the same sex and age (c). Our convention is the 93rd percentile. We say that if a kid has a given problem worse than 93% of his peer group that he could be meeting criteria for a diagnosis (d).*

4. *I'd like to show you some graphs that demonstrate where Monica stands on some particular problem areas (e). Given what I learned in the family interview, my individual interview with Monica, my review of the records, and the rating scales, I believe she meets criteria for (the number of) diagnoses (f). I'd like to discuss a little what causes these kinds of problems and how common they are (g).*

5. I then pause and say:

You probably have a lot going through your minds right now. Before I get to what we might do to help Monica with these challenges, what questions or comments do you have **(h)?**

The parents' questions usually invite a segue into the recommendations, but I try to make sure they don't have any other questions about the diagnostic formulation until I go forward. I then say:

6. *When I make recommendations, I like to pretend that you and I have an abundance of resources at our disposal. That is, I don't really consider practical issues like time and cost, but only focus on answering the question: "What might heal Monica as fast as possible?" After I review what I think would do that, and answer your questions about those recommendations, we can then consider what's practical* **(i).**

7. I don't always do this part; it sort of depends on how ambivalent I am about my impression. The more I'm in doubt or feel like I'm missing important pieces of information (e.g., the parents have resisted allowing teachers to complete rating forms), the more I'm likely to say the following: *I'd like to discuss how we might reconceptualize Monica's problems if this plan doesn't work. If you decide to do what we've just discussed, and it works, no worries. But, if you do as we discussed and Monica does not improve, or improve enough, that would probably mean . . .* **(j).**

8. I'll then pause and address any questions that the parents have, keeping an eye on the clock as I want to be sure to have at least 10 minutes to offer feedback to the kid. If the parents seem like they still have questions that we don't have time to get to, or if they just seem like deer in headlights, I'll say: *I want to be sure to have time to bring in Monica to go over what we've been discussing. But I know you probably have other questions. So, we can be sure to cover those first thing when I see you next.*

9. I then ask the kid to join us and say: *Monica, you know how you and I had time alone so that I could ask you questions? Well, I needed time like that with your parents, too. So that's what we were doing when they first came in. Then I shared with them some thoughts I have about you. I'd like to share some of those thoughts with you now as well.*

9a. *I'll tell you that I've certainly gotten to know you very well! See this chart* (motioning to what is usually a thick-looking folder), *this is all about* you. (I'll sometimes riffle through the folder, or act like I'm estimating its weight with my hand for effect.) *Plus, I have about another 30 or so pages of things about you on my computer that I didn't print out. I feel like I've just watched a movie about your life. And what all this tells me is how many strengths you have! This is what I think they are . . .* **(k).**

9b. *Okay, but it looks like you also have* (insert the number) *kinds of problems . . .* (l). *I'll tell you, I've been doing this for a lot of years so I know that sometimes I say things that kids don't agree with. Tell me, does part of what I've said sound off to you* (m)? *Okay, well, I also know that sometimes I think I'm explaining things well but I'm not; I'm being confusing. The only way I can check to see how good of a job I've done is to ask you to say things back to me. What am I saying are your strengths* (n)? *What am I saying the problems seem to be* (o)?

9c. *I've suggested to your parents some ideas about what we can do about these* (insert number) *problems . . .* (p). *What are your thoughts about that* (q)?

10. It's now time to wrap up. I'll end by directing a question to everyone:

Before we finish, does anyone have any closing questions or comments? . . . Well, I know that I've just shared a TON of information and that thinking about all of this can be a lot to do. So, do you want to take time to think through what you want to do before we schedule a next appointment, or would you like to schedule something now (r)?

Explanation

a. I think it's important to have parents wait with their questions. Otherwise, the session quickly becomes the tail wagging the dog. Though this can appear to be creating a small slight, both the tail and the dog tend to feel undone and stressed when letting the parents' questions structure the interview. Moreover, I don't want to forget things I want to say, and many of the questions parents want to ask I'll tend to get to on my own anyway. Having the writing material readily available is also a way of both alleviating parental anxiety (e.g., that a question will be forgotten if not asked) and showing respect.

b. If I had more time I'd review the strengths here as well. But, as the agenda is packed, I will review the strengths when the kid comes in. Moreover, the parents have brought their kid in to me in order to address problems first and foremost.

c. I find this to be a common worry among parents: that mental health professionals (MHPs) overpathologize kids. I once had a mom challenge me: "If Huckleberry Finn were alive today we'd diagnose him with attention deficit hyperactivity disorder, pump him full of drugs, and crush his wonderful distinctiveness!" Fortunately, an evidence-based assessment, the likes of which we are going over, accounts for this concern very well.

d. This cuts to the quick regarding why well-constructed behavior rating scales are an essential tool to child or adolescent MHPs who practice in an evidence-based fashion. One needn't be a psychologist to work with these rating scales. Sure, to give a Wechsler Intelligence Scale for Children or a Minnesota

Multiphasic Personality Inventory–Adolescent, one would need to be a psychologist. But these behavior scales are much simpler to use, though you'll need a little training to use them properly (e.g., coaching from your local friendly psychologist or a webinar by the publisher of the test). Also note that some parents do not know what a percentile is, so that may need an explanation. Recognize that more educated parents may also ask sophisticated questions about how the scales you're using have been constructed and validated, so be prepared; it's okay not to know the answers to these questions right away, but having easy access to the answers is important so that you can get back to them at the next appointment.

It should be noted that the norming of these instruments has an Achilles' heel: We can do a decent job comparing kids based on sex and age, but we do a terrible job comparing them based on other cultural factors, such as race. For diverse families, this is an important point to acknowledge as early in the process as is clinically advisable. There is also value in speculating to what degree, if any, you might subjectively adjust scores secondary to what you know about the multicultural issues in question, with all due caveats being offered.

e. I find offering this language to be one of the most alliance-enhancing activities that I do with parents. While the alliance is usually already pretty good by this juncture, this review can put it over the top. I also usually make a highlighted yellow line at the 50th, 84th (1 standard deviation in a normal distribution, which is a common subclinical cutoff), and 93rd (1.5 standard deviations in a normal distribution, which is a common clinical cutoff) percentiles for clinical scales, and at the 50th, 16th, and 7th percentiles for adaptive scales.

f. I've seen too many cases of clinicians avoiding using the actual diagnostic label for fear of sounding insulting. However, I just about always share the term with the parents for two primary reasons. First, I believe that to not do so is paternalistic. How would we feel if our physician kept back the name of a diagnosis for fear that we would feel insulted? Second, I very much hope that parents will educate themselves about the diagnosis, as doing so will usually make them better partners in the care of their child. To do this, they need the name of the thing, which brings to mind the Chinese proverb I shared at the beginning of Chapter 2.

g. The depth and breadth of this feedback varies across families. Some families are like I would be: I'd want to know as much about the relevant science as the clinician could tell me in the time that we have. For these families I'll copy articles, give links to science-based websites, and print out relevant sections of the *ICD-10*. Other families want to turn over all steering activities to me and get to the recommendations as fast as possible. For these types of families this can be a fairly brief discussion.

Regardless of how much the parents want to know about the relevant science, I try to address, sometimes explicitly but always implicitly, the ubiquitous parent-lunatic question: "Did I cause this?" Rare is a mental health problem in a kid that is caused by one thing. Moreover, engaged parents are the best-intended people on the planet, even when they make significant errors. So, the truth I have to share usually offers some combination of relief and hope.

h. I love questions. They offer opportunities for collaboration, alliance enhancement, and learning. The collaboration occurs when I can acknowledge the value of the parents' questions and how the underlying concerns are important in designing the intervention plan. The alliance enhancement occurs when I can offer an understandable and accurate answer. The learning occurs when parents ask me a relevant question that I don't know the answer to. Granted, after you've been doing this awhile, that doesn't happen as much. However, whether you are a grizzled vet or a practicum newbie, I think it's good to say something like this when you don't know an answer to a question: *Y'know, that's an awesome question and I don't know the answer to it as we sit here. But I am going to look into it and get back to you at our next appointment if that works for you.* Paradoxically, when a lean-mean-healing-machine can say "I don't know," it facilitates an impression that the clinician is self-confident and competent. On some level most of us realize that know-it-alls are often insecure.

i. Too many times I've heard MHPs *not* sharing a recommendation and giving reasons like, "I know they can't afford that, so I don't want to frustrate them." Or, "They have to drive an hour each way for that sort of a session and I know they're too busy for that." Or, and perhaps worst of all, "I know their insurance won't cover that so I'm not even going to suggest it." If you're in doubt about where I'm going with this, imagine that a loved one of yours had cancer and the treatment team told you about only those treatments *that they thought* would be a fit for you. I'm aggravated even writing this paragraph, so I can't even imagine how turned off I'd be if a clinician ever did that to me or someone I love. Parents have surprised me over and over again with their creativity, resilience, and resourcefulness when it comes to getting the care that their "baby" needs. Don't get me wrong, I'm not going to suggest pie-in-the-sky interventions the likes of which are only available to the uber-wealthy. I'm just talking about suggesting an intervention plan that is evidence-based and stands the best chance of healing the kid as soon as possible.

Once I'm done making the recommendations that pertain directly to the kid of concern, I'll sometimes add this remark (if one or more of the parental screens for psychopathology is positive): *Roberto and Paula, the same percentile thing goes for us adults as well. I'd like to show you charts regarding the instrument you filled out on yourself. I need to note that this instrument is not designed to diagnose so much as it addresses the question, "Might this person be suffering needlessly?" Roberto, this form suggests that you may be suffering needlessly.* (I review the graph and explain it.) *Let me ask you, if it was possible to feel better in a short period of time, could I interest you in having that discussion with a good clinician?*

j. What we do is a probabilistic enterprise. There is always contradicting data and all of us are wrong at least some of the time. Plus, the science is evolving. I know I thought, and was taught, things as a trainee that science has since disproven (e.g., young children don't suffer from depression, the best way to treat child defiance is play therapy). Humility is a personality attribute that not only serves us ethically, but it can also make us better clinicians. To be humble is not to lack confidence. It is to say that we appreciate that our minds, our science, and our art can be wrong, and often in surprising ways. So, if there is a viable theory of the child that captures some degree of interest in my mind, and assuming that sharing it would not be harmful, I share it.

k. This is one of my personal favorite moments in child clinical practice. First of all, the kid is bracing for a lot of bad news. I'm a "shrink," after all, and our culture suggests that shrinks are all about problems. So, I like being surprising in this way. But I also enjoy the effect on the parents and how bucked up the kid often seems to become. By the way, I don't generate this list just to be a nice guy. I do it to be objective, empathic, thorough, and accurate; to me, each of those words gets to the same place.

l. I usually don't use diagnostic language here, unless I'm dealing with a very mature teenager. Instead I use phrasing such as: ***Doing things when you don't feel like it, feeling worried a lot, often feeling sad, what you do when you get angry,*** and so forth.

m. If we offer a typical kid a "yes-no" type of question (e.g., "Does that sound right?" or "Do you agree?") that kid will take the easy out to move on with the conversation in order to get off the spot. But experienced MHPs know that differences not put into words will often be put to behavior. So, I press for differences to get them out in the open. If I get some answers, I'll get a full vetting, offer empathy, and then clarify further.

n. It's interesting to see what a kid remembers. If she struggles to remember her strengths, this can be a further indication of a mood disturbance, especially if the kid remembers the problems better. If that happens, I'll sometimes use that as a subsequent teaching point with the kid and the parents about how depression works. Regardless, I'll repeat back whatever strengths the kid didn't repeat and ask what she thinks about my impression of those strengths.

o. Interestingly, most kids can do a good job repeating back this feedback. Parents can be surprised when a kid does this, and agrees. Parents are used to battling with their kids about these issues. So, accessing the reasonable side of their kid in this moment facilitates a parental realization that their kid has an adaptive side as well.

p. Here I'll review only those recommendations that involve the kid. So, if I've recommended things like an evaluation for marriage counseling, I won't share that with the kid. I also use developmentally appropriate descriptions like: *I'm suggesting that you and I meet so that I can teach you some ways of not feeling worried,* or *I've recommended that you, your mom, your dad, and I meet to figure out how to cut down on all the arguing that's going on.*

q. Anything from a positive to a neutral response is good here. If a kid says she doesn't want to do this or that, I'll get a vetting of her concerns, provide empathy, and then state that it's really up to her parents, in consultation with her, to decide, but that I hope we'll do the thing because I think it would help reduce this or that symptom or problem.

r. I'd estimate that 85% of families decide to schedule the next appointment. But this is a lot to digest. So, some folks want to go home and think it all through first. If that's the case, I'll get a date by which they'll be back in touch so that I know whether or not we are moving forward. If I then don't hear from them by that date, I'll either call them for an update or send a letter.

What About Medication?

For most internalizing disorders, the extant science suggests that the optimal approach is a combination of pharmacotherapy and cognitive behavioral therapy (CBT). I share this information with the parents. When the kid has mild to moderate symptom expression, I'll take a neutral position regarding whether they might pursue such an evaluation. It's only when a kid is highly vegetative or reclusive that I'll lobby more actively for such an evaluation. However, my clinical experience suggests that when kids have mild to moderate symptoms, most parents will elect to try the CBT first as the kid will often end up not needing to take medicine.

TREATMENT PLANNING

If you don't know where you are going, you'll end up someplace else.
—*Yogi Berra*

For the early part of my career, I experienced treatment planning as being a pain in the neck. I thought of it as something mandated by accrediting bodies and insurance companies that distracted me and my clients from our meaningful agenda. However, I later did a complete 180 on that position. I now believe that treatment planning is *one of the most important* aspects of child clinical work. There are at least four benefits to treatment planning.

First, and perhaps most important, we keep our work accountable when we establish measurable goals. If three things are true, it's expected that we will reach these goals: (a) the diagnostic formulation is sufficiently accurate, (b) the interventions are informed by science and delivered artfully, and (c) the child and/or parents sufficiently adhere to the agreed-on interventions. If everyone is working well, but measurable progress is not occurring, something is amiss in the formulation. But it's harder to come to this realization if measurable goals are not first established.

Second, the presence of measurable goals makes it more likely that treatment won't continue on needlessly. What child or parent or family is ever problem free? Having measurable goals suggests that the work has been sufficiently helpful.

Third, having measurable goals in place creates the opportunity to have a highly rewarding and dynamic termination to the work. As experienced child MHPs know, once the work gets underway it can be hard to distinguish the forest from the trees. Thus, even I can be surprised when I break out a treatment plan and learn that we've met or exceeded our goals. To this day I can still end up privately thinking, "Man, this *&^% really works!" Of course, parents and kids are often totally blown away by the progress.

Fourth, a well-written treatment plan is a wonderful tool for dealing with petitions by parents or kids to terminate prematurely (see Chapters 16 and 17).

I form the treatment plan with whatever family member(s) I'm meeting with the most. For externalizing diagnoses (e.g., oppositional defiant disorder, conduct disorder) that is usually the parents for kids age 12 and under and the family for adolescents. For internalizing disorders (e.g., generalized anxiety disorder, dysthymic disorder), that is usually the kid of concern. As this book is geared more toward the latter than the former, I present the clinical scripts for developing a treatment plan for a kid. The form I use can be found in Appendix H.

This is the outline for treatment planning with a kid:

1. Review of impressions from the feedback session

2. Explaining the rationale for treatment planning

3. Soliciting the kid's input and developing problem and goal statements

4. Endorsement and cautions

5. Bringing parents into the loop

1. I typically start my next one-on-one meeting with the kid like this (keep in mind that the wording would be simpler for young children):

Hi, Monica. So, let me ask: Our last session, was it what you expected, better or worse (a)? . . . Did you and your parents discuss it afterward (b)? . . .

2. *Okay, I'm assuming that you don't want to see me for longer than is useful to you. So, the first thing I like to do is to have us agree on some goals for our work. By the way, what's a 'goal' (c)? . . . There are two reasons why I'd like to set up some goals. First, having goals will tell us if our work is helpful to you. Neither one of us wants to be doing this unless it really makes your life better. Second,*

having goals will let us know when we can think about stopping our work. Any questions about that? . . . Mind saying back to me the reasons we set up goals so I can make sure I explained it right **(d)**?

3. *Okay, how I like to do this is by asking you to imagine that we are in the future and that our work has been a home run, with the ball bouncing in the parking lot. I mean, it's just been outstanding how helpful it's been. And we have a video of your life at that point in time. What might we see on that video that would be different from a video of your life right now? I ask it this way because if you can see it on a video we can usually measure it. So, what would we see? . . . We have room for four goals, which doesn't mean that we can only work on four things. We are just looking for two to four good signs of a very improved life for you* **(e)**.

4. Once we have two to four goals written down, I'll say this:

Monica, great job in helping us to set some goals. Okay, now we both sign it. This isn't a legal thing. It's a way of saying that we both agree to work toward these goals **(f)**. *. . . Okay, now that we've done this, let's forget about these goals. These aren't a to-do list or things for you to now march out and try to get done. If what we do works, these things will just happen automatically. It's like if water is on a hill, in what direction does it move? . . . Right, it goes downhill. But, if a wall blocks the water it can stop flowing. However, if you remove the wall, no one has to command the water to flow downhill again. It just does. It's like that with these goals. If I've understood your problems right, and if you do the things I'll teach you to do, the goals should just happen naturally, like water flowing downhill. Any questions* **(g)**?

5. There is usually not a burning need to inform the parents about these goals right away. In Chapter 9, I review how I bring parents on board. However, clearly this is a matter of style rather than substance, so you may decide to share the treatment plan with the parents sooner. However, I usually wait until the first parent session to review the treatment plan, assuming the kid has given me permission to do so—and I can't remember a time when a kid didn't.

Explanation

a.   Like we saw in the individual evaluation session with the kid, most say as expected or better. "As expected" responses work for me, though hearing "better" often suggests that the feedback session instilled hope. However, I'm doing this primarily to rule out the "worse" answer. As I discuss throughout this book, it's better to have negative thoughts and feelings put to words than behavior. We can work with words but often are challenged to catch up with behaviors. If a kid says "worse," I try to get a full articulation of the concern(s), offer empathy (which sometimes leads to more words about the concerns), and then offer any reassurances or course corrections. A kid might say, "It just sounds like you're working for my parents, so you should meet with them, not me." Which would then allow me to say something like: *Boy, I hear where you're coming from. That'd suck to have to come here just to accomplish things that your parents want but you don't. However, I have some good news for you. You set the goals for our work, not your parents. So, I actually work for you, not them. You're my client, not them. And I can't tell them what you tell me without your say-so, except for those couple of exceptions I mentioned two sessions ago. So they may pay me, but I work for you. Bottom line: We don't work on squat if it doesn't help us to accomplish something that matters to you!*

b. Again, I'm mine sweeping. Sure, I might hear encouraging things like "Everyone said it went well and this is good," and that's nice to hear. But I'm mostly making sure parents haven't done things like complain about the cost, or yell at the kid for things she said, or that the family hasn't gotten into an argument about how the care will be prioritized over extracurricular activities. One of the delightful things about this work is that once you've seen one family you've seen one family; so, the mines can be *anywhere and everywhere*. Therefore, I prefer to deploy mine sweepers before my clinical ships are launched.

c. This is sort of like asking a kid to tell you how many days are in a week before you ask questions about weeks. We just want to make sure that the kid knows what a goal is. If not, we can say something like:

   A goal is something that you work toward. Like you study for a test to get a good grade. You practice at soccer so that you can help your team to win the next game. So, here we need to come up with what we are hoping will change in your life because we are working together.

d. I'll shoot you straight. I don't always do this, but I mean to always do this. That is, I mean to check to make sure that the kid has truly understood what I've said. I guess I'm like a lot of MHPs in that I *think* I'm being such a good teacher and that I'm being so very clear, when sometimes that is not the case. It saves so much time and energy, and does a lot to facilitate the alliance, to take a few moments to check.

e. I would argue that poor goals would be things like "increase self-esteem" or "get along better with my parents" or "become more popular." While clearly important domains, these goals are vague; and when it's time to review them, vague goals can leave everyone feeling "eh" and unsettled regarding whether they have been reached, because it is difficult to remember sometimes what things were like at the start of treatment. On the other hand, specific goals set the work up for a "shazam" moment when reviewing them later. While kids will often start with vague goals, we can help them to make the goals measurable. For example, this might be how a discussion could go:

Kid: *I'd be less afraid.*
MHP: *Awesome! I think that's a great idea. What would we see on the video that would tell us you were less afraid?*
Kid: *I don't know.*
MHP: *That's okay. Take your time. We're in no rush.*
Kid: *Well, I'd probably spend more time with friends.*
MHP: *Okay, now we're really getting somewhere. How many hours a week do you spend with friends now outside of school?*
Kid: *Hardly ever because I get too freaked out when I'm not at home or school.*
MHP: *So, like zero or near zero?*
Kid: *Yeah, unless they come to my house but they kind of get sick of that.*
MHP: *Okay, so right now (writing in the "problem box") you are spending zero hours with friends outside of home and school each week.*
Kid: *Yeah.*
MHP: *Okay, so if our work is successful, you'll spend at least how many hours a week with friends outside of home and school?*
Kid: *Eight?*
MHP: *That could happen, yes. But we want to set a minimum amount, or an amount that will happen even on busy weeks, even when you don't have a ton of time on your hands.*
Kid: *Two?*
MHP: *Would that be a major improvement, if you spent at least 2 hours each week with friends outside of school and home for at least 3 weeks in a row?*
Kid: *Huge. That'd be big.*
MHP: *Okay (writing it down in the goal box). Sounds like our first goal is finished.*

Sample imprecise goals	Transforming them into measurable goals
"Feel better about myself."	"Be able to look in the mirror for a minute without any negative thoughts or feelings."
	"I will ask out at least three girls on a date or land a girlfriend, whichever comes first."
"I won't feel so sad."	"I'll feel either sad or irritable no more than 10% of the day for a period of at least 2 weeks." (Granted, this is more of an internal phenomenon, but I find most kids can give an accurate report.)
	"I'll sleep at least eight restful hours a night and eat three solid meals a day for at least 2 weeks."

(continued)

(continued)

Sample imprecise goals	Transforming them into measurable goals
"I won't be so worried all the time."	"I'll be able to turn the lights off in rooms no more than once for a period of at least 2 weeks."
	"I'll be able to go to the bathroom in school whenever I feel the urge to go for a period of at least 2 weeks."
"I won't freak out so much."	"I'll yell no more than twice a week for a period of at least 3 weeks."
	"I won't throw anything or bang anything in anger for a period of at least 2 weeks."

f. Getting a signature is probably more useful for teens than children, but I do it for everyone for two reasons. First, it promotes buy-in. Second, if the kid later starts making sounds about wanting to stop before we are done, I don't go into salesman mode, I go into treatment plan review mode (see Chapter 16). Having the kid's signature on the document reminds her that these goals were not just my or her parents' dream for her.

g. This doesn't end up being a big deal for most kids. However, some anxious and/or achievement-oriented kids hear these goals as an adult directive to get going on a to-do list. And, if that would work, we probably would never have met the kid to begin with. Indeed, if we don't address this issue with such kids, our treatment starts freaking them out and they become a living caricature of the person who laments, "Shit! I said damn! Oh, *&^$, I just said 'shit'! . . . "

Two Closing Remarks

Sometimes kids struggle to come up with measurable goals. But, if you've followed the evaluation plan I reviewed in Chapter 2, you are usually already armed with tons of helpful data. That is, the kid has filled out rating scales that have indicated symptoms of concern. If the clinical gears start grinding, I'll break out these forms and start with the symptoms that seem most distressing to the kid. I might say something like: *Monica, on one of the forms you said that you have nightmares most nights. What would it be like to not have those anymore?* Moreover, I try very hard to not quote parental concerns unless (a) the kid comes up with nothing, (b) rating scales are of no help (not common), and (c) there is minimal or no estrangement or tension with the parent(s) in question.

The terms "at least" and "no more than" are critical phrases for treatment planning. "At least" is used for adaptive behaviors while "no more than" is used for symptoms. So, "at least" might be attached to physical activity, or studying, or socializing, and so forth. "No more than" will be attached to things like yelling or being avoidant or feeling sad. For the "at least" category, we say to kids: *This isn't to say that you won't have this happen way more. We just want to say that you'll do it at least this much each week in order to feel good.* For the "no more than" category, we say: *This isn't to say that it wouldn't be zero. It's just that you're human too and you're going to have off days and weeks. So, we want to put down what would be an amount that would show big-time progress and wouldn't totally mess up your life.*

TYPES OF TREATMENT CONTRACTS

I would argue that there are three categories of treatment contracts in kid clinical work: cure, management, and damage control. Deciding which is the primary category of a treatment plan is important because it influences how we communicate with the kid and his parents. Cure means that our goal is to eliminate the disorder(s) that are being treated. This is usually true for oppositional defiant disorder, mild to moderate conduct disorder, adjustment disorders, elimination disorders, most anxiety disorders, and mild to moderate unipolar mood disorders, though the relapse risk is significant. We are trying to manage (as we don't cure them) ADHD, pervasive developmental disorders, bipolar mood disorders, learning disabilities, some cases of posttraumatic stress disorder (PTSD) involving multiple traumas (e.g., incest), and schizophrenia. Sometimes we cure and sometimes we manage substance abuse disorders, obsessive-compulsive disorder, reactive attachment disorder, and eating disorders.

When discussing cure goals, metaphors like caging the internal enemy may apply (see Chapter 5), but the expectation is that ongoing treatment won't be needed outside of booster sessions. Thus, in cure intervention plans, the MHP and the family plan for a limited course of treatment. For management treatment contracts, kids and families are preparing for a marathon. One of the mistakes I've made, in treating juvenile-onset bipolar disorder, for example, is to not sufficiently prepare the family at the very beginning of treatment. If an athlete needs to run a marathon but trains for a 5K, that athlete increases the odds of becoming highly frustrated and unsuccessful. These discussions can occur through reviewing the treatment literature and my clinical experience, as well as by directing the family to quality psychoeducational materials.

But what about the third category of damage control treatment plans? "What are those?" you might be wondering. These are instances when we would wish to affect cure or management, but we are not provided with the means or resources to do so; however, we still can offer value. To be aware that this is the kind of treatment being offered, and to communicate about that openly with the family, does at least two things: (a) reduce MHP burnout and (b) reduce enabling resistance. Let me share a composite case to illustrate:

The kid was 16 years old and presented for treatment because the neighbor who had molested him was being released from prison; the man had been jailed secondary to the molestation. The teen had never received any mental health care. But, upon learning about the former neighbor's pending release, the teen started showing pronounced symptoms of PTSD. The evaluation also suggested that the teen was floundering in school, was starting to become promiscuous, and was defiant at home. The evaluation also suggested that the teen's single dad might have been suffering from bipolar disorder. Multiple recommendations were made: trauma-focused CBT for the teen to treat the PTSD, behaviorally oriented family therapy to treat the behavioral issues at school and home, consultation with the school and social service agencies (i.e., probation and parole and children and youth), and a mental health evaluation for the dad. After considerable discussion that spanned across three sessions, the dad made an informed decision to allow only one session a week for the teen to receive CBT. The thinking of the treatment team was that the MHP-trainee could be a harbor in the storm for this teen, which had value. The MHP-trainee then said something like this to the dad: "Jason, I'd really love to try to resolve all of Jackson's symptoms, and the recommendations I offered are designed to do that. But you've let me know that while you understand my reasoning, you disagree with it and only agree to bring him in for one 50-minute session a week of individual therapy. While I believe that falls significantly short of what Jackson needs, I still think that has value for him. In other words, I can try to be a harbor in the storm for him and try to keep things from getting worse. As long as you understand and agree to the fact that if we limit ourselves to this kind of a treatment plan, you may not see much improvement in Jackson's symptoms and may actually witness some of them worsening. Saying it succinctly, I'd be doing damage control. If you're okay with that I'm okay with that." The dad said he was okay with that. A few months later the dad came in and complained that he had been bringing his teen in for months without any improvement in his grades. The MHP-trainee then responded: "That is frustrating, Jason, isn't it? I mean, you really want to see Jackson do well in school, as do I. Let me take you back to our original discussion regarding the treatment plan. You may remember that I recommended both family therapy and school consultation to take care of that problem. If you'd like, I can review my reasoning now. . . . Certainly, I'm ready to go forward with those recommendations if you are ready to partner with me in taking a serious run at how Jackson is doing in school."

Of course, there can be many other reasons why a kid MHP is blocked from creating a viable cure or management treatment plan besides parental resistance: insurance plan limitations, system rules, legal mandates, and so forth. This is why I believe it's important to first communicate the best conceivable treatment plan before considering costs, parental attitudes, and context-limiting factors.

It's easy to script a formula for burnout: embrace responsibility for an important outcome (i.e., a kid's recovery) without having the power to reach that outcome (e.g., due to a resistant parent). Damage control treatment contracts recast everyone's expectations to be more realistic. I can't tell you how many times I've witnessed kid MHPs becoming burned out because of what seemed to be a self-imposed expectation to have divine powers. Damage control treatment contracts reduce the risk of MHP burnout. Moreover, notice how the dad in the previous example was communicated with in the vignette; it was a lot harder for him to tell himself that he was doing what his son needs (i.e., by the MHP not enabling that line of thinking). Moreover, the communication kept the tension where it belonged (i.e., with dad) and perhaps increased the chance that dad would come fully on board later.

I have only two caveats regarding damage control treatment contracts. First, there may be instances when resistance rises to the level of reportable neglect, in which case the local child welfare agency would need to be contacted. Second, sometimes a damage control treatment contract can be surprisingly beneficial. Therefore, we don't want to create a self-fulfilling prophecy where we are not open to such wonderful developments.

SIDEBAR 3.1

Puppets are a staple supply for child MHPs. For example, I use them if a child is too anxious or stressed to discuss a particular topic in an individual session. Instead of interviewing the child, I give us both a puppet. My puppet then interviews her puppet, creating a displacement that sometimes makes a difficult discussion more viable.

For this trick, I introduce my "mind puppet" Nanook. Nanook is a furry, soft wolf puppet that I have pictured on my practice website. (His name was generated by a survey I did with one semester's worth of undergraduate students.) So, you'll need a mind puppet also to do this trick the way that I do it. You'll also need to prepare four index cards. On one, write the word "red" in red marker. On the second, write the word "green" in green marker. On the third, write the word "blue" in blue marker. On the back of the green card write, "You will choose the color green." You can also color in a few shapes on each card, in that card's color, if you'd like. Put the three cards in an appropriately sized envelope. Then, on the fourth index card write the phrase, "You will choose the color red," and put that in the envelope too, on the bottom of the other three. Finally, write the phrase, "You will choose blue" on a pencil; of course, you'll need some manual dexterity to do this. You're now ready to do the trick.

I joke with kids that all good psychologists need a mind puppet and that Nanook has special powers that he can use to help me to do magic. I then take out the top three cards from the envelope, laying them face-up with the words "red," "green," and "blue" for the kid to see (be careful not to flash the back of the cards or to let the kid see that there is a fourth index card in the envelope), reading each card, and motioning with your pencil (making sure not to flash the writing that is on the pencil). I tell the kid that Nanook will get her to choose the color that he (Nanook) wants her (the kid) to pick. I then open Nanook's mouth and put it on top of the kid's head (this usually causes the kid to smile) and then I say: *Go ahead and say the color that Nanook has just put into your mind.* If the kid says "blue," show her the pencil, noting that there is no other writing on it. If she says "green," turn over the three cards and show what is written there. If she says "red," pull out the fourth index card, noting that the envelope has no other cards in it.

This is a delightful little trick that usually puts a smile on the face of kids of all ages.

REFERENCES AND BIBLIOGRAPHY

Achenbach, T. M. (2005). Advancing assessment of children and adolescents: Commentary on evidence-based assessment of child and adolescent disorders. *Journal of Clinical Child & Adolescent Psychology, 34*(3), 541–547.

Allen, A., Montgomery, M., Tubman, J., Frazier, L., & Escovar, L. (2003). The effects of assessment feedback on rapport-building and self-enhancement processes. *Journal of Mental Health Counseling, 25*(3), 165–182.

Birmaher, B., Bren, D. A., & Benson, R. S. (1998). Summary of the practice parameters for the assessment and treatment of children and adolescents with depressive disorders. *Journal of the American Academy of Child & Adolescent Psychiatry, 37*(11), 1234–1238.

Claiborn, C. D., Goodyear, R. K., & Horner, P. A. (2001). Feedback. *Psychotherapy: Theory, Research, Practice, Training, 38*(4), 401–405.

Clair, D., & Prendergast, D. (1994). Brief psychotherapy and psychological assessments: Entering a relationship, establishing a focus, and providing feedback. *Professional Psychology: Research and Practice, 25*(1), 46–49.

Connolly, S. D., & Bernstein, G. A. (2007). Practice parameter for the assessment and treatment of children and adolescents with anxiety disorders. *Journal of the American Academy of Child & Adolescent Psychiatry, 46*(2), 267–283.

Curry, K. T., & Hanson, W. E. (2010). National survey of psychologists' test feedback training, supervision, and practice: A mixed methods study. *Journal of Personality Assessment, 92*(4), 327–336.

Digiuseppe, R., Linscott, J., & Jilton, R. (1996). Developing the therapeutic alliance in child-adolescent psychotherapy. *Applied & Preventive Psychology, 5*, 85–100.

Elliot, S. N., & Busse, R. (1993). Behavior rating scales: Issues of use and development. *School Psychology Review, 22*(2), 313.

Harmon, S. C., Lambert, M. J., Smart, D. M., Hawkins, E., Nielsen, S. L., Slade, K., & Lutz, W. (2007). Enhancing outcome for potential treatment failures: Therapist–client feedback and clinical support tools. *Psychotherapy Research, 17*(4), 379–392.

Hawkins, E. J., Lambert, M. J., Vermeersch, D. A., Slade, K. L., & Tuttle, K. C. (2004). The therapeutic effects of providing patient progress information to therapists and patients. *Psychotherapy Research, 14*(3), 308–327.

Hawley, K. M., & Weisz, J. R. (2003). Child, parent, and therapist (dis)agreement on target problems in outpatient therapy: The therapist's dilemma and its implications. *Journal of Consulting and Clinical Psychology, 71*(1), 62–70.

Karver, M. S., Handelsman, J. B., Fields, S., & Bickman, L. (2005). Meta-analysis of therapeutic relationship variables in youth and family therapy: The evidence for different relationship variables in the child and adolescent treatment literature. *Clinical Psychology Review, 26*: 50–65.

Knaup, C., Koesters, M., Schoefer, D., Becker, T., & Puschner, B. (2009). Effect of feedback of treatment outcome in specialist mental healthcare: Meta-analysis. *British Journal of Psychiatry, 195*(1), 15–22.

Lambert, M. J., & Shimokawa, K. (2011). Collecting client feedback. *Psychotherapy, 48*(1), 72–79.

Lambert, M. J., Whipple, J. L., Vermeersch, D. A., Smart, D. W., Hawkins, E. J., Nielsen, S. L., & Goates, M. (2002). Enhancing psychotherapy outcomes via providing feedback on client progress: A replication. *Clinical Psychology & Psychotherapy, 9*(2), 91–103.

Long, J. R. (2001). Goal agreement and early therapeutic change. *Psychotherapy: Theory, Research, Practice, Training, 38*(2), 219–232.

Melton, G. B. (1981). Children's participation in treatment planning: Psychological and legal issues. *Professional Psychology, 12*(2), 246–252.

Palmiter, D. J. (2008). Child clinician's corner: Damage control treatment contracts. *The Independent Practitioner, 28*, 98–99.

Petrocelli, J. V. (2000). Review of scientist-practitioner perspectives on test interpretation. *Psychotherapy: Theory, Research, Practice, Training, 37*(1), 106.

Poston, J. M., & Hanson, W. E. (2010). Meta-analysis of psychological assessment as a therapeutic intervention. *Psychological Assessment, 22*(2), 203–212.

Reese, R. J., Norsworthy, L. A., & Rowlands, S. R. (2009). Does a continuous feedback system improve psychotherapy outcome? *Psychotherapy: Theory, Research, Practice, Training, 46*(4), 418–431.

Shirk, S. R., Karver, M. S., & Brown, R. (2011). The alliance in child and adolescent psychotherapy. *Psychotherapy, 48*(1), 17–24.

Tharinger, D. J., Finn, S. E., Hersh, B., Wilkinson, A., Christopher, G. B., & Tran, A. (2008). Assessment feedback with parents and preadolescent children: A collaborative approach. *Professional Psychology: Research and Practice, 39*(6), 600–609.

Tilsen, J., & McNamee, S. (2015). Feedback informed treatment: Evidence-based practice meets social construction. *Family Process, 54*(1), 124–137.

Tryon, G. S., & Winograd, G. (2011). Goal consensus and collaboration. *Psychotherapy, 48*(1), 50–57.

CHAPTER 4

Techniques for Facilitating Adherence and Responding to Resistance

For many years I gave two continuing-education workshops a month regarding kid clinical work. The number-one question I would get during the Q & A portions regarded how to deal with pain-in-the-neck kids and parents. In thinking about this I believe it's useful to compare the role of the parent with the role of the mental health professional (MHP). When helping parents to think through defiant behavior in their kids, we often say to them that if they think about defiance only after it starts, they are probably having to deal with more defiance than do parents who think about establishing compliance. The same thing goes for MHPs and client resistance. For this reason, I'd like to separate this chapter into two sections: facilitating adherence and responding to resistance.

FACILITATING ADHERENCE

You never know till you try to reach them how accessible men are; but you must approach each man by the right door.
—Henry Ward Beecher

Nonspecific Effects

What causes treatments to work? When considering this question I like to tell the story of Austrian physician and theologian Franz Friedrich Anton Mesmer (1734–1815) and his theory of animal magnetism. Franz argued that when a person's magnetism became misaligned, that person could develop an assortment of maladies. Thus, early in his career he would have his patients sit in bathtubs constructed to correct their animal magnetism. So many people were healed that Mesmer's treatment became the rage among the French aristocracy. Because of the interest and controversy the treatment garnered, King Louis XVI of France commissioned a panel of noted scientists, among them Benjamin Franklin and Antoine Lavoisier (often referred to as "the father of modern chemistry"). According to William Zeitler on www.glassarmonica.com, "The committee reported that Mesmer's results were due to his good salesmanship and the patient's imagination, and that his 'animal magnetism' was really the faith of the patient."

Using contemporary treatment models, what probably worked for some of Mesmer's patients was a collection of nonspecific effects. Nonspecific effects, when they derive from an artful and ethical clinician, are therapeutic practices that are not specific to any specific intervention model. In fact, such nonspecific effects are beneficial even when the stated intervention model is incorrect. Let me provide a ridiculous example to illustrate what I mean. Let's say I was to develop a roller-coaster therapy for treating kids with internalizing disorders. I tell parents that if they take their kid on two roller-coaster rides a week, for a period of 2 months, I'll cure their kid's internalizing disorder. Let's say in my treatment I do a number of things: I obtain informed consent regarding my goals and methods, I provide empathy and understanding of the kid's and the parents' suffering and context, I do as I say I'm going to do, I flexibly adjust to expressed concerns, I take good measurements, I give feedback as I go, and I'm generally kind. I would expect a sizable number of my kids to do better. Of course, a steely-eyed empiricist might challenge: "But Dr. Palmiter, have you established a *specific* benefit from the roller-coaster rides above and beyond what a kind and organized clinician might accomplish? Because, if not, why not tell parents that the treatment is to wear wool socks, as that would be much less expensive and inconvenient than your 16 roller-coaster rides?!"

This is why we get our shorts in a bunch regarding research. Evidence that a kid or kids are responding well to a treatment is a necessary but insufficient reason to say that it was the specific intended elements of that treatment that caused the benefit. What's remarkable is that the adult psychotherapy literature indicates that nonspecific effects garner more benefit than specific effects. According to a comprehensive review by Norcross and Lambert (2011), specific effects account for about 15% of the benefit, with common factors and expectancy accounting for 40% and 15%, respectively (the remainder is accounted for by changes in the client's life). I haven't found a similar summary of child clinical work. However, I believe it's reasonable to speculate that variance attached to specific factors wouldn't fall lower than it does with adult work.

Let's say the kid numbers end up looking like the adult numbers: 15% isn't much for specific effects, right? Well, in my experience, communicating knowledge of that 15% goes a long way to forming an alliance with parents, which I elaborate on later in this chapter. Moreover, when you're a parent-lunatic (see Chapter 1), you want every single tiny little morsel of value you can get for your kid. So, in approaching child clinical work, we want to maximize both nonspecific and specific effects, as doing so maximizes adherence and outcomes.

Elements of a Therapeutic Alliance

In thinking about these issues I've been influenced by Edward Bordin's (1979) classic paper, "The Generalizability of the Psychoanalytic Concept of the Working Alliance." In it, Bordin suggested that there are three elements to a therapeutic alliance: agreement about the goals, agreement about the methods, and the affective bond. In my experience this hits the bull's-eye, though the affective bond is multifaceted to a degree that makes it difficult to parse its elements; I also grant that the empirical literature on parent and kid alliance formation is young.

A challenge in kid clinical work is that the MHP needs to form an alliance with the parents, the kids, and, often, outside systems (e.g., school personnel, court personnel), many of whom may be at odds with each other. Moreover, what the MHP can do to produce an emotional connection with these folks can vary widely. This topic, by itself, could fill a packed volume. But here I offer a few suggestions.

▶ Reach agreement about the goals. In Chapters 2 and 3, I review how to do this in kid clinical work. This is usually a task targeted for the parents at the onset, as most kids are neutral or opposed to coming in. If kid clinical work required kids to say things like, "Yeah, seeing a therapist is a good idea" at the onset of the work, the large majority of the enterprise would come to a grinding halt. Yes, reaching some agreement about goals with a kid is critically important before starting intervention work (see Chapter 3), but not for the initial evaluation. For parents, however, reaching agreement about the evaluation goals is essential. Not only is the alliance promoted when they sign on with the goals, but doing so affords them a common ground with each other as well. The value of the latter cannot be underestimated in families where parents argue a lot about how to help their kid, which is a common occurrence in families where a kid has a persisting internalizing disorder (e.g., "If only you'd parent in the right way she wouldn't have these problems!").

Getting on the same page about goals is fairly easy, which makes it all the more remarkable when MHPs don't make the time to do it. Of course, parents don't say things like, "I want him to be more depressed," or, "I wish more people wouldn't like her." So, when we articulate specific goals that we have, across the clinical work, it's usually a very easy task to get on the same page with parents and, eventually, kids.

▶ Reach agreement about the methods. This is also something that I review how to do throughout this volume, beginning in Chapter 2. Garnering agreement about methods often takes more instruction, and back and forth, than reaching agreement about goals, during all phases of the work. Moreover, it is in the methods that parents are often in dispute with each other; indeed, they often come to first appointments primed to have the MHP act as Solomon in their dispute, or one parent is pro the *imagined* MHP stance while the other parent is against it. To elaborate on the latter point, some parents may have preconceived notions about what child MHPs believe and how they behave (e.g., that treatment always takes a long time, that coddling kids is advocated, that molehills are made into mountains, that punishments are verboten, and so forth). In these discussions we endeavor to be artistic teachers, skillfully communicating the relevant and extant science that pertains to the kid before us, while responding effectively to parent and kid concerns and attitudes.

Transparency and respect are two values that aid our efforts to reach agreement about goals and methods. We want our brains to be like a restaurant where you can look in and see what the chef is doing. Moreover, our task is not to get families to do the things that we believe are best. Our task is to communicate what we believe is best, relying on clinical experience and scientific evidence so that parents (and sometimes kids) can decide what they want to do. We aspire to be good communicators of the best information we have. We avoid pressuring, selling, and manipulating. We promote clarity in decision making, even when that clarity is different from what we advise.

▶ Create an affective bond. I should say that I think of this as both a cognitive and an affective bond. People not only feel some positive feelings for us and from us, but they also believe the work has value. This is why it has been my clinical experience that reaching agreement about the goals and methods contribute to the affective bond. Here are some other techniques that appear to facilitate this bond:

- Be organized. I speculate that parents feel especially comforted by organization, given how undone they often feel at intake. The methods for becoming organized are reviewed throughout this volume.

- Use empathy. Empathy is not compassion or sympathy. The latter is saying things like, "I'm sorry you're having to go through that." While that can be very nice, empathy is more powerful. It is saying back to a person an accurate representation of what the person's experience is, or what is sometimes called "connected knowing." What I do is try to imagine what it would be like to be this person, in the context under review, and share my understanding with the person. Empathy is to a person what the sun is to a spring bud: It facilitates opening up. The research suggests that the only folks who don't respond well to empathy are people afflicted with paranoid schemata. (My clinical experience is that some kids will also shrug off empathy if they believe that connecting with me is akin to losing a battle with their parents.) I wish I could suggest a script on how often to express empathy. Too little and the gears can grind. Too much and folks start feeling like we are a caricature of a therapist. It's a matter of feel, which I suspect most of us come to readily enough.

I don't believe empathy can be effectively inculcated in a therapist that doesn't naturally possess that ability. I do think, like the character Data from the *Star Trek: The Next Generation* series, it is possible to learn to make empathic remarks when not feeling empathy. But that appears to have limited value and takes a lot of effort to pull off. There is nothing quite like actually being able to experience a version of another person's life and to put accurate words to that perception.

- Use clarifications. Borrowing from Edward Bibring's model of therapeutic interventions, clarification means joining conscious material in ways that a client had not previously done for himself; this can be done through a question or a statement. This is not the same thing as making an interpretation, which involves making the unconscious conscious. It's easy for experienced MHPs to lose sight of how powerful clarifications can be for people; we MHPs make connections all the time and sometimes don't realize that lots of folks aren't used to doing that. For instance, let's say that an interview suggests that a kid is much more likely to request going to the school nurse on days that he has gym class, but no one in the family seems to have made that connection. Both of these pieces of data are conscious to all: The kid goes to the school nurse a lot and he has gym class, but no one has seen the association. So, an MHP might ask something like, "Roughly what percentage of the trips to the school nurse fall on the same days as gym class?" Clarifications offer the family new perspectives, which offers value and keeps them coming back.

- Find the middle ground between being thorough and being efficient. In a "managed cost" era (I think this term is more accurate than "managed care"), there can be formidable system pressures to rush. Procedures reviewed throughout this volume endeavor to be thorough without being frivolous about cost. I think all of us need to develop the skills to stand our ground on these principles.

On the other hand, kid MHPs can be vulnerable to being inefficient. For example, sometimes folks want to give us additional examples, or more details, regarding issues or experiences that we've understood—at least as much as we need to in order to meet the goals of the evaluation. Or, other clients are the sorts of people who like to tell us how a watch was made when we've asked for the time. I've seen trainees take much longer to do an evaluation because of a difficulty in knowing how to respond to these issues, often stating a desire "to show respect" or "to be empathic." However, unhelpful delays mean that it will take longer to get to feedback, treatment planning, and healing. This is not in the client's best interest. Should we linger in unhelpful ways we still get paid, and maybe even get paid more, but our clients are not well served. So we intervene. I'll usually say something like this: *Tanisha, it sounds like your boss often treats you in an unkind way and that that is a MAJOR stress right now. So, it's an important topic that we haven't come close to covering fully. However, for our purposes today I'd like to move on, because I have a lot of other ground to cover, and I want to make sure that we have the time for that. Actually, for the rest of the interview, I'd like your permission to be a little rude and interrupt you if I've gotten what I need on a topic. Would that be okay?* In my experience it has never not been okay. Actually, the challenge is to not let someone feel bad, as the parent sometimes responds with things like, "Oh, I go on too much a lot of the time," to which I'll say: *Not now you haven't. You were giving me useful information and answering my question about stress. And there were other important things to say on that topic. It's just that I got what I needed for today's purposes.* The script is an easy one: Kindly interrupt, give some empathy, give an indication why the information being shared has value, explain why you're interrupting, and ask for permission to do so again if needed.

During the intervention phase of cognitive behavioral therapy (CBT) work, we ask ourselves things like, "Does this discussion have value for reaching our goals?" "Do I need to change the agenda today because this is important to go over?" "Is this person stuck in a way that isn't helpful to her?" The answers to these questions will help you to ascertain whether you need to suggest a redirection to the discussion or adjust your agenda. I can't tell you how many people over the years have complained to me about a previous therapist letting them be the tail that wagged the dog. I'm guessing that these clinicians were motivated by desires to be respectful and kind. But it's certainly possible to let the work get off track by not considering these issues carefully.

- Demonstrate attention to details and manifest a good memory. Effective MHPs truly care. We pay attention and remember important things. Sometimes clients devalue their worth or imagine that we are too busy to remember important details. So clients will remind us or restate things. However, I just about always let my clients know that I already remember, jumping in and paraphrasing with things like: *I remember about Carol. She's the one you said dated your boyfriend while you guys were still together.*

- Reframe harsh judgments. Clients with internalizing disorders frequently bully themselves cognitively. Moreover, exhausted and depleted parent-lunatics often tear down their kids. Bottom line: Show me a harsh judgment and I'll show you an incomplete and inaccurate characterization. In my clinical lexicon, the following are either synonymous or highly related: being accurate, being thorough, being scientific, being empathic, and being kind. During the treatment phase, such thinking can be dealt with by interventions like thought testing or problem solving. During the evaluation phase, it might go like this:

Kid: *I suck.*
MHP: *How come you suck?*
Kid: *I failed math.*
MHP: *How come you failed math?*
Kid: *I just don't get it. Other kids get it. I don't. Never have.*

MHP: *Okay, so what you're telling me is that you're probably not on a path to work for NASA, but how does that mean you suck in general?*
Kid: *I don't know. Just a feeling I have.*
MHP: *When you get that feeling, do you forget about your strengths that we talked about earlier?*
Kid: *I guess so.*
MHP: *Okay, so you definitely have a thought that you suck sometimes. My guess is that we can do something about that. And I think we can probably do something about the math thing too—not that I'm going to try to convince you to work for NASA or anything. When I see you next time I'll share my ideas about that. For now, though, we can agree that you have lots of strengths and that the statement "I suck" is highly suspicious.*
Kid: *(Smiles)*

A parent example:

Mom: *He's SO LAZY!*
MHP: *What makes you say so?*
Mom: *He has to be pestered to do EVERYTHING: homework, chores, taking his meds. It's exhausting.*
MHP: *You do work very hard on this, don't you?*
Mom: *(Nods, getting tearful)*
MHP: *Do I have it right that he does his chores 50% of the time without a hassle and was on the honor roll in school up through the first quarter of this year?*
Mom: *Yes.*
MHP: *Okay, so dealing with these problems, given all the other things you're doing—working full-time, taking care of two other kids, running your daughter's Girl Scout troop—is exhausting beyond description. So, the legitimate problems you're seeing in Aiden make it seem like he's totally lazy sometimes. But I have the advantage of being distant from this, and I can see that lots of times he isn't lazy, as I know you know. You're just understandably overwhelmed right now. When I get to feedback I'll give lots of details about what I think is going on and, more importantly, what I think can fix things and get everyone feeling better.*

- Calmly going wherever the work needs to go. I think this becomes less and less of an issue the more miles an MHP travels down the clinical path. When newer to this work, however, there is a transition period of shifting from cultural norms to clinical norms. Cultural norms suggest that we don't ask people we've just met intimate questions (e.g., about their sex life, finances, race). Cultural norms also suggest that we change the topic when people start to get upset or indicate that they'd rather not discuss something. Therapy norms suggest that we need to work on ourselves (e.g., in therapy, in supervision) until we get to a place of relative calm in discussing difficult but clinically relevant topics. Clinical norms also suggest that when people show us pain that we need to explore it in order to understand its impact, its causes, and its potential cure (there is more on this later in this chapter), as long as by doing so we won't be making things worse—for example, in cases of serious posttraumatic stress disorder when it may take a long time to be able to hear a particular account.

- Endeavor to keep negative judgments out of the room. We MHPs are human, too. We may have our own moral judgments and perspectives about sexual orientation, abortion, parenting practices (short of reportable abuse and neglect), religion, politics, and so forth. When new to this work, many of us need to work on ourselves so that we don't judge our clients—even within our own minds, as the science of human communication suggests that negative judgments often get communicated and received, if only unconsciously. The statements I made previously about harsh judgments applies to us as well; this comes up a lot in kid work as it's all too easy to harshly judge ineffective parenting practices. I don't know that we ever *totally* arrive in this regard—I certainly haven't—but the ongoing and consistent effort to arrive improves our performance and reduces how often we stumble. Of course, we all share a responsibility to consider whether transferring a case is advisable when we are unable to pull this off with a particular client.

- Adjust goals and methods based on a client's concerns and feedback. As I shared previously, our task is not to sell and/or to manipulate. Our goal is to effectively communicate choices. Lots of times, after I've had my back and forth with parents, they'll decide to do things like not obtain teacher rating forms, not take their kid in for an evaluation for medication, reduce the frequency of needed treatment, and so forth. My question to myself, and stated out loud to the parents, is whether I still can offer value given how they wish to proceed. If (a) I believe the decision makers have understood my thinking on how the change(s) could impact the prognosis, (b) I believe I can still add value, and (c) the decision makers understand and agree with b, then I go forward, often offering statements like: *Y'know, you guys are the world's leading experts on your Aiden, so maybe you're right about this. Regardless, though, of what's right and what's not, I believe I can still be helpful doing it the way you'd like. So, let's proceed in the way you suggest. If it works, great. If it doesn't, we can always revisit this discussion.*

- Have fun with kids. I haven't seen any well-constructed studies that indicate having fun with kids is a mediator for therapeutic change. But, as I think it's possible to do this quickly and easily, and it seems to facilitate the alliance with kids, I look for opportunities to have fun. I discuss some of these methods in other parts of this volume (e.g., using magic, letting the kid direct us toward discussing fun topics some of the time). But I'll also do things like take a walk around the office, bring in my dog to a session, play a game of ping-pong, and so forth, making sure that anything fun we might do is not done in service of delaying the clinical task.

- Use humor. This is something to be cautious about. If you're adroit with using humor in your personal life and can objectively establish that you are funny (e.g., you've gotten that feedback routinely and it hasn't caused you to lose a friend), I'd suggest experimenting with integrating this skill set into your clinical work. Humorous perspectives and insights often pop into my head, so I'll share them if the timing seems right (e.g., doing so doesn't risk trivializing something). Moreover, humor can also be used to decatastrophize and to offer wisdom. So, I'll use it for those purposes as well. I also find that well-crafted teasing can go a long way towards forming a bond with teens.

- Emphasize that no good work can happen without the kid getting things that he wants. This is certainly made clear through treatment planning with a kid. Moreover, a kid experiencing symptom relief implicitly lets that kid know that the work prioritizes his getting better. Sometimes kids are conditioned to ignore adult talk and attend to adult walk, so it's a matter of feel regarding when and how I emphasize this point, but I always do.

- Assess for strengths and communicate the results. As I cover in Chapters 2, 3, and 12, this is a critically important strategy.

- Measure. Parents *love* when we measure and let them know where their kid stands normatively. While the psychometric enterprise can become problematic if it is turned into a religion, well-conceived measurements assist us in developing an accurate diagnostic formulation on a kid while facilitating the alliance.

- Maintain and stress the kid's confidentiality. This is discussed in the intake paperwork and during the one-on-one evaluation session with the kid. Before every parent consultation, I also go over with a kid what I'd like to cover and anything that the kid doesn't want me to share with his parents. Unless a kid is in significant danger, or there is a regulatory mandate to report, I respect a kid's wishes. Moreover, I'm very cautious about pressuring a kid to let me share something he doesn't want me to share, given the power differential in our relationship.

- Provide a cohesive, understandable model of the kid to both the parents and the kid. This occurs in the feedback session but often at other times as well. The MHP's model of a kid usually advances everyone's understanding and provides hope, both of which appear to be powerful nonspecific effects.

In sum, I endeavor to obtain informed consent about the goals and methods, promote insight through clarification, deploy empathy, maintain a pace that is both thorough and efficient, demonstrate attention to things that matter to the family, reframe harshness, explore sensitive but relevant topics calmly and kindly, avoid negative judgments (including privately), demonstrate flexibility with informed consent, have fun, use humor, emphasize that the kid needs to get something out of the work, assess for strengths, use rating scales, maintain the kid's confidentiality, and provide a cohesive and understandable model of the kid. (Notice, I could use all of these techniques to create my roller-coaster therapy, if I didn't care about being ethical, that is.) These procedures all promote nonspecific effects and are very powerful for creating and enhancing evaluation and treatment alliances.

RESPONDING TO RESISTANCE

People make plans; God laughs.
—*Yiddish proverb*

Chapters 16 and 17 cover a variety of specific situations involving resistance. Here I discuss some overview issues and techniques and go over how to engage resistant kids during the evaluation phase.

Some Coping Thoughts for MHPs

Healing yourself is connected with healing others.
—*Yoko Ono*

Research on this topic indicates that most clients hold back information from their therapists. If you've been in therapy yourself, you likely have done the same. There are a bunch of different reasons why this happens: The content is too embarrassing, the therapist might be offended or hurt, the health insurance company might find out, it's not worth the bother, it can be gotten under control without involving the therapist, and so forth. This same body of science also suggests that we MHPs do a poor job of guessing when a client has withheld something and even guessing what it is when we've been told that something has been held back.

Resistance offers a door into some of this unknown material. Imagine someone said to you, "Today your client is going to give you the opportunity to know something very important about him that you do not yet know." I imagine most of us would be energized for such a session. Keep in mind that if we bring our collection of nonspecific and specific effects to bear, and assuming we've properly understood the most important things about a kid, his family, and his context, we expect the work to go well. So, resistance tells us that there is something important *that we do not yet know*. The problem is that while this door is being illuminated, someone is often throwing holographic grenades at us. If we spend our time reacting to the grenades, by imagining that they are real, we don't walk through the door that offers such incredible learning. Of course, our reactions to the grenades can be referred to as countertransference. Let me say a little about that.

Transference is in every human relationship. We all bring relationship scripts from the past onto the stage of our current life. This is as inevitable as our breath. In behavioral treatments, we manage transference (e.g., responding effectively to resistance is an example of managing negative countertransference). In insight-oriented treatments, we study it to affect symptom relief. Countertransference is merely the type of transference that therapists experience. The correct question is not, "Is a therapist experiencing countertransference?" The correct question is, "What is the nature of a therapist's countertransference?" Countertransference can often be used to facilitate the work. Clients imagine that we are wiser than we are, or that we care more than we do, or that we can read their minds. Likewise, we MHPs can have a range of countertransferential reactions to our clients. For example, I fall in love (not romantically, thank God) with my clients routinely. I bless them sometimes as they walk out of my office, I sometimes pray for them, I sometimes have dreams about them, they sometimes annoy the crap out of me and I wish they would move to Cuba, and so forth. The follow-up question, then, as is the case with transference manifested in behavioral treatments, is: "Is the countertransference helping, interfering with, or having a neutral impact on the work?"

Few things can generate interfering countertransference quicker than resistance. We feel that our competence is being challenged, or that our clients are not sufficiently grateful, or that we are being dismissed, and so forth. The client's transference is *usually* a holographic grenade. However, our maladaptive countertransference turns it into a real grenade, which makes it harder to do the learning that is before us. But, if we can see the client's transference for what it is, we can take advantage of the opportunity that resistance affords.

This discussion illustrates one of the reasons that I number among those who lobby trainees to seek out personal therapy. We all have our vulnerabilities. For example, I've learned to be very cautious when I go above and beyond for a client (e.g., offering reduced fees, doing a school staffing pro bono) because I find that such offerings leave me subsequently more vulnerable to turning a holographic grenade into a real one. Moreover, I know I have to have a nap on days that I have clients who are slow to open up, lest I get sleepy in response to their transference. My two personal therapies have taught me about other vulnerabilities as well. Having this information reduces the odds that I will engage in maladaptive countertransference, though it still happens.

Bottom-line coping thought: "Okay, this is surprising. I can really learn a lot of useful things here if I do what I know."

If a clinician can heal, that clinician can be a pretty skillful warrior (e.g., I imagine surgeons could use a scalpel in a fight in a much more deadly way than most). Therefore, we MHPs need to be cautious not to use pseudo interventions as weapons. Take this exchange from a parent consultation as an illustration:

Dad: *We're starting 10 minutes late. I thought starting and ending on time is important to you! Will you be reducing my fee today?*

MHP: *I'm sorry. I had an unexpected delay. Would it be okay if we extended the session for 10 minutes?*

Dad: *I'd rather just take the reduced fee. I think you're being sort of hypocritical.*

MHP: *Y'know, Jordan, I know you shared that you had a dismissive and controlling father. I'm wondering if you're confusing me for him right now.*

In this example, the MHP is throwing a brick that portends to do a lot of damage to the relationship with that parent. Instead, the MHP might consider some of these strategies:

▶ Ask what the client is feeling. Whenever someone surprises me with anger, I use this question to both find out what's up and to give myself a few moments to think things through, instead of just reacting. I once had a dad get very angry, quickly, when I asked him about his relationship with an adult child. Asking him this question created the space for him to tell me he was upset and why (i.e., he was estranged from that child and it bothered him a lot).

▶ Use empathy. Ever have someone who you are upset with show you empathy in response? Granted, that is not a common human response to irritation. But it's very difficult to stay mad. For instance, the MHP in that parent consultation could have said, "Your time is very valuable, Jordan. And I have stressed the importance of starting and ending on time. You have cause to feel irritated." It's also true that the dad is probably overreacting, but everything just said is also true. Folks just tend to calm down and get out of fight-flight mode when receiving empathy. Not always, for sure, but often. After the client has told me what he is feeling, I try to use empathy next.

▶ Use reframing. I once heard the CBT master Donald Meichenbaum share a vignette that illustrated the power of reframing. He said he spent some time studying cult groups as they usually garner high levels of adherence. He reported that he attended indoctrination sessions held by Erhard Seminars Training (EST). He noted that sometimes someone would stand up, declare "This is BS," and leave. He then noticed that several of the EST personnel would follow that person into the parking lot and say things like this: "We had a leadership meeting this week and decided that we have some BS in our program. But none of us could put our finger on what it is. You seem to understand the BS. Would you mind helping us out by teaching us what the BS is so that we can get better?" We can wonder, did the cult members truly believe that they had BS in their program? I don't know, but I'm guessing not. However, we can take the same principle and use it ethically and effectively. Let's take an exchange that could happen after an MHP recommends a medication evaluation for a kid who has just been diagnosed with attention deficit hyperactivity disorder:

Mom: *There you guys go again. Drugs! Drugs! Drugs! What, if I take my kid in you win a casino trip this month from the drug company?*
MHP: *What are you feeling right now?*
Mom: *Pissed. I'm sick of how you guys are all in the pocket of Big Pharma.*
MHP: *I get why you're angry. I'd be angry too if I thought that my kid's needs were being set aside so that a clinician could personally profit.*
Mom: *Damn straight!*

MHP: *I have to say that I appreciate your openness with me. I wish more of my parents would be this open. And the passion that you are displaying to protect Aiden is admirable. If we are to work together, I hope I can count on that passion going forward, as it would be a major resource.*

The MHP's first response is to ask what the mom is feeling. While it's obvious, it gives the MHP a moment to collect herself. The second response is empathy. The third is the reframe. It's also true that the mom is being immature and attacking. However, the reframe is true as well. So, a reframe is saying back true things about what the person is saying that are disarming in some fashion. These sorts of interventions facilitate getting the client out of a regressed state and set the stage for the next intervention. Sometimes multiple empathic statements and reframes may be needed to move on.

▶ Explain goals and methods, using scientific evidence when available. Often this is better stated to be re-explaining or better explaining, as the MHP may have covered the ground already. But sometimes the information is being reviewed for the first time. The important thing is not to start with this technique. While the more mature and well-put-together clients can work with starting here, many will just take it as the MHP trying to win an argument. I'll eventually—after using empathy and reframing—say things like: *Tanisha, let's face it, we all do well to be skeptical of what drug companies assert. And, without having had the chance to review the relevant science, I'd feel exactly like you do. So, your opening stance is understandable. My hope is that if I could share with you a little more about the available science that you'd join me in agreeing that there could be a lot of value for Aiden in further considering this choice.*

▶ Make adjustments following informed consent. I covered this previously. Sometimes, the result is that we go with the client's flow.

▶ Apologize when that's warranted. Sometimes we miss the boat, make mistakes, and so forth. Acknowledging that and apologizing can be very helpful in such moments.

▶ Use humor. Again, humor should only be used by MHPs who are good at it, as poorly deployed humor can escalate the problem. For example, if I got on the same page with the drug-objecting mom and it felt like it would work, I might add at the end: *By the way, would you like to come along for the next casino trip?* I'd laugh, wave my hand, and then say: *Just kidding.* There is something about a moment like that that says to us both, "We're good now."

▶ Remain authentic. In efforts to soften a resistant kid, I've seen trainees try to go out of their way to be more relatable by changing themselves. I've had trainees wear their hair differently, sit differently, wear different clothing, use language that isn't natural to them, and so forth, all in an effort to form an affective bond. The available evidence and my clinical experience both suggest that this often has the exact opposite intended effect. It's remarkable how often authenticity, across the human interaction spectrum, is the better choice. Of course, if the MHP actually likes some of the same video games or movies or music, that's fine. For my own part, many of the things I like to do when I'm regressing in service of my ego overlap with things kids like, so I don't hesitate to use that. (Interestingly, I once had a teen challenge that I was BSing him about liking the Red Hot Chili Peppers. So, I broke out my iPhone and showed him my play list, which then caused him to say, in an admiring tone, "And you like rap also?" To which I said something like, "Nah, I just put it on there to manipulate dudes like you!" To which we both laughed.)

Engaging Angry Kids

This is the protocol I use for engaging the large portion of youth who angrily resist taking part in the first family interview. Most of the time, this protocol doesn't reach the end point as the kid starts participating earlier on. In what follows I'm taking you through the path of the most resistant kid. (You may recall from Chapter 2 that I like to begin the family interview with the kid.)

MHP: *What do you like to be called?*
Kid: *Aiden (a).*
MHP: *Aiden, how come you're here today?*
Kid: *I don't know (b).*
MHP: *Well, did your parents talk about where you were going today?*
Kid: *No (c).*
MHP: *Okay, well, do you know what kind of doctor/therapist/professional I am?*
Kid: *No (d).*
MHP: *So it wouldn't surprise you if I asked you to take off your shoes so I could examine your feet (smiling)? (e)*
Kid: *(Nonverbal reaction)*
MHP: *Well, I'm the kind of doctor/therapist/professional who helps kids with their problems. What kind of problems do you have?*
Kid: *I don't have any problems.*
MHP: *Aiden, everyone has problems. I have problems. Your mom and dad have problems. You have problems. Okay, let me put it this way: What small or unimportant problems do you have?*
Kid: *None. I DON'T HAVE ANY PROBLEMS (f).*
MHP: *Okay, well, it's good that I know how you think about this. Well, your parents have brought you in today, so they must look at things differently. Even though you might disagree with them, what's a problem they are going to say you have when it's their turn?*
Kid: *I don't know.*

MHP: *Okay, I guess you can't read their minds. But, make a guess.*
Kid: *I don't know.*
MHP: *C'mon, Aiden, I'm not asking you to know. I'm asking you to make a guess. I could guess. My secretary could guess. You can guess (g).*
Kid: *I DON'T KNOW.*
MHP: *(Turning to mom and dad) Would you guys mind excusing us for a minute and going out to the waiting room (h)?*
MHP: *Aiden, I'm starting with you as a way of showing you respect. I can already tell that when it's your parents' turn to talk they are going to have a lot to say. But I'm letting you get in what you think first . . . but listen, I can't make you talk. I don't even want to try. So, if you don't want to take part you can sit in the waiting room while I speak with your parents, and you and I can take another run at it the next time. So, do you want to stay in here and take part or wait in the waiting room (i)?*

Explanation

a. Even very angry kids will tend to answer this question. If I suspect I have a super angry kid I might ask, "Do you prefer to be called Aiden or something else?" I can't think of the last time it happened, but if the kid didn't want to answer this one, I'd just let it go.

b. The Excalibur of kids: "I don't know." This phrase often either stops adults dead in their tracks or makes them dance around the kid like hyperkinetic circus bears with lipstick and bad hair, asking a bunch of other questions. Later in the script I deal with this head on.

c. If a kid says "no," either the kid is lying (which is usually the case and will usually cause the parents to shift in their seats), or the parents feel bullied by the kid and were afraid to say where they were going, or the parents are just so overwhelmed they got the kid in the car without comment.

d. The chance is near zero that the kid has zero idea regarding what kind of professional the MHP is. If the kid truly doesn't know, she may be the sort of kid who walks through life missing major connections.

e. This is a style point. I like to tweak back a little bit, as if to say, "We both know you're yanking my chain right now." Most kids react to this comment with a barely noticeable smile.

f. A kid who gets this far into the protocol is either very angry, habituated to adult admonishments (i.e., through coercion cycles), or both. The main challenge here is to remain calm, even internally, as a calm response from an authority figure is probably not something the kid is used to when acting like a pain and is therefore less likely to reinforce the dynamic. Probably more familiar to the kid would be an authority figure who engages a coercion cycle by getting more harsh or insistent; also familiar might be an authority figure who acts

powerless in the face of the kid's anger. Likely to be less familiar is an authority figure who remains calm and effective.

g.   The thing that makes "I don't know" so powerful is that maybe the kid doesn't
     know or maybe the kid is being a pain; there's no way to discern the differ-
     ence. By turning the question into a guess, the MHP makes it clear that
     responding is within the kid's power. If the kid still refuses, the MHP is bet-
     ter able to confront defiance directly.

h.   I take a little private amusement from the fact that most parents, in this situa-
     tion, are happy to leave. It is as if they wish to say, "What a relief! Good! You
     deal with him!"

i.   Asking the parents to leave serves a couple of purposes. First, lots of angry kids
     view participating with the evaluation as losing a battle in their war with their
     parents. In such circumstances, as long as the parents are in the room, the kid
     will resist. Second, sometimes the kid has received a lot of negative reinforce-
     ment from his parents for defiant behavior (i.e., getting out of having to do
     something unpleasant by showing disruptive behavior). So removing them, at
     least for a few moments, can be like removing a reinforcing agent. Third, and
     related to the first two points, many angry kids are more likely to show their
     reasonable side without their parents in the room. Notice that it only takes a
     few moments to get to this point in the protocol, which is long before the kid
     has had a chance to get dug deep into an angry and defiant position.

     Authenticity and transparency often work very well for MHPs. Owning that
     the MHP doesn't have the power to force the kid to talk seems important here.

     I have had some years within my practice where no kids decide to wait in
     the waiting room. And I've never had more than two a year. Kids want to
     hear what their parents are going to say, plus the waiting room is boring, at
     least if a kid has to sit there for 90 minutes. Moreover, even when a kid chooses
     to go out into the waiting room, I'm okay with that for three reasons. First,
     I know that I'm likely to be able to engage the kid during the individual inter-
     view, as the questions during that interview are much less threatening.
     Second, in the second interview I have the opportunity to deploy my silver
     bullet for the werewolf of kid resistance: drawing on the computer. Third,
     I don't want to do a family interview with a kid acting out; I think this could
     suggest to the parents that I don't know how to deal with their kid's defiant
     behavior either.

     Anyway, most kids will start participating at some juncture. They may be
     angry and regressed, but they offer useful content.

Engaging Anxious Kids

This is the kid who doesn't talk due to anxiety, which is a very different scenario
from the kid who doesn't talk because of anger. The anxious kid often lets us know

about the problem before the first question is even asked. He'll bury his head in a parent's stomach, he'll clasp on hard to a parent walking into the consulting room, he'll hide his face from the MHP, and so forth. With this sort of a kid, my goal is to get some kind of communication going in the hope that it will become like a snowball rolling downhill. I might ask a question about how he wishes to be addressed. Or I might ask him to show me his age using his fingers. Or I might ask him to nod yes or no to a few questions. The first time, however, that the kid gets locked down with anxiety and won't respond, I let the protocol go. Defiance is usually under a kid's control, but debilitating anxiety is usually not. If I get to such a moment, I'll say to a kid something like this: *Aiden, I see that you're not comfortable being here. That's okay. I'm new to you. So, I'll ask your mom and dad some questions first. Feel free to stay there on the couch. But, if you'd like, I also have some toys over here* (motioning) *that you're welcome to play with. It's up to you.* I then start the parent interview. As I go along, the kid will often habituate to being in the room, at which point I'll float a question his way. If he scurries back to a defensive position, I'll let it go and wait for another moment later.

Of course, there are many other kinds of resistance that adults and kids can manifest. Addressing many of those is the mission of Chapters 16 and 17.

SIDEBAR 4.1

This is a card trick that will amaze many kids (and their parents and sibs, if they learn it well). I've adapted it from Gerry Griffin's DVD, *Complete Card Magic—Volume One: Beginner - 14 Easy to Learn Card Miracles.* Griffin calls the trick "Use Your Powers for Good." You'll need a deck of standard playing cards. I also use my mind puppet, Nanook.

Tell the kid to shuffle the deck as much as she likes. Then take the deck and, looking at the cards, say something like, "You sure shuffled these well." What you're really doing is determining which cards there are fewer of at the top of the deck: black (i.e., spades and clubs) or red cards (i.e., hearts and diamonds). For this description we'll say there are fewer red cards.

Take a red card from the top of the deck and put it on your left side face-up (we'll call it pile #1). Take a black card from the bottom of the deck and put it on your right side face-up (pile #2). Say to the kid something like this, "Nanook is going to now give you the power to know which cards are red ones and which ones are black ones without your looking at them." Then, make some contact with your puppet and the kid's head.

Now you are going to pick out only red cards from the top part of the deck and ask the kid if each one is either red or black (the cards will all be red); as the kid states the color, put the card facedown in that corresponding pile, stacking them like shingles, going down one vertical column (i.e., below either the red or the black cards that you had placed face-up). Your goal is to clear

(continued)

SIDEBAR 4.1 *(continued)*

out enough red cards from the top of the deck so that only black ones remain (say, 10 or so, but you can do fewer or more if you'd like). Once you've dealt enough out, then say you're going to switch things up. Push the stacked face-down cards on top of the displayed red and black prompt cards. Now put one of each of the opposite color cards face-up on each pile (so pile #1 will now have a black card face-up while pile #2 will have a red card face-up). Now say, "Let's see if you can use Nanook's powers to guess the color of the card without either one of us looking at it." Now have the kid guess what color each card is (but not look at it), stacking the cards down a vertical column on that color (of course, all of the cards are black at this point). Let the kid guess for a number of cards.

When done, all of the down-facing cards on the left side will match their face-up prompt. You just need to pick the bottom face-up card on the right pile (i.e., the face-up red card) and switch it to the top of the pile on the right. I do this by picking up that red card and using it to point to the piles on the left side, noting that you are making two of them (i.e., the pile under the red card and the pile under the black card on the left). When putting the red card from the right side back, you can switch it to the top and easily arrange the piles on the right side to match as well.

You should now have four piles, all of which match their face-up card. You can ask your kid, "What percent accuracy do you think you accomplished?" Kids will usually guess pretty low, which can cause you to joke that the kid should have more faith in your mind puppet. Then ask the kid to turn over the piles to see how accurate she was.

If you teach the kid this trick to use with others, it's especially important that she practice it first since it's easy to mess this one up. However, with practice, it commonly creates astonishment.

REFERENCES AND BIBLIOGRAPHY

Beutler, L. E., Harwood, T. M., Michelson, A., Song, X., & Holman, J. (2011). Resistance/reactance level. *Journal of Clinical Psychology, 67*(2), 133–142.

Bibring, E. (1954). Psychoanalysis and the dynamic psychotherapies. *Journal of the American Psychoanalytic Association, 2,* 745–770.

Bordin, E. S. (1979). The generalizability of the psychoanalytic concept of the working alliance. *Psychotherapy: Theory, Research & Practice, 16*(3), 252–260.

Broome, K. M., Joe, G. W., & Simpson, D. D. (2001). Engagement models for adolescents in DATOS-A. *Journal of Adolescent Research, 16*(6), 608–623.

Creed, T. A., & Kendall, P. C. (2005). Therapist alliance-building behavior within a cognitive-behavioral treatment for anxiety in youth. *Journal of Consulting and Clinical Psychology, 73*(3), 498–505.

Diamond, G. M., Liddle, H. A., Hogue, A., & Dakof, G. A. (1999). Alliance-building interventions with adolescents in family therapy: A process study. *Psychotherapy, 36*(4), 355–368.

Digiuseppe, R., Linscott, J., & Jilton, R. (1996). Developing the therapeutic alliance in child-adolescent psychotherapy. *Applied & Preventive Psychology, 5*, 85–100.

Garcia, J. A., & Weisz, J. R. (2002). When youth mental health care stops: Therapeutic relationship problems and other reasons for ending youth outpatient treatment. *Journal of Consulting and Clinical Psychology, 70*(2), 439.

Hogue, A., Dauber, S., Stambaugh, L. F., Cecero, J. J., & Liddle, H. A. (2006). Early therapeutic alliance and treatment outcome in individual and family therapy for adolescent behavior problems. *Journal of Consulting and Clinical Psychology, 74*(1), 121–129.

Hogue, A., Henderson, C. E., Dauber, S., Barajas, P. C., Fried, A., & Liddle, H. W. (2008). Treatment adherence, competence, and outcome in individual and family therapy for adolescent behavioral problems. *Journal of Consulting and Clinical Psychology, 76*(4), 544–555.

Jungbluth, N. J., & Shirk, S. R. (2013). Promoting homework adherence in cognitive-behavioral therapy for adolescent depression. *Journal of Clinical Child & Adolescent Psychology, 42*(4), 545–553.

Karver, M. S., Handelsman, J. B., Fields, S., & Bickman, L. (2005). Meta-analysis of therapeutic relationship variables in youth and family therapy: The evidence for different relationship variables in the child and adolescent treatment literature. *Clinical Psychology Review, 26*, 50–65.

Kazdin, A. E., Holland, L., & Crowley, M. (1997). Family experience of barriers to treatment and premature termination from child therapy. *Journal of Consulting and Clinical Psychology, 65*(3), 453.

Kazdin, A. E., & Wassell, G. (1999). Barriers to treatment participation and therapeutic change among children referred for conduct disorder. *Journal of Clinical Child Psychology, 28*(2), 160–172.

Kingery, J. N., Roblek, T. L., Suveg, C., Grover, R. L., Sherrill, J. T., & Bergman, R. L. (2006). They're not just "little adults": Developmental considerations for implementing cognitive-behavioral therapy with anxious youth. *Journal of Cognitive Psychotherapy, 20*(3), 263–273.

Meichenbaum, D., & Turk, D. C. (1987). *Facilitating treatment adherence.* New York, NY: Springer.

Nock, M. K., & Ferriter, C. (2005). Parent management of attendance and adherence in child and adolescent therapy: A conceptual and empirical review. *Clinical Child and Family Psychology Review, 8*(2), 149–186.

Norcross, J. C., & Lambert, M. J. (2011). Evidence-based therapy relationships. In J. C. Norcross (Ed.), *Psychotherapy relationships that work: Evidence-based responsiveness* (2nd ed., pp. 3–23). New York, NY: Oxford University Press.

Safran, J. D., Muran, J. C., Samstag, L. W., & Stevens, C. (1992). Repairing alliance ruptures. In J. C. Norcross (Ed.), *Psychotherapy relationships that work: Therapist contributions and responsiveness to patients* (pp. 235–254). New York, NY: Oxford University Press.

Shirk, S. R., Gudmundsen, G., Kaplinski, H. C., & McMakin, D. L. (2008). Alliance and outcome in cognitive-behavioral therapy for adolescent depression. *Journal of Clinical Child & Adolescent Psychology, 37*(3), 631–639.

Shirk, S. R., Karver, M. S., & Brown, R. (2011). The alliance in child and adolescent psychotherapy. *Psychotherapy, 48*(1), 17–24.

Spindel, C., Gabbay, V., & Coffey, B. (2008). Adolescent major depression: Challenges to treatment. *Journal of Child and Adolescent Psychopharmacology, 18*(3), 293–296.

Thompson, S., Bender, K., Windsor, L. C., & Flynn, P. (2009). Keeping families engaged: The effects of home-based family therapy enhanced with experiential activities. *Social Work Research, 33*(2), 121–126.

Webb, C. A., Auerbach, R. P., & DeRubeis, R. J. (2012). Processes of change in CBT of adolescent depression: Review and recommendations. *Journal of Clinical Child & Adolescent Psychology, 41*(5), 654–665.

Zeitler, W. (2009). *Franz Mesmer.* Retrieved from http://www.glassarmonica.com/armonica/mesmer.php

SECTION II

Engaging the Youth

CHAPTER **5**

Externalizing the Problem

Monsters are real, and ghosts are real too. They live inside us, and sometimes,
they win.
—Stephen King

Mental health professionals (MHPs) help clients battle successfully against their internal monsters and ghosts. This is part of the reason I love this quotation and use it often. However, the moment I use it most often is in introducing the technique of externalizing the problem. This is what I say to kids about it.

Ever hear of Stephen King? **(a)** *I love one of his quotes* (I then say the quote). *Stephen King realizes that EVERYONE battles with themselves . . . your mom, your dad, your teacher, and me. Everyone. We all do* **(b)**. *Last session we discussed how you struggle with* (whatever the kid's primary problem is) **(c)**. *So, we need to come up with a name for it that's unique to you, that describes what depression is like in your life. For example, I know one person who called his depression "the dementor," like from the Harry Potter movies. For him, his depression was like something that swooped in and sucked the life out of him, leaving him feeling like he was just a shell. I know another person who named her anxiety "the tarantula," because even thinking about a tarantula made her feel very afraid. So, when your depression is at its very worst, and it seems like there is none of you left over, what would be a good nickname for that attacking force? It could be an animal, a thing, something real, or something imaginary . . . really just about anything that describes it well works* **(d)**. (I wait for the kid to name something.) *That's awesome. I love it. Okay, now we need to describe the features of an iceman attack.* (I now grab a sheet of paper and draw a vertical line down the middle, putting the name— "the iceman"—at the top of the left side.) *Let's imagine the iceman has knocked you down and has his foot on your throat. I mean you are under a complete and total attack and it seems like there is none of you left. What words describe you in those* *moments* **(e)**? *That's a great description.* (I now write the kid's name at the top of the right column.) *Okay, now let's describe what you're like when the iceman is not around at all* **(f)**. *Awesome. Now read this sheet and tell me what you think* **(g)**.

Aiden, I'm now going to ask you a silly question. I use silly questions sometimes to make a point, so just play along. Not that you would ever do this, but if you ever got into a boxing match with (I name the grade of a kid the same sex but much younger; for example "a boy in the fourth grade" for a 16-year-old male) *... not that you'd ever do that, but if you did, who'd win* **(h)**? *Right, you would. But let's change the conditions. Let's say that you had to box that boy in a pitch-dark gym; it's so dark there that you can't even see the hands in front of your face. You're blind. And your arms are tied so tightly to your side that you can't move them. And your feet are tied up too, so you can't move around at all without falling. And the boy's arms and legs are free and he has night vision goggles. Now who wins* **(i)**? *Right, he'd win. That kind of describes what's been happening to you with the iceman. You've thought that your depression is you. You've believed a lie: That depression is who you are, instead of the truth: Depression is something that attacks you and his name is the iceman* **(j)**. *So, the iceman has been kicking your butt because you've thought it's you. However, what we've just done is to turn the lights on in the gym so that you can see your enemy for who he is. Now, the rest of the way, we are going to cut your arms and legs free. I'm also going to show you EXACTLY how the iceman attacks you. What you're going to find is that the iceman doesn't attack you in 104 ways. Actually, he only has a couple of ways of attacking you. And I'll show you that he isn't a very good fighter once you know what to do. I'm going to teach you how he gets you. And I'm going to teach you EXACTLY what you can do to avoid his attacks and counterpunch very, very well. Then, what you're going to find is that the iceman is as powerful over you as a fifth-grade boy. We can't kill the iceman, but we can cage him so that no one will ever know he's in your life unless you tell that person; that will stay the case as long as you continue to use the weapons I'll show you. What are your thoughts about this* **(k)**?

Okay (I give the kid a plain piece of paper with a box of crayons, pencils, and markers), *let's have you draw a picture with you and the iceman* **(l)**. *Okay, great. Aiden* (I take the externalizing sheet and the drawing and three-hole-punch them), *you're going to need a binder to put the stuff we make in. It's going to be your weapons manual against the iceman. So, long after we've stopped, you'll still have your binder to refer to so that you can remember all the weapons that I'll show you how to use. Bring the binder each time to our sessions* **(m)**.

At this point there is usually 10 or 15 minutes left in the session, so I'll say this about the structure of the sessions going forward:

Aiden, most sessions will have three parts. The first part is to go over your therapy homework for the week; your only homework this week is to get your binder set up. The second part is for me to teach you how to use a new weapon to use against the iceman. Then the third part will be for us to do whatever you want. We are at that point now, so we can do whatever you want with the time we have left today. Here are your choices. First, you can talk about something that's bothering you, of course. I'm a therapist, after all, and we love that kind of stuff (with older teens I *might* say the s-word, smiling). *Second, you can talk about anything else. This could be something you're interested in, or something like sports or movies, or anything at all* (n). *Third, you can draw, either on the computer or with paper and art supplies* (o). *Fourth, you can fill in one of these pictures I have* (p). *Fifth, you can play with toys I have in the office* (q). *Sixth, I can show you magic. Or seventh, I can teach you to do some magic* (r). *It's always up to you* (s). *Oh, and it's very important that you let me know when we start each session if you want to make sure to have time to talk about something important. I'll usually ask you about that, but if I forget, be sure to tell me so that I leave enough time* (t). *So, what would you like to do now?*

EXPLANATION

a. A lot of kids in my practice haven't heard of Stephen King, read one of his books, or seen one of his movies. If that's the case, I'll tell them a little about him.

b. For teens and sophisticated children I'll add this: *Show me someone who is not battling with himself and I'll show you someone who is in some pretty terrible circumstance like jail or homelessness. Everybody who is walking around with some degree of success battles themselves, me and your parents included.*

c. For the purpose of simplicity I'm going through this case as if the kid only struggled with depression. However, it's common to do two diagnoses at once (e.g., depression and anxiety). If so, I'll ask if the kid has seen the movie *A Christmas Story*, the one where the kid shoots himself with a BB gun. If not, I'll describe the bullies in that movie. I then go on and say something like: *The iceman is like the main bully, while the Tasmanian devil* (the hypothetical name of the anxiety) *is his sidekick in your life* (switch that up if the anxiety is more predominant). *They tag-team you to make you feel terrible. But, they are both easily caged, at least if I've understood you well and you do what we talk about. My part is to teach you to know what to do. Your part is then to do what you know.*

d. Kids sometimes will name a person: another kid or a family member they don't like, a bully, or even an estranged parent. However, I usually discourage that, as I don't want to complicate our discussions going forward. I also am very careful to not jump in with an idea, as many kids will take me up on that just to get out of the discussion. This is a sample of how one might deal with a kid who is either not getting it or being resistant at this point:

Kid: *I don't know.*
MHP: *That's okay, take your time, we're in no rush . . .*
Kid: *. . . I just don't know, I'm not thinking of anything.*
MHP: *It's good that you're not forcing it. Have you ever given someone a nickname that stuck, or known of someone who got a nickname that stuck?*
Kid: *Yeah.*
MHP: *Well, when those are good, and really fit a person and stick, they sort of just pop into your head and feel perfect. So, it's like that now, and we shouldn't feel like we have to rush it. Let's do this, think about a time that your depression felt absolutely terrible and at its worst.*
Kid: *When I didn't get invited to Jason's pool party but all my other friends did.*
MHP: *Oh man, that sucks. Okay, that sounds like what we need. Let's go back to that moment when you were feeling terrible about that. What did it feel like?*
Kid: *Like I had no friends and no one liked me.*
MHP: *So, pretty lonely?*
Kid: *Yeah.*
MHP: *What else?*
Kid: *I just felt heavy, like I couldn't get out of bed . . . and very, very sad. And, I started crying.*
MHP: *That was a miserable time, and I'm sorry you had to go through that. Okay, but this is good. We need a nickname for something that could make you feel very lonely, heavy, sad, and tearful. What could walk, float, slither, appear, or come into the room now that could make you feel that way, or be a good symbol for feeling that way? Feeling lonely . . . and heavy . . . and very, very sad . . . and like you want to cry?*
Kid: *I don't know. I can't think of anything.*
MHP: *Don't rush it. We have lots of time. Something that would make you feel very lonely . . . and heavy . . . and very, very sad . . . and tearful.*
Kid: *"The iceman."*
MHP: *I love it! Perfect! The iceman is the name of your enemy inside.*

I know it might seem like I'm assigning myself an easy case, among those kids who struggle with this process. But many kids don't even need a discussion like this. And among those that do, this is typically how it goes. Maybe once or twice every couple of years I might need to turn this process of coming up with a name into a homework assignment, but that is unusual. My speculation is that if the evaluation and treatment planning phases were less well designed, this first session might be more difficult. But, as it stands, it usually isn't that big of a deal to externalize the problem(s). The trick is to not take the bait of the kid's struggle and say things like, "What about 'the iceman'?" or "What about 'crusher'?" For this to have the wow factor, and to be of lasting value, the kid needs to come up with the name.

e. This part of the discussion usually flows pretty easily. I'm looking to fill up one-third to one-half of the left column of a sheet of paper. Kids will start saying things like "sad" and "afraid" and "moody." Synonyms are fine. Once I make sure to get the first three or four descriptions from them, I feel free to ask them if feelings, thoughts, and behaviors that I know are commonly affiliated with the disorder might apply, or that the kid has already acknowledged experiencing could be true. I'll say and ask things like:

- *Are you grouchy when the iceman owns you and there is none of you left?*

- *Ever have a really bad toothache or earache?* (Kid usually says "yes.") *So you know that when you have a really bad toothache it's hard to think about other people and their needs, right?* (Again, kids usually assent.) *We call that being "self-involved." When the iceman has you knocked down and has his foot on your throat, are you self-involved?*

- *Are you funny when the iceman is in charge?*

- *Are you a good friend when the iceman is calling the shots?*

- *Do you have any problems concentrating when the iceman is dominating you?*

And so forth. Sometimes a kid will say, "Well, sometimes I'm still a good friend and sometimes I'm not, it just depends." To which I'll reply: *Yes, because the strength of the iceman attacks can vary. Sometimes he mounts a small attack while at other times he really gets after making you feel terrible. But, we want to think about what you're like when you're being attacked the hardest. When the iceman is totally dominating you, are you a good friend?* At other times a kid will hesitate, and say things like, "I'm not sure, I still tend to be funny even when I feel terrible." To which I'll reply: *Okay, we won't put that one down. We don't want to write anything that isn't true.*

f. Coming up with the descriptions of how the enemy attacks the kid is not intellectually hard but can be emotionally draining. So, by the time we get to the right side of the sheet (see Table 5.1), the kid is usually ready to launch into it. I find kids complete more of the right side of the sheet than the left on their own, but they still often need my help. I try to do three things. First, I try to keep in mind what I've learned the kid's strengths are from the evaluation. So, I'll say something like, *Is it true that you're a very kind person when the iceman is not around?* Second, I try to ask if the antonyms of what's listed on the left side of the paper are true, though I usually don't line them up right across from their opposite on the paper. Third, I try to keep the two sides even. I don't think it's a big deal to go longer with the right side. I just like the symmetry and the suggestion that the iceman can be equally destructive if left unchecked. Table 5.1 indicates what the completed sheet would look like.

TABLE 5.1 Externalizing the Problem	
The Iceman	**Aiden**
Sad	Very friendly
Lonely	Active
Not funny	Happy
Can't concentrate	Positive
Thinks about suicide	Sleeps great
Self-involved	Social
Hopeless	Very funny
Doesn't sleep well	Gets after stuff
Poor appetite	Not self-critical
Not a good friend	Eats like a horse
Grouchy at home	Can't get enough fun
Not motivated	Hopeful
Doesn't like to have fun	Kind
Lazy	Generous
Negative	Never thinks about suicide
Mad at self	Mostly respectful to parents

g. This is one of my favorite moments in child clinical work. Many kids say things like "I can't believe how different they are." Or, "I guess it's like I'm two different people." Or, "Wow. I didn't realize how different I can be." To which I'll say: ***Not really. You're just Aiden. The iceman is not you. He's like a fever in your body that we need to cage.***

h. With some kids you need to go back and forth a couple of times. Something like this:

> **MHP:** . . . *who'd win?*
> **Kid:** *I'd never do that.*
> **MHP:** *Right, that'd be wrong to fight a boy much younger and smaller than you. It's a silly question. But work with me here. Though you'd NEVER do it, who would win that boxing match if you did?*

i. In my decades of using this technique and metaphor, I've never once had a kid say that he'd still win. But, as luck has it sometimes, probably the first person who buys this book will have the first kid that she tries this technique with have this happen. So, let me review what I'd suggest in that hypothetical scenario:

Kid: *I'd still win!*
MHP: *Really? You can't see. He can see. You can't move. He can move. You can't hit. He can hit. I mean even Batman would struggle with that one, right?*
Kid: *I'm not Batman. I'd still win.*
MHP: *Okay, I hear that. Let's add to it then. Let's say that you had a really bad case of diarrhea (making a funny face) . . . and a fever . . . and pus was coming out of your ears, so you couldn't hear either and you were, like, all feeling nasty and wickedly sick . . . but the kid felt at his very best. Who'd win now?*
Kid: *I guess he would then. . . .*

j. It's a feel thing, but I'll sometimes pause here and redirect the kid's attention to the sheet of paper to illustrate what a butt-kicking looks like. (For teens, I'll sometimes also substitute the word "ass" for butt, another feel thing.)

k. Okay, there's a lot to digest in this section. First, I like a weapons metaphor for most kids. I think they're often in the fight of their lives, and I like calling a spade a spade. I also like the term "weapons manual" for the binder we produce. But this is a style thing. You may prefer "tools," which is a common metaphor in the clinical literature. If so, you could use language like the "tools manual."

Second, as anxiety disorders usually have a high temperamental loading (and temperaments don't budge more than a little with time) and mood disorders have a high relapse rate and can have a high temperamental loading as well, I use the cage metaphor. I want the kid, and eventually his parents, to realize that the kid will likely need to continue using the cognitive behavioral therapy (CBT) and positive psychology (PP) interventions after we have met our goals. Also, if you're going to make a mistake, it's better to overprepare than the other way around.

Third, we are instilling hope. If you're new to being a therapist, you may be in doubt about how effective this work is. And, if so, join the club. Most of us have been there. But, the more experience you get with this, the more your confidence comes across. Along these lines, and depending on my feel of the situation with the kid, I might also add:

I've coached a lot, a lot of kids in their fight against enemies like the iceman. And, I'll tell you, when you know what you're doing, the iceman ain't so bad. Actually, he's kind of a wimp (I might use the p-word with older teens, which usually makes them laugh with what seems like partial relief). *So, you in?*

Fourth, most kids don't deploy a lot of words here. But their faces will often say it all. It's super awesome to be a therapist in these moments.

l.   Many kids will just take to this task and do the drawing. However, some ask questions. Here's what I've heard and some possible responses:

Kid: *Y'mean like inside me?*
MHP: *No, try drawing the iceman outside of you. (If the kid does this spontaneously, and that's rare, I'll accept it but then ask for another drawing with the enemy externalized.)*
Kid: *Include anyone else?*
MHP: *Nah, just you and the iceman.*
Kid: *Should we be doing something?*
MHP: *Totally up to you.*
Kid: *I don't draw well.*
MHP: *Yeah, me neither. But it doesn't matter here. Your best is plenty fine.*

I do this because I'll have the kid do a similar drawing in the termination session. It's then fun to compare the drawings. The enemy will often be smaller, or caged, or somehow indicated to be feckless, at least when compared with the first drawing. And, parents *love* seeing these two drawings at termination.

m.   For years I used clinical workbooks produced by others. And there are many very fine ones out there that can be quite comforting and helpful, especially when you're new to being a CBT therapist; you can find these books peppered throughout the References and Bibliography sections in this volume. However, I've morphed into the practice of creating a one-of-a-kind weapons manual for each kid. With the exception of the treatment plan, everything we produce goes in it, with me trying to remember to make copies for the chart. (I'll sometimes include the treatment plan if a kid lobbies convincingly for it, but I usually don't. I don't want a kid to think of it as a to-do list or to remember what we said our goals are, in case he wants to convince a parent that a premature termination is in order by declaring that he has reached goals that he hasn't.) When I come out to the waiting room I'll also ask the parent to get the kid a binder, pointing to the sheet we've produced. (You will also find in Appendix I a log that I use to keep track of which interventions I have covered with a kid and the date we went over them; this log helps me to keep easy track of which modules to consider as I approach each session.)

The large majority of kids in my practice don't care if their parents see what we've produced in this session (e.g., we're not charting how often they make out with a crush). However, if that is, or might be, a concern, I'll put the sheet in a manila envelope; most kids are pretty forward, though, about stating if they care about this issue. The large majority of parents in my practice also just naturally let their kid take the lead regarding what gets shared and what doesn't. However, if I have reason to believe that a given parent might be inclined to be snoopy, I'll invite him into the office and say something like: ***Bill, when we have our parent session I'll explain everything I'm doing with Aiden. For now, though, it's important that we treat Aiden's binder as*** *a very personal diary that only he and I look at. Is that okay?* I can't remember a time that it wasn't okay.

n. If kids elect to talk (e.g., instead of drawing or doing magic) but then struggle with what to talk about, I'll provide a little teaching about free association (see next paragraph). Freud aptly described free association as a quick path to unconscious, anxious, and clinically important material. This is a perfect illustration about how training in psychodynamic therapy can be extremely helpful even if you practice CBT, PP, and behavioral therapy 100% of the time. As a quick little exercise in free association, try this:

Identify the person you trust the most in your life and ask that person if you can do a brief exercise with him or her. Tell the person what you plan to do and that his or her task is just to listen closely until you're done. Then, try to say everything that pops into your head *without editing* for 10 minutes. If you're like most of the rest of us humans, you won't go long before you start editing yourself. Something will sound illogical (e.g., the thought is completely disconnected to the one that preceded it), or embarrassing (e.g., you find yourself attracted physically to your confidant but it's not that kind of a relationship), or potentially hurtful to the other person (e.g., the thought pops into your head that you wouldn't let yourself get as fat as your confidant), or boring to the other person (e.g., you start thinking about the laundry that's backed up at home). Psychodynamic therapists are trained to watch for the inevitable defense mechanisms that quickly come to bear when clients try to free-associate; they then interpret these defense mechanisms in order to get the free association back on line, which engenders useful thoughts and feelings (e.g., an elucidation of transference).

So, we are using such moments to touch base on where our kid's unconscious/anxious/transferential feelings and thoughts might be. This is a typical way it might go:

Kid: *I don't know what to say.*
MHP: *That's okay, just say whatever little thing pops into your head. It might seem boring, or embarrassing, or like I could get offended, but just say it anyway.*
Kid: *But I'm not thinking about anything.*
MHP: *Well, if you just relax and don't put any pressure on yourself, stuff will start popping into your head. Just go with it.*
Kid: *Well, I was wondering where you got your shoes.*
MHP: *Okay, I'll tell you in a minute. But tell me more about what you're thinking about my shoes.*
Kid: *Well, you said you like to coach baseball and I'm thinking you couldn't do that in shoes like that.*
MHP: *What might that mean?*
Kid: *Do you really coach baseball?*
MHP: *So, you're wondering if sometimes, just maybe, I might say things to you that aren't true.*

Kid: *I guess so. No offense.*
MHP: *No offense taken. Tell me, does it happen often that adults aren't truthful with you?*
Kid: *My dad lies all the time. I hate it.*

And so on. You see where this might then go: an exploration of the relationship with Dad, which can be very helpful later on when meeting with the parents; an MHP would also have the opportunity to reaffirm that therapy is a place where truth is pursued first and foremost, and that we both do well to only speak the truth to each other.

o. This is a staple of play therapy. So, let me share a little about my sense of the play therapy literature as well as my own experience with it.

My graduate training in child clinical at George Washington University had a heavy psychodynamic focus. Therefore, we learned a lot about how to think about and apply play therapy in working with kids. And, for my first couple of years doing therapy with kids, it's all I did. My experience and the literature suggest the same thing: used in the right situations and for the right kinds of problems, it is a very helpful type of treatment, especially if the parents are involved (e.g., filial play therapy). I have found that play therapy can be very useful for traumatized kids who can't tolerate the stress of CBT. It can also be indicated for kids with various kinds of speech and language disorders and for kids who are so resistant that the techniques I review for managing resistance don't work. And play therapy can be helpful for kids when CBT has failed for one reason or another. Finally, I find that it can be used nicely as an augment to CBT, which is how I use it in this context. The initial instruction is straightforward:

Aiden, there are only two things I'd ask when you draw something. First, make it totally pretend. So, try to avoid plots of movies and TV shows, unless you want to take them in a new direction. Also, try to avoid things that have happened to you, unless it's an event from your past that bothers you a lot. Second, I'll ask you to make a pretend story about it. Sound good?

This is another technique for discovering themes that are clinically relevant. Inevitably, the kid will produce a story that is relevant for his life. But, instead of discussing his life (i.e., we avoid linking the drawing to his life, unless he does, as that breaks the displacement) we discuss the characters in the story: what they are thinking and feeling, how they solve their problems, and other ways they might go about finding solutions that could be more adaptive, although the latter is done gently through questions. It's beyond the scope of this volume to cover all the details. If interested, seek out supervision or training from someone skilled in play therapy.

p. I have several books at hand (three volumes of the *Creative Therapy* books by Dossick & Shea, 1988–1995). These books are filled with partially completed drawings; the illustrations pull for material that might be clinically relevant. I'll let the kid choose the picture, make a copy of it, and have him fill it in. I then ask for him to make up a pretend story about it. This is yet another way of uncovering useful material. You could easily make your own pictures up as well.

q. This technique is akin to drawing in the play therapy world. I've seen and heard clinicians get their shorts in a bunch about the types of toys a kid MHP *should have*. I don't subscribe to that school of thought because I believe it is overstated. I just try to have some unstructured toys available (i.e., not board games and not toys with preordained stories attached to them). So, army men, medical kits, appliances, animals, puppets, blocks, and things like that. I keep a range available, but not so many that I can't store them easily in my cabinets, as I see adult clients also.

    In this approach, the kid plays out scenes while the MHP makes comments that are similar to the ones made when the kid draws: Skillful kid MHPs make empathic statements, provide clarifications about what's occurring, and offer gentle questions pertaining to various coping strategies being manifested in the play.

r. As I've discussed in Chapter 1, magic is fun, alliance enhancing, and can help kids develop a prosocial skill set.

s. If a kid says he doesn't know what to do, the response is pretty straightforward:

Kid: *I don't know what I want to do.*
MHP: *That's okay. Take your time. We're in no rush.*
Kid: *I don't know.*
MHP: *I hear that, but this is your call. Take your time. . . .*

    It is also noteworthy to me that when kids wish to discuss issues pertaining to having a minority status, they will often choose the time at the end of the session to do so. As I indicated in Chapter 1, I endeavor to always ask teens and families about their experience of living a minority status. One teenage girl, whom I call Aala, noted that being a Muslim in her high school was very difficult for her. She explained that she often had to respond to offensive questions and "jokes" about her religion. Moreover, she said she felt a pressure to never let the other kids know how much these exchanges bothered her. While working with the school system around these issues was part of the intervention plan, as was empowering Aala's voice with her peers, she would usually choose to spend time each session teaching me about the beauty of her religion. During the evaluation phase of the work I had expressed interest in her statement that she found her religion to be beautiful. I told her that I knew very little about Islam but would enjoy learning more if she cared to share; she then subsequently brought this dialogue to most of our sessions. My alliance with Aala was very strong, and I believe that had a lot to do with these discussions.

While we are on the topic of how sessions start, let me share that I open up many therapy sessions with the same question. This is typically how it might go at the start of a session:

MHP: *What's the best thing and what's the worst thing that has happened in your life since I last saw you?*
Kid: *Not much really.*
MHP: *Okay, but everyone has even little good and bad things that happen all the time. What's the best thing that's happened, even if it's really small, like a good meal or a friend said "hi" when you weren't feeling so hot?*

The kid shares and I ask a clarifying question or two and offer some empathy.

Then we continue:

MHP: *Now, what's the worst thing that happened, even if it was tiny, like having too much homework or someone was grouchy toward you?*

The kid shares, and I provide empathy and ask my clarifying question or two. If the vignette seems like something that is bothering the kid, I'll ask if he wants to talk about it at the end. If he says "yes," I ask for an estimate on how much time I should reserve to make sure we have enough time. We'll then talk about it at the end. However, if the worst thing seems like something that is preoccupying the kid's mind, I'll suggest that we might start the session by going over it. I've heard clinicians criticize CBT for being too structured or too robotic. However, that isn't the case in the hands of an artful therapist. This is just one example of how we adapt depending on what the kid's needs are.

t. This guideline reflects how CBT, artfully delivered, is flexible. If a kid has something important to discuss (e.g., a breakup, being upset by getting an F grade), we give it the time it needs.

ADDITIONAL COMMENTARY

It's almost as if we each have a vampire inside us. Controlling that beast,
that dark side, is what fascinates me.
—Sheryl Lee

This is the session I do after the evaluation and the treatment planning phases are completed. In the large majority of instances, this will be the fourth visit, as I do it in the same session as treatment planning (remember that the first three visits are allocated to the evaluation phase). However, if treatment planning or another agenda took up all the time, I'll introduce the concept and ask for the kid to think of the name as homework.

Examples of externalizing the problem can be found throughout the clinical literature. For instance, Neil Jacobson used to recommend this strategy in couples counseling when relationship problems could not be overcome via behavioral interventions: He referred to it as "turning the problem into an it." Likewise, when I worked on a National Institutes of Health (NIH)-funded project at George Washington Medical School that was investigating what psychosocial variables might prolong the lives of those diagnosed with kidney failure, we would encourage families with someone who was receiving dialysis treatment to set a place at the table for the kidney disease. Examples can also be found throughout the child clinical literature; see the References and Bibliography section at the end of this chapter for examples. Though this strategy has been around for a while, I find that many child clinicians have not been exposed to it. As I find it offers a rich clinical yield, I use it with anyone I'm treating in individual therapy, across the life span.

These are some of the clinical advantages that accrue from using this technique:

1. The kid's self-esteem is promoted. A key concept imbued in this strategy is that when a child is suffering from an internalizing disorder he is under attack. Asthma attacks the airways. Leukemia attacks the blood cells. Internalizing disorders attack the brain. Moreover, the attacking force *is not the kid*, just like leukemia isn't a person or asthma isn't a person. So we establish that the internalizing disorder *is not the kid*.

2. Parents are unleashed in expressing their anger and hurt feelings about the disorder(s). Those feelings are already there and are usually pronounced. However, many parents suppress them or feel shame about them. Their feelings can now be expressed. They don't feel rage toward their baby. They feel rage toward the disorder(s).

3. If I need to therapeutically confront the kid about succumbing to her internalizing problem, I don't sound as if I'm confronting the kid. I'm confronting the attacker. So, let's say Monica refused to get on the school bus because she was afraid. I don't need to say things like, "Monica, we talked about how your fears get worse when you avoid things you're afraid of," which can sound like I'm criticizing *her*. I can now say: *Wow, it sounds like the cobra knocked you down on Monday. We all have days like that. But let's say we were to go back into a time machine and you were going to use one of your weapons last Monday morning. Which one might you have chosen to defeat the cobra that day?* (By the way, I find this especially helpful when an internal enemy's method is to have my client lie, as is often the case with substance abuse disorders.)

4. Every technique I teach, and every exposure we do, can be couched as something to apply to engage a very winnable battle.

INTERVENTION TRACKING LOG

Once the evaluation is concluded, I attach a log sheet for tracking the interventions I've done with a kid to one of the chart surfaces (i.e., Appendix I). It allows me to quickly remember what interventions we've completed, the name(s) of the internal enemy(enemies), what videos I've shown the kid, and what magic I've either shown or taught the kid.

SIDEBAR 5.1

Knowing how to do a card force is a basic skill in magic. That is, knowing how to get a participant to select a specific card while having it appear that the selection was under the participant's control. If you search for "card force" at YouTube.com, you'll find a bunch of them. The simplest one that I've seen is called the cross cut force. The card you want to force is on the top of the deck. If you know how to riffle shuffle, do that a few times first, leaving the top card unchanged. Then put the deck down and ask the participant to cut the deck anywhere. So, now you have two piles. Pile A has the force card on top; let's say it's the ace of spades. Pile B is the other pile. Quickly take pile B and put it on top of pile A at a 90-degree angle; in other words, the two piles will now make a cross, with the ace of spades being on top of the bottom pile.

This is a cool way you can use a card force with a kid. Once you've scheduled your next appointment, write on a piece of paper, "Aiden will choose the four of clubs at our next appointment." Put the note in an envelope and mail it to yourself. You can also put sealing wax on the outside of it or tape it shut for effect. You can also write on the front, Don't open before (the date of your next appointment). Then take out the envelope and put it out on display. Then shuffle the cards as I've described, forcing the four of clubs. After you've done the cross cut, ask your kid client to notice that the envelope is sealed and the day it was mailed. Tell him that your mind puppet told you which card he would pick before he picked it. Then ask him to open the envelope. After he's read it say, "Let's look at the card that you randomly cut the deck to" which will be the top card on pile A, which is also the bottom pile. For effect, you can also have the kid look through the deck to ensure that there is no other four of clubs. The wow factor for this trick can be considerable.

By the way, for those of you who are trainees, this trick could be integrated into your applications for an internship or employment. As you explain that you integrate magic into your clinical work with kids, you could ask your interviewer if she'd like a quick demonstration of a trick you use. Next, force a card. Then, ask her to look at the classified ad section of her local newspaper for that day where it is written that your interviewer would choose that card. You might then joke that you never tell adults how you do a trick but you'd make an exception if the person makes you an offer.

REFERENCES AND BIBLIOGRAPHY

Ball, D., Piercy, F., & Bischof, G. (1993). Externalizing the problem through cartoons: A case example. *Journal of Systemic Therapies, 12*(1), 12–21B.

Bratton, S. C., Ray, D., Rhine, T., & Jones, L. (2005). The efficacy of play therapy with children: A meta-analytic review of treatment outcomes. *Professional Psychology: Research and Practice, 36*(4), 376–390.

Butler, S., Guterman, J., & Rudes, J. (2009). Using puppets with children in narrative therapy to externalize the problem. *Journal of Mental Health Counseling, 31*(3), 225–233.

Dossick, J., & Shea, E. (1988–1995). *Creative therapy* (3 Vols.). Sarasota, FL: Professional Resource Exchange.

Fristad, M. A., Gavazzi, S. M., & Soldano, K. W. (1999). Naming the enemy: Learning to differentiate mood disorder "symptoms" from the "self" that experiences them. *Journal of Family Psychotherapy, 10*(1), 81–88.

Fristad, M. A., & Goldberg-Arnold, J. S. (2011). *Psychotherapy for children with bipolar and depressive disorder.* New York, NY: Guilford Press.

Gottman, J. M. (1999). *The marriage clinic: A scientifically based marital therapy.* New York, NY: W. W. Norton.

Henley, D. (2007). Naming the enemy: An art therapy intervention for children with bipolar and comorbid disorders. *Art Therapy, 24*(3), 104–110.

Hoffman, R. M., & Kress, V. E. (2008). Narrative therapy and non-suicidal-self-injurious behavior: Externalizing the problem and internalizing personal agency. *Journal of Humanistic Counseling, Education, and Development, 47*(2), 157–171.

Keeling, M. L., & Bermudez, M. (2007). Externalizing problems through art and writing: Experience of process and helpfulness. *Journal of Marital and Family Therapy, 32*(4), 405–419.

March, J. S. (2006). *Talking back to OCD: The program that helps kids and teens say "no way"—and parents say "way to go."* New York, NY: Guilford Press.

Palmiter, D. J. (2007). Child clinician's corner: Externalizing the problem. *The Independent Practitioner, 27,* 142–143.

Tomm, K. (1989). Externalizing the problem and internalizing personal agency. *Journal of Strategic and Systemic Therapies, 8,* 1.

White, M., & Epston, D. (2004). Externalizing the problem. In C. Malone, L. Forbat, M. Robb, & J. Seden (Eds.), *Relating experience: Stories from health and social care.* London, UK: Routledge.

White, M., & Epston, D. (1990). *Narrative means to therapeutic ends.* New York, NY: W. W. Norton.

White, V. E. (2002). Developing counseling objectives and empowering clients: A strength-based intervention. *Journal of Mental Health Counseling, 24*(3), 270–279.

Zimmerman, T. S., & Shepherd, S. D. (1993). Externalizing the problem of bulimia: Conversation, drawing, and letter writing in group therapy. *Journal of Systemic Therapies, 12*(1), 22–31.

CHAPTER 6

Behavioral Activation and Sleep Hygiene

THE MODULAR TREATMENT APPROACH

Most of the chapters in this book regard specific stand-alone interventions. In my experience kids will pick two to three interventions to be their go-to strategies and leave the rest behind. This isn't to say that "the rest" don't get used. It also isn't to say that the underlying principles don't get used, either. It is to say that, like most of us, kids pick and choose what to keep and what to set aside based on their temperament, age, cost–benefit analysis, and context. A younger, action-oriented boy who tends to butt heads with his parents may be less likely to use thought testing but really get into behavioral activation; for an older, introverted, and academically minded young woman it may be the exact opposite. To learn more about this research, search with the term "goodness of fit." This is what I say to kids about it:

Aiden, today I'm going to give you the first weapon against the iceman. Ever hear of "jousts," as in knights jousting (a)? Well, as you may know, knights had multiple weapons to choose from, and they trained on them all. However, when it really counted they usually had their favorite weapons that they used, leaving the others behind. Ever see a movie or TV drama that showed that (b)? Right, well, it's the same thing here. I'm going to show you a bunch of weapons to use against the iceman, and I'm going to ask you to practice them all. However, when you do, you'll tend to have your favorite two or three that you'll go to the most, and that's okay. I need to show you many more though for two reasons. First, I never can tell which weapons will be a kid's favorite ones. I've tried guessing before but I'm not good at that (c). Second, as you get older or as your life changes you may change your mind. Like a knight may really like using a light sword when he's younger and quicker. But, as he gets older and stronger he may want to switch more to a heavy weapon (d). So I'll show you a bunch and then you'll use whatever best cages the iceman.

Explanation

a.   If the kid hasn't heard of jousting, I'll usually explain it. The only time I won't is if a child is too young to bother.

b.   If the kid knows what jousting is, but hasn't seen a movie or show depicting it, I may describe a scene, in an age-appropriate fashion.

c.   This is the case primarily with the more complicated interventions. I find just about all kids will use coping thoughts, just about all depressed kids will use behavioral activation, and just about all anxious kids use physiological calming. However, who uses what other interventions is somewhat of a crap shoot; moreover, how many interventions it takes to reach our goals also varies. For example, I remember one anxious little girl I was treating and thinking, "I don't think this kid–parent combination is going to get into thought testing very much," but the exact opposite ended up happening. They *loved* it. Likewise, I can think of another family when I thought they'd love doing problem solving together, but they acted like I was asking them to share a meal of sawdust when I went over how to practice the technique at home.

d.   The whole knight/weapons imagery thing I don't always say. It sort of depends on my intuition on how a given kid will respond. One could just as easily review how the kid's recreational life changed over time in terms of what the kid liked to do and the toys he preferred. For my part, I like giving the kid the material to put in a personalized binder; who knows when a given strategy might come in handy down the line.

BEHAVIORAL ACTIVATION

I think that success is having fun.
—Bruno Mars

There's no fear when you're having fun.
—Will Thomas

It's harder for a kid to be depressed if he is doing fun things. This is how I introduce behavioral activation to a kid:

Aiden, I'd like to show you a cartoon. This cartoon isn't meant to be funny. It's meant to make a point. (The cartoon is of a man looking at a bird, with the bird saying to the man, "I don't sing because I am happy. I am happy because I sing.")

What do you think it means **(a)**? *So the bird is saying he doesn't sing because he's happy. When he starts singing he may feel "blukh," but he makes himself sing and then he feels pretty good. But, one of the iceman's favorite ways of attacking you is to put this in your head: "Aiden, don't do that* (whatever used to be a fun thing) *because you don't feel like it." Have you ever had a family member or a friend ask you to do something that was supposed to be fun, but words like that were in your head? When was that? How did you feel after you made the decision to not go* **(b)**? *That was the iceman talking in your head! See, the iceman is a lying liar. Nothing out of his mouth is true, which you need to take on faith for now but I'll prove to you over time* **(c)**. *The iceman is using a true thing but changing it to try to hurt you. It's true that if you've had a day of working at school and on the baseball field and you come home it can feel pretty good to just chillax on the couch, in front of the TV, for an hour or so. That's kind of like getting into a warm bath after a long day of getting after it. That works and helps you to rest and recover. However, the iceman tries to change that and say, "Just rest, you don't feel like doing that," when doing that only makes you feel worse. So, a regular bath after a long day makes you feel better. But the iceman's bath sucks you down into the sewer and makes you feel worse, just like we saw with your example of the difference between when you went fishing and when you didn't. That's important for us to remember.*

Okay, so what we need to do is make a list of fun stuff that you can do; I'll be the secretary. There are usually three types of fun things. First, there are fun things you used to do but just stopped doing even though they might still be fun. Second, there are fun things you're doing now. Third, there are things you have never tried but might be fun if you did. Sound good? Okay, what do you do for fun these days **(d)**? *Are there fun things you used to do but have just gotten away from them* **(e)**? *Okay, what are some things you've never tried but might be fun if you tried them* **(f)**?*

Aiden, I'll tell you that there are both traps and wings on this list. Traps are things that the iceman can use to put you in a depression bath if you're not careful. Wings are things that help you to fly high above the iceman so it's harder for him to get you. Traps are typically things like watching TV, playing video games, goofing around on the computer, and other activities that you usually do by yourself and without much movement. Have you noticed a difference if you do those things just a little versus if you do them for hours on end? Okay, so I'm going to put an exclamation point next to those kinds of activities on our list **(g)**. *Now wings are things that involve some combination of being with other kids, moving around so that you sweat and breathe hard, and it's something you don't normally do. The more you have of those three, the bigger the wings are. So let's go through and put one, two, or three asterisks next to those activities that have one, two, or three of those types: social, physical, and novel* **(h)**. *So, looking at this list, what activities could you commit to doing this week* **(i)**? *Okay, I'd like to show you how we'll keep track of what you do and how it affects you. This is a form for doing that* (breaking out the form indicated later in this chapter). *It's easy-peasy to* *fill this in. This form will help us to keep track of how much fun you have and how effective it is in caging the iceman. The first column is just for saying what you did, like "Read Jurassic Park comic book." Then you see you give three mood ratings: "1" means you felt very sad; "7" means you felt very happy. So, you rate what your mood was before the fun thing, during it, and afterward. Finally, you rate how fun the activity was from 0 to 100: "0" is no fun at all; "100" is like the very best day of your life in terms of fun. You don't have to do this form during the fun thing; that might actually take away from the fun you're having. Just do it sometime that day. Lots of kids will do it just before bed. So, let's practice one. What's a recent example of some fun you had?* (We complete an example.) *Let's keep this in your binder.* (I'll three-hole-punch it at this point and insert it into the binder, giving him some blank forms.) *Over time, these sheets will really help us to understand which fun activities the iceman hates the most* (j).

Explanation

a.   When we mental health professionals (MHPs) work with a psychological truth for a while we can tend to forget that many people don't know it. I find that even a lot of adults struggle to accurately interpret this drawing (if you go to www.cartoonbank.com and enter "I don't sing because I am happy. I am happy because I sing." in their search engine the cartoon will come up). Some kids get it but most don't. But I feel a need to give a kid a shot at it in case he gets it on his own. If the kid says something like, "He sings when he's happy?" I'll say: *Good guess Aiden. What it means is that the bird. . . .*

b.   This can be a bit of a dance as depressed kids sometimes don't want to exert the effort to search their memory. This is an example of how it might go:

Kid: *No, I can't think of anything.*
MHP: *Well, what kinds of things do your friends like to do for fun?*
Kid: *Go to movies. Go out to eat. Stuff like that.*
MHP: *Can you think of a time that one of them invited you to go to a movie or go out to eat and you didn't go, even though your mom and dad would have let you?*
Kid: *Not really. My parents don't let me do much.*
MHP *Okay, well, what kinds of things does your family like to do for fun?*
Kid: *Play board games. Go to movies. Eat out. Go fishing. Stuff like that.*
MHP: *Can you think of a time that they wanted you to join them but you said "No"?*
Kid: *Last weekend my dad and brother wanted me to go fishing but I felt tired.*
MHP: *Do you like fishing?*
Kid: *Yeah, but I didn't feel like it then.*
MHP: *Right, so in your head was, "Don't do that, just rest instead."*
Kid: *Pretty much.*
MHP: *What did you do instead of going fishing?*
Kid: *I laid on my bed and goofed around on my phone.*

MHP: *If a 7 is very happy and a 1 is very unhappy, how did you feel lying on your bed, goofing around on your phone?*
Kid: *2 to 3, I guess.*
MHP: *When's the last time you went fishing?*
Kid: *About a month ago. We went to Lake Henry and I caught a bass.*
MHP: *So, if a 7 is very happy and a 1 is very unhappy, how did you feel that day?*
Kid: *6, I guess.*
MHP: *Exactly. The other day when your dad and brother wanted you to go fishing that was the iceman in your head. The iceman doesn't want you at a 5, 6, or 7. He wants you at a 1, 2, or 3, the lower the better. One of the weapons he uses against you to get you there is, "Don't do that fun thing 'cause you don't feel like it!"*

If my verbal dance with a kid doesn't generate a vignette, I'll bring in the parent who has brought the kid. Or, if it's an adolescent who has driven himself to the appointment, I'll call a parent. What I'll say to the kid to introduce this idea is: *Aiden, it's tough for you to remember a time when this happened. So, why don't we ask your mom/dad if s/he can remember a time?* I don't often get to this point with kids, but when I have they've always agreed. What I've found, then, is that the parent remembers an example almost instantly. Actually, the challenge is to try to keep the parent from offering a bunch of examples or saying things like, "Yeah, Aiden *never* wants to do stuff with us or his friends! That's part of the reason why we're here!" So, if you do this, be ready to interrupt once you have your example, so you don't find yourself having to deal with an angry kid who sees you as aligned against him with his parent.

c. Anytime I hear distorted thinking, especially of the self-critical type, I jump in with a declaration that the thought is an iceman thought. I say things like, *That's the iceman lying to you.* Or, *The iceman hates you and tries to make you think that's true when it isn't.* Or, with teens who have articulated some degree of suicidality, *The iceman won't be happy until he convinces you that you should take your own life.*

d. It is pretty easy for kids to understand having fun. Besides being interested in expanding the dosing of fun in a kid's life—and especially fun that is novel, physical, and social—I'm also interested in generating ideas that don't cost money and that the kid can do by himself on a school day, freeing both him and his parents from the burden of having to participate in or support the activity.

    What's interesting to note, as we begin to generate a list of fun activities, is how few items depressed kids generate on their own. The lethargy is easy to spot. Many of them also need help remembering what they like to do that's fun.

e. Sometimes the kid will offer a wonderful account that helps the agenda of this session. For example, one kid said, "I used to really enjoy Odyssey of the Mind, but my friend whose mom used to organize it moved away." (Odyssey of the Mind is a group activity where kids generate academic projects and enter them into competitions against other kids of the same age.) I would not have thought to ask this kid if he'd like to compete in Odyssey of the Mind. But, learning about it afforded me the opportunity to suggest to his parents to reengage that activity.

f. This is the money line of questioning and the one where I contribute the most. Each list I develop with kids is unique. Table 6.1 provides a list of fun activities to get you started.

TABLE 6.1 List of Potentially Fun Activities

Bowling	Drawing	Mindcrafting
Reading for fun	Kayaking	Writing plays
Swimming	Archery	Snowboarding
Ping-pong	Skiing	Photography
Going to a movie	Going to a water park	Crafting
Going to a museum	Texting friends	Playing volleyball
Geocaching	Hunting	Acting
Playing with a pet	Water skiing	Paintballing
Hiking	Snow tubing	Golfing
Biking	Going to a zoo	Singing
Fishing	Going to the library	Writing pretend stories
Playing pool	Camping	Water balloon fights
Shooting hoops	Boating	Making a snowman
Playing video games	Debate club	Skateboarding
Horseback riding	Shooting darts	Church youth group
Amusement parks	Playing board games	Running
Air hockey	Playing cards	Martial arts
Ice skating	Doing magic	Tennis
Going to an arcade	Listening to music	Badminton
Roller skating	Facebooking	Playing shuffleboard
Going out to eat	Snapchatting	Hopscotch
Going to a concert	Tweeting	Playing chess online
Track and field	Going online	freerice.com contests
Shopping	Listening to a comedian	Water gun battles
Getting nails done	Playing basketball	Playing with dolls
Target shooting	Playing field hockey	Play acting
Getting makeup done	Dancing	Going to fairs/bazaars

(continued)

TABLE 6.1 List of Potentially Fun Activities _(continued)_		
Going to the bookstore	Scouting	Writing poetry
Going to the coffee shop	Knitting	Getting a massage
Playing baseball	Pottery	Flying kites
Snorkeling	Building models	Going to a play
Shooting rockets	Making a tree house	Building a fort
Doing a friend's hair	Playing dress up	Croquet
Watching professional sports	Playing with a microscope	Making a tent in the home
Going to batting cages	Miniature golf	Going for ice cream
Collecting baseball cards	Walking along the beach	Watching a school game
Taking a day trip to a city	Working with playdough	Bird-watching

g. This might seem sort of obvious to adults, but many kids are clueless. If you have time, and depending on your kid client, there may be value in interviewing him about fun activities he's doing that might promote lethargy or a dour mood. The goal is to limit sedentary electronic pleasuring to 2 hours a day, which is the well-reasoned recommendation of the American Academy of Pediatrics. Also, see Chapter 13 for a discussion about how to engage the parents if the kid refuses to set aside significant dosing of sedentary electronic activity. For now, we put an exclamation point, or any symbol you want, next to these trap activities.

h. The brain releases higher doses of mood-lifting neurotransmitters when we socialize, are physically active, and are doing novel, fun things. Therefore, we want to focus the kid in this way. We can put one asterisk for each of these items that seem like they would be present for a given activity for the particular kid client. Table 6.2 indicates what a final fun activities sheet could look like for Aiden.

TABLE 6.2 Aiden's Fun Activities	
Reading for fun	Paintballing***
Swimming**	Water balloon fights***
Going to a movie*	Making a snowman***
Geocaching***	Martial arts***
Hiking**	Badminton***
Biking**	Playing chess online*

(continued)

TABLE 6.2 Aiden's Fun Activities *(continued)*	
Fishing**	Collecting baseball cards
Playing video games!	Going to fairs/bazaars**
Watching TV!	Flying kites**
Horseback riding***	Building a fort***
Amusement parks***	Making a tent in the home*
Going out to eat*	Going for ice cream
Taking a day trip to NYC**	Going to a zoo***
Playing baseball**	Doing magic**
Playing with a microscope	Listening to music
Going to batting cages**	Going online
Drawing	Building models
Going to a water park***	Making a tree house***
Texting friends*	Miniature golf**
Watching professional sports in person**	Water gun battles***
Going to the library	Playing with the dog

i. Most of my kid clients will readily agree to two or three things. But often they choose things like watch TV or play video games, which they had planned to do anyway. So I'll ask the kid for at least one thing he wouldn't normally do.

j. It's a judgment call whether or not to tell the parent about this tracking form. The younger or more disorganized a kid is, the more likely I'll say, before we go out into the waiting room: *Aiden, I'd like to let your mom know about this form so that she can maybe give you a reminder here and there to fill it in. Is that okay?* If it's okay, I'll say something like this to the mom: *Aiden and I have agreed about some fun things he's to do this week. This is the form he'll use to keep track of those things. Would you just give him a gentle reminder a few times during the week to fill it in?* That's as easy as it is most of the time; very young kids may also need the parent's help to complete it. If a kid says it's not okay to discuss it with his parent—and that is rare—I'll do two things. First, I'll check to see what the kid is concerned could happen if I engaged his parent; this can illuminate family issues that we'll eventually need to address. Second, I'll work on a plan for the kid to increase his odds of not forgetting to fill it in (e.g., setting an alarm on his phone, putting a sticky tab on his bathroom mirror) and I'll reach an agreement with him that we'll involve his mom if the plan we develop doesn't work, unless there is a significant clinical reason to do otherwise. Here's an example of how this sort of conversation might go:

MHP: *Aiden, I'd like to let your mom know about this form so that she can maybe give you a reminder here and there to fill it in. Is that okay?*

Kid: *No, not really.*

MHP: *Tell me what you're thinking.*

Kid: *I just don't want her to know.*

MHP: *Well, it's your decision. If you don't want her to know, that's it, I won't tell her. But tell me, what are you concerned could happen if I shared this with her?*

Kid: *She just wouldn't leave me alone about it. She'll ask, and ask, and ask, and ask, and yell, and ask and ask and ask!*

MHP: *What if I could get her to agree to never ask you more than once a day, would that make it okay?*

Kid: *She'll never agree to that.*

MHP: *I know, I know. But if squirrels could talk, and your mom agreed to bring it up only once a day, and stuck to that, would it then be okay to tell her or would you have other concerns?*

Kid: *I guess it'd be okay then.*

MHP: *So, if I get her to promise me first to ask you about it only once a day, and then to leave you alone about it no matter how you respond, could I ask her?*

Kid: *Alright.*

But let's say I do a variation of this same dialogue, but the kid still refuses to inform the parent. This is what I'd say at the point of the ultimate refusal:

Kid: *No, I just don't want to tell her.*

MHP: *Okay. Like I said, you're in charge of that decision. So, we won't tell her.*

Kid: *(Nodding)*

MHP: *However, we need a plan because you have a heck of a busy week and this is new to you. So it'd be super easy to forget to do it. What do you think is a way we could make sure you think about whether you have something to put down on the form each day?*

Kid: *I don't know.*

MHP: *Take your time, we're in no rush. . . .*

Kid: *Set an alarm in my phone?*

MHP: *Perfect! I love it! What time should you set it for each day and what should it say?*

Kid: *I guess set it for 8:30 at night before I go to bed, and DD form.*

MHP: *DD form?*

Kid: *Dr. Dave form.*

MHP: *Got it. Think that would work?*

Kid: *Yeah.*

MHP: *Good, let's go with that then. I think that will work, too.*

Kid: *Okay.*

MHP: *Aiden, we also need a backup plan. If this doesn't work, could we then involve your mom to remind you no more than once a day?*

Kid: *I guess. But this will work.*

MHP: *Gotcha, we have a plan.*

Table 6.3 indicates the form.

TABLE 6.3 Fun Activities Tracking Form

Name: _____

Week: _____

Mood rating: 1 = Very Depressed Fun rating: The more fun it was
            7 = Very Happy   the higher the number (0–100)

Type of Fun Activity	Mood Before	Mood During	Mood After	Fun Rating

Table 6.4 indicates what the form would look like completed.

TABLE 6.4 Fun Activities Tracking Form

Name: Aiden

Week: June 6–12

Mood rating: 1 = Very Depressed Fun rating: The more fun it was
            7 = Very Happy   the higher the number (0–100)

Type of Fun Activity	Mood Before	Mood During	Mood After	Fun Rating
Playing Xbox	4	5	4	50
Going to movies with Jake	3	6	5	70
Water park with family	4	7	6	90

Additional Commentary

If a kid's primary problem is depression, then this is the first strategy we review. If a kid's primary problem is anxiety, then I start with physiological calming (see Chapter 7). For anxious kids who are not also depressed, the timing of this module in the sequence of interventions is based on my intuition. I give it to all of them, as having fun combats all negative affect and can also provide helpful distractions. However, it's frontloaded in the treatments of kids struggling with depression.

I start with this intervention for depressed kids because doing so increases the odds of having an impactful start to the work. In my practice, most kids who are depressed will experience a lifting in mood if they make themselves do fun things. The kid benefiting from this technique at the start increases hope, grows the alliance, and increases treatment adherence, for both the kid and the parents.

Behavioral activation is a tried-and-true stable of cognitive behavioral therapy (CBT). I remember reading Beck's classic work on using CBT to treat adult depression in graduate school in the late 1980s; he hammered on the importance of this intervention. And, to date, I've never seen a CBT treatment manual for depression that didn't include some variant of behavioral activation. Moreover, just look at your own life for confirmation of this principle. If we grind, grind, and grind some more, and don't play adaptively, we break; when the break happens, how bad it is varies, of course. But we break. The same thing is true for kids, especially depressed kids. So we gift them with this information and intervention.

SLEEP HYGIENE

I've always envied people who sleep easily. Their brains must be cleaner,
the floorboards of the skull well swept, all the little monsters closed up in a
steamer trunk at the foot of the bed.
—David Benioff

A common presenting complaint among depressed or stressed kids is poor sleep. In my practice, kids most complain about a difficulty falling asleep, followed by a difficulty staying asleep. The most common scenario is a kid lying in bed, trying to sleep, with a busy mind that won't let him doze off. Some kids get to the point that they've given up on being able to get a good night's sleep and only lay down once they're exhausted, which is often midnight or after.

A good starting point is to consider what a good sleep schedule looks like. These are the nightly doses of sleep recommended by the National Sleep Foundation (NSF):

1 to 3 years old	12 to 14 hours
3 to 5 years old	11 to 13 hours
5 to 12 years old	10 to 11 hours
Teens	8.5 to 9.25 hours

The NSF elaborates on these guidelines here: http://bit.ly/1JshlIg. Regarding naps, I lobby for a 30-minute limit and usually encourage not going over 60 minutes or engaging in a napping habit that facilitates insomnia at bedtime. Sometimes parents will need to establish a behavioral system in order to get their kid to comply (see Chapter 13).

Also, a kid's pediatrician should be alerted if he snores, and I will often ask parents to ask their child's physician if nonpharmaceutical, time-released melatonin might be helpful to a kid who is struggling to fall asleep.

Over the years I've developed a handout that I work through with kids, teens, and parents to overcome some of the common clinical problems I see. As you'll note, it will need adaptation based on the age of your client. This is the handout:

Strategies for Combating Insomnia

David J. Palmiter, Jr., PhD, ABPP

www.helpingfamilies.com   www.hecticparents.com   @HelpingParents

1. Try to not have the TV on when falling asleep.

2. Try not to stay in bed, tossing and turning awake, for longer than 20 to 30 minutes (i.e., beds are for sleeping and should not become associated with a tortured experience).

3. Try listening to an audio recording of a book—one that is only of mild interest or slightly boring—as you're falling asleep; an alternative idea is to read a book of mild interest. This occupies your mind enough so that troubles don't bother you but not so much that you cannot fall asleep. Good choices might be books of movies you've seen or biographies of historical figures. If you use an audio book, make sure you set it to turn off after a set period of time.

4. Try listening to a tape of soothing sounds (e.g., the beach, rain, a forest, etc.), but make sure it turns itself off at some point. There are also multiple sound tracks available on iTunes and other servers.

5. Some people experience a sedating effect from consuming a light dose of non-processed carbohydrates just before bedtime (e.g., an apple).

6. Some people experience a sedating effect from a warm bath or shower just before bedtime.

7. Of course, you want to be sure you are sleeping in comfort (i.e., sleeping on a good mattress that isn't more than 5 years old; making sure the room temperature is soothing; making sure there are no loud, distracting noises).

8. Imagine yourself doing a relaxing repetitive activity as you're trying to fall asleep (e.g., fishing, walking on a beach, etc.); engage at least four of your senses by imagining the smells, touches, sounds, and sights.

9. Imagine yourself in an activity the next day that requires you to stay awake, but you desperately want to sleep (e.g., you're in a very boring math class or meeting and want so much to put your head down to nap, but you can't). Again, try to engage what your senses would experience when in that situation.

10. Some experience a sedating effect from lavender spray on the pillow.

11. If you wake up and can't get back to sleep, follow the same guidelines for falling asleep.

12. Ask your physician if you might benefit from taking a natural supplement such as time-released melatonin.

Once I've added physiological calming to the protocol (see Chapter 7), I'll also suggest that doing the exercise right before bed can be helpful for falling asleep. Collectively, these recommendations try to create a comfortable context, a relaxed body, and an unfettered mind. Several of the recommendations involve having the kid occupy himself with material interesting enough to take him away from his troubles but not so interesting as to keep him awake. Of course, other helpful steps might include an evaluation for a nonaddicting pharmaceutical or a sleep study.

SIDEBAR 6.1

Svengali decks are a staple in magic. You can buy such a deck for under $10 and sometimes even under $5. With this deck in hand there are a bunch of amazing tricks you can do and teach (e.g., search YouTube, or I like Oz Perlman's DVD on Svengali tricks found at www.penguinmagic.com). And you need zero skill to do them, other than to develop a patter. The tricks pretty much work themselves. Kids will respond to them by saying things like, "That's sick!" and "No way!"

Each Svengali deck has a focus card. Let's say it's the ace of hearts. When you look at the deck, you'll see that every other card is the ace of hearts. However, that card is cut to be a tiny, tiny bit shorter than the other cards. So, when you display the cards by holding them in one hand, with the face of the card on display toward the kid, in vertical position, and let them fall one by one into the other hand, the kid will not see any ace of hearts. They look like a normal deck.

This is a simple trick you can perform with this deck. Tell the kid that you want to form six piles from the deck you have, after you've displayed it in the manner I just shared. Tell the kid that you'll riffle through the deck with your thumb and stop to make a pile whenever he says "Stop." Remind him, though, that he needs to say it soon enough so that you can make six piles (you can always subdivide a pile if need be). It doesn't matter where you stop or how

(continued)

SIDEBAR 6.1 *(continued)*

you make the piles. The top card will *always* be the ace of hearts. Tell the kid to look at the top card on one of the piles, asking him to remember it. Then reassemble the piles. Cut the deck multiple times using the same riffling with your thumb method. Use your mind puppet, if you have one (see the trick attached to Chapter 3), to give your kid special powers. Now make six new piles, stating that his card is on top of one of them and he'll be able to pick the right pile. You can do this a couple of times, each time mixing the deck well in between. At the end, you can top it off by saying you can turn every card into the kid's selected card (if you ask the kid to not let you know what his selected card is throughout the trick, this can have an even bigger impact). Just move the top card in the deck to the bottom of the deck and display them in the opposite way than you did in the beginning (i.e., now the backs of the cards face the kid and fall one by one). Every card will now show as being the ace of hearts.

REFERENCES AND BIBLIOGRAPHY

American Academy of Pediatrics. (2006). Active healthy living: Prevention of childhood obesity through increased physical activity. *Pediatrics, 117*, 1834–1842.

Beck, A. T., Rush, A. J., Shaw, B. F., & Emery, G. (1979). *Cognitive therapy of depression.* New York, NY: Guilford Press.

Brent, D. A. (1997). *Cognitive therapy treatment manual for depressed and suicidal youth* (STAR Center Publications). Pittsburgh, PA: University of Pittsburgh Health System Services for Teens at Risk.

Cain, N., & Gradisar, M. (2010). Electronic media use and sleep in school-aged children and adolescents: A review. *Sleep Medicine, 11*, 735–742.

Chess, S., & Thomas, A. (2013). *Goodness of fit: Clinical applications, from infancy through adult life.* London, UK: Routledge.

Chu, B. C., & Harrison, T. L. (2007). Disorder-specific effects of CBT for anxious and depressed youth: A meta-analysis of candidate mediators of change. *Clinical Child and Family Psychology Review, 10*(4), 352–372.

Clarke, G. N., Rohde, P., Lewinsohn, P. M., Hops, H., & Seeley, J. R. (1999). Cognitive-behavioral treatment of adolescent depression: Efficacy of acute group treatment and booster sessions. *Journal of the American Academy of Child & Adolescent Psychiatry, 38*(3), 272–279.

De Sousa, I. C., Araujo, J. F., & De Azevdeo, C. V. M. (2007). The effect of a sleep hygiene education program on the sleep–wake cycle of Brazilian adolescent students. *Sleep and Biological Rhythms, 5*(4), 251–258.

Dimidjian, S., Hollon, S. D., Dobson, K. S., Schmaling, K. B., Kohlenberg, R. J., Addis, M. E., & Jacobson, N. S. (2006). Randomized trial of behavioral activation, cognitive therapy, and antidepressant medication in the acute treatment of adults with major depression. *Journal of Consulting and Clinical Psychology, 74*(4), 658.

Dobson, K. S., Hollon, S. D., Dimidjian, S., Schmaling, K. B., Kohlenberg, R. J., Gallop, R. J., & Jacobson, N. S. (2008). Randomized trial of behavioral activation, cognitive therapy, and antidepressant medication in the prevention of relapse and recurrence in major depression. *Journal of Consulting and Clinical Psychology, 76*(3), 468.

Ekers, D., Webster, L., Van Straten, A., Cuijpers, P., Richards, D., & Gilbody, S. (2014). Behavioural activation for depression: An update of meta-analysis of effectiveness and sub group analysis. *PLoS ONE, 9*(6), e100100.

Freij, K., & Masri, N. (2008). The brief behavioral activation treatment for depression: A psychiatric pilot study. *Nordic Psychology, 60*(2), 129.

Gawrysiak, M., Nicholas, C., & Hopko, D. R. (2009). Behavioral activation for moderately depressed university students: Randomized controlled trial. *Journal of Counseling Psychology, 56*(3), 468.

Gaynor, S. T., & Harris, A. (2008). Single-participant assessment of treatment mediators: Strategy description and examples from a behavioral activation intervention for depressed adolescents. *Behavior Modification, 32*(3), 372–402.

Hanley, J. L., & Deville, N. (2002). *Tired of being tired: Rescue, repair, and rejuvenate*. New York, NY: Berkley Publishing Group.

Hogendoorn, S. M., Prins, P. J., Boer, F., Vervoort, L., Wolters, L. H., Moorlag, H., & de Haan, E. (2014). Mediators of cognitive behavioral therapy for anxiety-disordered children and adolescents: Cognition, perceived control, and coping. *Journal of Clinical Child & Adolescent Psychology, 43*(3), 486–500.

Hopko, D. R., Lejuez, C. W., Lepage, J. P., Hopko, S. D., & McNeil, D. W. (2003). A brief behavioral activation treatment for depression: A randomized pilot trial within an inpatient psychiatric hospital. *Behavior Modification, 27*(4), 458–469.

Jakupcak, M., Wagner, A., Paulson, A., Varra, A., & McFall, M. (2010). Behavioral activation as a primary care-based treatment for PTSD and depression among returning veterans. *Journal of Traumatic Stress, 23*(4), 491–495.

Jan, J. E., Owens, J. A., Weiss, M. D., Johnson, K. P., Wasdell, M. B., Freeman, R. D., & Ipsiroglu, O. S. (2008). Sleep hygiene for children with neurodevelopmental disabilities. *Pediatrics, 122*(6), 1343–1350.

Lejuez, C. W., Hopko, D. R., Acierno, R., Daughters, S. B., & Pagoto, S. L. (2011). Ten-year revision of the brief behavioral activation treatment for depression: Revised treatment manual. *Behavior Modification, 35*(2), 111–161.

Malone, S. K. (2011). Early to bed, early to rise? An exploration of adolescent sleep hygiene practices. *Journal of School Nursing, 27*(5), 348–354.

Mazzucchelli, T., Kane, R., & Rees, C. (2009). Behavioral activation treatments for depression in adults: A meta-analysis and review. *Clinical Psychology: Science and Practice, 16*(4), 383–411.

McCauley, E., Schloredt, K., Gudmundsen, G., Martell, C., & Dimidjian, S. (2011). Expanding behavioral activation to depressed adolescents: Lessons learned in treatment development. *Cognitive and Behavioral Practice, 18*(3), 371–383.

Mindell, J. A., Meltzer, L. J., Carskadon, M. A., & Chervin, R. D. (2009). Developmental aspects of sleep hygiene: Findings from the 2004 National Sleep Foundation Sleep in America Poll. *Sleep Medicine, 10*(7), 771–779.

Mulick, P. S., & Naugle, A. E. (2010). Behavioral activation in the treatment of comorbid post-traumatic stress disorder and major depressive disorder. *International Journal of Behavioral Consultation and Therapy, 5*(3–4), 330.

Reynolds, E. K., MacPherson, L., Tull, M. T., Baruch, D. E., & Lejuez, C. W. (2011). Integration of the brief behavioral activation treatment for depression (BATD) into a college orientation program: Depression and alcohol outcomes. *Journal of Counseling Psychology, 58*(4), 555.

Rhodes, S., Richards, D. A., Ekers, D., McMillan, D., Byford, S., Farrand, P. A., & Wright, K. A. (2014). Cost and outcome of behavioural activation versus cognitive behaviour therapy for depression (COBRA): Study protocol for a randomized controlled trial. *Trials, 15*(1), 29.

Short, M. A., Gradisar, M., Wright, H., Lack, L. C., Dohnt, H., & Carskadon, M. A. (2011). Time for bed: Parent-set bedtimes associated with improved sleep and daytime functioning in adolescents. *Sleep, 34*(6), 797–800.

Stark, K., & Kendall, P. C. (1996). *Treating depressed children: Therapist manual for "taking action."* Ardmore, PA: Workbook Publishing.

Stepanski, E. J., & Wyatt, J. K. (2003). Use of sleep hygiene in the treatment of insomnia. *Sleep Medicine Reviews, 7*(3), 215–225.

Sturmey, P. (2009). Behavioral activation is an evidence-based treatment for depression. *Behavior Modification, 33*(6), 818–829.

Wallis, A., Roeger, L., Milan, S., Walmsley, C., & Allison, S. (2012). Behavioural activation for the treatment of rural adolescents with depression. *Australian Journal of Rural Health, 20*(2), 95–96.

Weinstock, L. M., Munroe, M. K., & Miller, I. W. (2011). Behavioral activation for the treatment of atypical depression: A pilot open trial. *Behavior Modification, 35*(4), 403–424.

CHAPTER 7

Physiological Calming and Mindfulness

PHYSIOLOGICAL CALMING

For fast-acting relief, try slowing down.
—Lily Tomlin

This is how I introduce and teach physiological calming:

Monica, I'd like to teach you a weapon that the cobra can't defeat. It may sound simple, but it is very powerful and you'll need to practice to get good at it. The weapon is to relax your body. If you can learn to make your entire body as soft and warm as a cooked piece of pasta, the cobra can't get you. Y'know how Superman can't defeat Kryptonite? Well, the cobra can't defeat this weapon (a). What I'd like to do is to show you how to get your body that way, then show you a way that you can practice it at home. Any questions (b)?

In a few seconds I'm going to ask you to sit back in the couch, put your head back, and close your eyes (c). Then I'm going to ask you to tense and relax certain muscles. When we are working on particular muscles try only to think about those muscles and what they are feeling (d). If you're like most of us, you may start to think of different things. That's okay. Don't worry or get upset about that. When you notice that, though, try to bring it back to what those muscles feel like (e). Okay, go ahead and get as comfortable as you can; close your eyes and put your head back (f).

15-Minute Script

I use this script for a child, younger teens, and older teens whose compliance portends to be dubious (g).

I'd like to begin by tensing both hands and arms as tight as you can ... make your fingers, hands, lower arms, and upper arms as tense as possible. Good effort. Hold it. Relax. (Total 15 seconds.)

Okay, now I'd like you to see how relaxed you can get your hands and arms. Without moving them, just try to use the power of your mind to get them totally relaxed and soft, like a cooked piece of pasta ... relax your fingers ... your palms ... your lower arms ... your upper arms. (Total 30–45 seconds.)

Okay, now let's tense your hands and arms again. Try to make them even tighter than the first time. . . . Pay attention to how they feel when they are like this ... good ... hold it ... let it go. (Total 15 seconds.)

Okay, now we are all done tensing your hands and arms. Just try to get them as relaxed as you can without actually moving them. . . . You're going to start to notice certain things about a relaxed muscle. One is that it starts to feel heavier. So, in a completely relaxed state it almost starts to feel like your arms want to fall out of your shoulder sockets from the weight of the relaxation ... try to focus on what your fingers, palms, lower arms, and upper arms are feeling ... try to use the power of your mind to get them as relaxed as possible. (Total 30–45 seconds.)

Okay, now we're going to move on to the next muscle group. As we do so, try to keep your hands and arms as relaxed as possible. Your arms may need to move a smidge to tense the next muscles and that's okay. But try to keep your arms and hands from moving. Okay, now let's tense your shoulders, neck, and face ... scrunch up your shoulders, tense your neck, scrunch up your face ... make everything all nasty and tight ... good effort ... hold it ... let it go. (Total 15 seconds.)

See just how relaxed you can get your shoulders, neck, and face by using the power of your mind . When some people relax their face their mouth wants to open. If you're one of those, let that happen ... relax your shoulders ... your neck ... your tongue ... your cheeks ... in a relaxed state it can almost feel like your cheeks want to slide off your face from the weight of the relaxation ... your eyes and your forehead. . . . (Total 30–45 seconds.)

Good, now let's tense your shoulders, neck, and face again. Go for even more tightness than the first time ... really go for it ... good effort ... keep it up ... relax. . . . (Total 15 seconds.)

Notice that your muscles are already starting to learn. They want to fall into relaxation as fast as someone falls into a warm pool ... the last thing your neck should want to do when completely relaxed is hold up your head ... your eyelashes can start to feel like they have little weights attached to them while your forehead becomes as smooth as a pond on a summer morning. . . . Another thing you can do to relax is to breathe in a special way. Instead of breathing into your chest, breathe into your belly. Imagine that your lungs are in your lower belly instead of your chest and breathe comfortably, but deeply, both in and out. Sometimes kids breathe deeply in but they forget to breathe deeply out. Also, after you breathe in, hold it for just a second or two before breathing out. By itself, this kind of breathing can stop a cobra attack. (Total 60 seconds.)

Okay, you're doing great. Let's move on to the next muscles. But try to keep the muscles we've already worked on nice and soft, like a cooked piece of pasta, even when we are tensing the new muscles. Go ahead and tense your belly and chest. Make those muscles as tight as possible. Almost like you're lying on the ground and someone is going to step on you, so you want to be like a rock in your belly and chest. (Total 15 seconds.)

Okay, good. Relax (h)*. Now let's get your chest and belly as relaxed as they've been in a long time while you're awake. You may start to notice that your breathing changes depending on whether you are tense or relaxed. When you're tense, your breathing becomes shorter and in your chest. When you're relaxed, your breathing becomes deeper and in your belly. Remembering this, by itself, can help you very much in your fight against the cobra ... think of each breath as almost a way to massage yourself using your body. ...* (Total 30–45 seconds.)

Okay, now let's tense your belly and chest again, going for even more tightness than the first time. Pay attention to how your muscles are feeling. When the cobra attacks you as hard as possible they can get like this, so you want to be able to recognize that ... good effort ... let it go. (Total 15 seconds.)

Now your chest and belly are all done tensing. See if you can use that information to get them that tiny bit more relaxed than they got the first time. Okay, now we've worked on your entire upper body ... you may be starting to feel almost like your body is becoming warmer, which is another thing that can happen for kids when their muscles are totally relaxed. ... Monica, let's circle back through the muscles we've worked on just to make sure that no tension has crept in anywhere. When I name the muscle, don't move it. Moving it makes you use your muscles and we don't want that right now. Just use the power of your mind to see if you can get the muscle a tiny bit more relaxed ... your fingers ... your palms ... your lower arms ... your upper arms ... your shoulders ... your neck ... your jaw ... your tongue ... your cheeks ... your eyes ... your forehead ... your chest ... your belly, which is receiving your breath gently and deeply and releasing it gently and deeply also. (About 75 seconds.)

Okay, now let's move on to your legs. Tense both legs as tight as you can. These are some of the larger muscles in your body, so really go for it ... good ... keep it up ... little more ... relax. (About 15 seconds.)

Okay, now relax your legs as much as you can ... focus your mind on what your legs feel like when they are totally relaxed. This is how you want to get all of your muscles if the cobra is trying to get you. You'll see, if you can do it, the cobra will go away. So, pay attention to what this feels like in your legs. ... (About 30–45 seconds.)

Okay, once more let's tense your legs. Really get after it. Like they are so hard someone could break a piece of wood across them ... good effort ... little more ... relax. (About 15 seconds.)

Great, now your legs are all done tensing. See if you can use that information to get them even a little bit more relaxed than the first time. Relax your upper legs . . . relax your lower legs . . . keep focused on what your legs are feeling. In a relaxed state, the last thing they want to do is hold up your body . . . make them like a warm piece of cooked pasta. (About 30–45 seconds.)

Okay, just one more group to go. Tense your toes, feet, and ankles as tight as you can. Scrunch up your toes. Make that whole area rock-hard. A lot of tightness can live in your feet and ankles, so pay attention to what they feel like all tensed up . . . good . . . hold it . . . let it go. (About 15 seconds.)

Good, now try to get your feet, toes, and ankles as relaxed as possible. It's like you're going to give yourself a foot massage with your mind . . . pay attention to what your toes are feeling . . . your feet . . . your ankles . . . good. . . . (About 30–45 seconds.)

Okay, last piece of tensing for today. Go ahead and tense your toes, feet, and ankles once again, going for even more tension than the first time . . . really go for it . . . almost done . . . let it go. (About 15 seconds.)

Phew, no more tensing. Just relaxing. In these next few moments see how relaxed you can get your toes, feet, and ankles. Get them all soft like a warm piece of cooked pasta . . . pay attention to how they feel in a completely relaxed state. (About 30–45 seconds.)

Okay, Monica, let's do one more pass through all of your muscles just to see if you can get them that tiniest bit more relaxed now that we are all done tensing. Remember, when I call them out, don't move them. Just use the power of your mind. Fingers and palms . . . lower arms . . . upper arms . . . shoulders . . . neck . . . jaw . . . tongue . . . cheeks . . . forehead, which should be completely smooth . . . chest, which is really not moving and is completely relaxed . . . belly, which is taking your breath in deeply and letting it out deeply . . . upper legs, lower legs . . . ankles . . . toes and feet . . . okay, as relaxed as you are, you might get that tiniest bit more relaxed by taking in a deep breath and letting it out slowly . . . once more. . . . (About 60–75 seconds.)

Okay, Monica, you can open your eyes. How do you feel (h)? *So, from 1 to 100, with 100 being as relaxed as you can be, what number were you at when you came in today? And now* (i)? *Awesome. So we want to get you to the point that you can get like you are now instantly, like* (I snap my fingers) *that. When you first started playing* (name a sport the kid plays or has tried multiple times), *didn't it feel like you weren't used to* (name an action like shooting a basketball or swinging a bat or rolling a bowling ball) (j)? *Right, it took some practice but then it felt easy-peasy to do, no? So it's like that here. It'll take some practice for you to get relaxed like* (snap of fingers again). *That's why I'd like you to do this at home three times this week. Here is a link I have for you to practice it* (k), *but I'll be sure to let your mom know also when we're done* (l). *We are building up what is called "muscle memory." So when the cobra attacks you don't tense-relax, you just relax everything instantly. Okay, so I just said a lot. Do you mind saying it back to me so that I know I said it right* (m)?

Also, when you do it at home, try to do it in a quiet place, in a comfortable chair or couch. Kick off your shoes, take off any jewelry, and make sure your clothes are all loose.

Okay, next I'd like to show you how we'll keep track of what you do and how it affects you. This is a form for doing that (breaking out Table 7.1). *It's easy-peasy to fill in. This form will help us to keep track of how relaxed you get doing this exercise. The first column is just for putting down when you did it. So, I'll fill in the first one: "(date) in Dr. Dave's office." Then you put down how relaxed you felt from 1 to 100 before you started* (insert number from 1–100 obtained from Monica). *Then you put in how relaxed you felt after you finished* (insert number). *It's usually best to do it right after each of the three times you do it this week so you don't forget. Is that okay? What days do you think you might do it? Could anything get in the way of doing it then* (n)?

TABLE 7.1 Relaxation Exercise Tracking Form (Audio file is at: http://d.pr/a/V4h4/bhaDLzP)		
Name: _____		
Week: _____		
Relaxation rating (0–100). Higher numbers mean more relaxed.		
Date and Place of Exercise	**Relaxation Rating Before**	**Relaxation Rating Right After**

Next week, we'll have a way of measuring how relaxed you can get your body, just like your doctor measures your height. But I'll explain that then. I mention it now just so that you'll know we'll have a way of knowing how good you're getting at this exercise, with practice.

Half-Hour Script

This is the script I use for older teens with average or better compliance (o). The script is essentially the same as the one I just reviewed, just with smaller muscle groups. This is the format:

▶ Hands and lower arms, tense twice each for about 15 seconds and relax twice each for about 30 to 45 seconds.

▶ Upper arms, tense twice each for about 15 seconds and relax twice each for about 30 to 45 seconds.

▶ Shoulders and neck, tense twice each for about 15 seconds and relax twice each for about 30 to 45 seconds.

▶ Face and head, tense twice each for about 15 seconds and relax twice each for about 30 to 45 seconds.

▶ Chest, tense twice each for about 15 seconds and relax twice each for about 30 to 45 seconds. Add the breathing instruction, about 15 to 30 seconds.

▶ Stomach, tense twice each for about 15 seconds and relax twice each for about 30 to 45 seconds.

▶ Circle back through previously relaxed muscles, about 45 to 60 seconds.

▶ Upper legs, tense twice each for about 15 seconds and relax twice each for about 30 to 45 seconds.

▶ Lower legs, tense twice each for about 15 seconds and relax twice each for about 30 to 45 seconds.

▶ Feet and ankles, tense twice each for about 15 seconds and relax twice each for about 30 to 45 seconds.

▶ Circle back through all muscles, about 60 to 75 seconds, and follow up with two deep breaths, in and out.

At different junctures during the relaxation phase I'll note that relaxed muscles tend to start to feel heavier and warmer. I'll also mention that it starts to feel like the teen's center of gravity is lowering when she relaxes. Finally, I'll ask the teen to notice the differences in her breathing when she is tense versus when she is relaxed. I also introduce the tracking form (Table 7.1) as well. So the older teen version is essentially the same as the kid version, just with more elaboration.

Explanation

a. I know it's a little dubious to equate the kid's internal enemy with a superhero and I don't always do it. It's a judgment call based on the kid (e.g., I'm more likely to do it for a boy who is into Marvel movies).

b. In the large majority of instances the kid has no questions. But it's respectful to ask.

c. Over the years I've found that if I just tell the kid to close her eyes and put her head back, it's a little abrupt for her. This is just my way of having the transition be less abrupt.

d. The three elements of a relaxed body are (1) relaxed muscles, (2) diaphragmatic breathing, and (3) an unfettered mind. By having the kid try to focus her attention just on her muscles, we are going for the third element.

e. This is a standard instruction in meditation and mindfulness exercises. Some achievement-oriented kids get a little mad at themselves for having their minds drift, so we encourage them to not worry about that.

f. Most kids do this simply enough, closing their eyes and becoming comfortable. However, others are fidgety, so I might need to add: *Monica, try to not move around as we do this. It won't take long at all.* If that doesn't work, I go forward anyway. Some kids also peek out of their eyes, pretending they are closed, so I might add, *Monica, close your eyes all the way so you can focus better on paying attention to what we'll be doing and can relax better.* If that doesn't work (and I can't remember a time when it didn't), I'll just go forward anyway; I'd expect the kid would lose interest and just end up closing her eyes anyway.

g. This script usually takes 15 to 20 minutes at the maximum. It's important to keep it brief to increase compliance with the practice routine at home. I try to use a soft, meditative tone during the relaxation phase and a normal to assertive tone during the tensing phase. Otherwise, this script tends to run itself.

h. At different points I will breathe out, loud enough for the kid to hear, making a swooshing sound. I do this to mirror the transition to the relaxation phase.

i. I can think of only one case, in my 25-plus years of doing this technique, that a client, of any age, didn't report feeling more relaxed as a function of doing this exercise. It's about as sure of an automatic as we get in child and adolescent clinical work.

j. I try to illustrate with some sport the kid plays or has tried. Bowling can also work for kids with near zero athletic experience. On the other hand, sometimes I'll get athletic kids, who are also a bit brazen in their temperament, who will assert that no athletic activity ever felt foreign. If so, I'll just ask, *Okay, you're a good athlete after all. So let me ask something different. Did you ever practice that sport? How come? . . . Right, practice made your natural skills grow even more. So it is here.*

k.   I recommend that you make an audio recording while doing the relaxation exercise. If you are tech savvy and have the energy to do it and the hardware at hand, you might record each time you do it with a kid and put it online, making sure to not say the kid's name. While I'm tech savvy, I don't have the energy to make a recording each time. So I've made one that I've put online using the Droplr service (www.droplr.com), which is currently free up to a certain storage limit. I then give this link to the kid it's to be found at the top of the tracking form. You could check mine out, but I think it better promotes your relationship with your kid client if she practices to a recording with your voice (feel free to use mine, though, if you'd like; *Note:* I use the label "toothless" as a metaphor for all internal enemies).

l.   Most kids readily agree when I ask each parent to do the exercise at least once with the child; this both offers support and prepares the parent for what I'll share in the parent session. See the discussion in Chapter 6 for a strategy if your kid client resists engaging a parent at this juncture.

m.   I don't always remember to do this, but I try to. We all spare ourselves problems later if we take the time to see how the kid has heard what we've said so that we can make any needed adjustments.

n.   This is another thing that I don't always do, but try to. Asking for obstacles in doing the homework allows us to partner with the kid, and sometimes the parent, to overcome these problems in advance. This goes a long way to enhancing treatment compliance and efficacy.

o.   This script is twice as long, coming in at about 30 minutes. It appears to promote deeper levels of relaxation and muscle memory. However, getting teens to do a 30-minute exercise, three times a week, in this day and age can be quite challenging. So I reserve the half-hour script for only my more mature and motivated teens. If I'm in doubt, I'll explain the choices and ask the teen which exercise she thinks would be better.

MEASURING RELAXATION

In the session following the physiological calming training, I use a biofeedback device for measuring how relaxed the kid can get. The word "biofeedback," in the child clinical world, can strongly activate many mental health professionals (MHPs), both for and against. I think that has a lot to do with how it is used, the cost, and the strength of the evidence base for how it is used. In this context I am using it as a cost-effective way to give a kid feedback on how relaxed she is getting (the references in the References and Bibliography section at the end of this chapter review the empirical base). I use the emWave system sold by heartmath.org, but other alternatives are available. In the example that follows, I'll use the script I use in teaching about the emWave.

I'll first check to see how many times the kid has listened to the audio file by checking the rating form. If the kid hasn't done it enough, I'll use some of the techniques that I cover in Chapters 4 and 14. But, whether the kid has done the practice or not, I move forward with the emWave session. This is what I say:

Monica, like I said in our last appointment, I'd like to check and see how relaxed you can get. A relaxed body sends signals that it's relaxed: The brain sends signals, the skin sends signals, and the heart sends signals. I have a device here that will measure how relaxed you get by measuring your heartbeat. It will measure it through the pulse in the tip of your finger. When I attach this device to your finger (motioning) *with Velcro, we'll be able to see how relaxed you can get. When I start it, one of three colors will come up: "Red" means not relaxed, "blue" means sort of relaxed, and "green" means relaxed* (a)*. If you're like most of us you'll start out in red, even though you may feel relaxed. Don't let that bother you. Just focus on three things: one, deep but comfortable belly breathing, both in and out; two, making all of your muscles like a cooked piece of pasta; and three, not thinking about stuff. The third thing can be the toughest. But, if you just focus on relaxing your muscles and your breathing, your mind will be clear enough* (b)*. Once you're mostly in green we'll do a game. It's called "The Garden." I'll show you it* (pulling up the garden module in the game section)*. You'll have 3 minutes to color in this garden. The more relaxed you are, the more quickly it will color in. The less relaxed you are the slower it will go* (c)*. When we get to this point you can either watch or just keep your eyes closed; if you keep your eyes closed I'll tell you what color you are in* (c)*. Once you can do this, we'll go to "The Balloon." I'll show you that also* (pulling up the balloon module in the game section)*. This balloon travels the world. You'll have 10 minutes to complete the journey. The more relaxed you are the faster the balloon will travel. The more tense you are, the slower it will go. There is music to go along with the trip, and sometimes it's sort of challenging music, just to see if you can stay relaxed even when it is playing* (d)*.*

Okay, let's attach it . . . now, just sit back, close your eyes, and try to get yourself like you're at the end of the relaxation exercise we did. Don't tense any muscles, just relax them. I'll give you a few moments before I start up the computer . . . (start the emWave, which also pings to different tones depending on the color)*. Okay, now that you're in green, let's go to the garden. Do you think you'll be able to relax more with your eyes open or closed? Okay, I'll give you a few moments to get into green again then I'll start it. Right away, you'll hear the garden sounds. . . . Okay, stay in green and let's see how you can do with the balloon. . . . You did great today, next week we'll. . . .* (e)*.*

Explanation

a.   You can readily find an image of how the dashboard looks with the emWave system by going to images.google.com and entering the search term "EmWave heart wave variability coherence."

On the emWave dashboard there are color bars that depict how often the kid is relaxed (a green bar), not relaxed (a red bar), and in between (a blue bar). Up at the top of the screen, near the left side, the dashboard depicts the challenge level. I start all of my kids out at the low challenge level and build up from there. I usually don't progress to the garden game until the kid is spending at least 50% of the time in green.

b. These are the three elements that the kid should focus on to get to green. Assuming kids are practicing the relaxation exercise at home, relaxing their muscles and the belly breathing are relatively easy to do. It is the clear mind that is the toughest of the three for most kids. These are some of the strategies I use, in progressive order (i.e., once the kid can get into green consistently, I don't have to go on to the next technique).

  • Eyes closed, focusing on either the breath or relaxing the muscle groups.

  • Eyes open, focusing on the details of the screen.

  • Eyes open, focusing on a candle or a virtual fireplace that I have on my iPad.

  • Eyes closed, imagining a pleasant, stress-free activity (e.g., fishing, walking along the beach).

  • Eyes closed, listening to a guided meditation.

I will also toggle the emWave's pinging on and off, depending on its effect on the kid; the same thing goes for my telling the kid, when her eyes are closed, what color she is at.

c. This is my favorite thing about the emWave system. The garden starts out as a grayscale image. The kid's task is to color it within the 3-minute time limit. The more relaxed the kid's body is, the quicker the garden colors in. As the garden game is timed, it says to a kid, "Ready, set, relax!" For years I relaxed kids in my office but had a sense that I wasn't preparing them for real life. In real life they need to learn to relax in demand situations. The emWave software does this.
It can take some kids a few weeks to get to the point that they can complete the garden module, while others nail it right away. I believe my task is to understand the obstacles that a kid is experiencing to accomplish this, as they are likely the same obstacles that interfere with getting relaxed in the kid's day-to-day life.

d. I love the balloon module. It is also a demand situation, but it challenges kids to remain relaxed longer (i.e., 8–10 minutes) and introduces some challenging music.
The number of sessions it takes for a kid to be able to do the balloon game varies greatly. Some do it in the very first session, while it can take weeks for

others. However, I'll only get one or two kids a year who can't complete it with sufficient work at home and coaching from me.

e. The emWave has multiple other modules, but I've found that once a kid can complete the balloon journey at the medium challenge level, she is also usually telling me that she is successful at consistently using relaxation to cage her anxiety.

For kids who seem to have a lot of success with this module, including using physiological calming well in between sessions, I'll discuss the option of purchasing the portable unit that comes with this system. This device, which has the footprint of a small handheld digital dictation machine, takes a pulse reading from the fingertip and flashes red, green, or blue readings. My first successful experience with it was with a Little League pitcher whose agitation on the mound would interfere with his performance. So, in between innings he would sit with this device on the bench and get into green.

MINDFULNESS STRATEGIES

Looking at beauty in the world is the first step of purifying the mind.
—*Amit Ray*, Meditation: Insights and Inspirations

If I deliver this intervention it is usually later in the treatment, after the core strategies of behavioral activation, physiological calming, coping thoughts, thought testing, and problem solving have been delivered and sufficiently practiced.

I usually start by estimating how much my client, based on her age and activity level, will be able to sit still. The younger and busier the kid, the more I'll keep the modules brief and movement oriented. The older and the calmer the kid's temperament, the more I'll include longer exercises that call for higher doses of stillness. Finally, how much we use them (ongoing) and practice them in session varies depending on how well the kid takes to them. Here I'll list six modules that I use and what I say to kids about them. Once you read them, you'll see it would be pretty easy to develop your own. It's all about being focused in the moment in a nonjudgmental way. (It would be very easy to design a tracking form, based on others you'll find in this volume, if your kid client gets into any of these exercises.)

Agitating Waits

Monica, have you ever been in a really long line or a traffic jam, when your car is barely moving? What's that like? Right, if we don't have something to play with, like a game or cell phone, it can seem like it's taking F-O-R-E-V-E-R. And if you have someplace you need to be the cobra can start to use it against you. So, let me share a little trick you can try. Pick out something around you and study the details of it. Like you might choose the sweater of the person in front of you in the line. Or you might pick the cracks along the side of the road if you're in the car.

Then, really study the details of them while you belly breathe in and out, comfortably and deeply. Like if we were to pick out something in this office, we might pick the rug. Let's look at a little piece of it now. What can you notice about my rug that you never noticed before? . . . Exactly. . . . What can you tell me about the colors and shading? What can you tell me about how different sections might feel to the touch? Notice any smudges or crumbs? Notice how you're feeling as we do this? I'm telling you that if you do this when you're trapped somewhere boring, it can make the time fly by like (I snap my fingers). *See if you can find a time this week to try it, and I'll tell your mom to give you a reminder, if that's okay.*

Mindful Eating

I have a dog named Dakota. How about you? Well, as you may know, when dogs eat, they gobble up food quickly. It's like the food goes from their teeth to the back of their throats, like (I snap my fingers). *It's almost like they don't even taste it. Well, as good as you've gotten with relaxing your body, there's other ways that you can chillax in other situations and, by doing so, enjoy those moments more. One of those is to really get into appreciating how wonderful food can taste. I have some apple slices for each of us today.* (For younger kids, or if I'm not sure whether dietary restrictions are in place, I'll have gotten permission to do this exercise from one of the parents.) *If you and I didn't think about it, we might eat them without noticing much. But, instead, let's first belly breathe a few times, deeply in and out, noticing how our breath feels coming in and leaving our bodies.* (You could also elect to get the kid into green on the emWave before starting this exercise.) *Now, let's bite about one half of the apple slice and chew it slowly, not swallowing . . . try to notice how wonderful it tastes . . . see how you might be noticing tastes that you wouldn't normally notice. Okay, go ahead and swallow it. Let's take a second bite, again eating it slowly and letting the taste fill up our mouths. . . . Let's do a second slice, but we'll add a little salt to it . . . bite half of it first . . . now the other half. What's it like to eat this way? How would you feel about taking the first six bites of your next three dinners doing this?*

Mindful Photography

Monica, there is so much beauty around us all the time. Did you know that? Did you ever take a picture with your phone and surprise yourself with how pretty it turned out? One way to focus on this beauty all around us is to look around your home, or your yard, or your neighborhood, or your school, for pretty things to take pictures of. To get in the mood, take three slow, deep, and comfortable belly breaths, in and out, then ask yourself, "Where is the beauty around me?" Then, when you find something, appreciate it for a few moments before you take out your phone or camera to take a picture of it. Afterward, enjoy the beauty for a few more moments before moving on. What do you think? How would you feel about taking at least nine pictures like this for this coming week and bringing them in to our next session?

Meditation

Monica, ever hear of "meditation"? Know what it is? . . . Meditation is actually a pretty easy thing to describe. It's just paying attention to something simple for some number of minutes. So, it could be your breathing or a candle, or your dog sleeping, or birds chirping in the morning or dew on the grass, or just about any-thing simple. What you want to do is set a timer for, let's say, 3 minutes (you can choose longer periods of time if your kid ends up enjoying this exercise or your intuition tells you she'll like it at the start, but I prefer to err on the side of shorter time units and to build from there) *and then pay attention to the thing while breathing, just like we did in the relaxation training I taught you. Remember how that breathing goes? With the relaxation weapon, you do that when the cobra has started in on you or when you think the cobra might be about to try to get out of his cage. But meditation is something you do just to be chillax and super calm. How does it feel to get like that? Right, I like it too. So, what do you say you try it three times this week? What might you study while you do your meditation?*

Body Mindfulness

Monica, just like you saw with the relaxation training, sometimes we don't always notice what our bodies are feeling, especially if our enemy inside starts to kick our butts. However, we can become pretty expert at tuning into what our bodies are feeling so that we can know what our bodies are trying to tell us. Another way to get good at this is to pay very close attention to how our bodies feel both when they are uncomfortable and when they are comfortable. To do this exercise you want to start by taking in three deep and comfortable breaths, in and out. Then, when you're sitting in something uncomfortable—let's say a hard chair at school or a wooden pew at church—sit up really straight, which probably won't feel that good. When you're in the comfortable seat, just sit in whatever way feels best. Then notice what every single muscle is feeling. Take at least 20 to 30 seconds with each of the muscle groups we used in the relaxation training. What's the mus-cle feeling? How does it feel in connection to the surface it's touching? Notice every little sensation before moving on to the next muscle group. During a day when you do this, do it once for an uncomfortable seat and once for a comfortable seat. Let's practice it now, once on my comfortable couch and once on the floor against the door. . . . What are you learning? What does this do for your sense of calm?

Beauty Walks

Monica, there is so much beauty around us all the time. Did you know that? One way to focus on this beauty all around us is to take a 15- to 30-minute "beauty walk." To get in the mood, take three slow, deep, and comfortable belly breaths, in and out, then start your walk wondering, "Where is the beauty around me?" Look for the little things. A pretty caterpillar crawling along, something green pushing its way out of cement, a tree with unique branches, a pretty sunset, and so forth. Then, when you find something, stop your walk for a few moments, belly breathe, and appreciate it before moving on and looking for the next beautiful thing. Don't worry about how far you get. This isn't about getting your body in shape; this is about training yourself to notice beauty. When you pay attention to beauty it's very difficult for the cobra to get you. How many beauty walks would be good to do this week? Where? For how long? Want to do it with anyone else or just by yourself? (If your situation allows for it, you and your client might go on a beauty walk together around your office.)

SIDEBAR 7.1

PK rings are another staple in magic; these are rings that are magnetic. You can get one from anywhere under $10 to $30, depending on the quality of the ring. As was the case with Svengali decks (see Sidebar 6.1 in Chapter 6), there are plenty of ideas on YouTube for how to use them, as well as professional DVDs you can purchase through online magic retailers.

One of my favorite tricks to do with a PK ring involves a bottle cap and a plastic water bottle. You'll need an empty water bottle with a label on it and two metal bottle caps that are significantly wider than the opening of the water bottle. Peel the label off partway and slit the bottle with a knife or razor, just enough so that you can insert one of the bottle caps inside it. After you've inserted the cap, glue or tape the label back into place so that the cut you made isn't visible. Next, position the cap within the bottle behind the label, using your hand with the PK ring on it to hold it in place. With the other hand, gesture that you have a bottle cap. Note that you are able to get the cap into the water bottle without bending it. Balance the cap on top of the bottle, ridges face-up, and on the count of three, do two things at the same time. First, palm the cap on the top of the bottle; the ridges on the bottle cap will make it easy for you to do so without closing your hand into a fist. Second, release the cap from inside the bottle; it should make a clunking sound as it hits the bottom of the water bottle. As you hand the bottle over to the kid for examination, drop your hand over a bag that you have placed by your side and release the bottle cap into it. This is a very easy trick to do and to teach—once you and your kid client possess a PK ring, that is.

REFERENCES AND BIBLIOGRAPHY

Barrett, P. M. (2000). Treatment of childhood anxiety: Developmental aspects. *Clinical Psychology Review, 20*(4), 479–494.

Beauchemin, J., Hutchins, T. L., & Patterson, F. (2008). Mindfulness meditation may lessen anxiety, promote social skills, and improve academic performance among adolescents with learning disabilities. *Complementary Health Practice Review, 13*(1), 34–45.

Bedell, W., & Kaszkin-Bettag, M. (2010). Coherence and health care cost—RCA actuarial study: A cost-effectiveness cohort study. *Congestive Heart Failure, 21*, 22.

Biegel, G. M., Brown, K. W., Shapiro, S. L., & Schubert, C. M. (2009). Mindfulness-based stress reduction for the treatment of adolescent psychiatric outpatients: A randomized clinical trial. *Journal of Consulting and Clinical Psychology, 77*(5), 855.

Bögels, S., Hoogstad, B., van Dun, L., de Schutter, S., & Restifo, K. (2008). Mindfulness training for adolescents with externalizing disorders and their parents. *Behavioural and Cognitive Psychotherapy, 36*(2), 193–209.

Bradley, R. T., McCraty, R., Atkinson, M., Tomasino, D., Daugherty, A., & Arguelles, L. (2010). Emotion self-regulation, psychophysiological coherence, and test anxiety: Results from an experiment using electrophysiological measures. *Applied Psychophysiology and Biofeedback, 35*(4), 261–283.

Burke, C. A. (2010). Mindfulness-based approaches with children and adolescents: A preliminary review of current research in an emergent field. *Journal of Child and Family Studies, 19*(2), 133–144.

Chu, B. C., & Harrison, T. L. (2007). Disorder-specific effects of CBT for anxious and depressed youth: A meta-analysis of candidate mediators of change. *Clinical Child and Family Psychology Review, 10*(4), 352–372.

Greco, L. A., & Hayes, S. C. (2008). *Acceptance and mindfulness treatments for children and adolescents: A practitioner's guide*. Oakland, CA: New Harbinger Publications.

Harnett, P. H., & Dawe, S. (2012). The contribution of mindfulness-based therapies for children and families and proposed conceptual integration. *Child and Adolescent Mental Health, 17*(4), 195–208.

Hastings, R. P., & Singh, N. N. (2010). Mindfulness, children, and families. *Journal of Child and Family Studies, 19*(2), 131–132.

Hofmann, S. G., Sawyer, A. T., Witt, A. A., & Oh, D. (2010). The effect of mindfulness-based therapy on anxiety and depression: A meta-analytic review. *Journal of Consulting and Clinical Psychology, 78*(2), 169–183.

Kendall, P. C., Choudhury, M., Hudson, J., & Webb, A. (2002). *"The C.A.T. Project" manual for the cognitive-behavioral treatment of anxious adolescents*. Ardmore, PA: Workbook Publishing.

Kendall, P. C., & Hedtke, K. A. (2006). *Cognitive-behavioral therapy for anxious children: Therapist manual* (3rd ed.). Ardmore, PA: Workbook Publishing.

Lee, J., Semple, R. J., Rosa, D., & Miller, L. (2008). Mindfulness-based cognitive therapy for children: Results of a pilot study. *Journal of Cognitive Psychotherapy, 22*(1), 15–28.

Lloyd, A., Brett, D., & Wesnes, K. (2010). Coherence training in children with attention-deficit hyperactivity disorder: Cognitive functions and behavioral changes. *Alternative Therapies in Health & Medicine, 16*(4), 34.

Lutz, B. (2014). An institutional case study: Emotion regulation with HeartMath at Santa Cruz County Children's Mental Health. *Global Advances in Health and Medicine, 3*(2), 68–71.

McCraty, R., & Shaffer, F. (2015). Heart rate variability: New perspectives on physiological mechanisms, assessment of self-regulatory capacity, and health risk. *Global Advances in Health and Medicine, 4*(1), 46–61.

Miller, A. L., Rathus, J. H., & Linehan, M. M. (2006). *Dialectical behavior therapy with suicidal adolescents*. New York, NY: Guilford Press.

Miller, A. L., Wyman, S. E., Huppert, J. D., Glassman, S. L., & Rathus, J. H. (2000). Analysis of behavioral skills utilized by suicidal adolescents receiving dialectical behavior therapy. *Cognitive and Behavioral Practice, 7*(2), 183–187.

Ratanasiripong, P., Ratanasiripong, N., & Kathalae, D. (2012). Biofeedback intervention for stress and anxiety among nursing students: A randomized controlled trial. *ISRN Nursing,* 2012. doi:10.5402/2012/827972

Schonert-Reichl, K. A., & Lawlor, M. S. (2010). The effects of a mindfulness-based education program on pre- and early adolescents' well-being and social and emotional competence. *Mindfulness, 1*(3), 137–151.

Semple, R., & Lee, J. (2007). *Mindfulness-based cognitive therapy for anxious children: A manual for treating childhood anxiety.* Oakland, CA: New Harbinger Publications.

Semple, R. J., Lee, J., Rosa, D., & Miller, L. F. (2010). A randomized trial of mindfulness-based cognitive therapy for children: Promoting mindful attention to enhance social-emotional resiliency in children. *Journal of Child and Family Studies, 19*(2), 218–229.

Semple, R. J., Reid, E. F., & Miller, L. (2005). Treating anxiety with mindfulness: An open trial of mindfulness training for anxious children. *Journal of Cognitive Psychotherapy, 19*(4), 379–392.

Shipherd, J. C., & Fordiani, J. M. (2014). The application of mindfulness in coping with intrusive thoughts. *Cognitive and Behavioral Practice, 22*(4), 439–446.

Thurstone, C., & Lajoie, T. (2013). Heart rate variability biofeedback in adolescent substance abuse treatment. *Global Advances in Health and Medicine, 2*(1), 22–23.

CHAPTER **8**

Coping/Happy Thoughts, Gratitude, and Crisis = Pain + Opportunity

BEGINNING SESSIONS

Once a kid has been given at least one technique, sessions tend to begin in a similar fashion. Especially early on in the work, I'll ask the parent who has accompanied a kid to a session, in the waiting area: *Tanisha, do you need any time with me?* I counsel parents to take me up on this offer if there have been any important developments that I should know about. It's rare for me to take more than 5 minutes with a parent, though.

Once the kid is in the consulting room I begin like this:

Aiden, what's the best thing and what's the worst thing that's happened to you this week (a)? *About how many iceman attacks did you have this week* (b)? *Which was the worst of them? Did you fight back* (c)? *How did you do with your homework from last week* (d)? *Is there anything that you want to make sure we have enough time to talk about today* (e)?

Explanation

a. As I explained earlier, you may need to emphasize that the best and the worst things could be trivial or that everyone has ups and downs each day and each week. Sometimes the worst thing that happened ends up being something that needs considerable time to unpack, but not often.

b. I don't ask "Did you have any iceman attacks this week?" as kids could easily become conditioned to say "no" just to get out of having to say more. Moreover, I've found that kids have no problem saying "none" if that's the true answer.

c. We are looking to gauge how well the kid did in using whatever techniques we have taught him. Sometimes he offers information on his own while at other times he'll have to be asked. Moreover, sometimes if he hasn't done well, I'll say, *Okay, I know how strong the iceman seems sometimes. Let's say we could go back in a time machine and you could have another shot at it. What's a weapon you could have tried to weaken the iceman then?* In the worst case scenario, I might need to reteach some technique, but that doesn't happen often.

d. Reviewing the homework, across the life of the treatment, tends to involve either (1) high fives, with reiterations of the value of the intervention, (2) a review of obstacles the kid experienced in doing the work (i.e., doing a psychological autopsy), (3) a discussion about the kid's engagement with the treatment, or (4) some combination of the first three.

e. I try to ask this question every session in case the kid needs extra time to discuss a topic of concern.

COPING THOUGHTS

If you count all your assets, you always show a profit.
—Robert Quillen

Behavioral activation (BA) and physiological calming (PC) are primarily behavioral interventions, though PC involves clearing one's mind and BA calls for a kid to overcome thoughts promoting lethargy. The module in this chapter is the first primary cognitive strategy. Like most other intervention sequences, we start with the easiest of the cognitive interventions and build from there. This is how I introduce it to kids:

Aiden, I'm going to ask you another one of my silly questions. Just go with it. Suppose you put on a pair of jeans that you hadn't worn in a year and when you buttoned them up they were so tight they hurt. What would be the very next thing you would do (a)? . . . Right, you'd take them off and put on a more comfortable pair of pants. Imagine how silly it'd be for a kid to walk around going, "Ow, these pants are tight and they really hurt. Ow! Ow!" Yet that's exactly what the iceman would have you do with the thoughts he puts into your head. There are times when painful thoughts are important to have because you're figuring stuff out. Like if you texted a friend to see if he wanted to go see a movie and he texted back cursing at you and telling you to leave him alone. In a case like that, you'd need to figure out what's going on, so you'd have to have some painful thoughts in your head. But that's not an iceman thought. Iceman thoughts are things like, "I'm so stupid!" Or, "I have no friends!" Or, "I'm so ugly!" They are thoughts that are very painful, are lies, and serve no good purpose. Later on I'll prove to you that iceman thoughts are lies. But, for now, we need a way to get rid of them. That's the weapon I'd like to show you today. So, just like you'd change an uncomfortable pair of pants, you're going to learn to trade a good thought for a painful thought. Before I teach you this, we could call this weapon "coping thoughts," or

"happy thoughts." "Coping" means to cope or to fight back with something use-
ful. Of course, you know what "happy" means. Which do you like better, "coping
thoughts" or "happy thoughts" (b)? Okay, coping thoughts it is.

We need to develop a list of three kinds of coping thoughts. First, we want to
write down some true things about you that, when you think about them, make
you feel good. Someone might say, "I'm very good at ice skating." Or, "Little kids
really like me a lot!" Or, "I'm pretty funny" (c). What are some true things about
you that feel good to think about (d)? . . . Excellent! Now, let's come up with some
true things about your life. Someone might think, "I have a great house by the
ocean." Or, "My dad is a great dad." Or, "My dog is awesome." What are some true
things about your life that feel good to think about (e)? Very good! Okay, the last
category is the one that changes the most. These are things you're looking forward
to. We only want to include things that are actually scheduled. Like we don't want
to put things like "having a family someday" because that's not scheduled yet. So,
what are some things that you're currently looking forward to (f)? Wonderful!

Here's the list—what do you think (g)? . . . Okay, here's how you use this weapon.
The next time that you have a painful thought that's in your head that is doing
you no good, and it just keeps playing over and over again (h), take out this list
and think about one of these things instead. Okay, Aiden, let's pretend like we
have a time machine here in the office. Let's go back in time to a moment that the
iceman was in your head with a painful thought and you might use one of these.
What is an example? . . . What thought did the iceman put in your head? . . . What
coping thought from this list could you have used (i)? . . . Okay, good, you're
really getting it. You know, I love my forms, so here's one for tracking your use of
coping thoughts this week. Let me explain it (j). Okay, let's use the example you
just came up with and fill in this form (k).

The really cool thing about this weapon is that you can use it just about any
time and in any situation. You can't always stop and do something fun; for exam-
ple, like in the middle of English class. And sometimes you can't relax all of your
muscles because you're using them, like in the middle of soccer practice. But this
weapon you can pretty much use all the time. Plus, it's easy-peasy to do it. The
only tough part is to get in the habit of noticing that the iceman is up to his tricks
and to use it to fight him. Any questions (l)? . . . Okay, just so I can make sure I
explained it well, can you say back to me how this weapon works? . . . What situ-
ations might come up this week when the iceman might try to get you and you
could use this weapon (m)?

Explanation

a. Sometimes kids will say, "Get mad at myself." Or, "Tell my mom." But, with a
little prompting, just about all kids will say that they'd change their pants.

b. It really doesn't matter which name a kid chooses, and some might change
their minds. But whatever the kid decides becomes the label at the top of the
sheet.

c. I try to pick examples of coping thoughts that would not be true for the kid before me. Otherwise, too many kids will just choose what I've said; it has more potential lasting value if the thoughts come from the kid.

d. Some kids will say things about their circumstances or what they are looking forward to; if so, I just remark that that's a good idea and will go into a subsequent category. As is usually the case, I'm writing down what they say as we go. I'm usually looking for four true things about the kid that feel good to him. Before the session, I'll prepare some ideas, based on the evaluation findings, just in case the kid struggles (usually as a symptom of a mood disorder); in these instances I'll say things like, *Your mom said that you're good at bowling. Is that true? . . . Does that feel good to think about?* Or, *in another session you told me that you're fast. Does that feel good to think about?*

e. Popular topics for coping thoughts are aspects of a kid's family, social network, house, and pets. But anything goes as long as it pertains to the kid's circumstances. Again, I'm looking for four cognitions and I've prepared some in advance, in case the kid struggles.

f. Anhedonic kids may particularly struggle here. So, I may need to ask things like, *Does your family have a vacation planned? What are you doing this weekend? What are you doing for* (name the next major holiday)*? Any plans for this summer?* Knowledge about a kid's extracurricular and social life can offer useful prompts as well.

This is an example of what a finished sheet could look like:

AIDEN'S HAPPY THOUGHTS

Things that are true about me

- I'm a very good baseball player.
- I'm funny.
- I'm a good friend.
- I sing well.

Things that are true about my life

- I have an awesome dog.
- I have great parents.
- I love my bedroom.
- I have over 10 good friends.

Things I'm looking forward to

- I'm going to Aunt Jackie's this weekend for a barbecue.

- Peter and I are going fishing next weekend.

- We are going to Wildwood Beach this summer.

- I'm getting inducted into the National Honor Society next month.

g. As is discussed throughout this volume, focusing on good things will often lift a kid's mood. So, it's not uncommon to have kids say things like, "I forget sometimes about the good things." Or, "I guess I have a lot that's good in my life." Or, "Yeah, I really love my dog." Depending on your intuition, your kid client's characteristics, and the time you have left in the session, you could always say, ***Why don't you pick one of these and draw a picture about it?***

h. The hardest part about this intervention is to get kids to recognize, in the moment, when they are having a repetitive, painful, and useless thought, so that they can stop it and use this strategy. Once a kid is shown how to do thought testing, that helps (see Chapter 10).

i. Most kids don't struggle with coming up with an example. After all, they often experience sadness, anxiety, and irritability. That's why they are before us. But, once again, it never hurts to prepare beforehand. During the evaluation phase, or even since, you would have been told about vignettes that pulled for negative affect. Just have a couple of those at the ready in case. Moreover, try to not accept "I don't know" as an answer and to give the kid sufficient time to try to come up with the vignette. (Silence is a powerful tool in kid clinical work, which is something trainees often need to become comfortable with.)

j. Table 8.1 indicates the form. It's self-explanatory. In the form there is a space before the word "thought" in the title so that you can insert whatever term the kid prefers. There is also a space at the top of the second column so that you can insert the name of his internal enemy.

k. Table 8.2 indicates what the form would look like once it is filled in.

l. Questions about the coping thought methodology are not common.

m. I ask the kid to say back to me what we've covered mostly to reduce the odds that the strategy will have flown out of the kid's mind by the time he gets home. But there is nothing like prompting the parent (who's in the waiting room) to remind the kid as I covered earlier.

TABLE 8.1 _____ Thought Tracking Form

Name: _____

Week: _____

Bother rating (0–100). Higher numbers mean it bothered you more.

Situation (What Was Going On Around You)	_____ Thought	Bother Rating	Coping Thought	Bother Rating

TABLE 8.2 <u>Happy</u> Thought Tracking Form

Name: <u>Aiden</u>

Week: <u>July 1–8, 2015</u>

Bother rating (0–100). Higher numbers mean it bothered you more.

Situation (What Was Going On Around You)	<u>Iceman</u> Thought	Bother Rating	Coping Thought	Bother Rating
I got an 83 on a math test.	You're an idiot!!	85	I'm on the honor roll for most report cards.	25

Additional Commentary

This is another staple of cognitive behavioral therapy (CBT) interventions. Thought stopping and thought substitution are examples of terms from the adult literature that have been used to describe this intervention. I've seen some kid CBT manuals focus on teaching about the difference between thoughts and feelings, using drawings of thought bubbles, and going through various vignettes. While I've conducted more of these kinds of sessions with kids than I can count, my clinical intuition is that the time spent doing these kinds of sessions has not been worth it. I think how and why stuff works is important to cover whenever we teach a kid an intervention. But I think that sometimes, as mental health professionals (MHPs), we sometimes value the former more than our kid clients. So, when doing this kind of didactic work on the difference between thoughts and feelings, I've felt sometimes like a teacher trying to get a kid to learn stuff he's going to forget soon anyway. For this reason, I focus more on the doing.

All that said, if you believe *for your kid client* that teaching about the difference between thoughts and feelings is important, then listen to yourself on that. It would be very easy to create your own materials. Just get a few pictures or drawings of kids interacting (e.g., from public domain images, magazines) and then draw some thought bubbles over the characters' heads. I'd start out with situations that are obvious (e.g., a kid smiling as a birthday cake with candles is being presented, a kid running from a barking dog). I'd also prepare a list of feeling words, longer for teens and shorter for children. You might start out with an example of a picture from your life, drawn with a thought bubble that you've filled in. You can then explain the difference between your thoughts and feelings, pointing to your list of feeling words. Then break out the pictures of kids that you've prepared and go through them with your client. You can then point out that the thought bubble is where your kid's internal enemy attacks him, and go from there using the methods I've shared.

In my experience, kids take quickly and well to using coping thoughts. Part of the reason is probably because it doesn't require them to stop life as much as some of the other interventions (e.g., thought testing). Moreover, many kids tend to generalize quickly to other kinds of coping/happy thoughts. For example, I recently had one of my teen clients say something like this, "Mrs. Robinson said she wondered where my head was at today and that started to make me feel sad, but then I just told myself that everyone has bad days and that her being grouchy probably didn't have much to do with me." I'll also use things like music videos to develop coping thoughts that fit a kid's situation (e.g., Billy Joel's music video of "You're Only Human [Second Wind]").

GRATITUDE

Feeling gratitude and not expressing it is like wrapping a present and not giving it.
—William Arthur Ward

I'd like to review just a few items from Chapter 1 about positive psychology (PP). Traditional clinical psychology addresses this question: "How can we understand and either reduce or heal this person's pain?" However, it is mostly silent on the question: "How can we produce happiness and experiences of meaning for this kid?" This is where the field of PP comes in, as it addresses this question: "What can a person do to feel happy and to have meaningful experiences?"

The literature within PP is scant when it comes to kids. However, the resilience literature is related, as resilience also appears to promote happiness and well-being. Granted, much of what promotes resilience in kids is determined by family, educational, and community variables. However, there are certain PP interventions that kids can do, within the context of CBT, that appear to be helpful. The first of these is to focus on gratitude. As I go through these techniques, you'll note that they are similar to the coping/happy thoughts intervention.

Gratitude Lists

This is how I introduce this intervention to kids:

Aiden, you know how you've been using happy thoughts when the iceman starts in on you (a)? Well, I have a new weapon that is sort of a supercharged version of happy thoughts. I say "supercharged" because coping thoughts are used to put the iceman back in his cage. But you use this weapon to thicken the bars on the cage. The weapon is called "gratitude lists."

Do you know what the word "grateful" means (b)? . . . So, a gratitude list is a list of things you feel grateful for. Let's make a list of things that you're grateful for from the past week. Things you're grateful for can be little things like a tasty burger or the sound of a bird chirping that you enjoyed one morning. Or, it can be big things, like taking a trip to an amusement park or getting an A on a midterm (c). What are you grateful for from the past week (d)? . . . Awesome list. So, Aiden, let's say a 7 is very happy and a 1 is very unhappy. As you think about this list, what do you feel? How did you feel arriving today? Okay, let's write down that number at the bottom of the list we just made (e). Aiden, a lot of us are like you. When we focus on what we're grateful for we feel better. We have two problems that get in the way, though. First, we are all SO BUSY. Because of this we just blow by things we're grateful for because we have to get our stuff done. Second, many different kinds of internal enemies—and remember, we all have at least one enemy inside—want us to focus on our problems, or what's not going right and well in our lives. So, many of us walk around thinking about what we have to do, our problems, how other people or situations have let us down, or how we've screwed up. And when you think like that a lot it opens the iceman's cage. But we can keep the doors on his cage closed, and even make the bars thicker, by having you focus on what you're grateful for, like we just did. What do you think? . . . Mind saying it back to me so I can check to see if I said it well?

There are a couple of different ways we can use gratitude as a weapon against the iceman. The first way I'd like to try is easy-peasy. It involves taking one day a week and writing down at least 10 things you're grateful for from that week (f). This is just like what we did, which we'll put in your binder. Would that be okay to do? When would be a good day to do it? Can you say it back to me what it is you're going to be doing and why? What could get in the way of doing this?

Explanation

a. Depending on how successful the kid has been with this intervention, I might ask for recent examples. If we've already had such discussions multiple times and the kid is using coping thoughts well, I'm less likely to do this. But, if the intervention is not well established, or there's doubt about that, it can't hurt to review it.

b. I'll just define it if the kid doesn't know, saying something like, *Yeah, "grateful" is sort of a fancy word. Grateful means when you feel glad or happy about something.*

c. There are kids who would scoff at the idea of enjoying a chirping bird or others who have never gotten an A on a major test, so you'll need to use your judgment about examples that the kid can relate to. However, I try to avoid examples that might have recently happened to the kid, as it's best if those come from him.

d. Like any similar exercise, the kid may need prompts such as: *Anything small or big happen at school today? . . . Earlier in the week? . . . Anything with your teacher? . . . on the playground? . . . in the cafeteria? . . .* This is an example of a composite list:

Aiden's Weekly Gratitude List
6/15/15

- Mom made me hot chocolate this morning.
- I got invited to Chris's party.
- I got an 86 in math on my report card, my highest grade yet.
- The town pool opened up yesterday.
- Dad came over for dinner.
- My dog was fun to play with yesterday.
- Jake told me that I'm the best shooter on our basketball team.
- The buns smelled fresh at lunch on Monday.
- I liked how my hair looked this morning.
- Taylor sent me a funny picture.

e. A rating would then be added to the bottom:

Aiden's Weekly Gratitude List
6/15/15

- Mom made me hot chocolate this morning.
- I got invited to Chris's party.

- I got an 86 in math on my report card, my highest grade yet.

- The town pool opened up yesterday.

- Dad came over for dinner.

- My dog was fun to play with yesterday.

- Jake told me that I'm the best shooter on our basketball team.

- The buns smelled fresh at lunch on Monday.

- I liked how my hair looked this morning.

- Taylor sent me a funny picture.

Mood before making this list: 4
Mood right after making this list: 6
(1 = very unhappy; 7 = very happy)

If a kid reports a neutral impact because he came to the session already feeling some degree of happiness, I'll ask him to imagine the impact of making the list if his mood had been rated at a 3 or a 4. If a kid reports a neutral impact but started out at a 3 or a 4, I'll explore more what happened that day and what might be the cause for him not feeling so hot. I'll then temper follow-up language based on that information. For example, let's say a kid says that he's at a 3 and stayed there, because he didn't sleep well the night before, is tired, and has a lot of homework to do that night. I'll point out that gratitude is like a helium balloon and that his stress is like a weight attached to the string, so it's tough for the gratitude to take off. I'll then temper what I say next in the script based on this information.

If a kid reports that his mood worsened based on making the list, it's likely that there is a problem that we need to discuss. For example, maybe making the list made him remember an ongoing stress (e.g., he only sees his father once a month and would like to see him more). If so, I'll stop the exercise and shift to problem solving (see Chapter 11), coming back to this intervention in a future session.

f. I've found that this is a good way to start as it's only once a week. The time commitment is light and it provides the bump in mood that we're looking for. There are other methods that can be tried as either an alternative or as an elaboration on this technique. These include:

- Writing down what the kid is grateful for each day, usually at the end of the day, as a bedtime ritual. Younger kids could make a drawing of something they are grateful for that day.

- Reflecting on what a kid is grateful for in the shower or bath each day. Prompts can be arranged (e.g., placing a waterproof reminder in the shower, asking a parent to offer reminders).

- Making a thank-you note, or a thank-you drawing, once every week for a couple of weeks.

Gratitude Letters

Acknowledging the good that you already have in your life is the foundation for all abundance.
—Eckhart Tolle

Of all the interventions I do and teach, this is one of my favorites. There are two ways to do this: with an engaged and psychologically minded teen and with a family. For teens I'll say this:

Aiden, I'd like to share with you a powerful way to use gratitude. It's called doing a gratitude letter. First, you need to find someone that you feel a lot of gratitude toward, but maybe haven't expressed it fully or recently enough. Then, you want to write a hand written letter to that person of about 300 words. It's important that it be hand written and not just written on a computer. It's more personal and intimate that way. And don't get hung up on it being PRECISELY 300 words, just about. In the letter, put down the things you're grateful for; it doesn't matter how recent it is. Then arrange to be with that person one-on-one and read him or her your letter. Don't chicken out and hand it over to be read. You read it out loud. One or both of you may start crying, but that's okay. What do you think? . . . Who might be a good person to write this for?

When done with a family, the instructions regarding how to write the letter are the same, though the length of it can be reduced for younger children or changed to a drawing for very young children. What's different is that people in the family take turns being the recipient of the letters. There are at least three ways to integrate this into the kid's CBT.

1. Arrange for the parent(s) and the kid to read their letters at the start or end of consecutive individual sessions.

2. Assign it as a task to do at home across weeks (i.e., one week per recipient).

3. Integrate it into augmenting family-level sessions (see Chapters 9 and 13).

Additional Commentary

The placement of this module in the sequence of interventions varies considerably based on (a) how a kid has done with other cognitive interventions, (b) the progress of the work, and (c) the characteristics of the kid, his family, and the context. For example, if getting a kid (and his system) to write down things is like pushing a pickup truck up a steep hill, with the parking brake on, in a thunderstorm, with no shoes on (experienced child clinicians know what this feels like), then I won't attempt a writing/drawing component. Or, if a kid has already met his goals I may keep this intervention for a booster session. Or I might just describe it to a parent near termination. Or, I may frontload this exercise more for teens who seem to be psychologically minded or never get to it for an action-oriented young kid who deplores self-examination. Despite what critics may lament, artfully applied CBT is very flexible and how it is implemented varies from kid to kid, at least when the MHP is an evidence-based artisan.

Gratitude letters open the door to a very powerful experience. I've done them, witnessed others doing them, and had more students and clients tell me about them than I can remember. Several outcomes are common: (a) one or both people cry, but in a good way; (b) the recipient treats the letter like a treasure; (c) folks report that the relationship is enhanced, no matter how good it already was; and (d) the author and the recipient of the letter experience a significant lift in mood and meaning. If you've not done one, I'd encourage you to try. If you feel like it, shoot me an e-mail telling me how it went.

CRISIS = PAIN + OPPORTUNITY

Your pain is the breaking of the shell that encloses your understanding.
—Kahlil Gibran

I have learned silence from the talkative, toleration from the intolerant, and kindness from the unkind; yet strange, I am ungrateful to these teachers.
—Kahlil Gibran

This is a module that can be helpful when an older kid or teen is trying to find perspective regarding painful events. Like many of the modules in this chapter, choosing if and when to use it is a matter of art. This is how it can be introduced:

Aiden, I'd like to make a list of the six worst things from the past that have ever happened to you (a). Okay, good. Now, let's take each one and consider whether there is any way that your life is better because of that (b). Now let's apply ratings. We'll go through each painful thing and give it a rating from 1 to 100, with 100 being the most pain you can feel (c). Good, now let's go through how your life was made better and rate those also from 1 to 100, with 100 meaning your life was improved as much as is possible (d). Our pain is like a dragon guarding treasure. The dragon has to have its way with us, clawing and hurting us, as we see here on your sheet; it's also made worse by what the iceman would say about it, if you listen to the iceman, that is (e). But the dragon finishes at some point and then the treasure is available. Aiden, let's go through these six bad things and how much they continue to hurt you (f). Okay, now let's go through the treasures. How much are they still giving to you (g)? Your experience is like most. The pain stops but the gifting continues (h).

Explanation

a. We want the kid to list past pains and not ones that are current. If a kid struggles to get to six, it's okay to stop at a smaller number. The exercise won't work as well if the pain is trivial, and not all kids have six significant painful things they can recount. Also, I'd stay away from any traumas that are promoting posttraumatic stress disorder (PTSD).

b. Psychologically minded kids get this right away. Moreover, psychologically minded teens can really take off with indicating how painful events opened the door to growth and opportunity. For other kids, they may need some prompting with questions like, *Janet dumping you—does that leave you better able to help a friend who goes through something like this?* Or, *Does losing your mom, when you were six, make you more grateful for having a loving father?*

c. Providing a rating is typically pretty easy for kids to do.

d. How easy this is will depend on how much the kid was able to identify subsequent upsides to bad experiences. If I start this module and my best efforts leave me feeling like the fruit on the tree has not ripened enough yet, I'm not beyond shifting gears away from this exercise and going elsewhere.

e. I'll sometimes ask for examples of things the iceman has tried to assert about past pains. This is a matter of feel.

f. If the event is in the past, and not affiliated with PTSD or unresolved grief, the pain ratings are usually pretty low.

g. If the kid was able to do the preceding steps well, these numbers usually look higher than the current pain numbers. The worst I've had happen is that some of the vignettes follow this prediction while others don't. I teach about the ones that do and then suggest that sometimes it can take a long time to reap the treasure. In the latter instance, I'll share this vignette (the wording here varies considerably based upon the age of the kid):

I know a person who generally got As in school but who had a teacher in the fifth grade that didn't care for him. This teacher gave him Bs and Cs and wrote on his report card that he was "weak in thinking skills." This was a source of significant pain for this boy. Flash forward 35 years and this boy, now a man, is a successful professional with two kids. His eldest child, like him, is a very good student in the fifth grade. One day she came home distraught with a C grade on a major exam. She was inconsolable as her father tried to help her to keep the grade in perspective. As he left her, and was doing some other work he had to do, he mysteriously came across his fifth grade report card. He took it to his daughter and showed her. Her eyes got wide as it was inconceivable to her that her father would have ever had less than a fantastic report card. She put her hand over her mouth, laughed, and hugged her father. In that moment, every little bit of pain he experienced from that report card, that was in the distant past for him, seemed to be so very worth it. Sometimes it can take awhile to find the treasure and, in those instances, the wait seems to make it all the more precious.

h.   Sometimes this point is self-evident at this juncture. If so, I just pile on. If not, I make the point by interviewing the kid about his experiences along these lines. I also sometimes augment this section by showing brief videos of examples, many of which are available on YouTube (e.g., search for videos on Nick Vujicic, a man born without arms and legs).

SIDEBAR 8.1

This is a trick that you can use to augment the coping thought module. I've adapted it from a trick on Luke Jermay's DVD *Emotional Intelligence*. You'll need either a deck of blank playing cards (usually available for under $5) or index cards. You want about 20 playing cards or index cards (I prefer the playing cards only because they hold up better). Cut half of them to be a *tiny* bit shorter than the other half, like is done with Svengali decks of cards (see the magic trick in Chapter 6). You'll want to create the following pairs of cards: happy-sad, peaceful-upset, joyful-miserable, calm-angry, brave-afraid, patient-impatient, generous-selfish, sociable-withdrawn, humorous-somber, and pleasant-grouchy. Write the positive affect on the short-cut card and its corresponding negative affect on a longer card, making sure to pair them together in the deck order. You will also need three blank pieces of paper, each about one-third of a size of a 8.5 x 11 sheet of paper, and a glass or bowl. You're now ready for the trick.

Display the cards for the kid, making sure to maintain the order and explaining that these are different feelings people have; you might have to define a couple of the words or substitute words that work better for your client. Then mix the deck as I described for the Svengali card trick (see Sidebar 6.1 in Chapter 6; the pairs will be maintained). Riffle through this small deck with your thumb while telling the kid that you'll stop where he says. Then have him take the top facedown card that he's told you to stop at, holding that part of the deck in your left hand. Ask him to remember it but not show you; as you do this, turn away and look to see what card you have in your right hand (the negative word, which will tell you what card the kid has selected). Ask the kid to think of a memory of a time when he felt that feeling strongly and was with someone else, then tell him that you'll use your mind puppet to read his mind. Once he says that he has a memory, put the cards aside and use your mind puppet (see

(continued)

SIDEBAR 8.1 (*continued*)

the magic trick in Chapter 3) to read his mind. As you have the mind puppet on your head (i.e., your mind puppet is telling you what the kid had been thinking), say that you're thinking of the main person he was with when he felt that feeling and then say you're going to write that person's name on the first piece of blank paper. On that paper write the positive affect you know the kid has chosen. Fold the paper and put it in the glass or bowl. Now ask the kid to say the person's name, nodding knowingly. Now tell him you're going to use your mind puppet to tell you about the month this happened in as you write the name of the person he just told you. Fold that paper up and put it in the glass or bowl. Then ask him to name the month, again nodding knowingly. Take the third piece of paper, using your mind puppet again, and say that you'd like for him to now focus on the feeling as you write the month on the piece of paper, but instead of writing the exact month, put down something like "end of January–early February" if he named either January or February (the approximation adds to the effect and many kids will subsequently say that what you've written is more accurate). Then put the third paper in the glass or bowl, mixing up the three papers. Have the kid pick out one of the papers and read it aloud, commenting that that's what your mind puppet told you. Then do the same for the second and then the third pieces of paper. After the kid expresses amazement, you can ask him what it felt like to remember such a good memory, further making the points from the coping thought module.

SIDEBAR 8.2

Commercially available magic tricks make for nice additions to your offerings. However, I'm mostly staying away from them to keep your costs down. One exception is my suggestion that you purchase the "Needle Through Balloon" trick available through www.magictricks.com; it is currently available for under $20. This trick allows you to insert a long steel needle through the end of an inflated balloon without it bursting, which can make for a nice teaching augment when doing the coping thought module.

Write coping thoughts on one side of the inflated balloon. On the other side of the balloon write thoughts generated by the internal enemy you're working on. Explain the balloon is like your kid's mood and the needle is stress. When the kid thinks of the coping thoughts, stress can't wreck his mood; demonstrate by inserting the needle in the way that doesn't burst the balloon. Then withdraw it and suggest that when the kid thinks of his internal enemy's thoughts his mood is wrecked, then touch the needle to the side of the balloon with the negative thoughts; it will burst.

REFERENCES AND BIBLIOGRAPHY

Alvord, M. K., & Grados, J. J. (2005). Enhancing resilience in children: A proactive approach. *Professional Psychology: Research and Practice, 36*(3), 238–245.

Armstrong, M. I., Birnie-Lefcovitch, S., & Ungar, M. T. (2005). Pathways between social support, family well-being, quality of parenting, and child resilience: What we know. *Journal of Child and Family Studies, 14*(2), 269–281.

Bonanno, G. A. (2008). Loss, trauma, and human resilience: Have we underestimated the human capacity to thrive after extremely aversive events? *Psychological Trauma: Theory, Research, Practice, and Policy, S*(1), 101–113.

Brooks, R., & Goldstein, S. (2001). *Raising resilient children: Fostering strength, hope, and optimism in your child.* Lincolnwood, IL: Contemporary Books.

Cohn, M. A., Fredrickson, B. L., Brown, S. L., Mikels, J. A., & Conway, A. M. (2009). Happiness unpacked: Positive emotions increase life satisfaction by building resilience. *Emotion, 9*(3), 361.

Emmons, R. A. (2007). *Thanks! How practicing gratitude can make you happier.* New York, NY: Houghton Mifflin.

Emmons, R. A., & McCullough, M. E. (2003). Counting blessings versus burdens: An experimental investigation of gratitude and subjective well-being in daily life. *Journal of Personality and Social Psychology, 84*(2), 377–389.

Froh, J. J., Sefick, W. J., & Emmons, R. A. (2008). Counting blessings in early adolescents: An experimental study of gratitude and subjective well-being. *Journal of School Psychology, 46*(2), 213–233.

Goldstein, S., & Brooks, R. B. (2012). *Handbook of resilience in children.* Berlin, Germany: Springer Science & Business Media.

Hogendoorn, S. M., Prins, P. J., Boer, F., Vervoort, L., Wolters, L. H., Moorlag, H., & de Haan, E. (2014). Mediators of cognitive behavioral therapy for anxiety-disordered children and adolescents: Cognition, perceived control, and coping. *Journal of Clinical Child & Adolescent Psychology, 43*(3), 486–500.

Hoy, B. D., Suldo, S. M., & Mendez, L. R. (2013). Links between parents' and children's levels of gratitude, life satisfaction, and hope. *Journal of Happiness Studies, 14*(4), 1343–1361.

Kendall, P. C., Choudhury, M., Hudson, J., & Webb, A. (2002). *"The C.A.T. Project" manual for the cognitive-behavioral treatment of anxious adolescents.* Ardmore, PA: Workbook Publishing.

Kendall, P. C., & Hedtke, K. A. (2006). *Cognitive-behavioral therapy for anxious children: Therapist manual* (3rd ed.). Ardmore, PA: Workbook Publishing.

Kendall, P. C., & Treadwell, K. R. H. (2007). The role of self-statements as a mediator in treatment for youth with anxiety disorders. *Journal of Consulting and Clinical Psychology, 75*(3), 380–389.

Layous, K., & Lyubomirsky, S. (2014). Benefits, mechanisms, and new directions for teaching gratitude to children. *School Psychology Review, 43*(2), 153–159.

Lyubomirsky, S., King, L., & Diener, E. (2005). The benefits of frequent positive affect: Does happiness lead to success? *Psychological Bulletin, 131*(6), 803.

McCarty, C. A., Violette, H. D., Duong, M. T., Cruz, R. A., & McCauley, E. (2013). A randomized trial of the positive thoughts and action program for depression among early adolescents. *Journal of Clinical Child & Adolescent Psychology, 42*(4), 554–563.

McCullough, M. E., Emmons, R. A., & Tsang, J. A. (2002). The grateful disposition: A conceptual and empirical topography. *Journal of Personality and Social Psychology, 82*(1), 112.

Nelson, J. A., Freitas, L. B., O'Brien, M., Calkins, S. D., Leerkes, E. M., & Marcovitch, S. (2013). Preschool-aged children's understanding of gratitude: Relations with emotion and mental state knowledge. *British Journal of Developmental Psychology, 31*(1), 42–56.

Norrish, J. M., & Vella-Brodrick, D. A. (2009). Positive psychology and adolescents: Where are we now? Where to from here? *Australian Psychologist, 44*(4), 270–278.

Ouweneel, E., Le Blanc, P. M., & Schaufeli, W. B. (2014). On being grateful and kind: Results of two randomized controlled trials on study-related emotions and academic engagement. *Journal of Psychology, 148*(1), 37–60.

Rash, J. A., Matsuba, M. K., & Prkachin, K. M. (2011). Gratitude and well-being: Who benefits the most from a gratitude intervention? *Applied Psychology: Health and Well-Being, 3*(3), 350–369.

Sheldon, K. M., & Lyubomirsky, S. (2006). How to increase and sustain positive emotion: The effects of expressing gratitude and visualizing best possible selves. *Journal of Positive Psychology, 1*(2), 73–82.

Sin, N. L., & Lyubomirsky, S. (2009). Enhancing well-being and alleviating depressive symptoms with positive psychology interventions: A practice-friendly meta-analysis. *Journal of Clinical Psychology, 65*(5), 467–487.

Thompson, R. A. (2012). *Nurturing future generations: Promoting resilience in children and adolescents through social, emotional, and cognitive skills.* London, UK: Routledge.

Tschann, J. M., Kaiser, P., Chesney, M. A., Alkon, A., & Boyce, W. T. (1996). Resilience and vulnerability among preschool children: Family functioning, temperament, and behavior problems. *Journal of the American Academy of Child & Adolescent Psychiatry, 35*(2), 184–192.

Tugade, M. M., & Fredrickson, B. L. (2004). Resilient individuals use positive emotions to bounce back from negative emotional experiences. *Journal of Personality and Social Psychology, 86*(2), 320.

SECTION III

Engaging the Parent(s)

CHAPTER 9

Parent Integration and Special Time

TIMING OF THE PARENT SESSION

*Does any new parent, even if you're not a first-time parent, ever really know
what to do?*
—Robert Downey Jr.

I wait to have a parent session until I have a solid 50 minutes worth of material to go over. Some of the questions to consider:

▶ How conflict-laden is the relationship between the parents? (The more conflict, the sooner the session will be.)

▶ How conflict-laden is the relationship between the parent(s) and the kid? (The more conflict, the sooner the session will be.)

▶ How psychologically minded and/or verbal is/are the parent/parents? (The more psychologically minded or verbal, the sooner the session will be.)

▶ How resistant is the kid? (The more resistant, the sooner the session will be.)

The most common scenario is to do behavioral activation or physiological calming (including introducing some kind of biofeedback), coping thoughts, and then the parent session (of course, these follow treatment planning and externalizing the problem).

PREPARING THE KID FOR THE PARENT SESSION

This is what I'll say:

Monica, next session I'm going to be meeting with your mom and dad. I'd like to talk with you about what I'll be going over with them. As you know, I won't be sharing anything without you saying it's okay. Would it be okay for me to tell them . . . (a)? Okay, good. Would it be okay if I told them about the cobra (b)? Okay, good. Then I'm going to be telling them about the weapons I've taught you for using against the cobra. So, let's go through those. I'm going to be going over how doing something fun is a weapon. Could I show them your list (c)? Next I'm going to teach them how we've been relaxing your body and measuring that. Is that okay (d)? Finally, I'm going to teach them about coping thoughts. Can I show them the ones you came up with (e)?

I'll next review with the kid what I believe her compliance has been like. If a kid is doing her homework well, then this will be limited to a brief discussion about whether reminders would be helpful. If the kid's compliance has been spotty, I'll say something like this:

Monica, you know how sometimes practicing your cobra weapons has been hard to do, given how busy you are (f)? Well, I know how much you hate it when the cobra takes over (motioning to the externalizing-the-problem exercise in the kid's binder). *Right, you hate when you get like this (g)? Well, maybe we can use your mom and dad to help you to work on practicing your weapons. So, that's something I'm going to go over with them also (h). Do you have any questions or things you want to say about my meeting with your mom and dad? . . . Can you say back to me why I'm meeting with them so that I can make sure I explained it right? . . . Okay, it's very important that you continue to practice your cobra weapons, so let's talk about that for a little bit (i).*

Explanation

a. What I might ask here is almost as varied as the number of flavors of ice cream. If there is something the kid has told me that . . .

. . . might help me with special time compliance, then I'll ask if I can share it (e.g., a kid has told me that she wishes her dad worked less).

. . . suggests there is a problem that I never discussed with the parent(s) before, then I'll ask if I can discuss it (e.g., a kid has told me that Mom is crying a lot, but the initial parent screen for psychopathology was negative).

. . . indicates the severity of the kid's internalizing symptoms is slowing the work, then I'll ask if I can share the symptoms of concern (e.g., a kid is vegetative and I want to revisit the possible value of an evaluation for medication).

. . . indicates the kid has a problem that is interfering with the work, then I'll find out if it's okay to mention it to the parents (e.g., a kid is spending excessive amounts of time doing homework and I need to develop a plan with the parents and school for dealing with that).

. . . suggests the kid is troubled by some stress that the parents don't know about but might help with (e.g., a kid is being bullied in school).

. . . suggests the kid has some idea in her head that the parents might help me to dispel (e.g., others don't have internal enemies).

In the large majority of instances, the kid will let me ask. In instances when a kid refuses, we might have a discussion like this:

MHP: *Monica, I'd like to share with your dad that you love spending time with him and wish he might find a way to work less. Would that be okay?*
Kid: *No, don't tell him that.*
MHP: *Okay, I won't. But, tell me, what are you worried could happen if I did?*
Kid: *He'd get angry at me for telling you.*
MHP: *What could happen if he got angry at you for telling me?*
Kid: *He'd yell at me when he got home.*
MHP: *I get it, you don't like it when he yells at you, so you don't want me to tell him something that might make him yell.*
Kid: *(Nods yes)*
MHP: *Well, let's say I could get him to promise to not yell, would that make it any better?*
Kid: *I don't know.*
MHP: *See, the thing is that I believe your dad loves you more than anything else in the world. And I think that he'd very much like to know about the important things that are on your mind, even if they upset him at first. And I think that he'd like to try to fix anything that needs fixing. So, I feel like it's pretty likely that if I told him that I had something important to share with him but that he had to promise to never yell at you about it, that he'd agree to that. Then I think he'd think about whether he could fix the problem. So, if could get him to promise not to yell, could I tell him then?*
Kid: *What if he promises then yells anyway?*
MHP: *Yeah, I guess that's a risk. But I don't think it's likely. Your dad seems to be a good guy to me who would work hard to keep his promises. But if he did yell after promising not to, then I would be on him about that and we'd know something important about him going forward. So it's a risk, but I think a very small one and one that I think is worth it. But, that said, it's still your call because it is your risk. I won't tell him if you still feel that way after hearing me out. What do you think?*
Kid: *Okay. But if he yells, I'll tell you.*
MHP: *Thanks, Monica. I'm going to work hard to make sure that you end up happy with this choice.*

If a kid won't agree, then that's that, as long as the issue at hand doesn't involve a risk of serious injury, abuse, or neglect. But it's still often possible to get to the same material more indirectly. One could ask such a parent things like, How's work going? How many hours are they expecting of you these days? What pressures does that add at home with you having to work so much? And so forth.

b. It's really only in kid–parent relationships that are highly conflict-laden, or with kids who start shaking their head "no" once my lips start moving, that I'll tend to get a refusal that can't be worked through. In the former case, special time can soften matters and we can turn to this later (see the text that follows). In the latter case, there may be a defiance monster to take on (see Chapter 13). Mostly, though, kids agree to this readily, including letting me show the parent the externalizing worksheet we made.

c. I'm not really asking for permission to discuss how behavioral activation is used, as that's information that has come from me to the kid. It's only information that has come from the kid to me that is in play for kid approval. If I need to, I'll make this point. What I'm looking for approval to share is the particular list of fun activities we've developed (see the text that follows).

d. I'll sometimes also ask if any parent has done the exercise with the kid, which is something I would have mentioned is a good idea in the waiting room after the physiological calming session. Families are pretty much always in run-and-gun mode, so it isn't a big deal to me if a parent hasn't done this following my slap-dash mentioning of it. It is just information that's useful to me before I explain the intervention to the parents.

e. Again, kids usually agree to this pretty readily. There's nothing controversial on the coping/happy thoughts list. It tends to be as controversial as puppies and rainbows.

f. This is a commonly used technique in psychotherapy. Artful mental health professionals (MHPs) set an empathic context before bringing up any undesirable behaviors. *Bob, I know you're working two jobs, raising three kids, trying to keep your wife happy, and helping your mom out when you can. So, it's like you're Atlas trying to hold up the world by yourself. Given that, it may sometimes feel overwhelming when a new stress appears, causing you to yell when you really don't want to.* It's the same technique here; it's effective across the life span. The one thing that's a little different with kids is that I'll state what I know to be some of the kid's top time commitments that could be interfering with doing the therapy practice.

g. This is another common technique across the life span. We're not selling. We are helping people to get where *they want to go*. If I ever start feeling like I'm selling, I try to refocus the discussion on the client's goals. In this context, kids nearly universally hate how they get when their internal enemy is winning.

h. This part of the conversation is for kids who are usually not complying, mostly because they are kids and a lot of what we've discussed in sessions flies out of their heads by the time they are back home. So, it's a developmental issue and getting a parent involved is helpful. Should a kid refuse after our back and forth, I'll say something like this: *Okay, Monica, I'll make you a deal. If you do your practicing this week, and your mom or dad confirm that with me, then I'll leave this alone. However, if your homework, soccer, and your other things you have to do keep getting in the way for another week, then I'll need to discuss this with your parents. Deal?* This is me making the kid "an offer she can't refuse" (I wish I could do a better job of impersonating Marlon Brando in *The Godfather*).

i. Homework could be agreeing on what fun activities the kid will do and/or how often she will do the relaxation exercise (i.e., depending on how the biofeedback data are looking), reviewing potential cobra attacks coming up, reviewing what coping thoughts might be used to get through, and any other tasks that might facilitate the kid taking her next steps forward toward her treatment goals.

Additional Commentary

Engaging the parents has numerous potential benefits: strengthening the parent–kid affective bond, enhancing kid compliance with therapy practice, resolving adjunctive issues that impact the prognosis of reaching the treatment goals, and increasing the odds that the kid will become skillful with, and continue to use, the cognitive behavioral (CBT) techniques, especially posttermination. In my decades of doing this, I can't think of a time when I wasn't interested in engaging the parents. The only instance in which I hesitate is if the relationship with the parent is too troubled (e.g., the parent has an active addiction) and the parent needs some treatment first. Otherwise, engaging parents, or parent-figures, is just too important to not do.

When I described the treatment course to the parents, during the feedback session, I would have said that I planned to meet them to give them updates and to engage them in the work, so it won't be a surprise when I ask to schedule this session. Assuming the kid has authorized it, I'll also ask the parents to bring the kid's binder to the next appointment. By the way, if your kid client really needs to not miss a week, and the family has the resources and motivation to comply, and you have the time in your schedule, you could always do two sessions in a week: the regular kid session and this parent consultation. There is rarely any harm in doing so; it's just that it may be too much for many families to engage in any given week.

THE PARENT CONSULTATION

The man (or woman) who can make hard things easy is the educator.
—Ralph Waldo Emerson

As you can tell from what you've read so far in this chapter, the agenda for these meetings can vary quite a bit. What I'll do here is describe what, for me, is a modal parent consultation outline:

    I. Agreeing on the agenda for the session

   II. Asking for updates

  III. Reviewing the to-date CBT modules

      a. Externalizing the problem

      b. Behavioral activation (when depression is the primary target) or physiological calming (when anxiety is the primary target)

      c. Coping/happy thoughts

  IV. A review of the special time technique

   V. A review of upcoming meetings

I. Agreeing on the agenda for the session. I usually open with something like this:

Roberto and Paula, it's nice to see you again. Before we start, I'd like to set an agenda for today. So let me review what I'm hoping we'll discuss and then see if you'd like to add to it or change it. First, I'd like to get an update from you about how Monica is doing. Then I'd like to share what I've been doing with her and how I believe it's been going. Third, I'd like to give you an exercise to do with her that will very much help our shared efforts. And, finally, I'd like to go over the next steps. How does that sound? Anything you'd like to change or add?

If parents say anything it tends to just be an update. Every now and again someone will add an agenda item, so we may do a back and forth so that I understand it and know how much time I need to leave to cover it; this usually pertains to some stressor that the parents wish to discuss.

II. Asking for updates. I will say something like this:

Okay, so how has Monica been doing? . . . What has she been saying, if anything, about our sessions? . . . Notice any improvements or worsening of symptoms? . . .

Most of the time parents will note a new event or two in the family, say the kid doesn't say much about the sessions and they don't pry, and remark on slight to moderate improvement. But if anyone has any concerns I make the time to talk about such.

III. Reviewing the to-date CBT modules. Assuming the kid has authorized such, and assuming the parents have brought the binder—I ask everyone to remember to have the parents bring this—I'll flip through it as I explain the modules. The scripts I use with the parents are often just a regurgitation of the ones I used with their kid. I just don't direct the script at them but review what I covered with their kid and what we came up with. I'll also ask them to not refer to anxiety, worry, or fear anymore, but instead to refer to cobra attacks. I then add:

Roberto and Paula, let me suggest what you might do if the cobra starts to rear its ugly head. Just ask Monica if it could be that she is getting upset because the cobra is after her. If she says "yes," then ask, "What weapon that Dr. Dave has taught you might work here?" You might then either salute her idea or ask about whether a particular strategy might work. If she says that she isn't experiencing a cobra attack, you can offer that you're not so sure and perhaps she might try a cobra weapon just to see if it could help. If Monica won't cooperate with you, just say something like, "Well, I'm sorry that you're feeling bad. I think it's the cobra at work, but I hear you that you don't want to fight it. That's not the way I'd go if I were you because I see it's painful, but I realize it's up to you. Let me know if you change your mind." Then separate from her. The problem is that if you continue to engage her you may end up saying or doing things that actually either strengthen the cobra attack or increase the frequency of cobra attacks. (This is what I'll say at this point to parents who have a kid whose primary problem is anxiety.) *I'd like to give you three examples of things that don't work.*

The first are reassurances. These can result in the exact opposite of the intended effect. Can you imagine how you might react if I said to you, "Don't worry about the ceiling collapsing on our heads. It's strong and won't fall down on us." You'd probably start thinking about the ceiling and wondering why I'd say that. And your level of tension would probably rise. In this context, a reassurance is like saying to a kid, "Time to start freaking out now."

The second is avoidance. We parents love our kids so much it makes us crazy people. When our kid hurts, most of us hurt worse. So, when our baby says that something is causing her pain, it's only natural to avoid that thing. The problem is that avoidance usually strengthens the cobra; it often makes the anxiety stronger, often spreading to other areas, at least in instances when the thing that is making her anxious is age appropriate and not truly dangerous.

The third thing is harshness. It often comes from a good motivation: You can't stand to see your baby hurting and you want her to feel better. But when she gets in her own way and won't listen to what's helpful, you understandably get frustrated. After all, no engaged parent is happier than her least happy child. So, you get frustrated and want to snap her out of it. But this rarely will work and often makes things worse.

(This is what I'll say to parents whose kid's primary problem is depression.) *I'd like to give you two examples of things that don't work.*

The first are reassurances. These can result in the exact opposite of the intended effect. If a kid isn't depressed, comes home with a low grade, says "I'm stupid!" and the parent offers factual contradicting information, the kid usually feels better. However, if a kid has an enemy like the iceman and the same situation occurs, parental reassurances are heard like, "You don't have any cause to feel depressed!" Which only makes the kid dig in deeper into depressive thinking and offer additional evidence that he is stupid. Which can then make the parent work even harder to prove the point, until both escalate to a point of significant frustra-tion. (Parents often nod their heads here, but if not, and I'm concerned they might not know what I mean, I'll ask for examples.)

The second thing is harshness. (I just repeat what I just reviewed regarding harshness with anxiety, adapted for depression.)

(Returning now to language for all parents.) *Now, what you CAN do is one of two things: First, you can ask if it's a cobra attack and see if you can partner with Monica on using her therapy weapons. Or, second, if she refuses, separate from her, exiting with an empathic remark like, "I'm sorry that you're making the choice to let the cobra win. Let me know if you change your mind." That's about all you can do. If Monica won't take separation as an answer and hounds you, you could consider putting her in a time-out, which is a technique I'll cover with you another time. Any questions? . . . Mind saying back to me how to respond to cobra attacks so that I can make sure I explained it well?*

IV. A review of the special time technique, which I've adapted from Russell Bark-ley's exercise in the *Defiant Children* treatment manual. For years I researched this question: What parenting strategies best promote resilience in their kids? At first I asked, What parenting strategies best promote happiness in their kids? But I learned that was a redundancy, as the same things that promote resilience also promote happiness. The result of this research, reflection, and dialogue with child clinicians and researchers was my parenting book *Working Parents, Thriving Families: 10 Strate-gies That Make a Difference.* Of the 10 parenting interventions in this book, my favor-ite one is special time, which is the first chapter. For a full accounting of the rationale for this module, I'd direct your attention there. For our purposes here, let me share what I say to parents about this technique:

Doesn't it seem like we parents are running and gunning more and more as each year goes by? For instance, there are survey data out there suggesting that fami-lies share more meals in automobiles than around kitchen tables and that the aver-age American father spends 9 minutes one-on-one each week with his teenage child. With all of this crazy busyness, we start buying into a false idea. The false idea is that the time we give to our relationships is the time that's left over after life's obligations have been met. The problem with that is that for most of us, there is no time left over after we've gotten done what we need to get done. So, that extra time is as mythical as a unicorn. For this reason we end up treating our relationships like cacti instead of the orchids that they are. But, if we treated an orchid like a cactus, we wouldn't blame the orchid when it inevitably showed symptoms. Yet, this is what we do with our relationships: We blame them instead of appreciating that we have a maintenance problem.

The exercise I want to review today is called "special time." It is designed to increase the odds that you will remain close to Monica, and she will feel valued by you, even though your life may feel like a grenade range.

The technique sounds simple to do but it is not. Special time involves spending one hour a week, one-on-one, with Monica doing nothing but: one, attending to her; two, proportionally and specifically praising her; and three, expressing positive thoughts and emotions toward her. You can do special time in one of two ways. First, you can wait until Monica is doing some activity that you can praise her for—for example, drawing, shooting baskets, playing a video game. Then saddle up next to her, watch what she is doing, proportionally praise that which you believe is praiseworthy, and express positive thoughts and feelings that you are having about her. If Monica is watching TV, and this is the only time you can do special time, have someone else turn the TV off 30 minutes before you wish to start special time. Monica is unlikely to just sit there but will start to do something that is more likely to be special time compatible.

The second method is just to tell Monica that you'd like to spend some special time with her, as she matters so much to you and you love her so; then ask her what she'd like to do that you can watch.

If you had a video recording of a parent doing special time well, only three verbs and their synonyms would describe that parent's behavior: attending, praising, and expressing positive thoughts and feelings. If you are doing special time well, you ought to be able to have your hands in your pockets, except to maybe rub Monica's back or tussle her hair. Special time is different from quality time. Quality time is a great thing. If there was more of it there'd be fewer prisons. But, when I'm sharing quality time with one of my children something else, besides my child, is capturing my attention. If I go to a ball game with my son I am giving him attention, yes, but I am also giving the game and our surroundings attention too. On the other hand, when I watch him, as a master-Jedi, battling the dark side of the force, and comment on his skill with a lightsaber, I'm doing special time. Quality time is 70% attention; special time is 100% attention.

During special time, avoid teaching, inquiring, sharing alternative perspectives, correcting, or moralizing. All of these are valuable parenting verbs, but they can be done during the rest of the week. Special time is just for attending, praising, and expressing positive thoughts and feelings. "I like your choice of color for that tree." "Great shot!" "I could never advance through those levels so quickly, very good." "I love spending time alone with you." "Your speed on those skates is remarkable." "Have I told you lately that no one matters more to me than you?" Start out trying to find something legitimate to affirm or praise every minute or so; you'll find the right dosing of praise that works for Monica, with practice.

Sometimes it might be hard to do special time while Monica is doing an activity. If so, you can do it during a conversation, but a very different kind of conversation.

During this conversation, you would be listening and pointing out only that which you value, appreciate, or admire: "I never looked at it that way." "You have a creative mind." "That's one of the things that I most admire about you, your loyalty to your friends." "I have a lot of respect for how well you handled yourself in that situation." If you hear things you don't like, bite your tongue and wait until you hear something you can value and endorse. You can offer alternative perspectives, teach, moralize, direct, and so forth, during the other 112 some odd hours of waking time during the week. So, doing special time during a conversation is akin to being an effective in-law: You say what you like and be quiet about the rest!

What I would ask is that you spend 20 minutes doing special time each day with Monica over the next week. After that, I'd suggest setting a target of at least one hour each week with her. It can be done all at once, which is how I do it, or you can break it up into segments—for instance, three 20-minute periods or two 30-minute periods. I refer to this hour as the minimal, weekly attentional requirement for any healthy family relationship. In our country we know how often to change the oil in our cars, how often to floss our teeth, and how much exercise we should get. We might not always do what we know, but we know what to do when we are acting with intention. However, ask around, "What's the minimal amount of undivided time that relationships need each week to do well?" Most people find the question foreign, never mind the answer. If we don't maintain our cars properly the indicator lights go off. The same thing goes for our relationships—it's just that we often misinterpret the indicator lights or, worse yet, blame them.

Imagine what it would be like to have someone whose opinion you value watch what you do for an hour and tell you, with sincerity, what he values about your performance. "Y'know it was hard for you to get up today. You were up late ironing our kids' clothes after a long day of putting them first. Not only did you get up without complaint, but you also maintained your patience throughout a trying morning and kept your focus on our son's needs. Have I told you lately how awesome of a mother you are?" Imagine one hour of that a week each week: authentic and accurate acknowledgment of the goodness of you by someone you care about. For many of us this could feel like coming upon a crackling, warm fire while traversing a frozen tundra. For kids it is incredibly powerful.

I've seen S-O-O-O many stories of special time having a transformative impact on a parent–kid relationship. People say things like, "I've found out how to be close again," or "I wish I knew about this years ago," or "This has taught me that I was being way more critical than I knew." Once you see the effect on your child you will be sold on the power of special time.

I will tell you, though, that sometimes kids fight it. I think this can happen for one of two reasons. Imagine that you had an ambivalent relationship with a boss and there was more tension there than you thought was healthy. Then, all of a sudden, the boss started acting really nice. It could throw you a little bit. You wonder, "What's going on?" "Is he setting me up for some bad news?" "Trying to *cut my hours?" "What's up with this?" So, some kids can be a little suspicious at the start. But, if the boss persists you'd find yourself just giving in. So it is, too, with your kid should she balk at first. I've worked with a lot of kids with some pretty hard bark on them, but I've never seen a kid not give in if a parent lovingly persists. Actually, my personal record is one especially willful 10-year-old girl who fought her parents on it for 3 weeks before she folded. The second reason is illustrated when you come out of a dark movie theater in the middle of a sunny and bright day. The sun is too much. It's lovely, but your eyes have to get used to it. Ever have someone close to you try to tell you how wonderful you are for a few minutes straight? I mean it's divine, but many of us can't take it and try to change the subject or water it down. Then, later on, we enjoy the comments and wondered why we needed to dilute them. So, too, it can be with special time, which is why you'll vary your dosing of verbal praise based on how your kid reacts to it. What do you think? . . . When could each of you do it this week?*

Common Questions and Concerns About Special Time

Parent: *I'm just so busy with work during times that Monica is free.*

MHP: *You do work so very hard for your family, don't you? It must be exhausting sometimes. Well, there are several things you could try. You could take her out for breakfast before school, or sit on her bed for 20 minutes at night before she goes to sleep. Plus, remember, we're only talking about 20 minutes each day this week. Later on, it throttles back to an hour a week, which many can do on the weekends much more easily.*

Parent: *She's just so angry with me, I think she's going to fight this.*

MHP: *Not an unusual problem, so join that club. Kids are tough sometimes. You open your veins for them and they despise you for how you do it. But, if you stay after it, and assuming I've understood Monica's problems correctly, this should work out fine. For now, you might try doing special time on car drives when you're taking her places. The lack of eye contact can be less intimidating. Or you can try arriving at a movie she wants to see, that you approve of, 20 minutes before the commercials start. Or . . . (here I might repeat the bed and breakfast ideas).*

Parent: *But what about my other kids?*

MHP: *I think special time is great for every kid.*

Parent: *OMG, I have four kids. Haven't you been listening to our schedules? How can I make 4 hours a week to do this thing?*

MHP: *That is a lot, isn't it? And I hear how overwhelming that sounds. But, let me change the question. Let's say you purchased an acre lot, the perimeter of which was adorned with beautiful rose bushes. You, having never owned rose bushes before, seek out a gardening consultation. Your consultant tells you that you need to water, prune, fertilize, and spray insecticide for each of the rose bushes. You then say, "OMG, but haven't you been listening to our schedules? How can I do all of that for an acre's worth of rose bushes?" There's just no getting around the maintenance needs of relationships, even though all of us, me included, try to do that from time to time.*

Parent: *This sounds easy to do, no?*

MHP: *It does sound easy, doesn't it? But, no, it's actually pretty hard to do consistently. The top-two traps I run into are, first, time—and saying things like, "I've got to find the time to do this." With special time, at least if it's done weekly, I have to say to myself, "What important thing isn't going to get done this week so that I make sure to have enough time to do special time?" The second trap is to confuse it for quality time. With few exceptions, the only thing that should be getting my attention, if I'm doing special time well, is my kid. Imagine the difference between two scenarios. In the first, you and your good friend go bowling, share some laughs, and have a good time. Fun, right? Good for your friendship, right? But, in the second scenario, your friend asks that you take a 20-minute break from the bowling as your friend has something to say to you. Your friend then spends that time, in an interactive way, telling you about your strengths and the value you hold in your friend's life. Different, right? Special time is much more intense with the attention and authentic acknowledgments.*

Parent: *So, you're implying that the two of us (gesturing to the other parent) should do weekly special time also?*

MHP: *What do you think?*

Parent: *I think we should. (Other parent nods.)*

MHP: *What do you think the impact could be if you did it each week across time?*

Parent: *Pretty amazing. (Other parent nods.)*

MHP: *Sounds like you have all the wisdom you need on that one.*

V. After having worked with the kid for a few sessions, and having gotten a feel for how the parent work will proceed, I will map out a rough schema of next steps. This review will often include things like: (1) when I might want to meet with the parents next, (2) about how many more modules I plan to do with the kid, including how many may need to include the parents, and (3) whether we'll need any augmenting interventions and how we might implement and integrate them (e.g., a school staffing). I try to make it very clear that this is only a rough draft of next steps and it is open to change based on emerging developments. I also try to leave time for any new questions or concerns the parent(s) may have, given the content I covered in this session. Later in this chapter I elaborate a little more on some of these issues.

Parent Sessions for Divorced or Separated Parents

This is one of the more complex topics that child MHPs deal with routinely. *In the ideal*, it's good to have all parents, including stepparents, involved in this session. However, there are common tensions that can interfere with this recommendation. What follows is a list of those issues that I've often seen and what I typically recommend to do about it:

▶ Problem: The birth parents continue to battle in the courts or otherwise maintain a hostile relationship. Common suggestion: therapy with the parents alone. This therapy would be designed to quell their conflict.

▶ Problem: One of the stepparents had an affair with one of the birth parents while that person was still married to the other birth parent. Common suggestion: individual therapy for the person who was cheated on, in order to get peace and perspective about that.

▶ Problem: One of the stepparents experiences harmony between the birth parents as a threat. Common suggestion: a consultation with that couple to see if one session could make a difference; if not, a referral for individual therapy for that stepparent and consideration of going forward with the parent work without that parent attending.

▶ Problem: One of the stepparents doesn't want to come in. Common suggestion: a phone call to that person to see if that could help (using techniques reviewed in other sections of this volume), but then going forward without that person if need be.

▶ Problem: One of the birth parents doesn't want to come in. Common suggestion: same strategy as preceding issue.

Once you have all of the cooperative parents in the room that you're going to get, it's just a matter of reviewing the material in pretty much the same way I have described so far. The only significant difference is that some parent(s) may not have the opportunity to do special time daily. In these instances, we take what we can get.

FUNERAL EXERCISE

Ever has it been that love knows not its own depth until the hour of separation.
—*Kahlil Gibran*

In my decades of doing this work, I've discovered that most people carry within themselves profound insights. However, they often don't know how to access this wisdom. Therefore, I liken my clients' minds to cottages in the woods that have deep wells of wisdom surrounding them. My job is to help them find the path to those wells. One such well of wisdom is the perspective of life through the lens of death. So, whenever an adult client tells me she doesn't have the time to do something we've agreed is advisable, I lay the following exercise on her, which I've adapted from Stephen Covey's *The 7 Habits of Highly Effective People*. Likewise, I use it with parents when I have time in this session or, in a subsequent session, if I'm told that life's obligations are interfering with doing special time consistently. (I'd estimate that I have time to do it in this session only about a third of the time.) This is what I say when I have time in this session or in a subsequent session:

Roberto and Paula, I've found that many parents struggle to make the time to do special time on a consistent basis. They very much want to do it—it's just that there's just too much to do each week. However, I've come across an exercise that really helps to create perspective regarding this problem with time. If it's okay with you, I'd like to close today with that exercise. What I'll ask you to do in a moment, if you're game, is close your eyes and imagine some scenes I'm going to describe. Try to imagine what each of your senses would experience in each scene, the sights, the sounds, the smells, and so forth. The only caution I'd say is that you wouldn't want to do it if you're struggling with depression or grief (a). Would it be okay to try it? . . . Okay, good. Put your heads back on the couch, get comfortable, and close your eyes. . . .

▶ *The first scene is in the morning of a sad day. It's sad because you're going to the funeral of someone you love a lot. It's not your spouse or one of your kids. But you love this person a lot, so you're sad. Imagine getting ready in the bedroom area of your residence.* (Allow 30–45 seconds.)

▶ *Okay, now you're in the kitchen area of your residence and you're going to make breakfast for yourself and those with whom you live. Imagine doing that and interacting with your family.* (Allow 30–45 seconds.)

▶ *Now you're going to commute to the funeral home. You're going to drive. It's a sunny and warm day. Imagine the route you'll take and the dialogue you'll engage in on the commute.* (Allow 30–45 seconds.)

▶ *Now you pull up to the funeral home and park your car. As you approach the home you notice family and friends standing about outside because it's a nice day. Imagine who you'll run into and the exchanges you'll have as you work your way into the home.* (Allow 30–45 seconds.)

▶ *Now you're inside the home, making your way to your seats. As you do so you run into other family and friends. Imagine those brief encounters.* (Allow 30–45 seconds.)

▶ *Okay, now you're in your seat and you decide to go up to pay your respects by yourself, leaving those you've traveled with behind. As you approach an open casket you have the shock of a lifetime. It's you lying in the casket. This is your funeral. It's your life that is now over . . . but you're lying in the casket conscious, thinking about what it has all meant. At first your thoughts turn toward what you celebrate about your life. What are those thoughts?* (Allow 45–60 seconds.)

▶ *Now, inevitably, your thoughts turn toward your regrets. What are your regrets now that your life is over?* (Allow 45–60 seconds.)

▶ *Now people who knew you well are going to stand and give an accounting of the meaning of your life. What might you hear?* (Allow 45–60 seconds.)

Okay, folks, we've done enough for my purposes, so you can open your eyes now (b). *The gift of death to the living is perspective. In my years of doing this exercise with many people I've yet to hear anyone say, "I wish I had more time to do laundry." Or, "I wish I could have worked more overtime." Or, "I should have gotten that leaky roof repaired sooner." No, people have thoughts that are probably very similar to the ones you're having. These are the same thoughts that people shared in texts and cell phone calls in the Twin Towers on 9/11 when they knew what they were facing. It's the same content that those on their deathbeds share, as in the book* **Tuesdays With Morrie** *or in the YouTube* Last Lecture *series. Death gives us acute perspective and wisdom. I would suggest that special time is a deathbed-compatible exercise and that many things that could interfere with it this week are probably not* (c). *I'm not going to ask you what thoughts and feelings you had doing this exercise, but you have the opportunity to share with each other on the drive home or later on, if you'd like, that is* (d).*

Okay, so in closing, let's review. You'll:

1. *Stop talking about Monica's anxiety and start talking about cobra attacks.*

2. *Look for opportunities to reinforce the therapy weapons I've taught her* (renaming what we've covered).

3. *Avoid reassurances, avoidance, and harshness—not that you are necessarily doing these things, just saying.*

4. *Each of you do 20 minutes of special time a day with Monica, for the next week, then throttle back to one hour a week going forward until she waves her little hand goodbye as she moves out of your home* (e).

Explanation

a. In the large majority of instances I'll have an informed inkling, from the initial evaluation, whether a given parent might be struggling with depression or grief. So, this language is mostly a caution I offer when I'm with an audience during a presentation. However, it never hurts to err on the side of caution. If a parent said that she was struggling with depression or grieving, I'd suggest that she just listen along and not do the exercise.

b. This exercise tends to generate powerful feelings and thoughts. The first couple of times I used it I felt ambivalent about it, wondering if I was being too manipulative. However, I surveyed several groups of parents that I was working with years ago and the unanimous feedback I received was that I should continue using it, as it focused attention on the key issues.

c. I think it's only after doing this exercise that this point has sufficient meaning attached to it. Before I started doing this exercise, parents would nod and acknowledge this point and then come in the next week telling me how their hectic family lifestyle kept them from doing special time. I don't hear this nearly as much, however, after parents do this funeral exercise. They've found their wisdom and don't need for me to lecture them about it; they'll still often struggle, as most of us do, but they understand what's at stake.

d.   I never ask parents to share the content of their imagery, as I don't need to know it—the themes are not that varied across people anyway—and it would be, in my opinion, voyeuristic to ask. However, I encourage them to consider the opportunity to share the content with each other.

e.   I often write this action plan down for parents and believe it's generally a good idea to do that.

ADDITIONAL PARENT SESSIONS

As you'll see in the chapters on thought testing and problem solving, I often teach kids these interventions with at least one parent in the room. However, when it comes to scheduling additional parent meetings I can offer some guidelines:

▶   As I've discussed elsewhere in this volume, it varies how many interventions kids need to reach their goals. But, whenever I've taught a kid a sufficient number so that reviewing them with a parent would take a full session, I schedule one.

▶   Parents become acculturated to the sort of material that is helpful for me to know. Hence, they will often call, or let me know at the start or end of a session, when they need to schedule an appointment with me.

▶   Additional sessions may need to be scheduled to deal with collateral concerns. These are some examples of what seems to be a near endless list of possibilities:

- A teen has graduated from high school and there needs to be a plan developed for going away to college.

- A parent plans to remarry and wants some guidance on how to discuss this with his child.

- A major surprising stress is about to happen and parents want help in figuring out how to parent around it (e.g., a decision to change the kid's school, parents have decided to divorce, a mom has been diagnosed with cancer).

- Parents have learned that a teen has started having sex.

- A kid has started to be bullied in school.

If you are new to this, it might seem overwhelming as you wonder, "What the *&^% would I do if that happened?!" But, to that concern I can offer three reassurances. First, you never need to be alone with this. Sure, if you have an assigned supervisor, or supervisors, you are prescriptively not alone. But, there are listservs, contacts with your state and national professional associations, and all sorts of professional groups and relationships that are available to you, often at no charge. One of the things that delights me as a psychologist is how generous colleagues are with their time and support when a difficult case or question comes along. So it's unlikely that you'd ever have to go at it alone, unless that's your preference. Second, once you've been doing this for a while, you start to delight in the fact that once you've seen one family you've seen one family (e.g., as I type this, I just had my first occurrence of a parent, at the point of a first interview with her adult child, treating that working and married and 50-something child like a 10-year-old). There is very little about this work that lends itself to going somewhere else mentally because you've already packaged that widget 5,006 times. Third, the principles underlying what we do remain the same, though the content and context before us varies widely. This is why, throughout this volume, I explain the whys of what I do. Once you have these schemata in place, you'll usually have a strong grounding for when surprising events happen. And, if not, you can call your colleague.

SIDEBAR 9.1

Yet another staple among magicians is invisible thread (IT), which you can purchase for under $5. This thread comes in a visible shoelace-thick single strand. However, that thread is composed of about a hundred singular ITs, each one of which is nearly impossible to see when using it to do a trick. To detach a single piece of thread you'll need a white background you can lay the thread on (so you can see it), scissors, and tape or sticky wax. Place the thicker strand on the white background and separate out a single thread (you may need a magnifying glass if your vision isn't sharp). Attach the end of that thread to a piece of tape or sticky wax. Then gently separate that single strand from the larger strand. For this trick you're going to want to cut the thread at a length that goes from the back of your ear to the top of where you would wear a belt. After you cut it (and make sure to keep it on the white background), tape the other end of the strand to the back of a Bicycle deck playing card, right at the center dot.

You now have one strand of IT, one end of which is attached to tape or sticky wax, and the other end of which is attached to the back of a playing card. Attach the tape to the back of your ear; if you wear glasses, attach it there. You'll note that the card just dangles at the top of your belt line. However, if you take one corner and give it a spin, it will rotate like a helicopter blade.

You can develop many different kinds of patter for this trick. I say that I've been working on manipulating air currents in the room by positioning my

(continued)

SIDEBAR 9.1 *(continued)*

> body in certain ways. I hold up the card, commenting that it's just an ordinary card (magicians are lying liars, but in a fun, prosocial way). I stand up, hunch over a little, point the toes of my right foot to the ceiling, and give the card a spin. After you've practiced it, you can move the card horizontally from hand to hand (motioning with your hand but not touching the card) by gently swaying your body, or even turn your body 360 degrees as the spinning card follows you around.
>
> On YouTube you can find multiple illustrations of tricks you can do with IT (e.g., spinning coins or floating napkins and dollar bills). If you'd like a good DVD that illustrates clever uses of IT, I'd recommend *The Art of Levitation* by Arthur Tracz.

REFERENCES AND BIBLIOGRAPHY

Allen, J. P., Hauser, S. T., Bell, K. L., & O'Connor, T. G. (1994). Longitudinal assessment of autonomy and relatedness in adolescent-family interactions as predictors of adolescent ego development and self-esteem. *Child Development, 65*(1), 179–194.

Amato, P. R. (1994). Father–child relations, mother–child relations, and offspring psychological well-being in early adulthood. *Journal of Marriage and the Family, 56*(4), 1031–1042.

Asarnow, J. R., Goldstein, M. J., Tompson, M., & Guthrie, D. (1993). One-year outcomes of depressive disorders in child psychiatric in-patients: Evaluation of the prognostic power of a brief measure of expressed emotion. *Journal of Child Psychology and Psychiatry, 34*(2), 129–137.

Barkley, R. (1997). *Defiant children: A clinician's manual for assessment and parent training* (2nd ed.). New York, NY: Guilford Press.

Burt, S. A. (2009). Rethinking environmental contributions to child and adolescent psychopathology: A meta-analysis of shared environmental influences. *Psychological Bulletin, 135*(4), 608–637.

Butzlaff, R. L., & Hooley, J. M. (1998). Expressed emotion and psychiatric relapse: A meta-analysis. *Archives of General Psychiatry, 55*(6), 547–552.

Clark, K. E., & Ladd, G. W. (2000). Connectedness and autonomy support in parent–child relationships: Links to children's socioemotional orientation and peer relationships. *Developmental Psychology, 36*(4), 485.

Cobham, V. E., Dadds, M. R., & Spence, S. H. (1998). The role of parental anxiety in the treatment of childhood anxiety. *Journal of Consulting and Clinical Psychology, 66*(6), 893–905.

Covey, S. (2004). *The 7 habits of highly effective people.* New York, NY: Free Press.

Dumas, J. E., & Albin, J. B. (1986). Parent training outcome: Does active parental involvement matter? *Behaviour Research and Therapy, 24*(2), 227–230.

Fergusson, D. M. (2003). Resilience to childhood adversity: Results of a 21-year study. In S. S. Luthar (Ed.), *Resilience and vulnerability: Adaptation in the context of childhood adversities* (pp. 130–155). New York, NY: Cambridge University Press.

Fiese, B. H., Tomcho, T. J., Douglas, M., Josephs, K., Poltrock, S., & Baker, T. (2002). A review of 50 years of research on naturally occurring family routines and rituals: Cause for celebration? *Journal of Family Psychology, 16*(4), 381–390.

Fristad, M. A., Davidson, K. H., & Leffler, J. M. (2008). Thinking-feeling-doing: A therapeutic technique for children with bipolar disorder and their parents. *Journal of Family Psychotherapy, 18*(4), 81–103.

Fristad, M. A., Gavazzi, S. M., & Mackinaw-Koons, B. (2003). Family psychoeducation: An adjunctive intervention for children with bipolar disorder. *Biological Psychiatry, 53*(11), 1000–1008.

Goldberg-Arnold, J. S., Fristad, M. A., & Gavazzi, S. M. (1999). Family psychoeducation: Giving caregivers what they want and need. *Family Relations, 48*(4), 411–417.

Levy-Frank, I., Hasson-Ohayon, I., Kravetz, S., & Roe, D. (2011). Family psychoeducation and therapeutic alliance focused interventions for parents of a daughter or son with a severe mental illness. *Psychiatry Research, 189*(2), 173–179.

Miklowitz, D. J., Axelson, D. A., George, E. L., Taylor, D. O., Schneck, C. D., Sullivan, A. E., & Birmaher, B. (2009). Expressed emotion moderates the effects of family-focused treatment for bipolar adolescents. *Journal of the American Academy of Child & Adolescent Psychiatry, 48*(6), 643–651.

Miklowitz, D. J., George, E. L., Axelson, D. A., Kim, E. Y., Birmaher, B., Schneck, C., & Brent, D. A. (2004). Family-focused treatment for adolescents with bipolar disorder. *Journal of Affective Disorders, 82*, S113–S128.

Nagi, C., & Davies, J. (2015). Bridging the gap: Brief family psychoeducation in forensic mental health. *Journal of Forensic Psychology Practice, 15*(2), 171–183.

Nock, M. K., & Ferriter, C. (2005). Parent management of attendance and adherence in child and adolescent therapy: A conceptual and empirical review. *Clinical Child and Family Psychology Review, 8*(2), 149–186.

Palmiter, D. J. (2007). Child clinician's corner: Working with parents. *The Independent Practitioner, 27*, 198–200.

Palmiter, D. J. (2009). Child clinician's corner: Special time. *The Independent Practitioner, 29*, 25–28.

Palmiter, D. J. (2011). *Working parents, thriving families: 10 strategies that make a difference*. North Branch, MN: Sunrise River Press.

Pavuluri, M. N., Graczyk, P. A., Henry, D. B., Carbray, J. A., Heidenreich, J., & Miklowitz, D. J. (2004). Child- and family-focused cognitive behavioral therapy for pediatric bipolar disorder: Development and preliminary results. *Journal of the American Academy of Child & Adolescent Psychiatry, 43*(5), 528–537.

Prinz, R. J., & Miller, G. E. (1994). Family-based treatment for childhood antisocial behavior: Experimental influences on dropout and engagement. *Journal of Consulting and Clinical Psychology, 62*(3), 645–650.

Rutter, M. (1999). Resilience concepts and findings: Implications for family therapy. *Journal of Family Therapy, 21*, 119–144.

Sander, J. B., & McCarty, C. A. (2005). Youth depression in the family context: Familial risk factors and models of treatment. *Clinical Child and Family Psychology Review, 8*(3), 203–219.

Smerud, P. E., & Rosenfarb, I. S. (2011). The therapeutic alliance and family psychoeducation in the treatment of schizophrenia: An exploratory prospective change process study. *Couple and Family Psychology: Research and Practice, 1*(S), 85–91.

Spence, S. H., Donovan, C., & Brechman-Toussaint, M. (2000). The treatment of childhood social phobia: The effectiveness of a social skills training-based, cognitive behavioural intervention, with and without parental involvement. *Journal of Child Psychology & Psychiatry, 41*(6), 713–726.

Utter, J., Denny, S., Robinson, E., Fleming, T., Ameratunga, S., & Grant, S. (2013). Family meals and the well-being of adolescents. *Journal of Pediatrics and Child Health, 49*(11), 906–911.

Wood, J. J., Piacentini, J. C., Southam-Gerow, M., Chu, B. C., & Sigman, M. (2006). Family cognitive behavioral therapy for child anxiety disorders. *Journal of the American Academy of Child & Adolescent Psychiatry, 45*(3), 314–321.

Zisser, A., & Eyberg, S. M. (2010). Parent–child interaction therapy and the treatment of disruptive behavior disorders. In A. E. Kazdin & J. R. Weisz (Eds.), *Evidence-based psychotherapies for children and adolescents* (2nd ed., pp. 179–193). New York, NY: Guilford Press.

CHAPTER 10

Thought Testing and the Serenity Prayer

If you look for truth, you may find comfort in the end. . . .
—C. S. Lewis

THOUGHT TESTING

I told my psychiatrist that everyone hates me. He said I was being
ridiculous—everyone hasn't met me yet.
—Rodney Dangerfield

Most kids receive this material from me with their parents in the room as it's just too complicated to do on their own, unless the kid in question is a psychologically minded and motivated teen. I did this for years without parents in the room and noticed that it's just too tough for most kids to do by themselves. The only times I don't do this with a parent in the room is when the kid has refused to have the parent come in—which is not common—or it seems like the kid is mature and intelligent enough to do the technique well enough on his own, which is the minority of kids, in my experience. The rest of the time, I ask the parent to come in. This is what I say:

Aiden, sometimes there could be a painful thought in your head that's true, while at other times a painful thought could be the iceman's. Like you might get a low score on a test that you didn't study much for and think, "If only I'd studied more I wouldn't have done so bad." So that's probably a painful thought that's true. On the other hand, you might then have a thought in your head like, "I'm stupid and a terrible student," which, given that you get good report cards, wouldn't be true and would be the iceman's lie. This weapon I want to show you today will help you to know if a thought is true or the iceman's lie. To teach you it, I need an example of a thought you had recently that was painful and you weren't sure if it was true or not (a). . . . Okay, so you were thinking that Jared doesn't like you anymore. That thought is like the top of an onion. You know how the onion has layers that you can peel off one at a time? Well, it's the same thing about your thoughts. So we need to get the thought that's at the middle of the onion (b). . . . Good. "I'm not a good friend." That sounds like a thought that's in the middle of the onion. We call that a "core thought" because the middle of the onion is the onion's core. Core thoughts are usually said in a few words and are all-or-nothing thoughts, or black-and-white thoughts about you, other people, or the world around you. Do you know what a black-and-white or all-or-nothing thought is (c)? So, other examples of painful core thoughts would be "all people are selfish," or "the world is evil," or "no one likes me," and so forth. Just like we figured out that your core thought is "I'm not a good friend." So we need to find out if that thought is true or the iceman's lie (d). The first step is to write down the thought at the top of the piece of paper (I write it down). *Next I draw a line down the middle of the paper. On the left side I want to put the facts that suggest you're not a good friend. By "facts" I mean things that a judge would accept in court or a police officer would write down. So, what facts show that you're not a good friend (e)? Okay, good. We have two so far. Anything else? Mom, how about you? Any other facts you can think of that support that Aiden here isn't a good friend? . . . You both sure (f)? . . . Okay, let's do the other side. What facts show that you are a good friend? Mom (g)? . . . Okay, notice that we couldn't think of more on the left side but I had to stop us on the right side because we have enough. Read this and tell me whether the thought that "I'm not a good friend" is true or not (h). Okay, Aiden. So, this is the iceman's lie. He won't stop until all you feel is complete and total depression (i). So you don't have to test whether this thought is true again, at least for a while, because you've just proven it's not true (j). If the iceman tries to put that thought in your head again, you can just remind yourself about this and either do something fun, use a coping thought, or do both. What coping thought might work for the lie that you're not a good friend (k)? Okay, you might be wondering, "But what if the painful thought turns out to be true?" Y'know, sometimes a painful thought does turn out to be true. And, guess what, I'll give you a powerful weapon to deal with those situations next week! See, the iceman has no move that we can't defeat. When you know what to do, he's as weak as a boy in the third grade (l).*

Okay, for this week, I'd like you to try to do two thought testings on your own. You want to wait until there is a painful thought in your head, then make sure you have the onion's core thought. Then write it down. Then put down the facts that suggest the painful core thought is true. Then put down the facts that suggest the painful core thought is not true. Then decide if it's true or the iceman's lie. If it's the iceman's lie, try to do something fun or use a coping thought to fight it. If it's true, just bring it in next week and I'll show you what you can do about that. Any questions? ... Mom, any questions? ... Okay Aiden, you can see this coming. Mind saying it back to me so that I can make sure that I explained it well?

Explanation

a. If I don't have a parent in the room and a kid struggles to come up with an example, I'll invite the parent in for just this part of the session, though not being able to come up with an example would cause me pause about whether the parent should stay in the session, as the sorts of kids who can practice this on their own can usually generate multiple examples on their own and don't need me to bring in their parent. Otherwise, I'll start with the kid, because most of the time he can come up with something. If his struggle becomes *significantly* uncomfortable for him, I'll ask his parent for an example, confirming with the kid that the parent remembers it correctly.

b. Most kids, or even adults for that matter, don't get to the core thought without help. This is a common way it might go:

Kid: *I said hi to Jared and he ignored me.*
MHP: *What do you think that means?*
Kid: *He doesn't like me anymore.*
MHP: *Well, Aiden, there could be lots of reasons why Jared didn't say hi back. He might have had a bad toothache, or maybe he just failed an exam, or maybe he was rushing to the bathroom because he had diarrhea. We don't know. BUT, let's say that was right, that he didn't like you anymore. What would that mean?*
Kid: *That I did something wrong.*
MHP: *If he really didn't like you anymore that also could be for multiple reasons. But let's say you did do something wrong and he didn't like you anymore because you did that. What would that mean?*
Kid: *I'm not a good friend.*
MHP: *So, could that be the middle of the onion, the thought "I'm not a good friend?"*
Kid: *Yeah, that's it.*

I find many clients, across the life span, when they get to the core thought have a nonverbal reaction that sort of says, "OMG, we just hit the nail exactly on the head!" If you get to the right place this becomes a very important exercise for the kid. First, many don't even fully realize that this is a schema that's been causing them pain. Second, it's really bothering the kid, and the fact that you're discussing it implies that he might be freed from it.

It's also important to have the parent witness the method of getting to the core thought. In my years of doing this, across the life span, getting to the core thought is an obtuse matter for many people. So it takes practice and the support of an artful mental health professional (MHP) to learn how to do it right, and consistently so.

c. I don't do this 100% of the time, but I probably should. I think it's worth the moments to drive home the characteristics of a core thought. These are operatic, mental tragedies. "I suck." "No one loves me." "I'm an idiot." "People are cruel," and so forth. They are some of the mightiest weapons that our internal enemies use against us, and they deserve to be called out for the vicious lies that they (usually) are.

d. This is another point that could sometimes use additional elaboration. We want a kid and/or his parent to appreciate that this is the go-to method for discerning the accuracy of painful thoughts. This can be an especially important point for parents with a history of trying to argue against an irrational thought, a methodology that often worsens the distress of kids with an internalizing disorder.

e. This is a very important moment in a kid's life. He is SO used to adults just arguing against pessimistic thinking. The fact that an adult is now saying, "Okay, what'cha got?" is surprising, and the results are usually pretty illuminating. In my experience, a kid usually has two to three facts, at the most, that support the negative thought. Generally, there's an event or two that are bothering the kid and his internalizing disorder would have him extrapolate wildly because of it. Seeing this for himself, instead of having an adult tell him, opens up a new universe, for both the kid and the observing parent.

Most kids (and many adults for that matter) will also need help separating facts from subjective judgments. This is an example of how that exchange might go:

MHP: *So, what facts support that you're not a good friend?*
Kid: *I invited Jake to my party and he didn't come.*
MHP: *How is that a fact that you're not a good friend?*
Kid: *If I was a good friend he'd have come.*
MHP: *Did he tell you why he didn't come?*
Kid: *No.*
MHP: *So, you don't know if his family was doing something that he had to be at?*
Kid: *I guess not.*
MHP: *And you didn't know if he couldn't come because he was puking his guts out because he had eaten some diseased cheese?*
Kid: *(smiling) I guess not.*
MHP: *Okay, so a judge wouldn't admit that evidence in court because it ain't a fact Jack. But you probably have some facts that suggest you're not a good friend. So what else ya got?*

Kid: *Well, another friend, Larry, invited me to his party and I lied and said I couldn't go when I could have gone. I just didn't feel like it.*

MHP: *Okay, that's a fact that supports the notion that you're not a good friend. So, we'll write that one down. "Lied to Larry and didn't go to his party." What else ya got?*

f. I hit this point pretty hard. To do so reinforces that the data for the negative thought are scant at best, in the large majority of instances. This is how internalizing disorders work. Now the kid is seeing this for himself instead of some adult preaching at him things that he doesn't want to hear. This also models for a parent how to proceed with negative thinking going forward. For a parent lecture to lead to behavior change, two conditions must be met: The kid doesn't have the information and the kid wants the information. In family life, how often are these two conditions satisfied? As both a recipient and an author of such lectures within my own family, I wonder (smiling as I type this).

g. Most of the time the kid just starts gushing data contradicting the thought. "I have about 12 good friends." "Susan told me I'm the nicest guy she knows." "I was elected class treasurer." I usually let the kid exhaust himself before I ask the parent if she has additional data. I'll also throw in things like, "On the forms the teachers filled out, they said that you show good leadership skills at school. Is that right?" Every now and again I'll need to have an exchange like this one:

Kid: *Becky smiles at me a lot.*

MHP: *Okay, but how is that a fact that suggests you're a good friend?*

Kid: *Well, she wouldn't smile at me unless I was.*

MHP: *I don't know, I mean there are some people who smile at everyone because that's how they are. Is there something else about your relationship with Becky that's more of a fact?*

Kid: *I guess not. We don't talk or anything. She just smiles at me.*

MHP: *Okay, so a judge wouldn't accept that as evidence that you're a good friend, so we can't use that one.*

I think exchanges like this are useful as they establish that we're not just about disproving things we don't find pleasant. We are, indeed, being objective. So, it enhances the credibility of thought testing to watch for opportunities to do this.

As I mentioned in the script, I usually don't exhaust this side as the data may continue to pour in long after the evidence is much more substantive on the right side. Table 10.1 illustrates how it would typically look at this juncture.

TABLE 10.1 Standard Thought Testing	
Core Thought: "I'm not a good friend."	
Facts Supporting	**Facts Contradicting**
I lied to Larry and didn't go to his party. I gossiped about Peter to Jake. Jessica texted and asked if she could call me about a problem, but I told her I had too much to do.	I have about 12 good friends. I was elected as class treasurer. Susan told me I'm the nicest guy she knows. 25 kids came to my last birthday party. My teachers believe that I'm a good leader. I don't tell others when a friend asks me to keep something secret. Lots of kids tell me about stuff that's bothering them. I'm one of the captains on the basketball team. My priest asked me to try to get other kids to join the church youth group.

h. In the large majority of instances, the kid says of the thought, "It's not true." Every now and again, I'll have a future psychologist before me and we'll have an exchange like this:

Kid: *There may be more on the right side, but gossiping about a friend is pretty terrible, so it kind of outweighs things like having teachers think I'm a good leader.*
MHP: *I hear that. So, let's assign a number to each. From 1 to 100, with 100 being the worst, how bad is it that you lied to Larry about the party?*
Kid: *70*
MHP: *Gossiped about Peter?*
Kid: *90*
MHP: *Didn't make yourself available for Jessica?*
Kid: *60*
MHP: *Okay, now let's do the other side. From 1 to 100, how good is it that you have 12 good friends, with 100 being the best thing?*
Kid: *80*
     (and so forth)
MHP: *Okay, now let's add them both up . . . okay, look again. Is the thought true or not?*

Table 10.2 illustrates what the sheet would look like at this juncture.

TABLE 10.2 Weighted Thought Testing			
Core Thought: "I'm not a good friend."			
Facts Supporting		**Facts Contradicting**	
70	I lied to Larry and didn't go to his party.	80	I have about 12 good friends.
90	I gossiped about Peter to Jake.	70	I was elected as class treasurer.
60	Jessica texted and asked if she could call me about a problem, but I told her I had too much to do.	85	Susan told me I'm the nicest guy she knows.
		83	25 kids came to my last birthday party.
220		65	My teachers believe that I'm a good leader.
		90	I don't tell others when a friend asks me to keep something secret.
		95	Lots of kids tell me about stuff that's bothering them.
		85	I'm one of the captains on the basketball team.
		60	My priest asked me to try to get other kids to join the church youth group.
		713	

i. For teens age 15 or older, or for younger kids who've thought about suicide, I'll add something like, *The iceman's endgame is suicide. He wants to convince you of so many terrible lies that he gets you thinking that suicide is the only way out.* However, if a parent is in the room and suicidal thinking is not a clinical issue with a given kid, I may not make this point unless I intuit that it could be helpful going forward.

j. This is an important point. If the kid is less than blown away (in a good way) by this exercise, I'll spend more time on it, saying things like, *Really, Aiden, the iceman is likely not done trying to put this thought in your head, maybe wrapping a different sort of onion around it. But we've just proven it's not true, so you don't have to bother with it.* In this moment we'll sometimes have an exchange like this:

Kid: *But I shouldn't gossip anyway.*
MHP: *How often do you do that?*
Kid: *Too often.*
MHP: *Okay, well, guess what? The next weapon I'm going to show you, called "problem solving," is useful for situations like that. So stay tuned, brother. We're going to get after that problem, too.*
Kid: *Okay. Good.*

k. The potential coping thoughts have already been developed: They are either already in the kid's binder (from the coping/happy thought session) or on the right side of the exercise that was just completed. By asking the kid we are encouraging him to make these connections for himself.

    In this moment you might also work out what fun things he might try to do if the thought popped into his head outside of school. This can also be a good moment to teach about distraction as a principle. If so, I'll do it like this:

    Aiden, remember when I asked you what you would do next if you put on a tight pair of jeans? . . . Right, you'd change them. So, that's what using your coping thoughts are like. You know, though, that coping thoughts and doing a fun activity have something in common: They both take your mind off the iceman's lie. That's called "distraction." The iceman says, "Hey! Aiden! Look at this painful lie! You suck!" Or, "People hate you!" Or, "You're so stupid!" But you don't have to think about those lies; you think about things that are true and make you feel good, like a coping thought or doing something fun. And when you do that, the iceman loses power and has to get in his cage, whimpering from the butt kicking you just gave him. But there are other distraction techniques. All you have to do is turn your mind to something that will keep it busy. Sure, it can be a coping thought or a fun thing, but it can be other things, like starting your homework or asking Siri to answer an interesting question for you or doing something nice for someone. Anything that is more interesting than the iceman's lie will work. And the iceman hates that! By the way, doing something nice for someone else is a strong weapon, by itself, against the iceman and something I'm probably going to teach you more about another time. What distraction weapons do you think might work for you? . . .

    It's also very helpful for a parent to hear this, as it may tap into a knowledge base that she has but forgot about. How classic is the old "distract the 2-year-old from the fascinating light socket" as a parenting intervention? (If you're not a parent, and end up becoming one, you'll see for yourself how much distraction is needed to maintain your sanity and keep you out of jail.)

    If not in this moment, it's easy to insert this instruction just about anywhere else that it fits. Just listen to—borrowing Theodor Reik's (1948) metaphor—your "third ear," or your intuition. Your intuition is an important tool that likely called you to this profession and is worthy of your nurturance and attention.

l. It never hurts to loop back and reinforce earlier metaphors. I find that all clients, across the life span, often feel powerless in the face of their internalizing disorder(s). We help them rediscover their power and grow in the conviction that if they consistently apply what we teach them—assuming we've properly understood their internal battles—they'll be fine.

Additional Commentary

Insanity: doing the same thing over and over again and expecting different results.
—Albert Einstein

Thought testing is a staple of cognitive behavioral therapy (CBT), though it can be called different things like "cognitive restructuring" or "reframing" or "being a thought detective." I don't believe I've ever encountered an evidence-based CBT treatment manual that didn't include it. And, over time, you will, and should, develop your own unique way of teaching it to kids. It's a remarkably powerful intervention.

The thing that is so radical for kids and parents to learn is that it doesn't work for adults to argue back against a kid's negative thinking. Sure, we adults can be squires in the fight, but the kid is the knight who wields the weapon. We parent-lunatics too often manifest Einstein's famous definition of insanity. Picture a fantasy for a moment. In the fantasy, there's a child, an attacking monster, and a sword. A parent rushes in, picks up the sword, and hacks on the monster. The monster isn't interested in the parent but only the child. With each hack the parent renders, the monster becomes stronger and more successful in its attack on the child. Sounds crazy, right? I mean, wouldn't the parent notice that and stop? But think about it from the parent's perspective. It never occurs to him to give the child the sword and to teach him how to use it. The parent's choices are to let it be—which is rarely a choice for a parent-lunatic who isn't too afflicted by his own psychopathology—or to hack away at the monster. Of course, he will often notice that his hacking makes the monster stronger, which then can cause him to become mighty frustrated and yell at the child metaphorical versions of, "Can you at least run the f**k away, or kick at the monster, or do f*****g something?!" This is part of what drives the parent–child alienation that often presents when kids have been suffering from an internalizing disorder for years.

Want to induce madness in a person (and this is a little bit of a review from Chapter 3 when I discussed damage control treatment contracts)? It's a fairly simple script: Make that person feel responsible for an important outcome but ensure that he doesn't have the power to reach it. In other words, get him to live the antithesis of the Serenity Prayer. This is what happens often when parents have a child with an internalizing disorder. As a parent-lunatic, I certainly care deeply about my kid's wellness and feel an indescribably deep sense of responsibility for it. So, if my kid isn't well, on some level, perhaps even unconsciously, I blame myself at least partially. Moreover, I assign to myself the responsibility to fix my kid's internalizing disorder(s). Yet, even if I'm a master parent, I can't do that for my kid. Only I don't know that and I try, and I try and I try, and I try some more, and I blame my spouse and my spouse blames me, and I blame teachers and maybe try some diets and pills and howling at the moon before, maybe, if I'm in the wise minority, I take my kid to see a good child MHP. But that usually takes years of dancing this terrible dance with my child, and our system, and his internalizing disorder(s) before I do that. So, he and I have probably experienced some damage in our relationship (which, by the way, is another reason why special time is so important to introduce in these cases).

We MHPs come at this from a brand-spanking-new angle, which most of the time proves to be highly relieving and empowering.

Finally, I'll also sometimes use videos to augment thought-testing products. For example, I enjoy showing teen girls, who have vanquished a thought like "I'm ugly," the Dove Beauty Bar videos of the forensic artist who compares the drawings he makes when women describe themselves to the drawings he makes when others describe those same women. It's powerful stuff, at least if you can suspend the judgment of that part of you that knows about research methodology.

SERENITY PRAYER

The truth is, unless you let go, unless you forgive yourself, unless you forgive the situation, unless you realize that the situation is over, you cannot move forward.
—Steve Maraboli

This is another elective module. I use it if I sense that a teen is overly stressed by trying to control important things that are not in his power.

The start to the Serenity Prayer offers a profound piece of wisdom:

> *God grant me the serenity to accept the things I cannot change; courage to change the things I can; and wisdom to know the difference.*

This is how I introduce it to my more mature and/or psychologically minded teen clients:

Aiden, ever heard of the Serenity Prayer (a)? You know, you can be someone who doesn't believe in God and still get a lot of use out of it. The word "prayer" is in the title, and you can use it that way, but you don't have to in order to get the benefit from it. Let's call it the SP for short (b). Let me fill you in on something the iceman tries to do to you. He tries to get you to think you can control important things that you can't control (c). Let me ask you another one of my silly questions. What do you think it would do to you if you told yourself it was your responsibility to make sure no kid in your entire school district ever got bullied? Seriously, you come to think that this is EXTREMELY important and it is 100% YOUR RESPONSIBILITY to solve. What might that do to you? I mean, just picture it and tell me what you think it would do to you (d). . . . Exactly, you'd go nuts. Stopping bullying is pretty important, and you could try to make your own contributions to that, but telling yourself you had failed as a person if you couldn't stop it altogether would probably make you sick. Can you imagine it? I mean, a person thinking such a thing might start to get very depressed (e)! But don't we all sometimes tell ourselves we need to control things that we can't control? I think it's probably as common as body odor. But, let's check, did you ever tell yourself that you're supposed to be in charge of something that you're really not in charge of (f)? So, the SP is really a supercharged kind of coping thought. The tough part is knowing what we can control and what we can't control. Obviously, trying to control all bullying that goes on in a school district is beyond anyone's capacity to control. But, at other times, it can be confusing. Maybe a friend is upset or a test is

IMPOSSIBLE, or your mom has a problem that you feel terrible about or something else. Can you think of a problem in your life, either now or from the recent past, that you were not sure whether you had control over (g)?

Explanation

a. Most teens haven't heard of the SP. If a kid has I'll ask him to share what he knows or remembers about it. Otherwise, I'll share it and ask what the teen thinks it means.

b. I'm careful to not sound like I'm promoting a theological perspective about whether or not there is a God. If a kid has already expressed a belief in God, then I just build on that, making sure to not sound like I'm leading but merely supporting. (If you've ever worked with an adult on ethically integrating that adult's spirituality into your psychotherapy, the approach is the same.)

c. I'll sometimes add a review of other things the internal enemy has tried to do to a particular teen, like engage in black-and-white thinking, encourage lethargy, lie to him about his efficacy, encourage avoidance, promote pessimism, or whatever else has been germane, using examples from our work.

d. Most teens with whom I do this module will answer this kind of question pretty accurately. But, an occasional teen might need some more questions to get there: *Well, do you think he'd be calm or nervous about that? Would he be able to pull it off? What might he tell himself if he thought he was supposed to be able to pull it off but couldn't?*

e. I'll use language that fits the particular teen before me. If it's a teen who becomes hyperkinetic when stressed, I might say, *He'd start running around like a hyperactive squirrel on crack!*

f. This segment isn't that script-friendly because there are so many different ways it could go. If you have a teen living in a family where codependency is active, that could come up. If you have a teen struggling with a tempestuous romance, that could come up. Or teens whose grades fall short of where they want them to be might mention that. So, let me give you an composite example from a 16-year-old regarding a popular one—divorce:

> **Kid:** *I used to feel it was my fault that my parents got divorced.*
> **MHP:** *Tell me what you used to think about that.*
> **Kid:** *I was six when they split up and my younger sister was four. It was terrible. My parents were fighting a lot. One of the things they fought about was me getting in trouble in school. So, when they told us that they were divorcing I thought it was because of me, which felt even worse because of how much it hurt my sister.*
> **MHP:** *Did you tell your parents that?*

Kid: *Sort of, I begged that I'd be better in school if they wouldn't get a divorce.*

MHP: *What did they say?*

Kid: *They said that my school problems had nothing to do with their divorcing, but I thought they were just saying that to try to make me feel better. I didn't believe them because I heard them fighting about that a lot.*

MHP: *So, what effect did thinking your parents' divorce was your fault have on you?*

Kid: *I had nightmares. I didn't want to eat anything. I quit basketball 'cause the last thing I wanted to do was run around with a bunch of little turds. I remember I felt like I was on my own. My parents tried to be nice and say nice things, but that didn't do much.*

MHP: *Looking back at it now, what do you think caused your parents' divorce?*

Kid: *Still haven't figured that out. Probably had a lot to do with my dad's drinking, but I don't know. I just know that it wasn't because of me. Yeah, my being a pain probably didn't help, but it didn't cause it.*

MHP: *How did you figure that out?*

Kid: *I guess just seeing how many kids have divorced parents and talking to Mr. Robinson, my history teacher, in sixth grade. His parents got divorced too, and I guess I could believe him when he told me what I was thinking was stupid.*

MHP: *So, and as we've discussed, the iceman tried to use your parents' divorce against you by making you feel responsible for it. You can see the iceman's cruelty. Even human enemies might give you a pass on the divorce thing, especially at age 6, but not the iceman. And it made you very sick, believing the iceman's lie.*

Kid: *Very sick.*

MHP: *So, the SP is a way to focus yourself on whether the iceman continues to try to use that sort of a weapon against you: trying to make you feel in charge of important things that you can't control. Going forward, the key question is, "Can I really control this thing?"*

Rationale

You know how dentists have been successful in getting the government to put fluoride into our drinking supply? Well, I wish there was a way of getting this construct into our thinking supply. So many types of psychological problems can emerge when a human tries to exert control over important matters over which that human has little or no control; it's no accident that this construct is used in just about all recovery programs.

One of my favorite books is *Breathing Under Water* (Rohr, 2001). In it, the author argues that all adults could benefit from working a 12-step program. His premise is that we all face important situations outside of our control that we try to control and that the 12 steps are the solution to this ubiquitous problem. As a scientist I can't empirically confirm that he's correct. As a clinician, and as a man trying to live on the high road, I believe he's right on the money. While I haven't helped any kid clients work the 12 steps, I have introduced the SP construct to teens with success. Actually, in some instances, it has felt to me like I'm helping the teen to develop an entirely new way of looking at the universe.

SIDEBAR 10.1

This is a card trick you can use to playfully suggest that you can tell when a kid isn't telling the truth. It's a trick I've adapted from a trick called Lie Detector on Gerry Griffin's DVD, *Complete Card Magic—Volume One: Beginner - 14 Easy to Learn Card Miracles*. If I suspect that a kid has told me a lie, I'll lightheartedly ask, *Are you sure?* And then I'll say that I can demonstrate my ability to intuit when his enemy is encouraging him to lie.

Have the kid shuffle a deck of playing cards. Then spell out "L-i-e" then "T-r-u-t-h" with eight cards, facedown. You'll end up with a pile of eight facedown cards. The kid then picks a card from the remainder of the deck, being careful not to show it to you. You put the selected card **third** within the pile of eight, so you now have a pile of nine cards (just break off the top two cards then flutter the rest into your left hand). These are the only nine cards you use in the trick. Put the other cards aside. Tell the kid, *It's up to you if you tell the truth or tell a lie in this trick. First, I'd like you to name the first part of your card. Each card has three parts, there's the King* (hold up one finger) *of* (hold up a second finger) *spades* (hold up a third finger). *Now, I'd like you to name the first part of your card. You can say the truth or lie.* Whatever the kid says, spell it out, so if the kid says "10" spell out t-e-n with three cards. Then put the remainder of the pile (in this case, six cards) on top of the three you just spelled out. Then say, *I'll spell out the second part, U-V* (smiling and spelling out two cards, then putting the other seven on top of those two). Then say, *Okay, you say the suit of the card* (you can name them if the kid doesn't know the four of them) *and you can say the truth or a lie.* Spell out the singular versions (no "s") of heart, spade, and diamond; spell out the plural of clubs and put the rest of the deck on top of it. Then say, *Okay, now I'm going to use my powers to find the truth.* Then spell out T-R-U-T-H. The kid's card is the "H." After the kid reacts, you can cycle back to the suspected lie, asking the kid if the enemy prefers the truth or a lie, revisiting what the kid has asserted.

By the way, if you develop a magic augment to your practice and want to add a fancier device for the same purpose, search the term "magic spirit bell" on ebay.com for a device that currently costs a little over $100.

SIDEBAR 10.2

There are many moments in CBT when a kid MHP helps to dispel an irrational thought. A nice little magic augment in these situations can be done with the use of a thumb tip, which is yet another staple among magicians. Thumb tips are merely hollowed out thumbs that can fit over your thumb; they are available in all skin pigmentations.

(continued)

SIDEBAR 10.2 *(continued)*

> To do this trick, secretly palm a thumb tip in one hand. Then have a kid write the dispelled irrational thought on a piece of paper (e.g., "I'm stupid). With the hand not holding the thumb tip, pick it up and say that the kid just made it disappear with thought testing, "Like this." Then make a hole with the hand holding the hollow thumb tip and push the paper down into the thumb tip. With the last push, use the thumb from the hand that picked up the paper, inserting it into the thumb tip. Then note that the thought has just vanished! Just keep the hand with the thumb tip moving and position it so the thumb, with the tip on it, always points right at the kid. (I'll also keep some extra thumb tips on hand—they are cheap—and give them out to any kid clients who are apprentice magicians.)

REFERENCES AND BIBLIOGRAPHY

Calvete, E., & Cardeññoso, O. (2002). Self-talk in adolescents: Dimensions, states of mind, and psychological maladjustment. *Cognitive Therapy and Research, 26*(4), 473–485.

Chatlos, J., & Estroff, T. W. (2001). Adolescent psychiatry and 12-step treatment. In W. Estroff (Ed.), *Manual of adolescent substance abuse treatment* (pp. 205–227). Washington, DC: American Psychiatric Publishing.

Hogendoorn, S. M., Prins, P. J., Boer, F., Vervoort, L., Wolters, L. H., Moorlag, H., & de Haan, E. (2014). Mediators of cognitive behavioral therapy for anxiety-disordered children and adolescents: Cognition, perceived control, and coping. *Journal of Clinical Child & Adolescent Psychology, 43*(3), 486–500.

Hogendoorn, S. M., Prins, P. J., Vervoort, L., Wolters, L. H., Nauta, M. H., Hartman, C. A., & Boer, F. (2012). Positive thinking in anxiety disordered children reconsidered. *Journal of Anxiety Disorders, 26*(1), 71–78.

Johnson, C. L., & Taylor, C. (1996). Working with difficult-to-treat eating disorders using an integration of twelve-step and traditional psychotherapies. *Psychiatric Clinics of North America, 19*(4), 829–841.

Kaufman, N. K. Rohde, P., Seeley, J. R., Clarke, G. N., & Stice, E. (2005). Potential mediators of cognitive-behavioral therapy for adolescents with comorbid major depression and conduct disorder. *Journal of Consulting and Clinical Psychology, 73*(1), 38–46.

Kazdin, A. E., Siegel, T. C., & Bass, D. (1992). Cognitive problem-solving skills training and parent management training in the treatment of antisocial behavior in children. *Journal of Consulting and Clinical Psychology, 60*(5), 733–747.

Kendall, P. C., & Treadwell, K. R. (2007). The role of self-statements as a mediator in treatment for youth with anxiety disorders. *Journal of Consulting and Clinical Psychology, 75*(3), 380.

Muris, P., Mayer, B., Den Adel, M., Roos, T., & van Wamelen, J. (2009). Predictors of change following cognitive-behavioral treatment of children with anxiety problems: A preliminary investigation on negative automatic thoughts and anxiety control. *Child Psychiatry and Human Development, 40*(1), 139–151.

Muris, P., Mayer, B., Snieder, N., & Merckelbach, H. (1998). The relationship between anxiety disorder symptoms and negative self-statements in normal children. *Social Behavior and Personality*, 26(3), 307–316.

Reik, T. (1948). *Listening with the third ear*. Garden City, NY: Garden City Books.

Rohr, R. (2001). *Breathing under water*. Cincinnati, OH: Franciscan Media.

Ronan, K. R., & Kendall, P. C. (1997). Self-talk in distressed youth: States of mind and content specificity. *Journal of Clinical Child Psychology*, 26(4), 330–337.

Rutter, M. (1999). Resilience concepts and findings: Implications for family therapy. *Journal of Family Therapy*, 21, 119–144.

Schniering, C. A., & Rapee, R. M. (2004). The structure of negative self-statements in children and adolescents: A confirmatory factor-analytic approach. *Journal of Abnormal Child Psychology*, 32(1), 95–109.

Sifton, E. (1998). The Serenity Prayer. *The Yale Review*, 86(1), 16–65.

Treadwell, K. H., & Kendall, P. C. (1996). Self-talk in youth with anxiety disorders: States of mind, content specificity, and treatment outcome. *Journal of Consulting and Clinical Psychology*, 64(5), 941–950.

Vaughn, C., & Long, W. (1999). Surrender to win: How adolescent drug and alcohol users change their lives. *Adolescence*, 34(133), 9–24.

Webb, C. A., Auerbach, R. P., & DeRubeis, R. J. (2012). Processes of change in CBT of adolescent depression: Review and recommendations. *Journal of Clinical Child & Adolescent Psychology*, 41(5), 654–665.

CHAPTER 11

Problem Solving

Problem solving is another staple of cognitive behavioral therapy (CBT). I usually cover it after I have done physiological calming, behavioral activation, coping thoughts, and special time. (Whether I do thought testing before or after is a judgment call.) The methodology for problem solving is a little bit different if it is done with an individual kid or in a family session. Hence, I cover each of those methods.

PROBLEM SOLVING IN A FAMILY SESSION

All happy families are alike; each unhappy family is unhappy in its own way.
—*Leo Tolstoy,* Anna Karenina

At a minimum I like to have the adults the kid lives with, and the kid, attend this session. However, it's ideal to have the other parents attend if there are two households, as long as everyone can be cordial. This is what I say:

I'd like to teach you guys an awesome way to deal with many kinds of problems that come up in a family. This method is classically used in situations when a kid wants to do something but the parents don't want to allow it, though it can be used in other situations as well. In order to teach you how to do this I need a recent problem that you had. This could be one you're dealing with now or it could be one from the past that you never really resolved; that is, time passed and you stopped thinking about it, but you never got on the same page about it. It shouldn't be a huge problem, just one of mild to moderate severity **(a)**. *What do you think would be a good problem to use* **(b)**? *. . . Okay, that's a good one. Monica, you wanted to go to a friend's house for a sleepover last Sunday but, Mom and Dad, you didn't want her to do that because it was a school night. Let's pretend that we could travel back to that Sunday afternoon and we could use this method to solve that problem. Let me show you a form that you can use to solve a problem like this one* (see Table 11.1) **(c)**.

TABLE 11.1 Problem Solving

Date: _____

Problem: _____

_____

Proposed Solutions (Do NOT evaluate until you have generated at least 10 ideas.)	Evaluations			
	+ −	+ −	+ −	+ −

1. _____   _____

2. _____   _____

3. _____   _____

4. _____   _____

5. _____   _____

6. _____   _____

7. _____   _____

8. _____   _____

9. _____   _____

10. _____   _____

11. _____   _____

12. _____   _____

The numbers of ideas with all +s	Give a score from 1 to 10 (10 is best)	Sum
	___ ___ ___ ___	
_____	_____	☐
_____	_____	☐
_____	_____	☐
_____	_____	☐
_____	_____	☐
_____	_____	☐
_____	_____	☐

Action Plan: _____

Okay, so the first step is to write down the problem. This is an important step because many families, when they sit down to solve a particular problem, end up talking about lots of other problems too, some dating back to the Old Testament. By writing it down, you are saying to each other that you will only be discussing this problem, at least until you are finished with it (d). So, each of you write down today's date and the problem we are working on (e). Okay, next is the trickiest part. We want to brainstorm. Brainstorming means coming up with as many possible solutions to the problem that we can WITHOUT EVALUATING THEM (f). This is what trips many people up when trying to solve a problem, evaluating while coming up with the ideas. Just like a light switch cannot be off and on at the same time, our brains cannot be fully creative if we try to evaluate at the same time. Imagine every time an artist completed a stroke on her painting she stood back and gave it a rating. It would be very hard for her to be fully creative. So too it is with solving problems. We want to think of as many ideas as we can to solve this problem, without evaluating them. Actually, we want to keep going until we have 10 ideas and 2 minutes of silence. That means we might have 3 minutes of silence between ideas six and seven, but we keep pressing on. And once we have 10 ideas, the ideas may still keep flowing, so we go with it until we have 2 minutes without a new idea coming forward (g). One other thing: We want to make sure that everyone has the same idea on each numbered line, so let's not go too fast. Okay, who has the first idea (h)? . . . Awesome. Now see these four lines on the top right of your form, under the word "evaluations"? Let's fill in Mom, Dad, and Monica on each of those (i). Now it's time to evaluate. Each of you, under your column, privately write either a plus or a minus. A plus indicates that the idea is at least a tiny bit okay in your mind. Of course, it might also be an awesome idea. It's just that you put a plus if it's at least a little bit decent. You put a minus sign if you think the idea is a bad idea. Go ahead and do your ratings, privately, without discussing them (j). Okay, time to share. What I'll do is name the number and you each say if you gave the idea a plus or a minus: Idea #1 (k) . . . Idea #2. . . . Okay, that's the first one that you all gave a plus to, so write that down below, on the bottom left on the first line under the words that say "The number of ideas with all +s" (l). Okay, you all think that four out of the 10 ideas are at least a little bit good. This is the mini-miracle of this problem-solving technique. In my decades of teaching families this method, I've had only ONE family that didn't have at least one idea with straight pluses, and that family wasn't really ready for this because they were still so angry at each other (m). It's amazing that when you take the time to do this how often you will find common ground, which makes it a lot harder to stay upset with each other. Okay, now let's see which of these ideas you like the best as a family. See the lines under "Give a score from 1 to 10" on the lower right? Good, once again write Mom, Dad, and Monica's names. Now, each of you give a rating from 1 to 10 for each of these four ideas. 10 means the very best while 1 means barely okay. And ideas can both have the same number—so, for example, you might have two ideas that are both 9s for you. . . . Good, now it's time to add them up. We'll put the totals in the boxes to the far right on each line (n). Mom and Dad, before you start problem solving you'll need to declare what kind of government you're running with the problem at hand. For many types of problems you'll likely decide that you're a democracy and the top idea or ideas win. However, sometimes the stakes are so high that you'll need to declare yourselves to be a benevolent dictatorship: In those instances, you'll promise to take the numbers very seriously, but you'll maintain the right to go in a different direction if you believe that's best (o). . . . So, for idea #2, what number did you each give? . . . Okay, so that totals up to 28, which we'll each put in the box to the far right. Finally, just discuss what you want to do, or what your "action plan" is and write that at the bottom. . . . So, it took us 20 minutes to do this exercise, including the time for me to teach you what to do. Last Sunday, how much time did this argument take? How much longer did it take for no one to be upset about it anymore (p)? So, it's a real no-brainer to say that this is the better choice. Actually, there are businesses that pay consultants a lot of money to come in to teach their workers how to do this. It's a pretty powerful tool for effectively resolving many types of conflicts (q). Monica, by the way, this is a very good weapon against the cobra. When there's a problem the cobra tries to get you super upset and worried about it, saying things like, "Martina won't be your friend anymore if you don't come over!" Or, "My parents are cruel and don't really love me!" Or, "I never get to have fun!" Did the cobra ever try to put those kinds of thoughts into your head (r)? But you can use this weapon to remove the teeth from the cobra's stinking, lying mouth (s). Okay, would you guys mind doing this twice this week? If no new problems emerge, just use ones from the past again. As this is sort of a tricky exercise to get into the habit of using, I feel better if I can see that you're doing it well on your own (t). Any obstacles that might come up in doing this? . . . Okay, take your sheets with you and here's another print-out of a composite problem-solving case (u).

Table 11.2 indicates what the final product would look like.

Explanation

a. Sometimes families are aching to take on a monster problem. This is often the case with teens. For example, a 15-year-old and her parents might be in a war over whether she should be allowed to car date an 18-year-old. Those are problems that can be taken on later, but they are too conflict-laden to use at this juncture. Here we are primarily trying to teach the method and what it portends to offer to a family.

 It's certainly okay, and even desirable, if the family picks a problem that is active. The shazam factor at the end is even higher in these instances. But I don't insist on it being a current problem as sometimes, at this stage in the work, the problems have often decreased considerably.

b. There can be a couple of minor challenges that can emerge at this point. The first is that the family says they can't think of anything. But I just keep saying things like, *That's okay. Take your time. We're in no rush.* Or, *It might be*

TABLE 11.2 Problem-Solving Example

Date: 12/6/15

Problem: <u>Monica wants to go over to Martina's house for a sleepover but it's a school night.</u>

Proposed Solutions (Do NOT evaluate until you have generated at least 10 ideas.)	Mom + −	Dad + −	Monica + −	+ −
1. <u>Monica sleeps over at Martina's house.</u>	−	−	+	
2. <u>Martina sleeps over at Monica's house this coming weekend.</u>	+	+	+	
3. <u>Monica does her homework and then invites Martina over for a couple of hours.</u>	+	+	+	
4. <u>Monica has Martina sleep over this coming weekend.</u>	+	−	+	
5. <u>Monica invites Martina to a movie this weekend.</u>	+	+	+	
6. <u>Monica does her homework and then calls Martina and invites her to FaceTime.</u>	+	+	−	
7. <u>Monica does her homework and then invites Martina to go get their nails done.</u>	−	+	+	
8. <u>Monica invites Martina to sleep over at her house instead.</u>	−	−	+	
9. <u>Monica does her homework and then goes over to Martina's house for a few hours to hang out and eat supper; then comes home.</u>	+	+	+	
10. <u>Monica goes out to dinner with her family instead.</u>	+	+	−	
11.				
12.				

The numbers of ideas with all +s   Give a score from 1 to 10 (10 is best)

	Mom	Dad	Monica		Sum
2	10	10	8		28
3	8	7	6		21
5	7	9	7		23
9	7	9	10		26

Action Plan: #2 & #9

something that you've mostly forgotten about because it's not bothering you, so just search your memory. There's stuff in there for us to use. Sometimes, I might remember a conflict I was told about; if I need to, I can also search through my evaluation notes for material. If so, I'll ask if a problem I had heard about might work—if they continue to struggle, that is. The second challenge that arises is a family suggests a problem that isn't workable for this method, either because it's too vague ("She's disrespectful all the time!") or it just isn't appropriate for problem solving ("He needs to get his grades up"). When these kinds of things are suggested I'll offer a dose of empathy but then redirect (e.g., *Yeah, though you may look at it differently, that is an important issue for you all. But, for this exercise, we need a specific example of an instance when Monica and you guys didn't agree about what she should do in a particular moment in time*).

c. I put a problem-solving form on a clipboard, with a pencil (in case of erasing needs), for each family member. If a kid is too young to write I might have her sit by me and watch me do her part for her.

d. To get this point, all you have to do is think about some of the "problem-solving" conversations you've had within your own family or with your significant other. They can get pretty convoluted. I find this is an easy sell with families, and they enjoy the Old Testament remark, nodding and smiling.

e. It doesn't matter if each person's wording of the problem is precise, as long as the gist of it is written down and they are able to remember later what it was they worked on. Some anxious or achievement-oriented kids worry about spelling or grammar, but I encourage them not to invest in such concerns.

f. For some kids you'll need to make sure that they know what the word "evaluate" means and define it if they are unsure or don't know.

g. This is a guideline that I refined through practice. If your experience suggests a different guideline, go for it. In practice, I'll stop the exercise once we are at 10 ideas, just to move things along. But I'll note that they would want to continue at home until they have the 2 minutes of silence.

h. It's remarkable how many times the kid, or a less psychologically minded or stressed-out parent, will suggest the first idea should be simply that person getting her or his way. If it's the kid, it's always interesting to see if the parent(s) will bite and retaliate. My estimation is that in about 50% to 60% of cases the first two ideas proposed are each camp's initial preference. Fine. We write it down, knowing that they'll see later that those ideas don't end up being moved forward.

   I try to let the family get as many ideas out as they can, making sure that everyone gets the space to contribute. For example, if Mom tends to be the dominant voice and just starts spit-firing out a bunch of ideas, I might say, *Paula, you're good at this! Take a break for a second and let's see what Monica and Dad might come up with.* In order to get universal investment, everyone would usually need to contribute ideas.

Depending on the family, I will sometimes suggest a ridiculous idea to emphasize that we are not evaluating. For example, for the sample in question, I might say, *Mom, we might arrange for you to get a hotel room and have Monica and Martina do their homework there and then stay with them.* (When we get to the evaluation phase I'll point out why I suggested that one, just so that they don't think I'm an idiot.)

Of course, anyone evaluating an idea gets a cheerful, *uh, uh, uh, no evaluating!* Likewise, if I see a parent suppressing what could be evaluation speech, I'll say something like, *Roberto, you're really getting this. It's hard to not evaluate but you're avoiding that nicely. The next step is to try to keep it even from entering your mind.*

i. Whether each person writes down everyone's name or just his or her own doesn't matter.

j. Most folks come to understand how to do the plus and minus ratings pretty easily, but some might need a little more explanation. Or some younger kids might need to come sit over by me so that I can help them (whispering, of course).

k. I really enjoy this part of the exercise. Without the mental health professional (MHP) saying a word about it, family members start to hear that one or more of the other family members are not the completely unreasonable jerks that they thought. They can actually find common ground!

l. There doesn't tend to be a lot of confusion in segueing to this part of the form, though every now and again you might run into a family that needs a little bit more explanation.

m. I'll tell you I really kicked myself when I taught problem solving to the family in question. The parents had not been doing much special time, Dad was stressed out from overworking, and Mom was depressed. The teen was also a pretty angry cat. Had I to do it over again, I would have worked more on having special time take root first. Had I done so they probably would have been more open to problem solving and my streak would still be going!

n. Again, families readily understand how to do this math. But a few families, here and there, will need a little bit more explanation.

o. Some teens get into the eye rolling when I use my "benevolent dictatorship" term. But I like it because it reinforces to everyone who is in charge a message that many families desperately need to have reinforced.

If I'm dealing with a family where the marriage seems to be in distress, I would have referred for an evaluation for marriage counseling in the feedback session. Whether that's the case or not, if I think there is a risk that parents will act out marital conflict in this session, I would create a side meeting with them first in order to coach them on how to handle this session (i.e., using psychodynamic nomenclature: give them some defense mechanisms). If they are able to keep those issues under control and not argue with each other in maladaptive ways in front of their kid, then we'll go forward. Otherwise, I'd just teach this technique with the kid and one of the parents or in an individual session with the kid.

p. Many parents make some of my concluding points for me, so I'll let them do that and merely agree with their insights.

q. Sometimes the family members are just nodding at this point, but sometimes they want to say more. So, I give them the chance to say more if they'd like.

r. Most kids will acknowledge having had those kinds of negative thoughts in these kinds of moments. The more psychologically minded ones will spontaneously offer examples. Sometimes the parent(s) will offer examples also; those are add-ons, as long as it doesn't come across like a criticism, in which case I'll reframe it and ask the parent if he has an internal enemy that ever talks to him like that as well.

s. As you can see by now, I take any opportunity I can to externalize and to characterize both the internalizing disorder and the kid's battle against it.

t. Having the family practice this problem-solving exercise is key. As the kid's internalizing disorder is often a top stress on the family, and as, at this juncture, that is often feeling much improved, some families may say that it's a struggle to come up with problems to work on. But I'll counter with the notion that it can be minor problems or problems from the past and that the primary goal is to practice. Whether they actually resolve a problem that is distressing them is, for this week, a secondary matter.

u. This is just another resource for them to have. I will also let them know about articles I have on my blog that might help (www.hecticparents.com), which you can feel free to print out if you'd like. Or I'll encourage them to read my parenting book, *Working Parents, Thriving Families* (and Chapter 6 in particular). Some of these resources I'll also sometimes put in the kid's binder. The primary goal is to give them what they need in order to remember what to do posttermination.

PROBLEM SOLVING IN AN INDIVIDUAL SESSION

*We cannot solve our problems with the same level of thinking that
created them.*
—Albert Einstein

*I'd like to teach you an awesome way to deal with many kinds of problems that
come up in your life. Monica, what would the cobra have you do if you got home
from school and realized that you had forgotten a book that you need to do your
homework (a)? Right, the cobra would have you freak out. Now you might relax
your body or use a coping thought, and those would help to cage the cobra, but
you'd still have a legit problem on your hands. So, this weapon is used when you
have a problem and the cobra is trying to get you to freak out about it, but you
prefer to solve the problem and move on. In order to teach you how to do that, I
need a recent problem that you had. It could be one you have now or it could be
one from the past that you never really fixed. It shouldn't be a HUGE problem,
because we want to start out with easier stuff. What do you think would be a
good problem to use (b)? Okay, so that problem I mentioned really happened to
you last month, huh? What did you do about it (c)? Okay, let's use that one, then.
Let's pretend that we could travel back to that night last month and I'll teach
you how to use this weapon called "problem solving." The first step is to write
down the problem at the top of the page (d). Okay, next is the trickiest part. We
want to brainstorm. Brainstorming means coming up with as many possible
solutions to the problem that we can WITHOUT EVALUATING THEM. Let me
just check, what does the word "evaluate" mean (e)? This can be hard to do. Monica, here's another of my silly questions: Can a light switch be off and on at the
same time? Right. In the same way, your brain can't come up with its best ideas
if we try to evaluate at the same time (f). We want to think of as many ideas as
we can to solve this problem, without evaluating them. Actually, we want to
keep going until we have 10 ideas and 2 minutes of silence. So what's our first
idea (g)? . . . Okay, we have 10 ideas. At home, you should keep going until you
also have 2 minutes of silence because sometimes the best idea can be the 11th or
12th one. But, for now, we can stop because we've done enough for me to teach
you how to use this weapon. Now we want to evaluate each idea. To do that, we
want to put a number from 0 to 10 next to each idea. A "0" means it's not a good
idea. A "1" means it's barely okay, while a "10" means it's totally awesome. And
different ideas can have the same number. Like, we might have three of these ideas
at a "9" or a "6." Okay, let me read them off and you tell me what number to put
next to them (h). . . . Now, look at this sheet and tell me what the plan would have
been last month if you had been able to do this. Okay, write the word "plan" and
then write what you just said under that (i). What do you think of this weapon? . . .
How helpful would it have been last month when you forgot your book? How long
do you think it took for us to do this? How long was the cobra at you about it last
month (j)? By the way, remember last week when I showed you how to do thought
testing? Remember how I said I'd give you a weapon for situations when the*

painful thought turns out to be true (k)? Well, it's this weapon. This is what you'd use. If thought testing ever showed that a painful thought was true the cobra would want you to freak out about it, but you don't have to—you just use this weapon. So, for this week, I'd like you to do two problem-solving exercises for me. Would that be okay? Is there anything that could get in the way of you doing this (l)?

Table 11.3 indicates what the completed sheet would look like.

TABLE 11.3 Monica's Problem Solving	
Date: 12/6/15	
Problem: <u>I forgot a book I need to do my homework.</u>	
Ideas	<u>Ratings, 0 to 10 (0 = bad idea; 10 = awesome idea)</u>
<u>1. Tell the teacher the next day why I couldn't do my homework.</u>	0
<u>2. Call my friend Selene and see if I could borrow her book.</u>	5
<u>3. Ask my mom if I could change schools.</u>	0
<u>4. Go to school 45 minutes early tomorrow, when the building is open, and do it then.</u>	7
<u>5. Ask my mom to take me to the school in case a janitor or someone can let us in.</u>	10
<u>6. Ask my friend Selene to take pictures of the pages I need in the book and send them to me.</u>	9
<u>7. Go to the library and see if they have the book.</u>	3
<u>8. Copy Selene's homework on the school bus.</u>	0
<u>9. Do my homework together with Selene using FaceTime.</u>	8
<u>10. Ask Selene if I could come over and do my homework there.</u>	6
Action Plan: <u>Try #5. If that doesn't work, try #6; if that doesn't work, try #9; and if that doesn't work, do #4</u>	

Explanation

a.   At this point in the work, the kid will usually quickly and easily review the negative self-talk that would be in her head. If not, you could always engage in a sequence like this:

> **Kid:** *I don't know.*
> **MHP:** *C'mon, Monica, you know to leave "I don't knows" at home.*
> **Kid:** *I wouldn't like it.*
> **MHP:** *Right, nobody would like that. I still have bad dreams like that from time to time. But, what would the cobra try to tell you about it?*
> **Kid:** *That I'll get into a lot of trouble.*
> **MHP:** *Anything else?*
> **Kid:** *That I'm an idiot for forgetting it.*
> **MHP:** *Okay, that sounds like the cobra, all right.*

b. Interestingly, I find that many kids will remember an example of having forgotten something they need to do their homework and suggest doing that one. That's okay with me, as long as they can give me enough particulars to indicate that they are being truthful.

c. This is an important question because if the kid solved it well, then problem solving will seem not worth the bother. We are listening for either a poor outcome or a mixed outcome. If the kid had a good outcome I'll salute the kid and the outcome but then ask for another example of a problem that maybe didn't turn out so well or had a mixed outcome.

d. Some kids, when they are on their own, try to do this exercise just in their heads. But those kids don't usually get the best outcomes, at least not consistently. So, I try to instill the habit of writing it down.

e. For some of your kids it's tempting to assume that they know what this word means. But I much prefer to err on the side of asking if I'm even a little bit in doubt. If I need to define the word, I'll just say something like, *To evaluate something means to decide if it's good or bad, useful or not.*

f. For some kids this could be moving pretty fast. So, it can be good to pause here and check the kid's understanding.

g. When I'm teaching problem solving to a family I may or may not introduce ridiculous ideas just to challenge them not to evaluate. But when I'm teaching this to kids one-on-one I just about always do. If the kid balks at the idea, I just use it as a reminder that we are not evaluating now. Later on I'll acknowledge that I suggested the idea just to make that point. Likewise, I can feel challenged if the kid suggests an idea that I know is fraught with problems. So, what's good for the goose. . . .

h. Most of the time this flows pretty easily and quickly. However, sometimes a kid rates what is clearly a bad idea as a good idea. So, an exchange like this might happen if the eighth idea in our example was rated as a good idea:

MHP: *"Copying Selene's homework on the bus."*
Kid: *9*

(The MHP waits until all of the ideas have been rated and then circles back to this issue so as to not condition the kid to try to read the MHP's mind.)

MHP: *Monica, you gave a 9 for copying Selene's homework?*
Kid: *Yeah, that'd be pretty easy to do and she wouldn't care.*
MHP: *What could happen if the teacher found out?*
Kid: *She wouldn't.*
MHP: *In your life, have you ever thought you wouldn't get caught doing something but you ended up getting caught?*
Kid: *Yeah, of course.*
MHP: *Well, so, what if the teacher did find out, even though you don't think that's likely?*
Kid: *She'd probably tell my parents.*
MHP: *And then what could happen?*
Kid: *They'd flip out.*
MHP: *Would they punish you?*
Kid: *Prob.*
MHP: *How do you think?*
Kid: *Take my cell phone or some stupid grounding.*
MHP: *From 1 to 10, with 10 being the most painful, how painful would that be?*
Kid: *Like an 8/9.*
MHP: *What about at school—any consequences there?*
Kid: *Could get a detention.*
MHP: *Give me a pain rating on that one.*
Kid: *Same.*
MHP: *Are 100% of the kids on the bus close friends?*
Kid: *No, some of them are idiots.*
MHP: *So, there's no knowing if all of them would keep it a secret if they saw you doing the copying?*
Kid: *Okay, maybe it isn't a 9; make it a 2 then.*

By the way, if you ever feel like you should be doing work, but can't bear it, check out episodes of *Columbo* on YouTube. *Columbo* was a popular TV series from the late 1960s and 1970s. He was a homicide detective who ended up being liked by even the people he arrested. His interviewing style is the one I try to adopt when I'm doing segments like I just reviewed. When a suspect would assert that he was at his mother's house at 6 p.m. but a videotape at a parking garage had him elsewhere, Columbo would present a confused demeanor to the suspect, asking him (the suspect) to help him to not be confused. It's an excellent interview style for what otherwise could be a needlessly confrontational moment.

i. The kid usually doesn't need much help to articulate a viable plan at this point. But, if she does, I'll offer it.

j. This part could go in a bunch of different directions. The main goal is to help the kid to understand that the inconvenience of doing this problem solving at home, and writing it down, is worth the bother.

k. I won't say this, obviously, if I haven't covered thought testing yet.

 A thought proven true in thought testing is not common; actually, I can't fill up two hands with examples of when the painful core thought proved to be true in doing thought testing with kids. I just like having a kid know that there is a backup plan should that happen. If I think a kid could use it, I'll give examples of painful core thoughts that could be true: "I have no friends at school," or "My dad is an alcoholic," or "I offend other kids a lot." I'll then suggest that problem solving could be used to address them.

l. This is old hat by now. You and your kid client know what the potential obstacles are and how to get around them. You just agree on the plan here.

Rationale

In research looking at what mediates benefits in family therapy, communications training and problem solving come out on top. This is a monstrously helpful technique. And it saves individuals and families all kinds of time and distress. It really is a little mini-miracle technique.

I realize there may be family-oriented therapists reading this book who might prefer for siblings to attend family sessions, including during the evaluation phase. I appreciate that an MHP gets extra data this way and can also try to be helpful with a wider range of problems that could be affecting the identified child client. However, my experience has been that not including siblings speeds things along during the evaluation phase without interfering with the primary evaluation goals and allows for a more focused approach to ameliorating the goals articulated on a kid's treatment plan. I appreciate that it's an arguable point, though. If you do decide to bring in siblings, you just may need a form that has more columns in it.

In terms of when to introduce it in a family session or an individual session, these are some of the factors I consider:

▶ Age, maturity level, and psychological mindedness of the child: The younger or less psychologically minded, the more likely I am to introduce this in a family session.

▶ The kid's track record with understanding and complying with the CBT techniques on her own: The more we've needed to use a parent, the more likely I am to introduce this in a family session.

▶ The level of conflict between the kid and the parents: The more conflict, the more likely I am to introduce this in a family session.

▶ How well the parents are getting along: As I mentioned previously, if I think they'll use this session to triangulate their conflict, I'm more likely to either introduce it to the child alone or just with one parent in the room.

If I'm on the fence, I go with the family session because of its potential value for the entire family. Even when I start with the family methodology I will review the individual method with the kid later, as she'll need the technique for effectively resolving individual problems.

SIDEBAR 11.1

Stripper decks are another staple of magicians, especially young magicians. These are playing cards that are narrower at the top of the card than the bottom. Hence, if one card is inserted back into the deck, narrow end down, with the rest of the deck being narrow end up, running two fingers along the side of the deck, from bottom to top, will cause the inserted card to rise out of the deck.

A very simple trick to show, and then teach, a kid is to have the kid pick out any four cards from the deck, with the deck arranged so that the wider end is at the top. Just make sure the kid picks them out in a way that doesn't turn them around (i.e., wide end stays at the top). Ask the kid to write the four cards down on a piece of paper, not showing you them. As the kid is writing them down, just turn the deck so that the narrow end is now at the top. Have the kid insert the four cards, one at a time, anywhere into the deck. You can then shuffle them, maintaining the wider–narrow arrangement. Ask the kid if she knows where the cards are in the deck, which of course she doesn't. Then run two fingers along the side of the deck, from the bottom to the top. The four cards will "magically" rise out.

As these decks are so cheap, I usually buy a bunch of them at once and hand them out to my apprentice magicians, encouraging them to look on YouTube for a bunch of other tricks that can be done with a stripper deck.

REFERENCES AND BIBLIOGRAPHY

Barkley, R. A., Edwards, G., Laneri, M., Fletcher, K., & Metevia, L. (2001). The efficacy of problem-solving communication training alone, behavior management training alone, and their combination for parent–adolescent conflict in teenagers with ADHD and ODD. *Journal of Consulting and Clinical Psychology, 69*(6), 926–941.

Barkley, R. A., & Robin, A. L. (2014). *Defiant teens: A clinician's manual for assessment and family intervention.* New York, NY: Guilford Press.

Brent, D. A. (1997). *Cognitive therapy treatment manual for depressed and suicidal youth* (STAR Center Publications). Pittsburgh, PA: University of Pittsburgh Health System Services for Teens at Risk.

Chen, S. Y., Jordan, C., & Thompson, S. (2006). The effect of cognitive behavioral therapy (CBT) on depression: The role of problem-solving appraisal. *Research on Social Work Practice, 16*(5), 500–510.

Davila, J., Hammen, C., Burge, D., Paley, B., & Daley, S. E. (1995). Poor interpersonal problem solving as a mechanism of stress generation in depression among adolescent women. *Journal of Abnormal Psychology, 104*(4), 592–600.

Denham, S. A., & Almeida, M. C. (1987). Children's social problem-solving skills, behavioral adjustment, and interventions: A meta-analysis evaluating theory and practice. *Journal of Applied Developmental Psychology, 8*(4), 391–409.

Friedberg, R. D., McClure, J. M., & Garcia, J. H. (2009). *Cognitive therapy techniques for children and adolescents*. New York, NY: Guilford Press.

Hogendoorn, S. M., Prins, P. J., Boer, F., Vervoort, L., Wolters, L. H., Moorlag, H., & de Haan, E. (2014). Mediators of cognitive behavioral therapy for anxiety-disordered children and adolescents: Cognition, perceived control, and coping. *Journal of Clinical Child & Adolescent Psychology, 43*(3), 486–500.

Kazdin, A. E., Esveldt-Dawson, K., French, N. H., & Unis, A. S. (1987). Problem-solving skills training and relationship therapy in the treatment of antisocial child behavior. *Journal of Consulting and Clinical Psychology, 55*(1), 76–85.

Kazdin, A. E., Siegel, T. C., & Bass, D. (1992). Cognitive problem-solving skills training and parent management training in the treatment of antisocial behavior in children. *Journal of Consulting and Clinical Psychology, 60*(5), 733–747.

Levenson, M., & Neuringer, C. (1971). Problem-solving behavior in suicidal adolescents. *Journal of Consulting and Clinical Psychology, 37*(3), 433–436.

Lochman, J. E. (1992). Cognitive-behavioral intervention with aggressive boys: Three-year follow-up and preventive effects. *Journal of Consulting and Clinical Psychology, 60*(3), 426.

Malouff, J. M., Thorsteinsson, E. B., & Schutte, N. S. (2007). The efficacy of problem solving therapy in reducing mental and physical health problems: A meta-analysis. *Clinical Psychology Review, 27*(1), 46–57.

Nezu, A. M. (1987). A problem-solving formulation of depression: A literature review and proposal of a pluralistic model. *Clinical Psychology Review, 7*(2), 121–144.

Nezu, A. M. (2005). Problem solving and behavior therapy revisited. *Behavior Therapy, 35*(1), 1–33.

Palmiter, D. J. (2011). *Working parents, thriving families: 10 strategies that make a difference*. North Branch, MN: Sunrise River Press.

Robin, A. L. (1981). A controlled evaluation of problem-solving communication training with parent-adolescent conflict. *Behavior Therapy, 12*(5), 593–609.

Robin, A. L., & Foster, S. L. (1984). Problem-solving communication training: A behavioral-family systems approach to parent–adolescent conflict. *Advances in Child Behavioral Analysis & Therapy, 3*, 195–240.

Robin, A. L., Kent, R., O'Leary, K. D., Foster, S., & Prinz, R. (1977). An approach to teaching parents and adolescents problem-solving communication skills: A preliminary report. *Behavior Therapy, 8*(4), 639–643.

Rutter, M. (1999). Resilience concepts and findings: Implications for family therapy. *Journal of Family Therapy, 21,* 119–144.

Shure, M. B., & Spivack, G. (1981). Interpersonal problem solving as a mediator of behavioral adjustment in preschool and kindergarten children. *Journal of Applied Developmental Psychology, 1*(1), 29–44.

Stark, K., & Kendall, P. C. (1996). *Treating depressed children: Therapist manual for "taking action."* Ardmore, PA: Workbook Publishing.

Stark, K. D., Reynolds, W. M., & Kaslow, N. J. (1987). A comparison of the relative efficacy of self-control therapy and a behavioral problem-solving therapy for depression in children. *Journal of Abnormal Child Psychology, 15*(1), 91–113.

Sukhodolsky, D. G., Kassinove, H., & Gorman, B. S. (2004). Cognitive-behavioral therapy for anger in children and adolescents: A meta-analysis. *Aggression and Violent Behavior, 9*(3), 247–269.

CHAPTER 12

Establishing and Growing Strengths and Acts of Kindness

ESTABLISHING A FOUNDATION

Ignore the negative voice inside you. Focus on your strengths.
—Lailah Gifty Akita

This is what I say to kids when introducing this topic:

Aiden, let's say the kids in your grade and school were to get into a sports tournament with kids in the same grade but from another school district. The kids from the winning school would be given an annual pass to their favorite amusement park. The tournament would consist of things like baseball, bowling, ping-pong, basketball, and a few other sports. Before the tournament started each kid would be required to say if he was going to play right-handed or left-handed, and then he'd have to stick to that choice. Which way would you choose to play (a)? Exactly. It wouldn't make sense to play left-handed because you wouldn't do as well. Because you want to win the park pass and help your team, you go with your stronger arm. Well, it's sort of like that in your fight with the iceman. You have parts of your personality, and skills, that are stronger and better than other parts. When you're using your strongest parts and having success, the iceman finds it very difficult to land any punches on you; you're just ducking and weaving too fast and landing too many punches yourself. But, when you're not using your stronger parts, you're moving more slowly and throwing fewer punches, making you an easier target for the iceman (b). So, we need to figure out what your top strengths are. You and your parents know a lot of them already that you've told me about, but I'd like to have you complete a couple of online tests at home so we can see if there are others. I'll tell your mom about them at the end of today (c).

They'll take you a while to finish them (d), *but I think you'll be happy with the results because we'll get even clearer about what your top strengths might be. We'll then be able to figure out how you're using them and how you might be able to use them more; believe me, that iceman will HATE that* (e).

Let's make a list. What are you REALLY good at (f)? *Okay, what's the evidence that you're really good at this* (g)? *Are there ways you can use each strength more* (h)?

Explanation

a. This is a simple matter of the kid identifying if he's right- or left-handed.

b. It would be possible to do this intervention without referencing the internal enemy, as is true of most of the interventions in this volume. However, it's important to conceive of interventions as ways of defeating or caging the internal enemy whenever possible.

c. Some older teens might be able to handle this on their own without their parents' help. I'll invite the teen into this deliberation. If the teen thinks he can do it on his own, that's what we do, bringing in the parent later only if that doesn't work.

d. There are five tools that could be of help here. Three of them—the *BASC-3*, the *Resiliency Scales for Children and Adolescents*, and the *Developmental History Form*—may have been completed during the initial evaluation. If so, they stand ready to use. The next two I'll describe here:

    • The *Values in Action (VIA) Youth Survey*. This measure, designed for ages 10 to 17, is currently available for free online. It measures 24 character strengths, has 96 items, and takes about 15 minutes to complete. Other information regarding this tool can be found in Appendix J.

    • The *Clifton Youth StrengthsExplorer*. This measure, designed for ages 10 to 14, is available by purchasing the book *StrengthsExplorer for Ages 10 to 14: From Gallup, the Creators of StrengthsFinder*. It measures 10 strength-based themes and reports back on each kid's conjectured top three strength-based themes. This instrument has 78 items and takes about 15 minutes to complete. The report also lists some possible action steps for further use and development of each of the top three strengths. See Appendix J for more information on this tool.

    For ages 15 and up, the companion assessment tool is *StrengthsFinder 2.0*. It has 180 paired, timed items (i.e., 20-second time limit per item), assessing 34 strength-based themes; it generates each respondent's conjectured top five strength-based themes. The report also lists some possible action steps for further use and development of each of the top three strengths. It also generates action plans for each conjectured strength. See Appendix J for more information on this tool.

When I think a kid can handle the work, I'll ask him, and his parent, to complete both measures in the same week. Otherwise, we'll spread it out across 2 weeks. Once the reports are available we are ready for the next phase.

e. I don't always do this, as it may make sense to wait for the results of the surveys to move forward. But, if a kid seems to have at least a couple of strengths readily available for review, I will begin a preliminary review now.

f. It isn't enough that a kid imagines he's very good at a thing as we are mining for true strengths. So, this an opportunity to consider supporting data. Has he won awards? Has he performed well in competitions? Has he been given special access (e.g., to experiences that less talented kids wouldn't be given access to)? Does it appear that he has received varied and objective feedback from nonfamily members? If these data are missing, I might make the time to query further with a parent, without the kid in the room. If the data are lacking we might arrange for a way of testing his ability (e.g., submit something for publication, enter a competition). At the end of the day if the noted strength does not appear to be a true strength, I'd just move on to the next possibility without dispelling the kid of the notion that the area under review is a strength.

g. If the kid is already consistently using the strength in a public way, great. There is little more to do here other than to hear about some success stories. However, it's remarkable how often a kid appears to have a true strength but is barely using it. I speculate that this is another product of the time crunch in families these days. So, I just want to begin the process of making sure that the kid is using the strength in consistent and public ways. As parental support is often needed, the kid and I will usually agree to partner with his parent(s) on a plan to make this happen.

STRENGTHS DEVELOPMENT PLAN

This is what I say (this can vary based on whether we did a preliminary review in an earlier session, before the survey results were available or reviewed):

Aiden, wow, we have a lot of information about your strengths. There's (a) . . . . I have a form here for us to use that I'll fill in (b). So, considering everything we have, what would you say are your strengths (c)? Okay, this is an awesome list. Now, let's try to figure out three very good ones that we can make sure you try to use regularly. Look at this list I have here. What would you say is the first one we might use (d)? . . . What's the second one we might use? . . . The third? Okay, now let's go through each one and I'll write down how you are currently using each one. How are you using strength #1 (e)? . . . #2? . . . #3? . . . Great. Now what facts are there that can be used to prove that these are top strengths of yours? We can use some of these reports or things you've done that we could see on a video camera, or anything that proves it's a strength (f). Let's start with #1 . . . #2 . . . #3 . . . Great. Now let's work on a plan for how you want to use them right now. This might just be continuing what you're doing or it might be doing new stuff also (g). Strength #1? . . . #2? . . . #3? . . . Wonderful. This is your plan for using your strengths. How do you think it would affect the iceman if you did this stuff (h)? . . . Right, HE WILL NOT BE PLEASED! Okay, finally, I have this tracking form for you to use. This week, write down what you did toward each of the action steps and rate your mood afterward. I have a form here, let's go through it (i).

Explanation

a. Here I just list out the sources of information before us. In the ideal circumstance this consists of the history I've been given, the *BASC-3*, the *Resiliency Scales for Children and Adolescents*, the parent's *Developmental History Form*, the *VIA Youth Survey*, and the *Clifton Youth StrengthsExplorer* or *StrengthsFinder 2.0*.

b. Table 12.1 illustrates the form.

TABLE 12.1 Strengths Development Form		
Name: _____ Date: _____		
Known strengths:		
Strength #1 & how it is being used	Evidence that #1 is a top strength	Action plan for strength #1
Strength #2 & how it is being used	Evidence that #2 is a top strength	Action plan for strength #2
Strength #3 & how it is being used	Evidence that #3 is a top strength	Action plan for strength #3

c. This material goes in the top section of the form. This is essentially a review as well as a brainstorming session. I wouldn't fret about it if a kid listed synonymous strengths. I also try to prepare for the session by being familiar with the evaluation findings and I take time to review the summaries of the VIA and Gallup tools. You can't have too many strengths. And it doesn't matter if we agree that everything a kid lists for this section is a strength.

d. We get more concerned about which three are picked out. The primary intention is to find three specific *top* strengths that the kid can make manifest in the world each week or most weeks. If a kid suggested a strength that I didn't think met these criteria I'd suggest that we consider it but then move on to something that might be more viable, explaining why and asking if that might be a better choice.

e. This is merely recording baseline measurable activity, which might be a lot or a little.

f. If the kid has already learned the thought-testing module, he is familiar with what a fact is. If not, I'll use some of the same language from that intervention to teach him (see Chapter 10). We'll both tend to contribute to developing these facts. If a kid says something like, "I'm just good at it," I'll respond with, *If we had a video recording of you using that strength, how could we tell that without anyone pointing it out?*

g. This is the step where the rubber meets the road. If the kid is already using the strength regularly, that's great. Kudos can be issued and the effects discussed. Otherwise, we can brainstorm on things the kid might do to enhance the application of that strength in the world (this brainstorming would be akin to the brainstorming portion of problem solving that was reviewed in Chapter 11). Table 12.2 illustrates what the form would look like upon completion.

h. Most kids readily understand how using their strengths would affect their internal enemy. I just agree with them and pile on a little in my next comment.

i. Table 12.3 indicates the form while Table 12.4 illustrates what a completed form would look like. It's pretty self-explanatory, other than to say that the fourth box, "Other," is there in case the kid wants to report on other strengths used that week.

TABLE 12.2 Sample of a Completed Strengths Development Form

Name: <u>Aiden Richards</u>   Date: <u>2/1/16</u>

Known strengths: kind, funny, baseball, spiritual, a leader, swimming, drawing, singing, basketball, giving, loyal, trustworthy, friendly, patient, respectful, caring, sensitive, reliable

Strength #1 & how it is being used	Evidence that #1 is a top strength	Action plan for strength #1
Baseball: starting shortstop and pitcher for Little League and travel baseball teams	▶ Selected to county all-star team ▶ Batted over .400 ▶ ERA under 1.0 ▶ Has always been a starter ▶ Lots of positive feedback from coaches ▶ "Competing" listed as a top strength on the StrengthsExplorer measure	▶ Continue playing baseball, hopefully on the middle school team ▶ Participate in winter baseball camps
Strength #2 & how it is being used	**Evidence that #2 is a top strength**	**Action plan for strength #2**
Spiritual: goes to church each week and prays every day; turns to God for help when troubles come	▶ Priest has said he hasn't seen many boys of the same age who are as spiritual ▶ "Spirituality" listed as a top strength on the VIA measure ▶ It has been very helpful	▶ Continue going to church each week, praying every day, and turning to God in times of trouble ▶ Apply to be an altar server ▶ Join the church youth group

(continued)

TABLE 12.2 Sample of a Completed Strengths Development Form (*continued*)

Strength #3 & how it is being used	Evidence that #3 is a top strength	Action plan for strength #3
Leadership: captain of the Little League and travel baseball teams	▶ Was elected by peers of two different baseball teams to be the captain ▶ "Organizer" listed as a top strength on the StrengthsExplorer measure	▶ Run for student council at the middle school ▶ Volunteer for a leadership role after joining the church youth group

TABLE 12.3 Strengths Development Tracking Form

Name: _____

Week: _____

Mood rating (0 to 100). Higher numbers mean more happiness and satisfaction.

Strength	Action(s) Taken	Mood Rating(s) After
#1	Date(s): Action(s):	
#2	Date(s): Action(s):	
#3	Date(s): Action(s):	
Other:	Date(s): Action(s):	

TABLE 12.4 Sample of a Completed Strengths Development Tracking Form

Name: _____

Week: _____

Mood rating (0 to 100). Higher numbers mean more happiness and satisfaction.

Strength	Action(s) Taken	Mood Rating(s) After
#1 Baseball	Date(s): Monday Action(s): Went to baseball camp	70
#2 Spirituality	Date(s): Every day, Wednesday, Saturday Action(s): Prayed, joined the youth group, went to church	Every day: 70–80 Wednesday: 85 Saturday: 65
#3 Leadership	Date(s): Wednesday Action(s): Voted to chair dance committee	90
Other:	Date(s): Action(s):	

TEACHING ABOUT WAIT

Self-doubt kills talent.
—Edie McClurg

WAIT—or Who Am I To?—is an acronym I first developed in producing and hosting a monthly television program on mental health issues titled *Mental Health Matters*. I would assemble three mental health professionals (MHPs) and a psychology graduate student and then interview them on a particular mental health topic. I would tell prospective MHP guests that they needn't do any research to prepare, though they could if they wished. I shared that my questions would merely be tapping their walk around clinical knowledge and experience. I was surprised at how many MHPs were reluctant to appear on TV secondary to self-doubt, or *"Who am I to* (WAIT) go on TV to discuss depression?" Moreover, when I was president-elect of the Pennsylvania Psychological Association, I reached out to previous presidents asking for advice on how to be successful. One of the past presidents, Dr. Emily Stevick, emphasized this point: "What I did learn was how many psychologists underestimated themselves . . . when I spoke to board chairs about running for Treasurer or President or etcetera . . . there was always a question about the ability to do so."

I've since discovered WAIT is *everywhere,* and that I suffered from it also until I became conscious of it. All the time, students (e.g., WAIT apply to Boston U's grad program?), colleagues (e.g., WAIT write a book?), and clients (e.g., WAIT ask that girl out?) give evidence of suffering from WAIT. WAIT puts a low ceiling on how a top strength can be made manifest in the world and we all deserve to vanquish it from our psyches. So, I encourage my clients to think BIG. I've had kids submit writings to national publications, encouraged high school students to raise their bar in the colleges they apply to, wonder with adult clients why they think of earning a desired degree as being outside of the realm of possibility, and don't even get me going on this notion of "this other unattached human is too grand for me to consider asking out." This most commonly comes up, in strength development work, when I suggest *what seems like* a bigger-than-life action step and a kid hesitates. I find it to be very rewarding to be the agent of a person becoming conscious of WAIT, discarding it, and accomplishing something special. I also find the process to be a mediator for meaningful life experiences.

ACTS OF KINDNESS

Kindness is the language which the deaf can hear and the blind can see.
—Mark Twain

This is another module that can be inserted at any point when the focus is on helping to lift a kid's mood. This might be to combat depression, to infuse more joy and meaning into a kid's life, or to teach an important lesson about how to engineer happiness. This is what I say:

Aiden, can you tell me a recent time that you did something nice for someone? I mean a time when you didn't have to be nice, but you went out of your way to be nice (a)*? Can you remember what you were feeling before you did that? Guess what your mood rating was beforehand, from 1 to 100, with 100 being as happy as you can feel* (b)*? How did you feel right afterward, including your mood rating* (c)*? Guess what, you already had a weapon against the iceman and you didn't even know it! It's called "acts of kindness," and you can do them just about* *whenever and wherever you'd like, making it a very convenient and easy-to-use weapon against the iceman. Let's make a list of things you might choose to do (d). Awesome. Are there any that you can try to do this week (e)? What do you think? Do you want to just remember what you did and how it felt, or is it helpful to write it down (f)?*

Explanation

a. Most kids can remember an example. The more recent the better, as the kid will feel more confident about his mood ratings. Depending on the kid, I'll sometimes prepare some examples that I know about, or I'll ask a parent for help if the kid struggles.

b. This is just the pre "act of kindness" rating.

c. Of course, this is the post rating. It would be unusual for a kid to report that it didn't feel good. If that happens I'd look to establish that this wasn't the work of the iceman, stomping on a flower the kid planted. I'd then try to have the kid, or the parent, come up with another example.

d. Of course, the range of what might be done varies as a function of the kid's age and maturity level. But here's a few ideas, some of which can be done with a parent or other family members depending on the age of the kid and the inclinations of the family:

- Do a chore for a sibling.
- Compliment a friend.
- Ask Mom or Dad if they need help.
- Offer to help a friend with homework.
- Invite a friend who is sad to do something fun.
- Hold the door open for some strangers.
- Offer to help a neighbor with yard work or snow shoveling.
- Volunteer at a pet shelter.
- Volunteer to altar serve.
- Give away toys to a charity.
- Let another person ahead of you in a line.
- Draw a picture or share a note for a waitress or waiter who did well.
- Send a thank-you picture or note for a teacher from the past who did a great job.

- Volunteer at a soup kitchen.

- Clean up something at home without being asked.

- Get some coupons for a free car wash and leave them in some windshields at a sports game with a note: "Enjoy, from a friend."

- Offer to brush your mom's or dad's hair.

- Nominate a favorite teacher for an award.

- Pick up the dog's poop without being asked.

- Donate some books to the local children's library.

- Give away some allowance money at church.

- Volunteer to help when people do fundraising events.

- Offer to massage your mom's or dad's feet (one or both of us smile at this one).

- Give out flowers to strangers at the mall.

- Help janitors clean up after the next school event.

It probably wouldn't take much brainstorming to double the size of this list.

e. How much I'd be looking for a kid to do would depend a lot on what other cognitive behavioral therapy (CBT) work there was to do for the week.

f. If a kid has done well with completing and benefiting from using tracking forms, I'll suggest using a form here as well. Otherwise, I don't lobby hard for the kid to do it and leave it up to him (he can usually remember what happened fairly well enough anyway). Table 12.5 indicates the form.

Additional Commentary

No act of kindness, no matter how small, is ever wasted.
—Aesop

The "helper's high" is an empirically supported and established adult phenomenon. While the literature on kids is limited (see the References and Bibliography section at the end of this chapter), clinical experience and generations of parent and educator counsel to kids suggest the intervention has value for youth as well.

TABLE 12.5 Acts of Kindness Tracking Form

Name: _____

Week: _____

Mood rating: 1 to 100 (100 = the most happiness)

What You Were Doing Right Before the Kind Act	Mood Before the Kind Act	Kind Act	Mood After the Kind Act

SIDEBAR 12.1

This is a nice little trick to teach when you only have a few seconds. You'll only need a dime and two nickels. Position the dime between the thumb and first finger of your right hand so that the entire face of the dime is visible to the kid. Position the two nickels behind the dime, but turned horizontally and stacked on top of each other; positioned this way, the kid can see the dime but can't see the two nickels hidden behind the dime. Comment that magic has all kinds of uses, including making change. Roll up your sleeves, if you have them, and show the dime and two open hands. Note that you have no other coins or materials on display. Then pull your open left hand across the front of the coins. As you do so, rotate and separate the nickels, positioning the dime behind one of them and displaying one nickel with each hand. (If this description is a little confusing, you'll quickly see how this works by trying it.) Young kids really enjoy how easy it is for them to do, with practice in front of a mirror, that is.

REFERENCES AND BIBLIOGRAPHY

Aknin, L. B., Hamlin, J. K., & Dunn, E. W. (2012). Giving leads to happiness in young children. *PLOS One, 7*(6), e39211.

Anderson, E. (2005). Strengths-based educating: A concrete way to bring out the best in students—and yourself. The confessions of an educator who got it right—finally! The quest for strengths. *Educational Horizons, 83*(3), 180–189.

Blechman, E. A., McEnroe, M. J., Carella, E. T., & Audette, D. P. (1986). Childhood competence and depression. *Journal of Abnormal Psychology, 95*(3), 223–227.

Bouffard, T., Marcoux, M., Vezeau, C., & Bordeleau, L. (2003). Changes in self-perceptions of competence and intrinsic motivation among elementary schoolchildren. *British Journal of Educational Psychology, 73*(2), 171–186.

Bromley, E., Johnson, J. G., & Cohen, P. (2006). Personality strengths in adolescence and decreased risk of developing mental health problems in early adulthood. *Comprehensive Psychiatry, 47*(4), 315–324.

Brooks, R. B., & Goldstein, S. (2002a). *Nurturing resilience in our children: Answers to the most important parenting questions*. Burr Ridge, IL: McGraw-Hill.

Brooks, R. B., & Goldstein, S. (2002b). *Raising resilient children: Fostering strength, hope, and optimism in your child*. Burr Ridge, IL: McGraw-Hill.

Cox, K. F. (2006). Investigating the impact of strength-based assessment on youth with emotional or behavioral disorders. *Journal of Child and Family Studies, 15*(3), 278–292.

Exline, J. J., Lisan, A. M., & Lisan, E. R. (2012). Reflecting on acts of kindness toward the self: Emotions, generosity, and the role of social norms. *Journal of Positive Psychology, 7*(1), 45–56.

Finamore, D. (2008). *Little Miss Sunshine* and positive psychology as a vehicle for change in adolescent depression. In L. C. Rubin & L. C. Rubin (Eds.), *Popular culture in counseling, psychotherapy, and play-based interventions* (pp. 123–139). New York, NY: Springer Publishing Company.

Graybeal, C. (2001). Strengths-based social work assessment: Transforming the dominant paradigm. *Families in Society: The Journal of Contemporary Social Services, 82*(3), 233–242.

Greener, S., & Crick, N. R. (1999). Normative beliefs about prosocial behavior in middle childhood: What does it mean to be nice? *Social Development, 8*(3), 349–363.

Jones, A. L. (1998). Random acts of kindness: A teaching tool for positive deviance. *Teaching Sociology, 26*(3), 179–189.

Layous, K., Nelson, S. K., Oberle, E., Schonert-Reichl, K. A., & Lyubomirsky, S. (2012). Kindness counts: Prompting prosocial behavior in preadolescents boosts peer acceptance and well-being. *PLOS One, 7*(12), e51380.

Lee Duckworth, A., Steen, T. A., & Seligman, M. E. (2005). Positive psychology in clinical practice. *Annual Review of Clinical Psychology, 1*, 629–651.

MacConville, R., & Rae, T. (2012). *Building happiness, resilience, and motivation in adolescents: A positive psychology curriculum for well-being*. London, UK: Jessica Kingsley Publishers.

Masten, A. S., & Coatsworth, J. D. (1998). The development of competence in favorable and unfavorable environments: Lessons from research on successful children. *American Psychologist, 53*(2), 205–220.

Mruk, C. J. (2006). *Self-esteem research, theory, and practice: Toward a positive psychology of self-esteem.* New York, NY: Springer Publishing Company.

Obach, M. S. (2003). A longitudinal-sequential study of perceived academic competence and motivational beliefs for learning among children in middle school. *Educational Psychology, 23*(3), 323–338.

Otake, K., Shimai, S., Tanaka-Matsumi, J., Otsui, K., & Fredrickson, B. L. (2006). Happy people become happier through kindness: A counting kindnesses intervention. *Journal of Happiness Studies, 7*(3), 361–375.

Palmiter, D. J. (2010). Child clinician's corner: Pursuing competence. *The Independent Practitioner, 30*, 32–33.

Park, N., & Peterson, C. (2006). Character strengths and happiness among young children: Content analysis of parental descriptions. *Journal of Happiness Studies, 7*(3), 323–341.

Peterson, C., & Seligman, M. E. (2004). *Character strengths and virtues: A handbook and classification.* New York, NY: Oxford University Press.

Pressman, S. D., Kraft, T. L., & Cross, M. P. (2015). It's good to do good and receive good: The impact of a "pay it forward" style kindness intervention on giver and receiver well-being. *Journal of Positive Psychology, 10*(4), 293–302.

Rath, T. (2007). *StrengthsFinder 2.0: A new and upgraded edition of the online test from Gallup's Now Discover Your Strengths.* Washington, DC: Gallup Press.

Rutter, M. (1999). Resilience concepts and findings: Implications for family therapy. *Journal of Family Therapy, 21*, 119–144.

Seligman, M. E., Rashid, T., & Parks, A. C. (2006). Positive psychotherapy. *American Psychologist, 61*(8), 774.

Seligman, M. E., Steen, T. A., Park, N., & Peterson, C. (2005). Positive psychology progress: Empirical validation of interventions. *American Psychologist, 60*(5), 410.

Steel, P., Schmidt, J., & Shultz, J. (2008). Refining the relationship between personality and subjective well-being. *Psychological Bulletin, 134*(1), 138–161.

Steen, T. A., Kachorek, L. V., & Peterson, C. (2003). Character strengths among youth. *Journal of Youth and Adolescence, 32*(1), 5–16.

Taylor, T. L., & Montgomery, P. (2007). Can cognitive-behavioral therapy increase self-esteem among depressed adolescents? A systematic review. *Children and Youth Services Review, 29*(7), 823–839.

Thompson, R. A. (2006). *Nurturing future generations: Promoting resilience in children and adolescents through social, emotional and cognitive skills* (2nd ed.). London, UK: Routledge.

Werner, E. (2006). What can we learn about resilience from large-scale longitudinal studies? In S. Goldstein & R. B. Brooks (Eds.), *Handbook of resilience in children.* New York, NY: Springer.

White, V. E. (2002). Developing counseling objectives and empowering clients: A strength-based intervention. *Journal of Mental Health Counseling, 24*(3), 270.

CHAPTER 13

Defiant Kids

SETTING A CONTEXT

If you want children to keep their feet on the ground, put some responsibility on their shoulders.
—Abigail Van Buren

For kids age 12 and under, only the parents meet to do this work. For teens, the work is done in a session with the teen and the parents. This intervention is *not* ideal for kids who meet diagnostic criteria for oppositional defiant disorder (ODD) or conduct disorder (CD). Those kids need more (see the "Additional Commentary" section later in this chapter). This intervention is for kids who are not complying with doing their cognitive behavioral therapy (CBT) homework and for whom the other interventions in this volume have not been able to resolve that problem. In my clinical experience, these kids often show milder forms of defiance at home or school as well. As these interventions can help clean up these issues, parents tend to highly value them. However, before starting this work I would have given the kid notice, a week or two beforehand, saying something like this:

Monica, I know how important defeating the cobra is to you. And when you're here in sessions I notice how hard you've been working on that. This is why we are seeing some positive changes (a). But I also notice that you're a busy girl. You have homework to do, you deserve and enjoy time to relax each day with your friends online, you're playing soccer, and you have friends you want to see (b). For these reasons, you often don't get to practice using your cobra weapons. Have I understood that correctly (c)? However, I have a way to help with that. I've found that if we get your parents more involved they can help make a difference. What I mean by that is that I can work with them on setting up a system where you earn rewards for doing your therapy practice (d). But I can't tell at this point. Should we involve them or do you think you can start making the time to do your therapy practice on your own **(e)***? Okay, let's agree to do this. If you do your therapy practice each week, going forward, we won't involve them. But if you miss any weeks, that will tell us that you need their help, then we'll bring them in. Deal* **(f)***?*

Explanation

a. Here I would usually list any positive changes we've discussed. At this point in the work depressed kids are usually doing more fun activities, or anxious kids are usually using physiological calming to quell anxiety attacks, or a kid is generally feeling less sad or worried. These sorts of benefits are common even if a kid isn't working much in between sessions.

b. This is just a list of how the kid spends her time after school and on weekends.

c. Empathic feedback like this not only supports accuracy and thoroughness, but it also reduces the odds of sounding like another scolding adult. Because of that kids will rarely disagree. Should you get a kid who disagrees with you and says something like, "Nah, I just think this stuff is stupid," I'd break out the treatment plan and review how important these goals remain to the kid. If that didn't work, I'd press on with engaging the parents.

d. There will actually be two kinds of rewards, should it come to it: the kid earning things that she is currently taking for granted (e.g., access to a cell phone) and things that she would actually think of as a reward (e.g., earning money for a desired purchase). It is remarkable how many kids think of things like cell phones and video games as constitutional rights. However, that doesn't need to be addressed at this juncture, unless a kid asks something like, "What do you mean by 'rewards'?"

e. Most kids will elect to try on their own. But if a kid says that this help would be welcomed, then we'll just agree to start it at the next session.

f. Essentially the kid is being given a chance to avoid parent support, as that such engagement is usually unwelcomed in kid-dom. If parents are ultimately to be brought in, this agreement, in advance of that development, makes it later seem more fair and respectful to kids.

Additional Commentary

Kids who meet diagnostic criteria for ODD or CD need additional interventions. In these instances, the default is to have two therapists: one to do the CBT and one to do the behavioral treatment for ODD and CD. The reason for the default of two therapists is that the mental health professional (MHP) doing the family level behavioral work, for periods of that work, can often be perceived as a bad guy by the kid, which then interferes with the CBT. There have been instances when I've done both kinds of work for a given family, but those have usually been in situations when (a) I can't find a viable choice of therapist to do the other work or (b) a given kid or family gives me the sense that the risk of my becoming a bad guy is very small. Of course, I also involve the parents, and sometimes more mature teens, in this decision making about whether there should be one or two therapists.

My reading of the scientific literature as well as my clinical experience suggest that behaviorally oriented family therapy (BOFT) is the treatment of choice for ODD and mild to moderate CD. The treatment of choice for severe CD is multisystemic therapy (MST). I would only do BOFT for a case of severe CD if MST wasn't a choice and the parents understood my concerns about the prognosis for using that treatment. There are many viable choices for BOFT manuals, some of which I've listed in the References and Bibliography section of this chapter.

In the ideal scenario both treatments would proceed at the same time, meaning two sessions a week. However, if that isn't practical, I usually would treat the externalizing symptoms first and follow up with the treatment for the internalizing symptoms, unless the internalizing symptoms are severe (e.g., the kid is refusing school or is suicidal). The reason I would generally prioritize the treatment for the externalizing symptoms is (a) they are highly distressing to the family system, (b) the treatment is generally briefer than the CBT, and (c) the resolution of externalizing symptoms often, in my clinical experience, resolves at least some, and sometimes all, of the internalizing symptoms. In the latter instance, regularly getting in trouble can be the primary fuel for the internalizing symptoms. So, if you cut off that supply, spontaneous remission of at least some of the internalizing symptoms is possible.

PARENT WORK WITH KIDS AGE 12 AND UNDER

I think it's important to show a husband and a wife together, in a room,
raising children, because you don't see that anymore.
—Tyler Perry

The goal here is to set up a token system. For some kids this may prove to be overkill. But I prefer to overkill a problem and then throttle back, rather than the other way around, which risks stressing everyone out and weakening the alliance. (I'll say more on this in the "Additional Commentary" section.)

So, this will be a session with just the parents. In the waiting-room chat before this session, I would have indicated that the next session is a parent session and explained, in front of the child, that the child and I have agreed that she needs parent support to do her therapy practice and that I'll explain how to do that in the next session. The same commentary I offered in Chapters 2 and 9 regarding which parents would be involved applies here as well. This is what I say in the parent session (I've adapted this script from Barkley's *Defiant Children* treatment manual):

Mom and Dad, how are things going with Monica **(a)**? *This is what I see* **(b)**. *Any thoughts or questions about that* **(c)**? *Okay, so I'd like to set up a program that incentivizes Monica's compliance with her therapy practice. However, this will also be an opportunity for you to incentivize Monica's compliance with your* *expectations at home, including academic work. This is a little complicated, so I'm only going to explain part of it at first, then show you a printed example, then restate a few things, and then wrap up. Here's a clipboard and pen so that if you have any questions as we go along you can write them down. I've found that I won't forget anything, and will often answer most questions anyway if I just finish what I have to share before I get to your questions. I'll also make sure to get to any remaining questions you have when I'm finished. Ready* (d)?

What we are going to create is a 24/7 reward program. There are several steps. The first step is to list out what you expect of Monica. There are usually three things. The first are chores. The second are any grooming responsibilities that she is currently not doing like she's supposed to. The third regard any negative behaviors that you'd like for her to stop. The second step is to make a list of rewards. These can be things that you are currently providing for Monica that she's taking for granted, like access to video games and a cell phone, but it also includes things that you may not currently be providing for her, like the purchase of a new softball glove or a video game. There are three kinds of rewards. First, there are things that you'll allow her to have access to on most days: things like watching TV or playing video games. Second, there are pleasures that might come up only once a week or every 2 weeks, like going out to eat or allowing a sleepover. Then there are more long-term rewards, which may come up only once a month or longer, like a trip to an amusement park or the purchase of some desired toy. So, you make your list of responsibilities: chores, inconsistent grooming, and negative behaviors to stop. Then you make your list of rewards—daily, midterm, and long-term. You can't have too many rewards and want at least 15 of them; don't worry, these rewards will compete with each other. Just like you don't have enough money to buy everything you desire, nor will Monica. It's just that you want Monica's eyes to get big when she sees these rewards, as that will help to motivate her compliance.

Now you're going to decide on your currency. Given that Monica is X (age of the kid), *I'd suggest that we use Y* (e). *The more difficult or challenging a task is for Monica to do, the more chips you'll assign to it, using a range of 3 to 20 chips. Then you'll do a calculation whereby you'll take two-thirds of the chips she can earn every day and disperse that among the daily rewards. I know that's a little confusing, so this might be a good time to review an example* (please see Table 13.1).

So, in this composite case, the responsibilities are on the left side and the rewards are on the right side. On the left side you can see that there are chores like making the bed, doing homework, and cleaning up toys. There are also grooming responsibilities with which this kid is struggling, like taking a shower. You wouldn't want to include any grooming responsibilities that Monica is doing well because we all just do those things without expectation of a reward. It's just that we include them for now until she has them mastered. Once she's doing that kind of grooming consistently and well, you'd remove it from the token system. Next we see examples of negative behaviors to stop—hitting her brother in the morning and evening. For the negative behaviors, you'll need to decide how chronic of a problem it is. If it isn't chronic—occurring only once or twice a week, let's

TABLE 13.1 Sample Token System, Chips

Responsibilities (** = Required Every Day)	Reward	Privileges (** = Available Every Day; Bold = Midterm Privileges; Italics = Long-Term Privileges)	Cost
Make the bed**	5 chips	Television**	5 chips
Get dressed Sunday morning	10 chips	Xbox**	10 chips
Take a shower**	8 chips	Computer usage (for fun)**	5 chips
Brush teeth**	6 chips	Playing outside**	5 chips
Complete homework**	10 chips	Riding bike**	8 chips
			→ Totals 33
Don't hit brother in the morning**	7 chips	**Going out to eat**	40 chips
Don't hit brother in the afternoon and evening**	7 chips	**Renting a DVD**	40 chips
		Buying a CD	40 chips
Don't beg when company is over	3 chips		
Clean up toys	3 chips	**Staying up one extra hour on the weekend**	30 chips
Stay seated during dinner**	3 chips	**$5.00**	35 chips
Go to bed on time**	3 chips	*Sleepover*	50 chips
Do therapy practice	15 chips	*Going to Discovery Zone*	60 chips
		Getting a new bike	1,740 chips
		Getting a laptop	2,300 chips
		Take a trip to Dorney Park	1,000 chips
Total chips from activities that are required each day: 49 chips			
2/3 (rounded): 33 chips			
Bank a week if spends all of daily chips (1/3 of 49 times seven plus the weekly tasks): 145 chips		It is important to construct both responsibility and reward cards that specify expectations and limitations for rewards (e.g., when they can be accessed, time limits, etc.).	

say—you'd just list it once. But if it happens throughout the day, you want to split it in two, into morning and evening blocks, like I've done in this table, so Monica is incentivized to gather herself for the second half of the day if she's lapsed in the first part of the day. Now you see that the parent has set chip values. Not knowing this kid, we can see that getting dressed on Sunday morning must be a real struggle because it's earning 10 chips. Likewise, cleaning up toys must not be a big parental challenge or difficult for the kid to do because it's only earning three chips. On the right side we can see the rewards. The ones this kid has access to each day are in plain text. The midterm rewards are in bold while the long-term rewards are in italics. Don't get bothered by the extravagance of these rewards because, like I mentioned before, no kid will be able to earn enough chips to do them all regularly, as you'll see in a moment.

Now we can see that the things this kid is expected to do each day have two asterisks next to them. If you do the math, and add up those chip values, you'd get 49 chips, which is depicted at the lower left of the sheet. Now the parent takes two-thirds of that number, approximately—you can round—which in this case is 33 chips, and disperses that among the daily rewards. The more a kid enjoys doing a thing, or the more it taxes your time or resources, the more expensive it should be. So, we can see that this kid must really love playing on her Xbox system more than the other daily pleasures as that one is twice as expensive as any other daily reward. Now what the parent did was to figure out how many chips this kid would be banking each week, if she's an angel. We have the one-third left over from the daily responsibilities, plus the chips from the nondaily responsibilities that come up each week. You can see, on the lower left, that that number is 145 chips. Next, the parents figure out how often they want the kid to have access to the midterm and long-term rewards. There are two kinds of mistakes to avoid. If the chip values are set too low, you'll feel like you're a slave to this system and it will exhaust you. If you set the chip values too high, it will seem to Monica like it's too difficult to earn the rewards and she won't be motivated. It's the middle ground you're looking for. I find that most parents have a good intuition about where that middle ground is and do a good job with that.

Okay, the next thing you're going to need are chore and reward cards. Chore cards specify what appropriate task completion looks like. You can use index cards for this. For example, on a "making the bed" chore card it might list "everything off the bed," "all sheets and pillows put on neatly," and "done before eating breakfast." This spares you Monica saying that she made her bed but it's not up to scratch. It should also include how long you expect the task to take; you're not looking for Monica to break any speed records, but putting a time limit on it helps you to deal with passive resistance. Reward cards likewise specify any limitations you want to place on access to the rewards. So, for example, for the "going out to eat" reward, a parent might have a reward card that reads, "Only on Fridays if there are no previously scheduled events and a car is available." This spares you from having Monica complain that you're not being fair when she wants to spend her points on a reward that isn't practical to deliver at the point in time that she asks for it. Reward cards also allow you to put limits on sedentary electronic pleasuring. For my own part, I think the recommendation of the American Academy of Pediatrics is spot on. They suggest limiting such activities to 2 hours a day. I believe their thought is that if a kid is spending more time than that each day watching TV or playing electronic games she is probably short-changing other important activities like homework or being physically active.

What I suggest you do is write a rough draft on your own and then set it aside. Then sit down with Monica and say something like, "Honey, we think you're doing well in so many things these days." And list them. Then say, "We also think that you could be even more successful in certain areas, like doing your therapy practice. So, we want to create a way to reward you for your hard work. We'll explain as we go. First, let's make a list of the things that we expect you to do. What are those?" Then you'll walk her through her responsibilities, trying to get her to say them before you go through the questions you ask; if she says the responsibility first, you'll get less eye rolling and resistance. Though, you may need to remind her of a few things. Then you can say something like, "Okay, now what are the things that we either are giving to you that are fun or which you're not getting now but would like to get?" Again, you may need to ask her some questions to get her to say things like "watching TV." But she may very well think of some midterm and long-term rewards that you didn't. So, including her ideas would be important to do. After you have your lists, tell her you need to take a break and then finalize your math.

You can then come back to her and explain, "Monica, whenever you do these responsibilities you're going to earn these chips. These chips are going to be your money around here. Because then you can use them to spend on these rewards." You can then go through what earns what and what costs what. You can present her with her bank. An empty plastic gallon jug of milk, with the top cut off, usually works fine. You can say, "Whenever you do something on this side, be sure to tell us. We'll look to see that you did it and then put chips in your bank. Then, when you want something on this side, just tell us and we'll go to your bank and see if you have enough chips for it. These here are chore cards; they tell you what you need to do to earn chips for your chores. These are your reward cards. They tell you when and where you can buy your rewards."

You can keep Monica's bank somewhere that she can see it but can't get easy access to it, like the top of the refrigerator, for example. We don't let her keep the bank because it becomes your nightmare if she loses chips that she's earned. It's okay to let her periodically count her chips for herself, or do the Scrooge thing and run her fingers through her chips, but always under your supervision. Of course, you want to keep your central bank somewhere that she can't get access to it. If you notice that she did a responsibility and she didn't tell you, it's okay to give her the chips. But, if she doesn't tell you, and you didn't notice it, she's lost her opportunity to earn chips. The alternative is to incentivize lying. This is business, and you need to put eyes on it.

Let me tell you that there are two easy ways to sink this ship. The first is to advance her chips on the promise that she'll do a responsibility later. There are usually no advances in this system, because if she doesn't have enough chips for a daily or midterm reward, that often means that she's dropped the ball on the responsibility side somewhere along the line, or just chose to spend heavily in other areas. So, advances can do things like reward ball-dropping behavior. The second is to deny her something she's earned and that meets the specifications of a reward card, outside of moments that she is tantruming, because you're mad at her. It's a simple rule to keep in mind: If it's not earned it's not granted. If it's earned it's granted.

The first time Monica doesn't have enough chips for a daily or midterm reward she may want to direct the language of punishment at you. She might say, "Why are you doing this to me?" Or, "Why are you punishing me so much?" Or, other things along those lines. In the language of punishment, you have all the power and are deciding, often arbitrarily, when and how to deploy it. You want to respond with the language of reward, which will be to say calmly and empathically things like, "Monica, I'm sorry that you don't have enough chips to watch TV. You may remember that you didn't make your bed this morning. If you had, you'd now have enough chips to watch TV. I'm really sorry that you did that to yourself, as I know how much you enjoy TV. But tomorrow is a new day and I'm hopeful that you'll make a better decision for yourself then."

When it comes to the therapy practice responsibility, I will let you know, in our waiting-room consult each week, if Monica earned her chips for that responsibility each week.

There are so many sidebar benefits to a token system. First, kids learn about budgeting their resources, with some amusing results sometimes. For instance, I once had a TV-obsessed—or that's how her parents put it—10-year-old girl decide to go 3 weeks without watching TV because she was saving up for a new bike. Also, this language of reward instills responsibility. As a university professor I'm amazed at how many young adults expect me to protect them from the consequences of their choices because they are nice people who mean well and try hard. At the tender age of X (insert age) you are teaching Monica that her desired outcomes, each and every day, are contingent on the choices SHE makes. You just can't buy that kind of value.

Don't take away any chips for the first week. Later, we can discuss punishment strategies if they are needed. For now, this is reward only.

Okay, what questions do you have (f)?

Explanation

a. It's common for parents to remark on what's better. That's what we are expecting and listen for. If they say that nothing is better, the next segment becomes even more important.

b. I would have prepared, in my mind, a summary of how Monica is working in session and any symptom improvement that I've noted. (Of course, if nothing is truly improved it suggests a need to loop back to the evaluation findings and the treatment plan.)

c. If you are on the same page with the parents, great, and that's usually what happens here. If they have concerns about progress, those would normally need to be addressed before pushing on. If so, other chapters in this volume will give you ideas about how to proceed.

d. Some parents may offer a question, but I encourage them to wait on that until I get through my spiel. Tail wagging dog sessions usually start with good intentions (e.g., being respectful) but slow progress and ultimately stress the treatment alliance.

e. For kids age 8 and under, chips are usually advisable. These kids usually need the tangible touch and sight of the chips to maximize motivation. Older kids have the cognitive maturity to be sufficiently motivated by points. In the previous example (Table 13.1), I proceeded with a chip system. Table 13.2 illustrates what a point system could look like.

    Instead of chips in a jug it's points in a bankbook, with a range of 20 to 200. Everything else is just about the same.

f. Here are some common questions and suggested responses:

Parent: *What about our other kids? Should we do this with them also?*
MHP: *If you have the energy, fine. But if you don't, I wouldn't worry about it as long as the amount of rewarding is approximately even across your kids. Just like your kids need different pant sizes to be comfortable, they need different parenting approaches to be successful. One size doesn't fit all in pants or parenting. So, if you have the energy to do a token system with all your kids, awesome. If not, no worries. Besides, no matter what you do, each of your kids will complain that you favor the other one from time to time; that's just the nature of sibling life.*
Parent: *What if she sneaks into our stash and steals chips?*
MHP: *Let's not even make that a possibility. If there's a risk of that, keep it locked in one of your cars or in a safe or something like that.*
Parent: *What do we do if we're going to watch a movie as a family? Do I make her spend her chips?*
MHP: *No. The guideline is that if it's something you're planning to do as a family it's a freebie.*
Parent: *Should we include things like going to softball practice, which she loves, but there's a team component?*
MHP: *There are a few kinds of activities, even though they're pleasurable, that you wouldn't want to include. The first are experiences that you very much want Monica to do because they are good for her. I once had a mom who had a daughter with a reading disorder. A fun ritual they had was to go to the library on Saturday and read together. For that kid, it would have been a mistake to include that in the token system because the mom needed for her daughter to do that each week. Another thing to avoid are experiences that you've paid money for and you'd be irritated if Monica didn't go—if you paid for a month's worth of softball coaching, let's say. Otherwise, I'd err on the*

TABLE 13.2 Sample Token System, Points

Responsibilities (** = Required Every Day)	Reward	Privileges (** = Available Every Day; Bold = Midterm Privileges; Italics = Long-Term Privileges)	Cost
Make the bed**	100 points	Television**	100 points
Get dressed Sunday morning	200 points	Xbox**	195 points
Take a shower**	150 points	Computer usage (for fun)**	75 points
Brush teeth**	125 points	Playing outside**	100 points
Complete homework**	200 points	Riding bike**	150 points
			⟶ Totals 620
Don't hit brother in the morning**	150 points	**Going out to eat**	500 points
Don't hit brother in the afternoon and evening**	150 points	**Renting a DVD**	500 points
		Buying a CD	525 points
Don't beg when company is over	40		
Clean up toys	50 points	**Staying up one extra hour on the weekend**	350 points
Stay seated during dinner**	20 points	**$5.00**	500 points
Go to bed on time**	30 points	*Sleepover*	1,000 points
Do therapy practice	200 points	*Going to Discovery Zone*	800 points
		Getting a new bike	45,000 points
		Getting a laptop	60,000 points
		Take a trip to Dorney Park	30,000 points
Total points from activities that are required each day: 925 points			
2/3 (rounded): 620 points			
Bank a week if spends all of daily points (1/3 of 925 times seven plus the weekly tasks): 2,600 points		It is important to construct both responsibility and reward cards that specify expectations and limitations for rewards (e.g., when they can be accessed, time limits, etc.).	

side of making Monica earn it, which she will have every opportunity to do. Her choices determine if she has the chips she needs.

Parent: *Should I take away her going outside, even if I could use the peace and quiet?*

MHP: *I'm really glad you asked it that way because it allows me to make an important point. You're not taking away anything. Monica is either earning or not earning her rewards. And, yes, if she didn't have enough chips to go outside and play with her friends I'd bite the bullet on that one, reminding her that she would have had enough chips if only she had done X and that you're hopeful she'll make a better choice for herself going forward. In the short run this taxes you more, but this approach should leave you in the black over the long run.*

Parent: *When should we start?*

MHP: *As soon as you can. You might let Monica start earning her chips this week, but not make her buy stuff until next week. Or, you can start her out with one day's worth of chips to get her going. But I'd start as soon as possible.*

(Some of these latter points I'd also include in the default review if they seem germane.)

Additional Commentary

It's remarkable how much a motivated kid can improve her performance. And a token system reorganizes a kid's world so that compliance is a lavish banquet and defiance is a walk in the desert. In these instances parents don't have to lobby their kid to choose the banquet instead of the desert; she just does.

PARENT WORK WITH KIDS AGE 13 AND OLDER

I take a very practical view of raising children. I put a sign in each of their rooms: "Checkout Time is 18 years."
—Erma Bombeck

For teens the preferred method is to establish a contract. This is done in a family session with the parent(s) and the teen. This is what I say to teens and their parents:

Monica, how are things going? Mom and Dad, how are things going in your minds? Yeah, this is some of what I think . . . (a). Okay, as I mentioned last time, today's appointment has the purpose of forming a contract between you, Monica, and your parents. Everybody benefits. Monica, you benefit because you feel less hounded and pestered. Also, you get more control over your privileges and rewards and don't have to rely as much on Mom or Dad being in a good mood. Mom and Dad, you benefit because Monica more consistently does as you expect and you don't have to act as much like a prison warden. If any of that seems mysterious, I promise you it'll clear up by the time we're done today.

Monica, the first step is for you and I to make a list of what would be fair for your parents to expect of you. Mom and Dad, you'll have a chance to weigh in later; for now, just let the two of us do this as you listen. Okay Monica, what would be fair for your parents to expect of you (b)? Great, now, let's go over your privileges, and I mean that in two ways. First, what are the things they are currently providing for you and what are the things you'd like to be able to earn that you don't yet have (c)? Okay, Mom and Dad, it's time for you to weigh in. Let's go through the responsibility side one-by-one and see if you'd like to make any changes (d). Great, now let's do the reward side of things (e). Awesome. Okay, now Monica, let me ask, do you get an allowance? Would you like to earn one (f)? Mom and Dad, if it was properly earned, would you be okay with Monica having an allowance (g)? Great, think for a few moments about what would be fair; feel free to text each other, or to pass notes, as we talk. Monica, I need you to think of something that you'd like to be able to earn, having your parents purchase it for you. It could be a piece of sports equipment, or a video game, or some experience, or whatever. While I do some work, think about that and I'll ask you in a couple of minutes (h). Table 13.3 indicates what my notes might look like.

TABLE 13.3 Monica's Contract

Responsibility	Reward
Academic duty Complete at least 110 minutes of homework each day, with a quality effort and no complaining.	Can earn up to 2 hours on the computer, for leisure, that day. Doing homework 3 out of 5 days, plus working 1x with Math teacher, earns up to 2 hours on Saturdays. Doing homework 5 out of 5 days, plus working 3x with Math teacher, earns up to 3 hours on Sundays.
Vacuum duty Vacuum all carpets, and dust room, between Friday night and Saturday night, 8 p.m.	Use of iPad the following week.
Take care of room Pick up dirty clothes and water bottles by bedtime each day and put away clean laundry (from laundry room) within the same day, when parent indicates laundry is done.	Can watch TV or play Xbox the next day (combined with playing on the computer, cannot exceed 3 hours, except on Sunday, when it cannot exceed 4 hours if homework was done all week).
Do therapy practice.	Access to the cell phone at home the following week.
Outdoor duty Cut the backyard grass, water plants, and wash Dad's car between Friday night and Sunday night, 8 p.m.	Can go out with friends at least once the following week as long as parents approve of the activity.

Okay, here is how I've paired things up. What I've tried to do is pair the tasks that are hardest to do with the rewards that you value the most, Monica. But we can change any pairing that you all would like (i). Mom and Dad, did you come up with an allowance (j)? Monica, did you come up with something to earn (k)? Great. So, Monica, I'd suggest you get two bonuses. The first bonus would be an allowance. So, if you do everything you're supposed to do in a given day, that's $4 that you've earned. Therefore, you can earn up to $28 a week. When would you like your payday to be? Mom and Dad, is that okay with you (l)? The DOUBLE bonus, then, is that you'd earn a dollar a day toward the purchase of jewelry (m).

Mom and Dad, you'll need some grid paper (n). The rows on this sheet are each responsibility, while the columns are the days of the month. First thing is to go through and cross out any cells that aren't needed. So, for example, most cells across from the vacuuming duty will be crossed out. Then, Monica, whenever you do something, you let your Mom or Dad know so that they can put a checkmark in that cell on the grid. Mom and Dad, if you notice that Monica completed something and she didn't tell you, it's okay to note it on the grid. But let's say it's a very busy day and you do your homework, Monica, but they don't notice, and you forget to tell them, and then it's the next day and you're like, "Oh, Mom and Dad, I did my homework yesterday," it's too late—you wouldn't get the credit for that day's homework. So, it's sort of like employees having to punch their time cards to get paid. Sure, if a boss notices that they were at work and forgot to punch in or out, the boss could choose to do it for them. But, otherwise, it's on the worker. Any questions about that (o)? Monica, let me just repeat and elaborate on something I said earlier. I don't know if you figured this out yet, but EVERY reward in this contract is 100% under your control, with only one possible exception that I'll review another time. You know (looking at the kid) that what you're allowed to do can change based on the kind of a day your Mom or Dad are having. But, not now. They are agreeing (looking at Mom and Dad) to surrender all control over your rewards. You are master and commander of your rewards (p). Oh, and the therapy practice deal is something that you and I—mostly me, but I'll involve you—will decide if you did each week. Fair (q)? I'll only add one other thing. All functioning relationships require goodwill. Monica, there may be privileges or rewards you'll want that aren't in this contract. Likewise, Mom and Dad, you may ask Monica to do things that aren't listed here, either. This is where goodwill comes into play. If everyone does what they can to be cooperative and kind, these moments tend to be relatively drama-free. If not, you can just use the problem-solving technique to deal with them (r).

Explanation

a. The explanation is the same as the one for starting a token system.

b. This mostly is a straightforward matter. Experienced and wise kid MHPs are like experienced and wise kindergarten teachers. We know that if you ask most humans, in moments of calm, what's fair to expect of them, they'll usually do a good job, and sometimes are even more strict with themselves than the authority figure planned to be. The only hitch I consistently run into here regards time spent on homework, at least for kids whose academic performance is compromised. This is how that dialogue will commonly go with a teen:

Kid: *Do my homework.*
MHP: *Right. What would be a good minimum to do each night?*
Kid: *Just until it's done.*
MHP: *Yes, sometimes you'd have to go over the minimum, but what would be a fair minimum in case you got it all done in school and nothing is assigned or almost nothing is assigned?*
Kid: *Don't need a minimum.*
MHP: *Y'know, Monica, there are just about always tests or quizzes around the corner, or projects that are due later in the quarter. Let me share something. The research suggests that a good amount of time is 10 minutes times the grade you are in. So, given that you're in 11th grade, that's 110 minutes. During that time, on nights where you have nothing else due the next day, you'd study for tests, go over notes, do the work toward a longer-term project, and so forth.*
Kid: *That sounds stupid.*
MHP: *I hear that. You don't want to waste your time, after all. I'll tell you, though, that sort of a habit will also better prepare you for college. But think about it for a few minutes and we'll get your parents' thoughts when it's their turn to weigh in.*

The vast majority of parents will want to insist on a minimal amount of homework time. Most kids will grouse, and there may be an adjustment period, but it's mostly not a big deal. If parents decide to capitulate to the kid's wishes, I might set a few minutes aside with them to make sure they are making an informed decision. But I believe our task is to share information and to peacefully go along with whatever a family decides once they know our thinking, as long as we still have a positive contribution to make and there is no reportable abuse or neglect going on.

c. This is usually also a fairly straightforward task. Sometimes, like is the case with younger kids, teens need to be prompted to think of their cell phone as a privilege, but that's done easily enough most of the time. Like with the homework time allotment, I'll also need to engage a teen with questions like, *Should there be a total limit on how much time you spend playing video games?* And, *What's a fair curfew?* The ensuing discussion is similar to the one I just reviewed on homework, with me getting the teen's take, offering empathy, offering my perspective, getting the teen's reaction, and then deferring the decision to the parents. In the case of sedentary electronic pleasuring, the discussion is very similar to the one I shared about setting up the token system.

d. Were I to guesstimate an average, I'd say that 85% of what the teen has offered is okay by the parents. They may tweak here and there, in which case I'll ask the teen if the tweaks sound fair. In the less common situations when the teen balks, I'll encourage the family to have a discussion about the issue with me serving as a communications coach. If they lock down, and that happens quite infrequently, it can serve as an opportunity to practice the problem-solving technique reviewed in Chapter 11.

e. Again, parents usually only offer a few tweaks here.

f. In my practice many kids say "no." At first this surprised me. But over time I've come to a view that many kids are just used to going to their parents and having an open account. So, they may not see value in having an allowance. If so, I ask them if they'd *mind* getting an allowance, which they almost always don't mind.

g. If parents hesitate, or they look at me as if to say, "Why are you introducing this as a topic?" I'll say something like this: *I think allowances are a good thing. It sounds like how it is now is that Monica just asks whenever she wants something and you, if it's a reasonable request, grant it. However, allowances begin to teach things about money management and prioritizing expenditures. If you did this, and it would be my suggestion that you do, Monica would become more responsible for spending her own money on elective purchases and not have such an open account with you.* The latter point usually allays parent concerns, as I think they were imagining that I was suggesting that they add to their weekly expenditures.

h. For some kids this is an easy question. In other households, where teens are already being lavished with goods, it can take the kid some time to come up with something. Another thing that can cause some pause is if the kid is still anhedonic, in which case I'll invite the parents into the discussion and we'll brainstorm what the teen might like to earn as a double bonus.

i. Families just usually go with my pairings, but sometimes they'll have some sound reasoning that suggests a change. There is usually little drama generated at this juncture.

j. Sometimes a kid is given this as homework, but most of the time the kid and the parents can come up with something.

k. Sometimes they'll ask me for my opinion regarding an amount for the allowance, but there isn't a less or more psychologically sound number, other than avoiding obvious and extreme ends of the continuum. The only thing I usually do is suggest making the number easily divisible by seven (i.e., the days in a week).

l. I can't think of the last time a parent objected to the teen's selection for the payday. To ask creates another empowerment moment for a teen.

m.   Bonuses and double bonuses are very important. On a given day or week a teen may feel like a given reward isn't important to her. So, we need to create a contract where blowing off a given responsibility causes multiple deprivations. Most families figure this out on their own, but if a parent balks here, I'll explain it. Once everyone agrees, I write in the bonus and the double bonus at the bottom of the contract.

n.   Grid paper is available at most office supply stores, but most folks just make up their own.

o.   The immediate reason for establishing this guideline is to deincentivize lying. But it also adds to the yield of the teen learning personal responsibility.

p.   Besides the rewards, this way of conceptualizing the contract is a major selling point for a teen, and I always emphasize it. The exception I allude to refers to groundings (discussed in the subsequent section on Punishment), but I don't get into that discussion now as it just causes, in my clinical experience, needless complications and consternation.

q.   I ask for the teen's assent here in order to be respectful. I can't think of the last time when a teen didn't agree. But, should that happen tomorrow, I'd just use one of the previous scripts I reviewed (i.e., involving getting a statement of the teen's concern[s], providing empathy, providing clarification, and encouraging discussion with the parents if needed).

r.   A need to do problem solving usually doesn't present itself. But, if it does, it's easy to bang one out in 10 to 15 minutes, at least if the family is practiced with the technique.

Additional Commentary

There isn't much to add here. As long as the diagnostic formulation is accurate (e.g., there are no complicating factors like conduct disorder or an addiction) and the responsibilities and rewards are specific and well conceived, comprehensive contracts tend to run themselves.

PUNISHMENT

If a punishment module is needed, I'll do it in a separate session. While such work is a staple of treatments for ODD and CD, it usually is not needed in these cases. Even so, I offer this section because you may end up having some use for it. I won't review my wording but just explain the techniques.

Response Cost

Response cost is used in a token system. It is usually not established until the token system is up and running for at least one week in order to keep the reward component primary. It is merely a take away of the same amount of chips or points a kid would have earned if she had done the responsibility as expected. This is explained to the kid up front and is used for those two or three responsibilities for which the kid's performance is spotty. If you have a kid who needs a response cost for more items than that, something is amiss (e.g., the parents aren't doing special time, there is more marital conflict than the original evaluation suggested). So, let's say a kid earns 10 chips by brushing her teeth, but she's consistently not doing it. The parent adds a new column of a take away of 10 chips if the kid doesn't brush her teeth as expected. This is a *one-time* deduction per occurrence; in other words, the parent doesn't deduct additional chips if the kid gets mouthy about the first deduction.

Time-Out

Time-out is used for children and not usually for teens. There are two paths to time-out. The first path involves a child not complying with a parent's directive. The first command is issued as normal (i.e., as few words as possible, specific and calmly, firmly delivered, with eye contact, giving the kid some advance notice if possible). If the child resists, the second command is issued 5 seconds or so later, with the threat of time-out and the parent adopting a terse tone of voice. If the child still doesn't get going 5 seconds later (i.e., "one thousand one, one thousand two . . ." counted inside the parent's head), the parent tells her to get into the time-out chair. The child sits in the time-out chair, which should be something relatively uncomfortable, like a dining room chair, for a minimum sentence of one minute for each year she has lived out-side of the womb; the parent does not declare the minimum sentence or set a timer, because that makes it less comfortable of an experience for the child. To get out of time-out, two conditions must be met: the child has to be sitting in the chair quietly and she must agree to comply. If both conditions are not satisfied the parent adds another minimum sentence but without announcing it, as that could needlessly escalate the child. The parent keeps privately cycling through periods of minimum sentences until the child meets both criteria.

The second path to time-out is the child does something significantly inappropriate (e.g., damages a sibling's toy). That's a straight shot to time-out. The child sits there for the minimum sentence until two criteria are met: She is sitting there quietly and expresses remorse. In this instance it would also be important for the parent to engage the child in a plan of reparation once everyone is calmed down, which may not be when time-out is over. It's not good for a kid's development to merely apologize; for her sake, she should make it right. Making this a collaborative exchange is ideal, but the parent may need to impose the reparative plan if the kid resists.

The time-out chair should also be positioned so that it is away from anything entertaining and the child can't grab and throw stuff. No one should interact with the child while she is in time-out. (Want to set up a reward program for getting a child to say disrespectful things to a parent? Put her in time-out and make sure the parent gives her attention when she says the disrespectful things.) The real intervention with time-out becomes the threat of it. Children appreciate that it's better for them to simply comply with a command than it is to do time-out and then comply with the command. For other issues that can come up, I recommend that you see one of the treatment manuals in the References and Bibliography section of this chapter or search at my blog site, www.hecticparents.com.

Grounding

This is the punishment for teens. Grounding occurs if the teen does something significantly wrong (e.g., skips first period in order to go out to breakfast). The grounding involves not being able to access earned rewards for a period of a couple of hours to 2 or 3 days. It's important that the parent not set groundings that are not enforceable (e.g., a parent is not around to monitor), so the timing is important. If a teen does something that seems to warrant a grounding for a longer period of time, that's usually signaling a need for the MHP to become involved in understanding what happened and how to best address it.

SIDEBAR 13.1

Marked playing cards are yet another staple of magicians. My favorites are Phoenix Decks. They are marked in multiple ways, allowing for more kinds of tricks; they are currently available for under $5.

A great DVD for showing a range of tricks with Phoenix Decks is *Release the Power: Phoenix Cards for Magicians* by Christian Schenk. One of the simpler tricks on the DVD is titled "Don't Blink." The kid shuffles the deck. The cards are then spread facedown. The kid picks one. Ask the kid to hold it up and stare at it for a minute, making sure to memorize it. As the kid does this you can spot what the card is by looking at the back of the card. Then ask the kid to put her card back into the deck and shuffle it, noting that you're not touching anything and haven't seen the face of the card. Get out your mind puppet (see the trick in Chapter 3) and have it infuse you with the power to read the kid's mind. Tell the kid that when you display the selected card she should **scream in her head 'That's it!' but not out loud**. Then turn the cards face-up, one at a time, noting that you will be listening for her to scream in her head, "That's it!" As you flip over cards that are not her card, note that you're not hearing her screaming, so her card must not have come up yet. When you get to her selected card, exaggerate a response like, **Whoa! You didn't have to scream that loud!** Do this while laughing. It's usually a big hit.

REFERENCES AND BIBLIOGRAPHY

Barkley, R. A. (2013). *Defiant children: A clinician's manual for assessment and parent training.* New York, NY: Guilford Press.

Barkley, R. A., & Robin, A. L. (2014). *Defiant teens: A clinician's manual for assessment and family intervention.* New York, NY: Guilford Press.

Baumrind, D. (1971). Current patterns of parental authority. *Developmental Psychology, 4*, 1–103.

Baumrind, D. (1991). The influence of parenting style on adolescent competence and substance use. *Journal of Early Adolescence, 11*(1), 56–95.

Brooks, R. B. (2006). The power of parenting. In S. Goldstein & R. B. Brooks (Eds.), *Handbook of resilience in children.* New York, NY: Springer.

Christophersen, E. R., & Vanscoyoc, S. M. (2013). *Treatments that work with children: Empirically supported strategies for managing childhood problems.* Washington, DC: American Psychological Association.

Cooper, H. (2007). *The battle over homework* (3rd ed.). Thousand Oaks, CA: Corwin Press.

Fonagy, P., Target, M., Cottrell, D., Phillips, J., & Kurtz, Z. (2002). *What works for whom: A critical review of treatments for children and adolescents.* New York, NY: Guilford Press.

Hoeve, M., Dubas, J. S., Eichelsheim, V. I., Van der Laan, P. H., Smeenk, W., & Gerris, J. R. (2009). The relationship between parenting and delinquency: A meta-analysis. *Journal of Abnormal Child Psychology, 37*(6), 749–775.

Huebner, A. J., & Howell, L. W. (2003). Examining the relationship between adolescent sexual risk-taking and perceptions of monitoring, communication, and parenting styles. *Journal of Adolescent Health, 33*(2), 71–78.

Kahn, J. H., & Garrison, A. M. (2009). Emotional self-disclosure and emotional avoidance: Relations with symptoms of depression and anxiety. *Journal of Counseling Psychology, 56*(4), 573–584.

Kazdin, A. E., Siegel, T. C., & Bass, D. (1992). Cognitive problem-solving skills training and parent management training in the treatment of antisocial behavior in children. *Journal of Consulting and Clinical Psychology, 60*(5), 733–747.

Lamborn, S. D., Mounts, N. S., Steinberg, L., & Dornbusch, S. M. (1991). Patterns of competence and adjustment among adolescents from authoritative, authoritarian, indulgent, and neglectful families. *Child Development, 62*, 1049–1065.

Laskey, B. J., & Cartwright-Hatton, S. (2009). Parental discipline behaviours and beliefs about their child: Associations with child internalizing and mediation relationships. *Child: Care, Health, and Development, 35*(5), 717–727.

Michelson, D., Davenport, C., Dretzke, J., Barlow, J., & Day, C. (2013). Do evidence-based interventions work when tested in the "real world"? A systematic review and meta-analysis of parent management training for the treatment of child disruptive behavior. *Clinical Child & Family Psychology Review, 16*(1), 18–34.

Querido, J. G., Warner, T. D., & Eyberg, S. M. (2002). Parenting styles and child behavior in African American families of preschool children. *Journal of Clinical Child & Adolescent Psychology, 31*(2), 272–277

Rueter, M. A., & Conger, R. D. (1998). Reciprocal influences between parenting and adolescent problem-solving behavior. *Developmental Psychology, 34*(6), 1470–1482.

Shucksmith, J., Hendry, L. B., & Glendinning, A. (1995). Models of parenting: Implications for adolescent well-being within different types of family contexts. *Journal of Adolescence, 18*(3), 253–270.

Simons, R. L., Simons, L. G., Burt, C. H., Brody, G. H., & Cutrona, C. (2005). Collective efficacy, authoritative parenting, and delinquency: A longitudinal test of a model integrating community- and family-level processes. *Criminology, 43*(4), 989–1029.

Steinberg, L., Blatt-Eisengart, I., & Cauffman, E. (2006). Patterns of competence and adjustment among adolescents from authoritative, authoritarian, indulgent, and neglectful homes: A replication in a sample of serious juvenile offenders. *Journal of Research on Adolescence*, 16(1), 47–58.

Steinberg, L., Elmen, J. D., & Mounts, N. S. (1989). Authoritative parenting, psychosocial maturity, and academic success among adolescents. *Child Development*, 60(6), 1424–1436.

Weersing, V. R., & Weisz, J. R. (2002). Mechanisms of action in youth psychotherapy. *Journal of Child Psychology and Psychiatry*, 43(1), 3–29.

SECTION **IV**

Final Phase and Termination

CHAPTER **14**

Using Exposures

ENGAGING THE KID

He who is not everyday conquering some fear has not learned the secret of life.
—Ralph Waldo Emerson

This procedure is used for kids who are treated for anxiety. This is what I say:

Monica, you've done such a great job fighting back against the cobra (a)*. This is why the cobra has been mostly leaving you alone. However, now we need to go to where the cobra lives, bang on its door, and call it out for a butt kicking. We do this by making a list of the situations in which the cobra has tended to try to attack you. I'll explain more as we go* (b)*. What kind of situations tend to bring on a cobra attack* (c)*?*

This is a list of common exposures among anxious youth:

▶ Getting on the school bus

▶ Answering the door at home when someone knocks

▶ Going down to the basement by myself

▶ Introducing myself to another kid I don't know

▶ Talking to a guy I'm attracted to

▶ Asking a friend, face-to-face, to do something on the weekend

▶ Asking a clerk at a store where something is

- ► Sleeping in my bed by myself

- ► Answering the house phone when I don't know who it is

- ► Ordering pizza from the house phone

- ► Raising my hand in class

- ► Missing a shot in a basketball game

- ► Staying in the car by myself when my mom goes into a store

- ► Going to a strange city (accompanied by a parent or teacher)

- ► Giving a speech

- ► Giving a wrong answer in class

- ► Being late for something

- ► Being left with a babysitter

- ► A thunderstorm

- ► Asking to change my order at a restaurant

- ► Eating something that's dropped on the floor

- ► Petting a dog

- ► Going to the doctor's office

- ► Being home alone

Okay, this looks like a good list (d). *Next we need to give each of these situations a number that lets us know how hard the cobra attacks you in these situations. Let's go from 1 to 100. A "1" means that the cobra is barely, barely doing anything. A "100" means it's the hardest attack that the cobra can do. So, you give the number after I name the situation.* This is what this list could look like.

Cobra Fear List

- ► Getting on the school bus 75

- ► Answering the door at home when someone knocks 50

▶ Going down to the basement by myself 60

▶ Introducing myself to another kid I don't know 70

▶ Talking to a guy I'm attracted to. 95

▶ Asking a friend, face-to-face, to do something on the weekend 45

▶ Asking a clerk at a store where something is 80

▶ Sleeping in my bed by myself 85

▶ Answering the house phone when I don't know who it is 40

▶ Ordering pizza from the house phone. 60

▶ Raising my hand in class 70

▶ Missing a shot in a basketball game. 95

▶ Staying in the car by myself when my mom goes into a store 35

▶ Going to a strange city (accompanied by a parent or teacher) 50

▶ Giving a speech 99

▶ Giving a wrong answer in class 95

▶ Being late for something 65

▶ Being left with a babysitter 67

▶ A thunderstorm. 50

▶ Asking to change my order at a restaurant. 80

▶ Eating something that's dropped on the floor 50

▶ Petting a dog 30

▶ Going to the doctor's office 35

▶ Being home alone 80

So, what we want to do is to have you deliberately put yourself in these situations and then use your weapons to defeat the cobra. These are called "exposures" because we are exposing you to the cobra to show that you're stronger and can defeat the cobra. Don't worry, we'll start out with the easier things and build from there. And, once you've defeated the cobra in these situations, we are all done with our work (e)! So, look at this list. Let's pick two for you to do this week (f). Okay, good, you'll pet your cousin's dog this weekend at their house for at least 10 minutes and you'll answer the phone at home three times when you don't know who it is, if the opportunity arises anyway. Now, what weapon or weapons can you use when you do these two exposures (g)? That sounds awesome. I think this is going to go well. Let me show you this form that we can use to track your exposures (see Table 14.1).

TABLE 14.1 Exposure Tracking Form

Name: _____

Week: _____

Situation Before the Exposure (Around Me and Inside Me)	Exposure	Strength of Cobra Attack at the Start (1–100)	Weapon(s) Used	Strength of Cobra Attack at the End (1–100)	Situation After the Exposure (Around Me and Inside Me)

So you can see in the first column that you want to put down what was going on before the exposure, both around you and inside you. So, a kid might write, "I was watching TV and felt calm," or "I was doing homework and thinking I don't like my math teacher," or "I was playing with my cat, feeling happy and thinking she's an awesome cat." So, you have the situation, like watching TV, and then you could be thinking things, feeling things, or both. Then you put what exposure you did. So, this week we said you'll list when you pet your cousin's dog and each time you answer the phone. Then, as you start to do the exposure, the cobra will likely try to lie to you in some way, trying to make you like this (point to the right side of the externalizing problem sheet from the kid's binder). *So, write down how strong the cobra was at that point. Of course, you'll use the weapons we just talked about, which you'll put in this column. Then, when the exposure is done, put down how strong the cobra was at that point in the fifth column. Finally, you'll put down what was going on inside you and outside you in the last column. What questions do you have, Monica? Would you mind saying back to me how to fill in this sheet, so I make sure I explained it well* (h)?

At the end today, we'll review that this is our plan with your mom (i).

a. This is a chance to review progress to date. A review of treatment plan goals might also be helpful here.

b. I avoid mentioning the exposure part up front because kids who are both intelligent and resistant will be hesitant to name exposure opportunities if they'd just as soon not bother with them.

c. In my experience, most kids will need significant help developing a comprehensive list. Many anxious kids are just so used to avoidance that they've forgotten what they are afraid of. Moreover, some of the exposures might seem far-reaching for some kids (e.g., asking a clerk for help in a store).

d. Obviously this list will look different depending on the age of the kid (e.g., dating anxiety, appropriateness of being left home alone). In subsequently explaining the exposure sequence to a parent, I will also ask for the parent(s) to add to the list as they are among the world's leading experts on where the cobra resides. No list can be comprehensive. However, it's desirable to create as comprehensive of a list as you can regarding developmentally appropriate exposure scenarios. To reiterate, this would not include things that are inherently scary or developmentally inappropriate (e.g., horror movies, gory graphics on the news).

e. Whether you augment this discussion with a review of the treatment plan is a matter of clinical judgment. In my experience, most kids are neutral or positive about stopping the work. However, if you have a kid you suspect may take termination as bad news, you can modify what you say, indicating something like, *Once you've completed the exposures we can think about whether it's time to spread out how often we meet.*

f. In my decades of doing this work, I've never had a kid go for too much, too fast here. That said, should it happen tomorrow, I'd suggest that we build slowly, perhaps using a sports training metaphor. It's important that this discussion include details about when and how the exposures will be completed, together with potential obstacles that could emerge.

g. Physiological calming and coping thoughts are the two popular techniques for supporting exposures; however, kids can vary regarding what helps them to do an exposure. The research on exposures suggests that the exposure itself is the mediating factor. However, we are trying to make the kid as comfortable as possible when doing the exposure, lest we encourage resistance or discouragement.

h. I don't use this tracking form for every kid. At this point in the work it will be clear whether a kid fills out forms well and benefits from doing so, or whether getting her to do it is like pulling teeth. The main thing is that the kid does the exposures in the way we discuss.

i. Involving the parent is often key with doing exposures, which we are about to get into.

ENGAGING THE PARENT

Your job as a parent is not to make your child's way smooth, but rather to help her develop inner resources so she can cope.
—Ellyn Satter

Here are the three most common scenarios:

▶ The kid is motivated enough, or compliant enough, to do the exposures on her own. Among anxious kids this group is the least common. Most anxious kids are conditioned to do what they need to do to remain comfortable and distress free, which is the opposite of doing exposures (i.e., avoidance). But sometimes we run into a kid who has sufficiently owned the battle against anxiety (i.e., is motivated) or who just wants to be a "good student" (i.e., is compliant); such kids may not need much parental support beyond praise and a gentle reminder here and there. In these instances, the contact with the parent may be minimal and limited to keeping the parent in the loop and confirming that the exposures were completed.

▶ The kid is engaged in the work but doesn't like the discomfort of doing the exposures, at least once she gets past the easy ones. For these kids it's often enough to bring the parent in at the end of the session (e.g., the last 10 minutes) to discuss what the week's exposures are. This would include a review of the rationale, the specific plan we've developed, how the parent might support the exposures, giving the parent the chance to add exposure opportunities, including at home, and any obstacles the parent is aware of so that we can develop a plan for overcoming them. For these kinds of kids the review of the exposure homework the following week is sometimes best done with the parent in the room; not always, but often.

▶ The kid has needed a token system or a contract to do her therapy practice consistently. For these kids it's often advisable to bring the parent into the session with a good 15 to 20 minutes left and to discuss, in addition to the issues mentioned in the previous bullet point, how to integrate the exposures into the behavioral program. For a token system I'd maximize the point value (i.e., 20 chips or 200 points) and add a response cost right from the beginning. As I reviewed earlier, the downsides from overdoing this are usually less significant than the ones affiliated with not bringing enough parental support to bear. For a contract system, I'll rework it so that doing the exposures earns the kid what matters most to her; it might also be a good moment to find another double bonus or even to add a triple bonus. With most teens I'll also emphasize even more that completing the exposures is the path to being done with our work and freeing up more time in her schedule each week. This is how I might introduce bringing in the parent to a kid like this:

Monica, as we've seen, you're a busy person and it's helpful to involve your mom in supporting your efforts to do your therapy practice. So, I think it's a good idea to involve her here as well. I'm going to bring her in now and suggest that you be rewarded for doing these exposures and see if she has any ideas about other places where the cobra might be lurking.

This is also a time to reinforce for a parent that avoidance and excessive reassurances often make things worse. To the former point, I encourage parents to be on the lookout for ongoing opportunities for doing exposures; some of these might even be considered microexposures (e.g., a mom once told me that she asked for her 10-year-old daughter to go up to the register at a diner to pay the bill while she was still sipping her coffee at the booth). To the latter point, excessive reassurances can also be signaling parental anxiety. When it is difficult for a parent to quell it, I sometimes reintroduce the question of whether a parent might benefit from his own cognitive behavioral therapy (CBT). Also, if there is one parent who is more activated along these lines, I'll ask for the other parent (when available) to accompany the child on certain exposures (e.g., taking the child to the bus stop).

EXPOSURE NUANCES

Do the thing you Fear to do and keep on doing it . . . that is the quickest and surest way ever yet discovered to conquer Fear.
—*Dale Carnegie*

Certain exposures require additional support or dialogue. I'll review some of those here.

▶ Getting on the school bus: School-based exposures, which can also include things like going to school, using the bathroom at school, playing on the playground, and so forth, sometimes require systematic desensitization. This means chunking the exposure into manageable units when the end point provokes panic in a child. With each unit, the child is exposed to it and learns to relax during it (i.e., getting into green, to use the emWave metaphor) before moving on to the next chunk. So, for getting on the school bus, chunks might include waiting at the bus stop with a parent, then waiting at the bus stop with a parent in a car close by, then sitting on an empty school bus (I find that many school districts are cooperative in making such arrangements), and then getting on the school bus. Chunking can serve not only a child but also an anxious parent.

▶ Pursuing romantic interests: Many teens need help in learning how to do what I call "the low-risk flirt." This is another sort of chunking, but with a more interpersonal focus. I'll suggest that teens manufacture reasons to be in touch with their crush: missing homework, advice about studying for tests, inquiring about practice locations, and so forth. Teens can be taught to "accidentally" manage to sit in the crush's vicinity at lunch, to watch the crush at an extracurricular event and follow up with a text, and so forth. It's also *very* helpful to let the teen know that just about everyone goes through versions of these anxieties. I remember being a college student and being very surprised to learn that female creatures feel as much anxiety about these things as dudes; I also remember, around the same time, giving a talk to a group of teen girls and having them express surprise that guys feel the same anxieties. I have some pretty funny stories of dating failures that I'll share and I also encourage parents to share their stories. If you're interested in reading more on this topic, I wrote a chapter on helping teens overcome dating anxiety that you can find listed in the References and Bibliography section at the end of this chapter.

▶ Sports-related performance anxiety: Anxious kids catastrophize mistakes, which causes both poorer performance (because of worries) and meltdowns (because of projecting this perspective onto observers and teammates). Therefore, the exposure encourages them to deliberately make nonconsequential mistakes, but without telling anyone. So, a golfer might purposefully slice a ball into the woods, a tennis player might deliberately double fault, or a pitcher might intentionally walk a batter, but without anyone knowing, except parents. (If the coach is intelligent and psychologically minded and has a caring and good relationship with the athlete, that person might be brought onboard. If you can partner like this, the coach can help the kid to identify the moments to make the mistake. In these instances, the coach's almost unperceivable smile at the kid, after the kid has made the mistake, reinforces that it's no big deal. But, in this sports dad's experience, such coaches are in the minority.) Just like all exposures, the kid uses her CBT tools (e.g., physiological calming and coping thoughts) to calm herself. I encourage the kid to do this at points in the contest when the mistake won't affect the outcome or significantly disadvantage anyone. I once had a top-performing golfer, who was stressed out about landing a college scholarship, significantly improve his performance, and land his college scholarship, once he completed this exposure. The player gives a little—in order to get to a more relaxed mental place—and then receives a lot.

▶ Academic-related performance anxiety: This is essentially the same as the previous bullet point. However, the one potentially confounding factor is that sometimes a kid can also be anxious about raising her hand in class *at all*, correct answer or not. If so, it's important to disempower that anxiety first, before taking on this one. It's the same script: Wait until the moment is essentially nonconsequential and then give the wrong answer to the teacher's question, without letting the teacher know about it. Both this and the sports exposures needn't be done frequently to work. There is something about doing it on purpose that causes a kid to take better note of the fact that no one really cares, or at least that's what most of my kid clients end up learning.

As a professor, I encourage my students to try it. It's stunning to me how many young adults remain hesitant to think out loud in class, even when a guy like me will reward them for doing so, regardless of whether I agree with them or whether they've answered one of my questions correctly. Moreover, I do a lot of media work. I end up giving the same message to anxious co-interviewees or rookie interviewers, sometimes sharing funny stories about my mistakes on camera, noting whimsically, "Nobody cares." So many of we mental health professionals (MHPs) also need performance-based exposures to chill out!

SESSIONS GOING FORWARD

The number of variations in the work at this juncture makes it more challenging to offer a frame. Once the exposure phase begins with anxious kids the sessions become much less structured. These are the additional goals that I usually have in mind when the primary goal has become completing an exposure sequence:

▶ Teach skills from positive psychology. I confess to still being somewhat fuzzy where to draw the line between reducing pain (i.e., traditional clinical psychology) and promoting joy and meaning (i.e., positive psychology), and which interventions do one of these or both of these and which interventions do one or both for which kids and under what circumstances. However, I generally consider any interventions I haven't covered by the exposure phase, with anxious kids, as elective. I use that word "elective" as I wouldn't be starting the exposure phase unless the kid and parent(s) were telling me how improved the kid's anxiety-based symptoms are. Sure, one could still press on teaching all uncovered interventions at that point, but it's difficult for kids and parents to invest the needed energy to come to sessions, pay for sessions, and do therapy practice when the kid seems to be doing so well. So we start the exposure phase. But there is time we can use to teach the kid these elective interventions. It's common for me to have not gotten to some combination of strength building, using gratitude, acts of kindness, crisis = pain + opportunity, mindfulness, or the Serenity Prayer. I might spend time augmenting with these, based on what my intuition is suggesting might be maximally beneficial for a given kid.

▶ Use expressive modalities to resolve lingering intrapsychic conflicts. This is where training in play therapy can be very helpful. I use it as an augment. Kids might do open-drawings (including on the computer), play with unstructured toys, or complete drawings on stimuli that are started (e.g., see Chapter 5). Doing play therapy is not something I can teach you how to do here, however. Among the interventions I do with kids, it is the most complex. I agree with those who argue that play therapy is best learned by practicing it under the supervision of a qualified play therapist.

▶ Work on interpersonal exposures. These can include introducing oneself to another kid, asking a friend to do something fun, and so forth. Kids worry that they will be experienced as an unwanted intrusion or that they will say or do something embarrassing. One way to disempower some of this is to encourage the kid to say what she would feel if the roles were reversed. Anxious folks, almost to a person, end up saying that they'd have a kinder and more understanding reaction than they imagine they'd receive from others. Sometimes that's all a client needs to understand the key issues; but if the person still hasn't gotten it I'll playfully challenge with something like: *So, what, you're a way better person than other people?!*

This is how a dialogue might go with a kid on this topic:

MHP: *Monica, what bad thing does the cobra tell you could happen if you asked Consuela to go with you to see a movie?*
Kid: *She might be busy and not like it.*
MHP: *Not like it?*
Kid: *Yeah, like feel pressure to go with me.*
MHP: *How might she feel if she thought you were pressuring her?*
Kid: *Angry at me.*
MHP: *Okay, so the cobra is trying to tell you that asking Consuela to the movies will make her angry?*
Kid: *Yeah.*
MHP: *Well, let's turn that around to check it out. What if when you got home tonight Consuela called you and asked you to go to the movies?*
Kid: *I'd be happy.*
MHP: *But don't you have a lot to do this weekend? I mean, I know your mom is planning your aunt's birthday party and you have both soccer practice and a soccer game, plus your brother has his tutoring.*
Kid: *I know, I might not be able to go.*
MHP: *How would that make you feel?*
Kid: *Maybe a little frustrated that I couldn't go.*
MHP: *How would it make you feel toward Consuela?*
Kid: *Fine, I'd just want her to know that my not going wouldn't have anything to do with her.*
MHP: *So, you wouldn't be mad at her for asking you to do something when you're busy?*
Kid: *No. How could she know? And, even if she knew, I'd still want to be included.*

MHP: *I see. You wouldn't want her deciding for you that you couldn't go. You'd want to be asked and have the chance to work it out?*
Kid: *Yeah.*
MHP: *See where I'm going with this?*
Kid: *I guess. The cobra had me fooled.*
MHP: *EXACTLY. If ever you want to know how another kid might react to a thing, ask yourself how you might react in that same situation. That won't always work, but it's a heck of a lot more likely to be more true than the cobra's lies.*

▶ Sleeping in her own bed. If a contributing underlying dynamic is marital tension or parental anxiety, then such will need to be empathically named and a referral made. This is also an exposure that might require systematic desensitization if a kid experiences debilitating anxiety. I've done sequences like this: parent sleeps in kid's bed until kid is asleep; parent sits in a chair in the kid's room until the kid is asleep; parent sits in the chair for a couple of minutes less than it takes for the kid to fall asleep; parent sits in the hallway for the same amount of time; parent sits in the hallway for half the time. What's amazing is that sometimes the kid, in the middle of the sequence, will say things like, "I'm okay, you don't have to."

▶ Give a speech. In some survey research, people rate their anxiety about giving speeches to be higher than dying! If a kid is not taking a class where a speech is scheduled, and I have a motivated family, I'll propose approaching a teacher about arranging for the kid to give a speech for extra credit, perhaps sharing the context with the teacher (again, if the teacher seems bright, psychologically minded, and caring). When most anxious kids (and adults for that matter) can effectively give a speech without experiencing impairing anxiety, we're usually close to the finish line.

▶ Ask a clerk for help in a store. This is an exposure you can also chunk over time if need be. You can start with the kid asking a clerk while within the parent's eye-line. Then build to the parent being in the store but not in sight. Then the parent is in the car. Then the kid (now a teen) goes to the store by herself to ask the clerk. This also promotes the family instilling a culture of exposures. What families learn is that this ends up being pretty easy to do if they stay on it, which is true of just about any wellness routine.

▶ Eat something that dropped on the floor. This comes up for kids who may not meet criteria for obsessive-compulsive disorder (OCD) but whose worries about germs are impairing. Before setting this one up, I'll need to introduce likewise germ-phobic parents to some of the research on germ exposures (e.g., see the relevant chapter in the book *The Secrets of People Who Never Get Sick*).

▶ Pet a dog. Sometimes I'll need to coordinate with a parent on finding a dog that has a zero chance of biting a kid, or even growling at a kid. My dog,

Dakota, is like this, so I'll use him sometimes in my practice, which is located in my home.

▶ Thunderstorms. Exposures like this offer the opportunity to further develop distraction techniques, like doing something fun.

Kids, and their parents, may also need help developing ancillary skill sets during the exposure phase of the work. Though it isn't possible to develop a comprehensive list, here are some examples:

▶ Learning to think adaptively about sexual orientations that are not heterosexual. In these discussions I reintroduce the bell-shaped curve, which was covered in the feedback session. I suggest that our culture has an unfortunate tendency to pathologize certain human interests and experiences that are not in the middle of the curve. This is a conversation that usually happens with a teen and her parents:

Monica, this is a bell-shaped curve (demonstrating one and explaining the percentiles). *For most traits and skills most of us fall in the middle. How well we can shoot a basketball, our height, how long we live, and so forth. Unfortunately, when it comes to human sexuality we have a cultural bias of thinking that those interests that are common are healthy, while those that are not common are not. That couldn't be more wrong. Let's say you told me that a woman's sexual interests fell at the 50th percentile: Maybe she likes tall, dark, handsome, and mysterious men. Then you asked me how healthy her sexuality is. Y'know, I couldn't tell you based ONLY on that information. Maybe she pursues her interests in ways that are healthy and adaptive. On the other hand, maybe she offers sex to every such man she meets. One just can't tell how healthy her sexual interests are based on how common they are. It's all in what she does with her interests. The same thing goes with interests that are less common. I once knew a heterosexual married man whose sexual interest was pregnant men. That image was very appealing to him. He shared that with his wife and she was all about supporting that; so it was an interest that they effectively integrated into their sex lives and it went very well. If that same man started trying to pick up strange women, through websites, let's say, in order to act out this interest with them, then I'd say that's not healthy. So, your interest in women is the same way. It is neither inherently healthy nor unhealthy. It is your interest, and trying to pretend otherwise could make you sick. Ultimately, whether your interest becomes healthy or not all depends on what you do with it.*

Some parents may need to consult with a wise clergy person to reconcile misgivings; I try to help in identifying such clergy. Parents may also need to hear that their parenting strategies (e.g., monitoring) don't need to be different as a function of their teen's sexual interests. Moreover, there may need to be discussions regarding the pros and cons of coming out to various people and in various situations. Finally, the family may need the services of support organizations like Parents, Families, and Friends of Lesbians and Gays (PFLAG).

▶ Becoming physically fit. Obese kids or kids who are physically inactive may need help changing. If the family has the means, consultations with nutritionists or physical trainers may be in order. I try to maintain a referral list of those who have been successful doing this kind of work with kids. One key point: Think "physical activity" and not "exercise." As is the case with a lot of content in this volume, you can find supplemental information on my blog, www.hecticparents.com.

▶ Developing better study skills. Kids may need tutoring services. For example, many high schools offer peer tutors at no charge.

▶ Preparing for a competitive application for colleges. Lots of families don't know how to facilitate their kid turning in a competitive application for college. As it only takes a few minutes, I'll share what I know, suggest resources, offer referrals, and help a family to develop an action plan that suits a particular kid's interests and aptitudes.

▶ Helping a kid know how to effectively apply for internships or jobs.

▶ Aiding in expanding a kid's extracurricular interests. The work on developing strengths helps here (see Chapter 12).

Another activity that commonly occurs is preparing a kid for termination. Mostly, this is a joyful task. For instance, we might start tapering off how often we meet, agree on an intervening schedule of exposures, and discuss when we might shift to a booster session phase.

NUANCES WITH OTHER POPULATIONS

Obsessive-Compulsive Disorder

The exposure sequence is similar for these kids. The piece that gets added is response prevention. That is, the exposure includes not doing the ritual on exposure to the trigger. As with any exposure sequence, we start out easy and build. For example, a kid, prior to doing any exposures, might only do a hand-washing ritual 30% of the time when touching a doorknob that looks dirty. So, that would be a good one with which to begin.

Single-Event Posttraumatic Stress Disorder

This section is for kids who were functioning well prior to a single-event trauma. For kids who have been exposed to multiple-event traumas (e.g., incest), a more specialized approach that extends beyond the parameters of this volume is warranted (see the References and Bibliography section at the end of this chapter for resources).

For these kids, there is a need to develop an exposure list that is based on the traumatic event. For example, I once worked with a teen who was the victim of an attempted rape. She foiled the assailant but was traumatized by the experience. This is the sequence we developed:

▶ Parking several blocks away from the site in the car

▶ Parking one block away

▶ Smelling the cologne of the attacker at home (she knew what it was)

▶ Smelling the cologne of the attacker parked one block away

▶ Walking by the attack site from a distance

▶ Sitting down, and smelling the cologne, within eye-line of the attack site

▶ Walking through the attack site

▶ Sitting down at the attack site

▶ Sitting down at the attack site smelling the cologne

Sometimes the exposures can be imaginal, done in the office or at home. If your practice parameters allow for such, you could also explore accompanying your client for some of the exposures. Another discussion to have is whether it's advisable to have the parent accompany the kid; much of this depends on the age of the kid, the nature of the exposure, and the quality of the relationship with the parent. So, for a child who needs transportation and who is close to a parent, it makes sense for the parent to be involved; in these instances, finding ways for the parent to disengage from her own anxiety can be part of the exposure sequence. In the case I just reviewed, the client was an older teen who could transport herself; she preferred to keep her parent out of the exposure sequence as she didn't want to upset her mother (the parent had declined a referral for her own care).

SIDEBAR 14.1

> I like having a collection of attention-grabbing tricks for kids that are both easy to learn and can be done with household items, like playing cards and coins. One of my favorites is done with two rubber bands. Just about anywhere a kid

(continued)

SIDEBAR 14.1 (*continued*)

might find herself, two rubber bands can usually be acquired. This trick is called "Magician's Handcuffs" or "Crazy Man's Handcuffs." While it is very simple to learn and to do, and the impact is great, it's nearly impossible to describe how to do it by writing a description. Fear not, though. On YouTube, just use the search term "rubber bands magicians handcuffs revealed" or "crazy mans rubber band magic trick revealed" and you'll find a video teaching you the trick. Here is one such link: http://bit.ly/1LnChhO.

REFERENCES AND BIBLIOGRAPHY

Albano, A. M., & Kendall, P. C. (2002). Cognitive behavioural therapy for children and adolescents with anxiety disorders: Clinical research advances. *International Review of Psychiatry,* *14*(2), 129–134.

Barrett, P. M., Dadds, M. R., & Rapee, R. M. (1996). Family treatment of childhood anxiety: A controlled trial. *Journal of Consulting and Clinical Psychology, 64*(2), 333–342.

Chu, B. C., & Harrison, T. L. (2007). Disorder-specific effects of CBT for anxious and depressed youth: A meta-analysis of candidate mediators of change. *Clinical Child and Family Psychology Review, 10*(4), 352–372.

Cohen, J. A., Mannarino, A. P., Berliner, L., & Deblinger, E. (2000). Trauma-focused cognitive behavioral therapy for children and adolescents: An empirical update. *Journal of Interpersonal Violence, 15*(11), 1202–1223.

Courtois, C. (2010). *Healing the incest wound: Adult survivors in therapy* (2nd ed.). New York, NY: W. W. Norton.

Forsyth, J. P., Barrios, V., & Acheson, D. T. (2007). Exposure therapy and cognitive interventions for the anxiety disorders: Overview and newer third-generation perspectives. In D. C. S. Richard & D. Lauterbach (Eds.), *Handbook of exposure therapies* (pp. 61–108). Atlanta, GA: Elsevier.

James, A. A., Soler, A., & Weatherall, R. R. (2005). Cognitive behavioural therapy for anxiety disorders in children and adolescents. *Cochrane Database of Systematic Reviews, 4*.

Kendall, P. C., Choudhury, M., Hudson, J., & Webb, A. (2002). *"The C.A.T. Project" Manual for the cognitive-behavioral treatment of anxious adolescents.* Ardmore, PA: Workbook Publishing.

Kendall, P. C., & Hedtke, K. A. (2006). *Cognitive-behavioral therapy for anxious children: Therapist manual* (3rd ed.). Ardmore, PA: Workbook Publishing.

Kendall, P. C., Hudson, J. L., Gosch, E., Flannery-Schroeder, E., & Suveg, C. (2008). Cognitive-behavioral therapy for anxiety disordered youth: A randomized clinical trial evaluating child and family modalities. *Journal of Consulting and Clinical Psychology, 76*(2), 282–297.

Kendall, P. C., Robin, J. A., Hedtke, K. A., Suveg, C., Flannery-Schroeder, E., & Gosch, E. (2005). Considering CBT with anxious youth? Think exposures. *Cognitive and Behavioral Practice, 12*(1), 136–148.

Koch, E. I., Gloster, A. T., & Waller, S. A. (2007). Exposure treatments for panic disorder with and without agoraphobia. In D. C. S. Richard & D. Lauterbach (Eds.), *Handbook of exposure therapies* (pp. 221–245). Atlanta, GA: Elsevier.

Lauterbach, D., & Reiland, S. (2007). Exposure therapy and posttraumatic stress disorder. In D. C. S. Richard & D. Lauterbach (Eds.), *Handbook of exposure therapies* (pp. 127–151). Atlanta, GA: Elsevier.

March, J. S. (1995). Cognitive-behavioral psychotherapy for children and adolescents with OCD: A review and recommendations for treatment. *Journal of the American Academy of Child & Adolescent Psychiatry, 34*(1), 7–18.

March, J. S. (2006). *Talking back to OCD: The program that helps kids and teens say "no way"—and parents say "way to go."* New York, NY: Guilford Press.

Mineka, S., & Thomas, C. (1999). Mechanisms of change in exposure therapy for anxiety disorders. In T. Dalgleish & M. J. Power (Eds.), *Handbook of cognition and emotion* (pp. 747–764). New York, NY: John Wiley & Sons.

Ollendick, T. H., & King, N. J. (1998). Empirically supported treatments for children with phobic and anxiety disorders: Current status. *Journal of Clinical Child Psychology, 27*(2), 156–167.

Palmiter, D. J. (2013). Reducing dating anxiety in adolescents: Clinician's response. In S. Walfish & L. Grossman (Eds.), *Translating psychological research into practice: A desk reference for practicing mental health professionals* (pp. 408–412). New York, NY: Springer Publishing Company.

Perrin, S., Smith, P., & Yule, W. (2000). Practitioner review: The assessment and treatment of post-traumatic stress disorder in children and adolescents. *Journal of Child Psychology and Psychiatry, 41*(3), 277–289.

Pina, A. A., Silverman, W. K., Fuentes, R. M., Kurtines, W. M., & Weems, C. F. (2003). Exposure-based cognitive-behavioral treatment for phobic and anxiety disorders: Treatment effects and maintenance for Hispanic/Latino relative to European-American youths. *Journal of the American Academy of Child & Adolescent Psychiatry, 42*(10), 1179–1187.

Saunders, B. E., Berliner, L., & Hanson, R. F. (Eds.). (2004). *Child physical and sexual abuse: Guidelines for treatment.* Charleston, SC: National Crime Victims Research and Treatment Center.

Shortt, A. L., Barrett, P. M., & Fox, T. L. (2001). Evaluating the FRIENDS program: A cognitive-behavioral group treatment for anxious children and their parents. *Journal of Clinical Child Psychology, 30*(4), 525–535.

Spence, S. H., Donovan, C., & Brechman-Toussaint, M. (2000). The treatment of childhood social phobia: The effectiveness of a social skills training-based, cognitive-behavioural intervention, with and without parental involvement. *Journal of Child Psychology and Psychiatry, 41*(6), 713–726.

Stone, G. (2012). *The secrets of people who never get sick: What they know, why it works, and how it can work for you.* New York, NY: Workman Publishing Company.

U.S. Department of Health and Human Services. (1994). *Treatment for abused and neglected children: Infancy to age 18.* Retrieved from https://www.childwelfare.gov/pubs/usermanuals/treatmen

Wood, J. J., Piacentini, J. C., Southam-Gerow, M., Chu, B. C., & Sigman, M. (2006). Family cognitive behavioral therapy for child anxiety disorders. *Journal of the American Academy of Child & Adolescent Psychiatry, 45*(3), 314–321.

CHAPTER 15

Termination and Booster Sessions

CONTEXT

There is no real ending. It's just the place where you stop the story.
—Frank Herbert

Treatment manuals may imply that cognitive behavioral therapy (CBT) takes X number of sessions for anxiety and Y number of sessions for depression. However, artful practitioners of these manuals would nearly universally agree that kids vary considerably regarding when they are ready to terminate. These are six developments that tend to emerge when we are nearing termination:

▶ Kids being treated for depression are reporting very few, if any, attacks from their internal enemy and also are having regular experiences of joy. However, we are especially looking for examples of a kid beating back depression with his CBT techniques, lest we confuse improvement with the natural course of depression, which often includes periods of remission.

▶ Kids being treated for anxiety are going through their exposures like a hot knife through butter. The only thing we need to be cautious about is what psychodynamic therapists call "a flight into health," one manifestation of which can be a kid saying and doing what he needs to do to free up one or more hours each week. Again, we are looking for evidence that a kid experienced some dosing of anxiety at the start of an exposure and used CBT techniques to quell it and complete the exposure.

▶ Just about all of the kid's energy in session is invested in nonsymptomatic concerns. Of course, it's important to ensure that the kid isn't merely avoiding painful or anxiety-provoking material. If a kid is truly better, this should be clear across multiple sources of information (e.g., parents, teachers, the kid's dreams, and the kid's play).

▶ My private review of the treatment plan leaves me suspecting that the goals have been met or are almost met. Of course, there's just no knowing for sure without inquiring of the kid and his parents.

▶ I'm struggling to think about what a kid needs in a given session (because he is doing so well) and I'm having increasing periods of boredom within the session. (As I discussed in Chapter 4, countertransference is a helpful tool. I love doing this work and find it so interesting. So, if I'm bored it may mean that we are nearing termination.) However, this guideline only works if my self-care is reasonably good. Otherwise, what feels like boredom could really be sleepiness or distraction.

▶ The kid or the parent(s) start asking when we'll be done. If it occurs in isolation, without any of these other signs, this isn't likely an indication that termination is advisable. As I discuss throughout this volume, most kids are neutral or opposed to treatment. Dogs bark, kids grouse. Moreover, parents who are overscheduled and stressed will often experience initial relief in the early phases of the work and start thinking that the kid is well enough and that the treatment is a stress that can be shredded from their weekly schedule. Both of these developments are as common to kid mental health professionals (MHPs) as weeds are to landscapers.

Here I'm talking about when questions about stopping are accompanying the other features I listed. The one thing to be cautious about is our own biases regarding treatment length. That is, I think all kid MHPs fall into one of two camps: inclined to end too early or inclined to linger too long. In my case, it's the former; I'm at risk to become too aligned with the kid's and parents' wishes to be finished. So, if a parent or kid has beat me to the punch and brought up termination first, I'm cautious. But, the protocol that follows next can often get to the bottom of things nicely.

INTRODUCING TERMINATION TO A KID

When you need me but do not want me, then I must stay. When you want me but no longer need me, then I have to go.
—Nanny McPhee

Aiden, what's the best and what's the worst thing that happened this week (a)? How many iceman attacks did you experience this week (b)? How do you think our work is going in terms of caging the iceman (c)? Yeah, I've been thinking that it's going well also. Remember how when we started we wrote down some goals for our work (d)? Well, why don't we look at them and see what's going on. Okay, so let me ask, how long is it taking you to fall asleep each night and then how many hours are you sleeping (e)? . . . *Okay, so you've caged the iceman pretty well then. How's that feel* (f)? *Aiden, it is so important that you and I figure out TOGETHER what makes the most sense to do at this point. It's not my job to make a recommendation about what to do based on only what I think* (g). *It's very important that I suggest to your mom and dad what we do based on what you and I BOTH think. What do you think about us meeting less often* (h)? *So, how would it work for us to meet next in 2 weeks? Then, if things are like they are now, we meet in 1 month? Then if that works, 6 months* (i)? *Okay, that's what I'll run by your mom and dad to see what they think because they need to take part in this decision also* (j). *Your mom and dad might not see it the same as you and me and, if so, we'd have to talk about that. But, assuming they agree, we're talking about mostly stopping our work. How's that feel* (k)?

Explanation

a. As I've discussed throughout this volume, this is a standard way of opening many sessions. However, for teens that are invested in the work, and doing well, I'll sometimes open by saying, ***Where's a good place to start?***

b. When a kid is ready for termination this is a happy question. Either there have been no such attacks or they are few and far between. In other words, the internal enemy has been effectively caged.

c. There are so many different ways that kids respond. Some take this as a throwaway question, like someone greeting them with a "How are you?" Moreover, they've likely had experiences of adults asking questions like these just as a way of getting to what the adult thinks and wants to do. In these instances, I let them know that I *really* want to get their sense for how they are doing in their battle against depression and/or anxiety. Many kids who are ready for termination will speak with confidence about how well they are doing and why. However, if they haven't connected their improved standing with using the cognitive development (CBT) techniques, I'll ask them questions that look to draw out their thinking about that: ***Does stuff in your binder have anything to do with that?*** Or, ***How did you manage to cage the iceman so well?*** Or, ***How come you're better, do you think?*** I would not be as disposed to move toward termination if a kid doesn't report that his improved standing is affiliated with his use of CBT techniques—unless he's quite young and has a parent who stays on top of his using them—or, worse yet, he can't identify any reason why he's better or attributes his improvement exclusively to things outside of his control (e.g., he has a better teacher now). I worry that terminating under such terms would leave a kid too vulnerable to relapse.

   Experienced and wise child MHPs are like experienced and wise parents. It mostly doesn't cross our minds to expect to hear acknowledgment for our contributions. If they come, it's very nice (more for parents, though). If it doesn't, eh, so what? We take our meaning and reward from seeing how the kid is doing. However, when you first start this work and are trying to form your identity as a therapist, it's natural and even expected to be looking for kudos. That's okay and might even be a little weird if it wasn't there. Just tell your supervisor/colleagues/therapist about it so that you're less tempted to ask things like, "Have I helped you, Aiden?"

d. It's only a small portion of the future psychologists of this world who remember what goals we set at the start of the therapy. That's okay. Kids are kids. I just remind them, bringing back to mind the metaphor(s) deployed at that time (e.g., the video recording of the future that was discussed in Chapter 3).

e. It's very important to not ask things like, "We said you'd be sleeping at least 8 hours a night and that it would take you no more than 15 minutes to fall asleep, so how's that going?" Thinking like a kid is important here. If questions are asked that way, kids who are better and kids who are not better are both likely to say that the goal has been reached, with the latter knowing that such an answer renders a quicker path toward stopping. It's much better to ask for the raw data and not prompt a kid with "the right answer."

Of course, we will also go through these with the parent(s). But, if a goal is not met, then that becomes the focus. Unlike the start of treatment, when I ask a kid to put the goals out of mind, lest they become like a to-do list that is gutted out with willpower, we can focus more explicitly on any specific obstacles that might be at play. So, maybe this is a moment when focusing on the sleep hygiene is in order. Or there may be specific skill sets or issues that need to be addressed.

If a goal is met, I then go on to the next one, asking the question in the same way. I wait until I've reviewed all the goals before I circle back and review where the kid was previously at, as well as what goals we established. I do it this way so as to not establish a response set for giving happy answers early on.

These are some of my favorite moments in kid work. As is the case with adults, many forget the specifics of how bad it was initially. They've also usually forgotten the specific goals. So, to review them all together often blows kids away. This is part of the reason why I emphasized developing specific problem and goal statements in Chapter 3. There's no shazam without that *blam*. Kids say things like, "Oh my God, I forgot how bad it was!" Or, "Really? I did that?!" Some get tearful, in a good way, of course. Others just quietly smile from ear-to-ear and nod. It's pretty cool to see.

f. As I just indicated, this part often just happens automatically. But, if not, I ask. No need to rush here. Savor. Praise. Enjoy together.

For younger kids I'll also sometimes ask them to do a drawing with their internal enemy, as we did during the externalizing the problem module. You know those fitness programs that show the before/after pictures? Well, we do our before/after drawings of their internal enemy, but without prompting for a recollection of the first drawing. Kids will often draw their enemy as smaller than before, or behind cages or in other defeated positions, and then tell accompanying stories.

g. I can't stress enough how important it is to have a kid understand that he is involved in this decision. Kids are used to adults saying things like this without it really being true. It's often more like the adult is saying, "Parrot back to me what I want to hear." So there's lots of different ways I may try to instill collaboration, depending on what I think is needed. But I stay in this space until I feel confident that the kid feels empowered. Finally, the wording I use here is adjusted based on the age of the kid (e.g., the wording I've illustrated in the script would probably be too difficult for a younger child).

h. The response I expect most often is something like, "That sounds good," together with a smile. However, sometimes kids express reluctance to meet less often. I find there are three common reasons why this happens. First, a kid is really ready to stop but either oversubscribes his improved standing to me and/or underestimates his efficacy going forward, posttermination. This is how an exchange about this could go:

Kid: *I'd rather not cut back.*
MHP: *We absolutely won't if that's not a good idea. But, tell me, what are you concerned could happen if we cut back how often we meet?*
Kid: *I need to be able to tell you about my week.*
MHP: *What's good about doing that?*
Kid: *So, you can tell me what I did right and wrong.*
MHP: *Hmmm. When's the last time I pointed out how you could battle the iceman better?*
Kid: *I don't know.*
MHP: *Give it a few minutes. It's important. When was the last time?*
Kid: *A month or so ago.*
MHP: *So, you've been kicking the iceman's butt on your own, with only high fives from me, for about one month?*
Kid: *Yeah, I guess so.*
MHP: *Have your mom and dad been giving you any high fives about that?*
Kid: *Not really. I don't tell them as much.*
MHP: *What if you did tell them as much, and they gave you the high fives?*
Kid: *That might be okay.*
MHP: *What if we try it, and we can talk about this with them? Then, if it works—great. We try this plan. But, if it doesn't work, and you win less often, we can go back to meeting weekly. How's that sound?*
Kid: *Okay, I guess. That might work.*

Second, I've become an important attachment figure and the kid doesn't want to experience the loss. In these instances, a kid may express palpable distress (e.g., crying, panic) or regresses significantly in between visits. In these instances, I'm prompted to explore questions like these:

1. How consistently is special time being done (see Chapter 9)?

2. Is the kid engaged enough with friends?

3. Are the kid's strengths being made manifest enough in the world (see Chapter 12)?

I've never had a case, when this obstacle to termination is at play, when all three of those questions are answered positively. So, the area(s) of vulnerability become the new focus of the work.

Third, I've missed the mark and the kid is not skillful enough in the CBT techniques to terminate. This is usually made clear when the kid comes back and has regressed secondary to not using his CBT techniques to control his internalizing symptoms. In these instances, I loop back to a review of each, with new practice assignments, until the skills take better root.

It's important that we all attend to our countertransference when kids express distress at the notion of separating from us. Just like an anxious parent can consciously or unconsciously believe it makes sense for an anxious kid to want to metaphorically, or literally, clutch to her leg, we can, if we're not careful, be unduly influenced by our countertransference.

i. The pacing I suggest here is purely a matter of intuition. I will usually suggest skipping a week as a first step. But the sequence I'll propose after that varies. The protocol I reviewed here is one I'd use when I'm confident, especially after doing the treatment plan review and hearing the kid's perspective, that the kid is doing well. On the other end of the continuum, when termination seems advisable but I'm having some doubts, I might suggest that we meet every other week for now and see how it goes.

j. This consultation with the parents is done in the subsequent parent meeting (which I'll review next). I can't think of a time when a kid gave me even a little bit of push back.

k. This is time for the kid to express any feelings of loss, if he's having them. For most kids this is just a joyful moment. But, for others, their sense of joy and accomplishment can be intertwined with feelings of loss and gratitude. If the latter kinds of feelings are present, I don't keep pressing until a kid puts voice to them; that's not how some kids are wired. But I open the door, maybe even making an empathic remark or two such as, *Y'know, Aiden, many kids really enjoy starting the process of meeting less. However, some also feel, at the same time, like it can be a little hard to see me less. Not always, but sometimes. Do you have any of those kinds of feelings?*

INTRODUCING TERMINATION TO THE PARENTS FIRST

The wound is the place where the Light enters you.
—Rumi

Most of the time I proceed first in the way I described in the previous section. However, there are instances where I'll begin the discussion of termination with a parent instead of the kid. These are some of those circumstances:

▶ A kid is consistently resistant. Throughout this volume I've been discussing how to deal with resistant kids. And these techniques just about always work with this population of kid clients. However, if I've had to continue to bring such techniques to bear throughout the work, I know that a kid cannot be counted on to engage me in a objective review of whether or not it makes sense to stop. Moreover, if I introduce the topic of termination and that proves to be a bad idea, the intensity of the resistance can worsen. In these instances I've found that it's better to discuss the possibility of termination with the parent(s) first.

▶ The chance that a kid will regress when this topic is introduced is significant. In these instances I prefer to think through the possibility of termination with the parent(s) first.

▶ There's a good chance that a parent will become anxious or upset about the notion of termination. This work can be so marvelously transformative that some parents have a lot of concern that the risk of regression is significant. Just like I believe it is not respectful to push a kid out the door as he's clutching desperately to it, the same thing goes for parents. It's not that I let a parent unilaterally decide how long the work will go. It's just that I don't unilaterally make the decision, either.

▶ Whether termination is advisable or not is cloudy. I don't bring up termination unless enough of the factors I've mentioned are in play. However, sometimes the number of them is not what I'd like it to be, or I'm not sure about some of them, or there are other complicating factors that I need to talk out with the parents (e.g., a remarriage is pending, the kid is about to start high school, a parent is new to a recovery program).

In short, if I have significant doubts I start with the parent(s). I will schedule a separate session with them to do this. Here is what I say when they come in:

Tanisha and Bill, thanks for coming in today. Let's set an agenda. I'd like to get an update from you regarding how Aiden is doing and how special time is going (a). Then, I'd like to update you again on what I've done with him since you and I last met. After that, there's another topic I want to bring up, but I'd like to wait a little to introduce it **(b)**. *Is there anything else you'd like to add to our agenda* **(c)**? . . . *Okay, the third topic is whether or not it makes sense to move our work into a termination phase. That means, meeting less frequently, with an eye toward possibly stopping* **(d)**, *which may or may not include booster sessions every 6 months or so. This is a decision that we all need to make together. This is NOT about me deciding alone. So, what do you think? Is Aiden ready for us to start scaling back* **(e)**?

Explanation

a. This is a standard introduction for any parent treatment meeting past the first one. Special time is *so important*. They may not leave me doing it, but they rarely leave me not knowing why doing it is important. Moreover, if they've been slow to get it up and running, I would have given them the funeral exercise by now (see Chapter 9) and had me reference their wisdom from that exercise. Moreover, if we have set up a token system or a contract, we'll review that as well.

b. Again, this is a standard part of the opening. The only reason I don't mention termination right here is that I've found many parents can't help but jump right to that topic when they are giving me their update. And I prefer to hear the data in the rawest form I can, without having parents adjust it through the lens of a possible termination. Otherwise, I've found the data can be skewed depending on whether a parent favors or doesn't favor termination.

c. They rarely have something to add. If they do, it's usually a new conflict or a crisis. If so, this discussion might entail me reminding parents, through kindly questioning, that they already possess the skills they need to deal with the problem. If the latter isn't true and there's a new kind of problem, or the parent doesn't really know how to handle it, then the termination agenda is put on hold until this agenda can be addressed.

d. The insertion of the word "possibly" is done solely to set the stage that this is a collaborative decision. Parents are conditioned to be passive in the face of clinical feedback provided to them by dentists, pediatricians, school psychologists, and so forth. Not with us. Not in this moment. This is collaborative.

e. I wish it were possible to give a tight summary of what happens next. But I find that it varies widely in kid work. The modal response is metaphorical hugs and kisses. They are thrilled with the progress and wish to erect a statue in the downtown square honoring the work. However, there are many other kinds of things stated; some of these issues I reviewed in the kid section. Here are some of the other things parents can sometimes bring up:

- Looking for reassurance that their kid is not getting the boot out of treatment. This is just a matter of affirming how collaborative this decision is.

- Looking for reassurance that if we go to booster session mode they can still call to schedule an appointment, before the booster session, if they feel the need. I'd say this concern comes up a lot. I then issue the reassurance and they rarely end up using it; it's sort of like a psychological spare tire. Parents don't want to leave home without it but it rarely gets used.

- Expressing concern about developmental hurdles that are coming up in the future. Will he be ready to go to high school, date, drive, go to college, and so forth? Will he ever end up on the FBI's 10 Most Wanted list? I jest about the last one, but remember, we engaged parents are lunatics. The script is similar across the board: empathy, followed by directed questioning designed to remind the parents what they know and the resources they have at their disposal, followed by reassurances. One of the ways anxiety attacks its host is to promote worry about some important (usually far off) future event. The anxiety works that way because there is no way to reason specific solutions to possible and unknown future problems. In these instances the parents usually just need reassurances that, while it's hard to know what they'll say and do in this or that scenario, they have the skills and the resources they need to do well, including using their spare tire.

- Providing good evidence that entering the termination phase is premature at this juncture. Maybe there have been new important developments. Maybe the kid has been snowing me about the data, driving my decision to bring it up for review. If so, we deal with whatever problem is at hand.

In those instances when the parent work has included a treatment plan we'll certainly review that as well, following the same script I reviewed in the preceding kid section.

INTRODUCING TERMINATION TO PARENTS SECOND

At the end of the day, the most overwhelming key to a child's success is the positive involvement of parents.
—Jane D. Hull

If the termination discussion with a kid has gone well, the discussion with the parents goes well almost all the time. Once I'm done with the kid, I'll switch places with the parent and go over what the kid and I discussed, including going over the treatment plan. Any concerns the kid has raised about stopping can be reviewed as well. Sometimes new issues come up, the like of which I reviewed in the previous section. If so, the kid will be brought back in so that these can be discussed. Most of the time, though, the parent does a lot of head nodding and expresses gratitude.

THE LAST SESSION PRIOR TO STARTING BOOSTER SESSIONS

There are many different kinds of discussions that can ensue in this visit. Some of the more common things that come up:

▶ If we haven't yet, we'll make a list of the kid's weapons against his enemy, perhaps highlighting the ones that are most successful for him. This goes in the very front of his binder.

▶ We'll often go through the weapons, with me asking the kid to teach me how each one is used and when.

▶ A kid will sometimes draw a picture of him and his enemy at this point in time. Or a kid may choose to draw a picture with a story; these drawings usually provide insight into how the kid is experiencing the termination.

▶ We review risks for relapse. Each kid is different, but some common themes are not practicing the techniques and letting self-care go off-line. I'll also sometimes say this to a kid: *Aiden, if ever you are trying to figure out whether to do something or not, ask yourself what the iceman would prefer for you to do. Then, just do the opposite.* I'll then go over some examples from the recent past and some potential scenarios going forward.

▶ As mentioned earlier, with kids who are being treated for anxiety, I try to instill an attitude of looking for opportunities to do ongoing exposures. It's music to my ears when a kid and his parent review exposures they are doing on their own.

▶ We go over when it might be a good idea to call for a session before the next booster session. I've learned over the years that kids, and their parents, are at risk to think that coming back in before the next scheduled booster session could equate with failing. So it's important to review when it would make sense to come back in:

• The CBT techniques are not controlling the internal enemy.

• Accomplished treatment plan goals are being undone.

• There is a new and toxic stress that has come into play that the CBT techniques are not successful in managing.

I'll say to the kid something like this: *Aiden, let's say that the iceman gets out of his cage and you are struggling to get him back in. If that happens, what might the iceman try to tell you about the idea of coming back in to see me?* Believe it or not, most kids will quickly say things like, "He wouldn't want me to come back in." I'll then ask things like, *Why do you think the iceman wouldn't like that?* And, *Would the iceman try to tell you that coming back in to see me would mean that you screwed up and are a failure?* We then reaffirm that the correct path to doing the right thing is often a simple matter of figuring out what the enemy wants and then doing the opposite. (I love it when teens are a fan of the TV program *Seinfeld*. If so, I just kiddingly refer to the character George Costanza's conclusion that to be successful in life all he had to do was the opposite of what his intuition was calling for him to do.)

Being a self-studied MHP comes in very handy here. The more self-studied we are (e.g., through a personal therapy), the more we won't let our own interpersonal style and preferences unduly influence what a kid needs to do in this session. For example, in earlier phases of my career I think I'd too often squelch a kid's need to express gratitude. The more we've examined ourselves the more we can just let the kid say or do whatever reasonable thing he needs to say or do.

BOOSTER SESSIONS

Healing is a matter of time, but it is sometimes also a matter of opportunity.
—Hippocrates

This is a common sequence for how I get to the booster session phase: Have a session in which termination is discussed, meet 2 weeks later, meet 1 month later, meet 6 months later, meet 6 months later, and so forth. Of course, this sequence can be altered based on a given kid's and family's needs and preferences.

These are some of the agenda items I have in mind for booster sessions:

1. Is there anything that the kid or the parent(s) came to the booster session wanting to discuss? Often this overlaps with one of the next three potential agenda topics. But, if not, I make sure to give whatever they've brought in the attention it deserves.

2. Are there any important developments that have happened in the kid's or the family's life that could use my input? Of course, there are always important developments. However, often they are just happy or meaningful events that the family merely wants to share. I'm listening for any events that could use my help. Maybe a kid has a new teacher that scares her, or a teen has started dating and the parents need help developing a monitoring protocol, or a kid has become an Eagle Scout and is wondering about whether to come out to the scout master in charge. One of the delightful things about kid clinical work is how varied these issues can be.

3. How is the kid doing in keeping the internal enemy, or enemies, caged? For kids treated for depression I'm listening for how he deals with new stresses, his mood fluctuations, and how often he enjoys himself. For the kid treated for anxiety I'm listening for whether a culture of exposures has continued and whether any avoidance coping styles have crept back in.

I'll review which CBT techniques the kid is still using and offer any tweaks that seem advisable. The techniques will often have morphed to less potent variants. If the kid is symptom free I'll leave it there. However, if there has been any regression or emergence of new symptoms, I do a review of those techniques that I think would be most helpful at that point.

I'm listening for how well the parent(s) coach the CBT techniques and whether they are avoiding behaviors that enable the internal enemy (see Chapter 4).

4. I'll ask about any significant stresses that we dealt with during the main treatment phase: academics, social, athletic, and so forth. If there was anything that was an acute bother to the kid or the family, I'll check in to see how that thing is now going.

5. I'll touch base with the parents about whether they are still doing special time. Many of them see this coming and, if they have stopped, will start doing it again before the booster session. Rather than get preachy, I'll ask them to review for me what they've heard from me about the value of special time. If they can say that back well, I don't hassle them about it, regardless of whether they are doing it. If they've forgotten why special time is important I try to find artful ways of reviewing the reasons. If we have the time, I'll also do the funeral exercise with them if we haven't done it yet (see Chapter 9).

   Of course, if we created a token system or a contract system I'll review that with them as well. Often they'll say that they set it aside because they don't need it any longer. Or they set it aside but suggest to me that the kid's behavior indicates they should bring it back on board; if so, we go over any new parameters. Or sometimes they've kept it going but need to go over some tweaks with me as circumstances in the kid's or the family's life have changed.

6. Often one or more of these agenda items creates a session that has full value for the kid and/or the parent(s). However, if we still have time after going over the topics, I'll turn my attention to how the kid might use a positive psychology (PP) intervention that we never got to.

7. Although it's not really an agenda that I usually cover with the kid or parents directly, I'm very interested in having them feel like the session has value for them. And if it doesn't (usually just because things are so fabulous), I'll wonder with them if we should not schedule another booster session and just transition to them calling me on an as-needed basis. If the session seems to have sufficient value, I'll usually say, *So, should we schedule again for 6 months?*

Starting With the Parents

I'll just about always bring the parent(s) in first. If I start with the kid, or the kid and the parents together, sometimes I don't end up learning about, or give sufficient time to, something important on the parents' mind (e.g., the parents may not want to be as open about a topic in front of their kid). If I need to bring a kid in to join them, before meeting with the kid alone, that's always easy to do (e.g., there is a dispute and perhaps they could use some time problem solving with me). When I bring the parents in I usually say something like this:

Nice to see you guys! So, let's set an agenda for the few minutes we have before I bring in Aiden. Of course, I'd like to get an update from you about how Aiden is doing (a). I'd also like to hear how he's doing with his depression (b) and how you guys are doing with special time (c). Is there anything that you're wanting to discuss (d)?

Explanation

a. This is tapping the second agenda item that I mentioned in the "Booster Sessions" section.

b. This is tapping the third agenda item that I mentioned in the "Booster Sessions" section. What I'm really hoping is that the parents will be the first ones to say "iceman." This tells me that the externalizing methodology has taken root. If they don't, I will say it and see if they are still working with that concept. When we go over this, I'll review any significant triggers that were relevant during the primary treatment phase; this covers the fourth agenda item I mentioned. Finally, I'll ask questions like, *So, what do you do when Aiden comes to you with something that he's sad over? Or, How often would you guys say you arrange for Monica to do an exposure? Or, Have there been any times that Aiden has been sad that your efforts seemed to make things worse? Or, Are there any situations that Monica is avoiding these days because they upset her?*

c. This is tapping the fifth agenda item that I mentioned in the "Booster Sessions" section. Again, many parents see this coming. So, the parents who have really understood special time will do things like differentiate it from quality time and review their ongoing struggle with doing it consistently (no one bats 1.000, including child psychologists who write training books); for these parents, I offer empathy, support, and maybe an idea or two. Otherwise, I'll do some review while offering empathy, support, and maybe an idea or two.

d. This is tapping the first agenda item that I mentioned in the "Booster Sessions" section.

   Sometimes parents also need reassurances that they are doing a good job. If so, I'll do things like challenge popular concepts like "work/life balance" or show them a YouTube video on parental self-criticism (e.g., http://bit.ly/1ONPHqu).

Bringing in the Kid

After I've finished with the parent(s), and I try to limit the parent portion to 15 to 20 minutes at the most, I bring in the kid. Usually, this is just a matter of switching seats. But, if there is a conflict or something else that could use a family meeting, we'll do that. Otherwise, these are some of the questions I ask the kid:

▶ *Aiden, nice to see you, dude! Is there anything you want to make sure we have time to talk about today* **(a)**? *So, what's the best and worst things that have happened in your life since last February 10* **(b)**?

▶ *How's it going in your battle with depression* **(c)**?

▶ *Was there anything that you were wanting to make sure that we talked about today* **(d)**?

▶ *How's it going with X, Y, and Z* **(e)**?

▶ *Aiden, you know our work has mostly been about caging the iceman. And it sounds like you're doing outstanding in that. So, when the iceman is caged you're not tricked into being sad or angry* **(f)**? *But, what about feeling happy? How often do you feel happy* **(g)**?

▶ *So, we still have X minutes left. What would you like to do* **(h)**?

Explanation

a. This is very important to ask. Many kids have a specific problem or issue they want to discuss. Of course, whatever it is should be prioritized.

b. This is tapping the second agenda item. I always have the date at the ready from our last appointment. Kids often don't remember how long ago we last met, and they need that frame of reference to appreciate what I know and what I don't know.

c. This is tapping the third agenda item. As was the case with the parents, I'm hoping the kid names his enemy first. If not, I'll ask if he remembers the name of his enemy and then ascertain how much he's still working with that concept.

d. This is tapping the first agenda item. Sometimes I ask this question first or second. It's a feel thing.

e. This is tapping the fourth agenda item. Of course, X, Y, and Z are the given stresses or developmental challenges we previously worked on. I'll also bring up any developmental hurdles that might be emerging, given the kid's age, and see what the kid is thinking or feeling about those.

f. At different points in the care, we would have covered realistic sadness, anxiety, and irritability and differentiated such from the work of the internal enemies.

Sometimes this differentiation needs a review. This could be how such a review might go:

Kid: *I felt sad when Jake moved away.*
MHP: *He's your best friend, I know.*
Kid: *Yeah, I miss him a lot and am sad.*
MHP: *Feeling sad over having a friend move away makes all the sense in the world. That's not necessarily the iceman working on you. Jake is important to you, so having him move away makes you feel sad. That's healthy. But, let me check, do you think the iceman is trying to tell you anything about that?*
Kid: *That I'll never have another close friend because I'm a freak.*
MHP: *Are you a freak?*
Kid: *No. I did thought testing on that one. A lot of kids like me.*
MHP: *Will you ever have another close friend?*
Kid: *Yeah, I guess so. I can see that's the iceman. I just miss Jake. There will never be another Jake.*
MHP: *Yeah, there will never be another Jake. That part is real. It's also true that there will be other close friends. Not better or worse than Jake, just different. And they'll matter a lot, too. You have a big heart, and there's lots of room in there to care about lots of other people.*

g. I don't always get to this question, and sometimes skip it altogether for younger kids. But, if I do, it's usually serving as a prelude to covering one of the following modules from this volume: gratitude, kindness, or strengths; I'm particularly fond of introducing gratitude letters if the kid has never done one (see Chapter 8).

h. This closing is done just like it's done in many of the individual sessions with kids. However, many kids want to see, learn, or discuss magic. Actually, I've had instances when other agendas have filled up the session and I've had to extend a couple of minutes because a kid said something like, "What? No magic today?!"

Additional Commentary

At least for me, termination can activate countertransference like few other things. For example, for years I didn't offer booster sessions because I was concerned I would come across like I was trying to sell something; I set aside the evidence in the literature because of my countertransference. Fortunately, I got over that. But there are many other kinds of risks if we are not careful:

▶ We might solicit more feedback than has value for a kid or family.

▶ We might cut off expressions of gratitude and loss because we are made uncomfortable by them.

▶ We might schedule more meetings than a kid needs because of our fiscal or psychological needs.

▶ We might push a kid out sooner than is advisable because of our fiscal or psychological needs.

In short, self-examination is key, as it always is when doing kid clinical work. I know I may be overdoing this point, but it's just that critical. This self-examination won't necessarily weaken or eliminate the thoughts or feelings we are having that could interfere with the work, but it will allow us to make better decisions by not responding to those factors. Talking these things out with a supervisor, a therapist, or a colleague can also be very helpful.

The bottom line is that this is a wonderful phase of the work. Some of my favorite memories of things people have said have occurred in termination or booster sessions. I often think, "I can't believe I'm getting paid to do this!"

SIDEBAR 15.1

This is a simple card trick to teach kids that has a strong impact. You just need a deck of playing cards, your mind puppet (see the trick reviewed in Chapter 3), three slips of paper, and a glass. Ask the kid to shuffle the deck as much as he wants and to then give it to you. As you're talking and motioning, spy the bottom card; for the purpose of this illustration, let's say it's the four of clubs. Now, say that you can use your mind puppet to read his mind regarding the cards that he picks. Spread the deck and ask him to choose any card, being careful not to show you. Then, use your mind puppet to read his mind. Write "four of clubs" on the first piece of paper. Fold it up and put it in the glass. Then ask him to put his selected card face-up on the side of the deck; let's say it's the 10 of spades. Ask him to pick a second card, again not showing you. Have your mind puppet read his mind on that one. Write "10 of spades" on the second piece of paper, fold it, and put it in the glass. Tell him that you'll pick the third card and show neither of you. Pick the four of clubs from the bottom of the deck (if you're comfortable with forcing cards, you could always shuffle the deck and force what was the bottom card), but position it facedown next to the two face-up cards. Say that this time, your mind puppet will read the card and share the information with you, without either of you seeing the card. After gesturing with your mind puppet, write "queen of hearts" on the third piece of paper, putting it in the glass and mixing up the three scraps of paper. Then have the kid pull out the pieces of paper and read them; after he does so, turn over the third card.

Should the kid pick the bottom card (never had it happen), you can just modify the trick by what you write on the scraps of paper and by picking up the deck, motioning and talking, and spotting the new bottom card.

REFERENCES AND BIBLIOGRAPHY

Asarnow, J. R., Jaycox, L. H., & Tompson, M. C. (2001). Depression in youth: Psychosocial interventions. *Journal of Clinical Child Psychology, 30*(1), 33–47.

Barrett, P., Healy-Farrell, L., & March, J. S. (2004). Cognitive-behavioral family treatment of childhood obsessive-compulsive disorder: A controlled trial. *Journal of the American Academy of Child & Adolescent Psychiatry, 43*(1), 46–62.

Birmaher, B., Brent, D. A., Kolko, D., Baugher, M., Bridge, J., Holder, D., & Ulloa, R. E. (2000). Clinical outcome after short-term psychotherapy for adolescents with major depressive disorder. *Archives of General Psychiatry, 57*(1), 29–36.

Clarke, G. N., Rohde, P., Lewinsohn, P. M., Hops, H., & Seeley, J. R. (1999). Cognitive-behavioral treatment of adolescent depression: Efficacy of acute group treatment and booster sessions. *Journal of the American Academy of Child & Adolescent Psychiatry, 38*(3), 272–279.

Davis, D. D. (2008). *Terminating therapy: A professional guide to ending on a positive note.* New York, NY: John Wiley & Sons.

Gearing, R. E., Schwalbe, C. S., Lee, R., & Hoagwood, K. E. (2013). The effectiveness of booster sessions in CBT treatment for child and adolescent mood and anxiety disorders. *Depression and Anxiety, 30*(9), 800–808.

Hayward, C., Varady, S., Albano, A. M., Thienemann, M., Henderson, L., & Schatzberg, A. F. (2000). Cognitive-behavioral group therapy for social phobia in female adolescents: Results of a pilot study. *Journal of the American Academy of Child & Adolescent Psychiatry, 39*(6), 721–726.

Leijten, P., Raaijmakers, M. A., de Castro, B. O., & Matthys, W. (2013). Does socioeconomic status matter? A meta-analysis on parent training effectiveness for disruptive child behavior. *Journal of Clinical Child & Adolescent Psychology, 42*(3), 384–392.

Lewinsohn, P. M., & Clarke, G. N. (1999). Psychosocial treatments for adolescent depression. *Clinical Psychology Review, 19*(3), 329–342.

Schmukler, A. G. (Ed.). (2013). *Saying goodbye: A casebook of termination in child and adolescent analysis and therapy.* London, UK: Routledge.

Storch, E. A., Geffken, G. R., Merlo, L. J., Mann, G., Duke, D., Munson, M., & Goodman, W. K. (2007). Family-based cognitive-behavioral therapy for pediatric obsessive-compulsive disorder: Comparison of intensive and weekly approaches. *Journal of the American Academy of Child & Adolescent Psychiatry, 46*(4), 469–478.

West, A. E., Henry, D. B., & Pavuluri, M. N. (2007). Maintenance model of integrated psychosocial treatment in pediatric bipolar disorder: A pilot feasibility study. *Journal of the American Academy of Child & Adolescent Psychiatry, 46*(2), 205–212.

SECTION V

Surprising Events and Special Circumstances

CHAPTER **16**

Surprising Events With Kids

Teenagers. Everything is so apocalyptic.
—*Kami Garcia*

One of the most delightful things about kid clinical work is the number of surprising things that can happen. No matter how many years I do this, there are still surprises. Sure, the frequency of surprising events goes down with time (e.g., when you're a trainee it can feel like they happen multiple times each week!), but they keep coming. What I'm attempting to do in this chapter is to provide enough of a range of examples so that the underlying principles become clear; this way, even when a new kind of surprise happens that I don't cover here, you hopefully will be left with a rationale to ground you.

I'd strongly urge you to consider what you might do in each situation before you read my thoughts; better yet, have a discussion with others before reading what I think (or even afterward). If you try to work this through for yourself first, it's more likely that you'll better remember what you want to do should it happen to you.

Before I start, let me suggest three guiding questions to consider when surprising situations arise: (1) What is my goal? This one can anchor you in many stormy moments. Maybe your goal is to provide empathy. Maybe your goal is to have the client be able to partner with you in the design of the work. Or you might have a different goal. But, being conscious of the goal(s) can be very helpful in guiding your words and actions. (2) What is the client trying to accomplish or to communicate? When it comes to resistance, the surface-level communication is often not *the* communication. A client may ask if you're gay, but *what is she really asking?* A client may put on her headphones to listen to music, but *what is she really trying to communicate?* (3) How can you use the exchange to promote the clinical work?

So, here are some vignettes for you to consider:

▶ **A kid tries to listen to her portable music player, use a cell phone, do homework, or otherwise tune the mental health professional (MHP) out. Pick**

**one of those and consider: What would you do? Would you respond differ-
ently if you were meeting alone with a kid versus if you were meeting with
the kid and a parent?**

Any appointment with a parent in the room: What's interesting here is to
see how the parent(s) will respond. Most parents will take over and correct
the kid's behavior. It seems like kids expect this when it happens and don't
put up too much of a fuss. However, if the parents shrug their shoulders, I
would turn to the kid and say something like: *Monica, put that away.* If the
kid doesn't listen—and many will if the MHP projects sufficient authority
and doesn't project fear or self-doubt—I'll say to the parents: *Folks, I can't do
the interview if Monica is doing that. So, I'd like for you to jump in here
and help.* I really can't think of the last time that didn't work. Hypothetically,
if it didn't work, I'd ask the kid to leave the room for just a moment and then
suggest to the parents that they establish a contract with the kid—for instance,
you earn your cell phone (or some other very desirable privilege) for the next
24 to 48 hours by participating in the interview. If that didn't work, and now
I'm really stretching my imagination, I'd give the kid the choice of either stopping the behavior or sitting in the waiting room while I interview her parents. Later the kid can be interviewed about what she is feeling and what the
behavior is communicating (see Chapter 4).

Appointments with the kid alone, evaluation phase: If a kid does this with
her parents in the room the kid might be challenging the parent, the therapist, or both. But, in this instance, it's a straight up challenge to the MHP.
Sometimes it's done with an aura of, "Hmm, I wonder how you'll handle this,
MHP," while at other times is seems to be a pretty clear "F-you!" I deal with
it in a similar way to how I just illustrated. I'll ask the kid to knock it off. If
she won't, I'll ask if she needs for me to bring her parent(s) into the office to
cease the behavior. If she still won't, I'll go out into the waiting area and
say something like, *Paula, Monica is doing her homework and won't stop.
Would you mind coming in and taking it from her?* I've never had an instance
where that didn't solve the immediate problem. I then might take the occasion to review what the kid is feeling about being there or else review how
I'm trying to be helpful to the kid. But, if a kid is set on being irritable, I just
press on with the task at hand.

Appointments with the kid alone, treatment phase: This is rare. It suggests
that a treatment alliance either hasn't been established or has been ruptured.
In the latter instance, I'll say things like, *Monica, what's happened that
you're upset with me?* Or, *You're letting me know that you're upset with me
but not with your words. I wonder what is making using your words so difficult?* Or, *Hmmm. You're upset about something, clearly. Does it make you
feel anxious to use words to tell me about it?* Most of the time, if this won't
work, I'll just insist that the kid knock it off, using techniques like I just
reviewed. However, if the treatment is longer term (e.g., play therapy with a
kid, insight-oriented therapy with a teen) I'll first get a parent to remove the
materials the kid is using (e.g., music player, books). If the kid then refuses to

talk, I'm more likely to break out a book and read, hoping that extinguishing the behavior might work, making sure that the parent has ensured that the kid hasn't entered the consulting room with some entertainment or homework. In such instances I'll say as I start to read, *Monica, I see that it's important to you that we stop our work for now. I mean, I'd like to continue it, but I respect your choice. I'm going to start reading my book now, but if you change your mind, just start talking or give me a signal and we can pick back up.* I've never had this go on for more than two sessions. If it did, we might have to develop a behavioral program with the parent (see Chapter 13).

▶ **A kid says she needs to go to the bathroom. What would you do? What if it became a pattern?**

With the parents in the room: Parents are usually a great judge for whether this is resistance or reflects a real need. I'll usually follow their lead. If a pattern seems to be emerging, I might say something like, *As you guys are paying for every minute, and as we all want to get the most out of our time as possible, and as Monica often needs to go to the bathroom while we're meeting, what would you think of arriving a couple of minutes early next time so that she can make herself comfortable before the session starts?*

Meeting with the kid alone: For younger kids, the first time it happens, with obvious signs of distress, I just say, *Sure.* For older youth the same thing, unless we have 15 minutes or less to go in the session, in which case I might say, *There's about 15 minutes left in our session. Could it wait or is this more urgent?* And then do whatever the kid wants to do. If it gets to be a pattern, I might say something like this: *Monica, have you noticed that you tend to need to go to the bathroom often during our sessions?* Unless the kid has a related medical problem, she'll usually just acknowledge the fact without much commentary. So I'll next ask how the kid is experiencing our sessions, seeing if any adjustments are warranted so that she is more comfortable. Otherwise, I'll suggest to the parent that they arrive early enough for her to go before we begin the session.

▶ **A kid lies down on your couch. What would you do? Would it matter to you if the kid left her shoes on or took them off?**

Unless I have a good reason to think otherwise, I think of this as acting out. Therefore, I handle it the same way that I handle bringing in homework or other direct challenges. To me, it wouldn't really matter if a kid kept her shoes on or kicked them off.

▶ **A youth starts to misuse office furniture or materials. What would you do? Would you handle it differently if damage was being done?**

With a parent in the room: Rarely does a kid try to damage furniture (e.g., gouging wood with a pen). It's more likely that a kid will try to amuse herself by tipping a lamp or putting dirty feet up on a table. My first approach is to wait to see if a parent will intercede. If she doesn't I will, with a simple instruction like, *Monica, don't tip the lamp like that.* Most of the time that works. If not, I'll ask the parent to intercede. If that didn't work, then I'd ask the parents to set up a contract with the kid (as discussed in the previous example).

With a parent not in the room: For younger kids who may simply not know better, I'll just ask them to stop, but bring in a parent if need be. For older kids or teens I'm more likely to ask the kid to stop and follow it up with something like, *I wonder what you're trying to accomplish today by* (behavior X)? The goal is to try to have the kid put words to the feelings and thoughts that are driving the behavior. But I don't chase this for long if the kid can't or won't participate in it. I just have her knock it off and look for evidence of an alliance problem, with an eye toward understanding and repair.

▶ **A child tries to sit on your lap. What would you do? Would it matter to you if the kid just sat there talking or if she put her head on your chest and her arms around your neck?**

I've never had this happen with a parent in the room. It's usually happened when I'm working with a younger kid who is struggling with attachment issues. Sometimes MHPs new to kid work believe that the only two choices are to be kind (i.e., go along with it) or be mean (i.e., deny it). But I don't think it's that simple. First of all, we MHPs generally prefer to work with words rather than to work with behaviors, at least when they are available to us. We can do more precise and better work with words. Second, it is *very easy* for adults to misconstrue the nature of the physical contact, even when it has been 100% innocent. For these two reasons it is my style to say this to a child who is approaching me to sit on my lap, maybe even holding her hands if she has gotten that close: *Monica, I love it that you feel comfortable with me and like me. I feel the same way about you. You're a great kid! Because I like you so much and want so much to help you to put the cobra in its cage, I'd rather that you didn't sit on my lap. It's just a lot easier for us to work that way. Would that be okay?* For kids like this there is also often concomitant work going on to develop the quality of their attachments or to expand upon them.

▶ **A kid starts to partially disrobe to show something on her skin. What would you do? Would your response vary depending on the part of the body that was being disrobed?**

I'm considering here the layer of clothing directly in contact with the kid's skin. This is usually attempted by younger kids, though some older kids and teens with poorer impulse control or judgment may try to do this as well. I just jump in quickly with, *Oh, that's okay. I don't need to see it. Your description is fine.* Again, it's just too easy for adults to misconstrue the nature of the disrobing, even if no sensitive parts of the kid's body are exposed.

Of course, taking an item of clothing off is different from rolling up a sleeve or a long pant leg. I wouldn't generally feel a need to jump in if a kid started showing me something that way.

▶ **A kid asks if you have children, are married, are Christian, are gay, and so on. Imagine one of those questions coming your way. What would you do?**

This is a good place to ask yourself, "What is the client really wondering about?" In the vast majority of instances, she wants to know that you will be accepting and/or that you have sufficient knowledge to be helpful, though sometimes it can be to make sure you don't have some objectionable characteristic or won't judge her. All things being equal, your having personal experiences that overlap with the client's is often helpful. However, that value is often overvalued, as it doesn't remotely compare to things like artful clinical skill and knowledge of the relevant science. Moreover, even when the answer to the asked question seems like it would be well received, I prefer to answer *the real question.* Not only does answering the real question spare a clinician from having to answer other veiled questions (because the real question hasn't been addressed), but it also keeps the clinician from walking on land mines. In the latter instance, imagine an exchange like this between a teen and an MHP:

Teen: *Are you a Christian?*
MHP: *Yes* (sensing that the "right" answer is true).
Teen: *So, you believe that sinners go to hell?*

I would prefer this:

Teen: *Are you a Christian?*
MHP: *Monica, if you want to know I'll tell you. But, before I go there, tell me, what would it be like for you if I was, versus if I wasn't?*
Teen: *If you weren't I don't think you could understand where I'm coming from. Or you might also think I'm weird.*
MHP: *So it's very important to you that I understand you and that I don't judge you unfairly?*
Teen: (Nodding)
MHP: *Any good therapist, whether Christian or not, needs to be able to show you that he understands you and accepts you for who you are. Actually, I would think that any therapist who couldn't do that probably shouldn't be your therapist. So, I promise to work hard to both understand you and to use that understanding to accept who you are, no matter where that takes us. Does that sound like an okay answer?*

Most kids would drop it there, as the *real* question has been addressed, at least for now. However, if a kid pressed—which isn't common at all—and to avoid going back to the land mine, I might suggest this:

Teen: *Are you a Christian?*
MHP: *Yes.*
Teen: *So, you believe that sinners go to hell?*
MHP: *What do you think?*

Teen: *I think they go to hell, and that I might be headed there.*
MHP: *Wow. That sounds very important. What happened?*

If the teen pressed with the MHP's views about hell, I might suggest saying something like, **Monica, I don't even think about that when we're talking. I'm just so focused on helping you** (insert one of the goals, including perhaps a general statement about caging an enemy) **and thinking about how your views of hell relate. I think if we started talking about something else, like what I think about this or that, it'd really cut down on my ability to help you.** But what about if the kid presses for religious affiliation and the MHP's answer is not the "right" answer. It might go like this:

Teen: *Are you a Christian?*
MHP: *No, I belong to another religion. But I have lots of clients who don't belong to the same religion as me, and we do well together, just like I have lots of clients who are different from me in other ways also* (insert other differences like sexual orientation, political leanings, history of illnesses, sports teams liked, and so forth, whatever fits). *What matters to me is whether I can understand where you're coming from, how your religion fits into your life, and value that. I know that I can but I also appreciate that you have to form your own opinion about that as we work together.*
Teen: *Well, in your religion, do sinners go to hell?*

In wrapping up this section, let me say that some clinicians elect to disclose nothing about such matters after answering the real question and being pressed for more specifics. I've experimented with that style myself. *For me (and maybe not for you),* I've found that I feel like I'm coming across as a control freak/authority figure/a-hole if I don't share a little in this context. So I do. But, if that doesn't work for you, do it your way. As I've said, there are many kinds of styles that work equally well, and we all do well to find those styles that work best with our temperaments and clinical model.

▶ **A kid asks if you have other child clients. If you answered that, would you also answer a question about how many? If yes, would you answer a question about how many of the same age as the client? What would you do?**
Again, we want to get to the *real question.* Imagine you wanted to know if a person liked or hated you. To find that out you asked what sports team he liked. He answers, but you still can't tell. So, you ask another question, as the *real* question hasn't been addressed. On and on it goes until one of you gets frustrated or you get some sort of a reasonable sense for the answer to your *true* question. We MHPs know that many questions are not *the real* question, so an exchange might go like this:

Kid: *Do you have other kids you see besides me?*
MHP: *I'll answer that in a few minutes if you'd like, but tell me, what would it be like for you if I did and what would it be like for you if I didn't?*

Kid: *I don't know. I guess I'd like it if I was the only girl you saw.*

MHP: *What would be nice about that?*

Kid: *I don't know. You'd be able to better remember things I say and not mix me up with the other girls.*

MHP: *So, that's important, isn't it? It's important that I remember what you say and not confuse it with things other girls say?*

Kid: (Nodding)

MHP: *Well, I'll tell you, Monica, even if I had like three kazillion other kids that I saw, and I had 20 billion things to do the day I saw you, I think it would still be very, very important for me to not forget what you say and to not confuse you with other girls. More than that, it'd be important for you to be the ONLY girl on my mind, and the only thing on my mind, when I'm meeting with you.*

Kid: (Smiling)

MHP: *Does that answer your question well enough?*

Kid: (Nodding)

Depending on what we were doing in that session, I might follow up with a discussion on how often the kid feels unattended to or unimportant to others, with an eye toward developing interventions for fixing that.

If the kid still wanted to know the answer to the first question, which isn't common, I'd say something like, *Yes, I have other kids I see. But when I'm with you, I'm not thinking about any of them.* If the kid pressed with other questions about the other clients, I'd say something like, *Monica, if another kid I see had any questions about you I'd have to tell her that I can't say, because what I do with you is private. So, that's why I can't say anything more about the other kids I see, though I certainly understand why you'd be curious about that.*

▶ **A kid runs up to you in public to interact. What would you do?**

This isn't common, as most parents of younger kids would rein them in before they could do this. But sometimes a kid might squirt away or have a distracted parent. Or, sometimes the kid is older and out in public without her parents. The first reaction I'd suggest is whatever reaction the MHP would offer to a kid in her personal life in that same circumstance. In other words, I'd suggest offering a genuine greeting that fits your style. Much of the time, that's all a kid wants and she'll go on her merry way. If a kid started to strike up a conversation, I might say something like, *Monica, I think that's interesting, and I have something to say about it. But, can we wait until I see you this week 'cause I don't want to rush and I also want to make sure that no one can hear us?*

I've not had this happen, but what would you suggest an MHP do if a teen client started to try to engage the MHP, together with another teen friend, about a given topic? Think about it for a moment before reading on.

In a case like that I'd try to have an authentic first reaction, then ask if I could talk to my client alone for a second, stating something like this, *Monica, I so value our relationship and I really don't know how to preserve what we do if we bring someone else in on it, especially out in public. That said, if you'd like to talk about this more, we can when I see you this week. For now, though, I kind of have to get going.* I'd then wave bye to the friend saying something like, *It was nice to meet you Michelle!* Besides the fact that such a moment would not offer us many tools that we rely on (e.g., confidentiality), there are just too many ways that continuing such a dialogue could go badly. I know it may seem like staying and chatting would be harmless and could promote the alliance, and in many instances it might, but what if the other teen went home and posted something on social networking sites about Monica's cool therapist? Or what if Monica told her parent that the MHP did a helpful "mini session" with Monica and her friend at the mall? Or what if Monica's friend told her own parent that Monica's therapist agreed with her on some point with which the parent differs? In my view, there's too much potential downside for very little potential upside.

▶ **A kid asks if you can come to watch him or her at an extracurricular event. What would you do? Would you ever? If yes, when? If not, why not?**
This vignette has too many permutations to script. But I can share the questions I'd be asking myself:

• What's the reason the kid wants me to see her? Is it simply that I'm an important person in her life and she likes to have her important people see her do well? I'd be inclined to accommodate that sort of a motivation if I conveniently could. Alternatively, is it that her own dad is absent from her life and I'd be filling a void? I'd be less inclined to try to sate that need by attending, as such a solution isn't lasting and sets a kid up for disappointment later; moreover, I'd want to focus on more viable solutions to that very important need.

• What might the parents' attitudes be about it? Some parents would welcome it while others would be freaked out, even if the MHP remained anonymous. The parents' wishes obviously matter.

• Is it convenient for me to do it? The less convenient, the less likely I am to want to do it. I've learned the hard way that overextending for my clients leaves *me* vulnerable to countertransference that interferes with the work.

• Do I want to do it? Yes, we get to ask this question! Sometimes we just don't feel like it and that's okay.

• Can we agree on a protocol? I would generally prefer not to sit with the family so that I'm not burdened by thinking through how to react to small talk and introductions to other family or friends. I also like to leave myself free to come late and leave early. This is just my style. If I thought that my style might cause offense then I'm less likely to do it.

If I agree to do it, we'll discuss the protocol and get on the same page. If I decide not to do it, I'll just provide empathy for the request and communicate why I'm not going, with an eye toward emphasizing any advantages for the kid, including the preservation of an effective treatment protocol.

▶ **A kid bakes cookies for you. Would you accept them? If yes, would you eat them? If no, what would you say if the kid asked how they tasted?**

You may note that certain themes are woven throughout this chapter. Whenever a kid *acts* toward the MHP the first reaction is usually best if it is prosocial and authentic. A second theme is that MHPs do well to determine what the behavior means for the client and how the various choices the clinician has might affect both the alliance and the treatment plan. Most of the time this scenario comes up around the holidays or other special occasions. Typically, I'd accept the cookies, sample them later, and report back my enjoyment (if I enjoyed them, that is, but it's really hard to mess up cookies). The only situations that might realistically come up that would cause me pause are these:

- The kid is being generally resistant. I'd want to rule out that the cookies are acting out an apology or I might wonder, if the kid has such leanings, what ingredients might be in the cookies.

- There is no occasion for the cookies. Again, I'd just want to be sure that I'm not making it harder to get to relevant thoughts and feelings by accepting the cookies. In these instances, hybrid solutions are also sometimes possible: We explore what the cookies mean and, assuming it's not then problematic to do so, I'd accept them.

- The cookies were purchased from a boutique bakery and are expensive. The formula for costly gifts is straightforward: First, express empathy for the client's perspective about the gift; second, express gratitude; and third, explain why accepting the gift could dampen the efficacy of the work while looking for opportunities to compromise (e.g., maybe we each eat one cookie during the session but the kid takes the rest home). Sometimes these discussions also have to happen with the parents, either separately or together with the kid.

- The kid, or her parents, have a history of acting out in the treatment in ways that have been problematic for the alliance or the treatment plan goals. For example, one divorced parent might be trying to win over the favor of the MHP over the other parent. Or a teen might be acting out a crush on the therapist. Or the teen despises coming in but the parent makes a show of a gift in order to rub the teen's face in it. Again, the script would be empathy, then gratitude, then explanation, and then *possible* compromise.

▶ **A kid asks you to not allow other kid clients to dismantle a Lego object she has made. The kid has put a lot of effort into making this object and**

has started developing a story about it that she wants to continue next session. What would you do? (A similar request can be made when a child asks for the MHP to hang something she has made in the office.)

This is how an exchange might go:

Kid: *Can you make sure no other kid touches this?*
MHP: *What would it be like if I didn't let anyone do that, and what would it be like if I let other kids play with all the Legos?*
Kid: *I just want to play more with this and I don't have enough time today.*
MHP: *That stinks, doesn't it?*
Kid: *Yes.*
MHP: *So, if I let other kids touch this it might seem like I'm not realizing that this really matters to you.*
Kid: *Yes.*
MHP: *I understand that. I'd probably feel the same way in your shoes. Here's the thing, though. How would you feel if you came to a session and I said you couldn't play with all the toys or you couldn't sit in some of the furniture or you could only use two pieces of paper?*
Kid: *I wouldn't like that.*
MHP: *It might feel like I was cheating you somehow.*
Kid: *Yeah.*
MHP: *That's what it would be like if I told other kids they couldn't play with all the Legos. Monica, it's possible that no kid will touch that between now and when you next come in—it's just that I can't forbid a kid from being able to use everything here, just like I would never forbid you, either. But it would still stink if someone else did decide to play with those particular Legos.*
Kid: *Oh, okay.*
MHP: *How are you feeling about it now?*
Kid: *Not good, but okay I guess.*

If a kid was still fretting about it I might inquire how often she feels unattended to or mistreated, with an eye toward developing interventions for addressing these themes in her life.

▶ **A kid tries to link with you on a social networking (SN) site. What would you do?**

You'll note in my intake paperwork that I have a SN policy (see Appendix A). But kids don't usually read those documents. That's why if you're working with kids who regularly use SN, it would be a good idea to say something like this if you feel it could be coming: *Monica, I also want to let you know that you might see that I'm on some social networking sites. In order for me to be your therapist, and stay good at my job, I wouldn't normally link up with any of my clients on those sites. Not only would I be concerned about my client's privacy, but I do a better job when everything I say happens just in this room.* This would be another illustration regarding how pursuing adherence is less complicated and difficult than responding to resistance. If a kid requested linking on SN and I hadn't said this to her, I'd express empathy and gratitude and then explain. If I had already said this to a kid, and I still got the request, it might go something like this:

MHP: *Hey, Monica, I notice I got a request on Facebook from you.*
Kid: *Yeah, I thought it'd be cool to link.*
MHP: *That would be cool, wouldn't it? And I really like what it says about how you feel about our relationship.*
Kid: *Thanks. Yeah, I like you okay.*
MHP: *Turns out I'm not as big of a loser as it first might have seemed* (laughing)!
Kid: *Yeah* (smiling).
MHP: *Great. Let me just check in on something. I covered a lot of stuff when we first started working together, so it's okay if the answer is "no," but do you remember what I said about how I handle social networking sites with people I'm doing counseling with?*
Kid: *A little.*
MHP: *What do you remember?*
Kid: *That sometimes you don't do it 'cause you think it's not a good idea.*
MHP: *Thanks. That allows me to clarify. And I'm sorry if I said anything that made it seem like a* sometimes *thing. It's pretty much an all the time thing, because I'm concerned about your privacy and I can do a better job for you if our conversations aren't scattered like the leaves on a lawn and are focused when we meet here. So that's why I haven't responded, even though I really enjoy it that you feel comfortable enough to ask.*
Kid: *Oh, okay. No biggie.*
MHP: *Sure? I want to make sure you don't think I'm freezing you out or anything.*
Kid: *No, it's okay. I get it.*

Let's say the kid in this example did remember the policy and remembered it correctly. Then the conversation might go like this:

MHP: *Yeah, you remember that pretty well. So, tell me, Monica, given what you know about how I handle that, what do you think caused you to make the request anyway?*
Kid: *I don't know. Thought it'd be nice, and not all rules are real rules. So, figured it couldn't hurt to check.*
MHP: *Yeah, I hear you. Not all rules are real rules. I know how much that is true at the universities I've worked at, and I'm guessing it might also sometimes be true at your school and maybe even at home?*
Kid: *Umm-hum.*
MHP: (Chuckling) *Well, this one is a real rule. But just for one reason—it's what works best for you* (repeating the reasons).

Kid: *Okay, that's cool.*

MHP: (Repeating the double checking language)

▶ **A teen asks if she can bring her boyfriend to the next session. What would you do? If you'd do this, would your answer change if you knew the parents objected to the boyfriend? If you'd do this, would your answer change if it was a lesbian relationship and the kid hadn't yet come out to her parents?**

This sort of stuff happens semi-regularly in different guises. The situation is a kid introduces a proposal for a modification to the treatment methodology. The question might be, "Can we go for a walk instead of meeting in here?" Or, "Would you be willing to call my coach for me?" Or, "Can I sit where you sit and you sit where I sit?" And so forth. These are all proposals to change methods, which then leads us to wonder what goal(s) the kid has in mind for the method change. We then consider how that goal fits in with our agreed-on goals and whether there might be any side effects to consider. So, it might go like this:

Kid: *Can I bring my boyfriend to the next session?*

MHP: *Interesting. Tell me, what good thing might we accomplish if we brought him in?*

Kid: *I think he could verify that my dad is a jerk to me. I mean, I know he sounds reasonable when he talks to you, but Jason sees how he acts when we're at home. So you'd get to know better how my dad really is.*

MHP: *So, you're concerned that maybe I don't fully appreciate how your dad affects you and that Jason might help me to better get that?*

Kid: *Exactly.*

MHP: *That would feel nice, wouldn't it, to be sure that I got how your dad impacts you?*

Kid: *A lot.*

MHP: *Well, let me check something first. Let me share with you how I think your dad affects you and see how well or how poorly I've understood. Is that okay?*

Kid: *Sure. Go for it.*

MHP: *I think you know that your dad loves you and that he does a lot of good stuff for you, like pay for your activities and drive you places and go to your games. But you also believe that he is too impatient and that he explodes too often. Then, when he explodes, he says things that hurt you deeply and erases all the other good stuff that he has done. How you feel then makes you badly want to live with your mom instead, even though it would mean changing schools and not seeing some of your friends as much. It's just that it hurts you so much when he says those things in anger, like you're stupid and lazy and have to stop acting like your mother.*

Kid: (Showing tears and nodding)

MHP: *I'm glad I get it, but I'm not glad that that's something that's in your life. Monica, I promise you that I've started working with your dad on this stuff and will continue; I've started challenging your dad—hard. And he's been very open, even though I've been tough on him. I think he's been as open as he's been because I'm only taking him where he already wants to go.*

Kid: (Crying and nodding some more)
MHP: *I want to talk more about this, but let me just check. Is there any other reason you wanted to bring in Jason?*
Kid: *No, not really.*
MHP: *So, maybe we want to wait on that for now and just get back to your dad.*
Kid: *Sounds good.*

Or our exchange could go like this:

Kid: *Can I bring my boyfriend to the next session?*
MHP: *Interesting. Tell me, what good thing might we accomplish if we brought him in?*
Kid: *He thinks I'm abusing drugs when I take medication for my ADHD. I've given him stuff to read, but he says it comes from people who are paid by drug companies. But I think if you spoke with him he might get it and stop hounding me about it.*
MHP: *It really upsets you when he does that hounding?*
Kid: *A LOT.*
MHP: *And you're thinking that maybe I might be able to get him to see it differently, and that if I could lead to him hounding you less it would reduce how much stress is in your life?*
Kid: *EXACTLY.*
MHP: *Have you spoken with anyone else about this idea?*
Kid: *Yeah. My mom and dad said it's up to you, and my boyfriend said he'd come in; I think he's actually curious to meet you. He said his parents are cool with it, too.*
MHP: *Would you be okay with signing a release so that I could speak with him during one of our sessions?*
Kid: *Yes! You'll do it, then?*
MHP: *Sure. I think you have a good goal for bringing him in and it sounds like you've gotten everyone on board.*
Kid: *Thank you!*

In this last vignette, and depending on your state's regulations and the kids' ages, you might need to get the consent of the boyfriend's parents and/or have the kid client's parents sign the release as well.

What about those scenarios where the parents either don't like the crush or the kid identifies gay but the parents don't know that? Let's take the latter and let's assume that the teen client has at least one good goal for bringing in her crush. This exchange would be inserted into, or added onto, one of the previous ones:

MHP: *How are you feeling these days about your parents knowing that you identify yourself as a lesbian?*
Kid: *I still don't want them to know. They'd FREAK out and send me to Bible camp hell or something.*
MHP: *So, what if they found out that you brought Rachel in to speak with me?*
Kid: *How could they?*

MHP: *In my experience you never know. Someone could spot you guys walking in. Or your parents might insist on seeing my file, or Rachel's parents find out somehow and call up your parents, or who knows? It's just a risk.*

Kid: *That's okay. I'll take it.*

MHP: *Here's the thing, though. It's also a risk to our work. If your parents found out they could very well lose faith in me. You know how much I support your right to choose your romantic partner, and I also like what you tell me about how suitable Rachel is for you. But, you've also told me that your parents would freak out if they found out. So, if they found out that I met with Rachel and you, and I didn't keep them in the loop . . . it's just too risky that they'd torpedo our working together, and I have to keep that as a top concern.*

At this point the kid would either agree, and we'd be done, or the kid would give other arguments for bringing Rachel in. In this case I'd make sure I understood her thinking, reflecting that understanding back to her, provide empathy, and then explain my rationale as to why I need to not bring Rachel in (unless the teen thought of something that trumped my concern). Another thing to keep in mind is that states have differing requirements regarding parents' rights to access a kid's chart; your knowledge of those laws could affect what you say as well.

I'm not a big fan of secrets in family therapy. When I'm given one it feels like I'm holding a porous bag of fecal matter (which is why I generally don't meet with individuals when doing couples counseling and, when I do, we agree that there are to be no secrets). For example, consider the implications if I met with Rachel and Monica and then Monica, in a subsequent drama-filled argument with her parents, declared: "Even Dr. Palmiter has met her and likes her!" So, I stay away from such scenarios unless I have a very, very strong and important reason to do otherwise.

To review, these are the steps: (a) get a full articulation of the method and goal(s) that the kid has in mind; (b) reflect back what you've heard, checking to make sure you've heard it correctly while offering empathy; (c) consider how well the goal supports, interferes with, or has a neutral impact on the treatment goals and your alliance; (d) consider possible side effects; and (e) if you think it isn't a good idea, say why and offer a better method for reaching the goal, including perhaps explaining how a method already onboard might do a better job (e.g., it would more quickly reach the goal or not include as many potential side effects).

► **A kid, mesmerized by the video camera in a training clinic consulting room, performs for it by playing the drums on her buttocks. What would you do?**

This is one of my favorite supervision memories. The supervision group, me included, got a good laugh from this footage; that laughing was probably further fueled by how at a loss the therapist trainee was in knowing what to do (she joined in also); I'm even smiling now as I type this story.

As surprising and unusual of an event as it was, it was fairly easy for the group to help the therapist know how to proceed going forward, and without much input from me. It was suggested that the therapist get a full exposition of the kid's fantasies about who was watching and the viewer(s)' imagined responses to the performance, giving empathy for what the kid offered and then clarifying how the videos are used. This happened early on in that treatment. And, like most treatments where taping is occurring, the video camera quickly dropped out of consciousness for the kid (and the therapist) as the work became more engaging and important.

I encourage you to consider other possible vignettes with colleagues and/or supervisors, especially if you are in training.

SIDEBAR 16.1

There are many permutations of "the magician's choice" in magic. This is one of them that I am adapting from David Copperfield's wonderful *Project Magic Handbook*. He titles the trick "Anyone Can Read Minds." You need any seven objects, a piece of paper, a pen, and your trusty mind puppet (see the magic trick in Chapter 3).

This trick involves placing seven objects in front of a kid. Tell her that your magic puppet is going to give you the power to predict the future. Then make a show of having your magic puppet temporarily imbue you with the power to predict the future. Let's say one of your objects is a pencil. With an all-knowing look on your face, write on the piece of paper "only the pencil will remain." Fold the paper and ask the kid to put it in a pocket but not to look at it. Now tell her that you will each take turns picking two objects by holding two hands over them; once one of you has done so, the other person says which of the two to eliminate.

You go first, putting your hand over any two objects *except the pencil*. The kid then chooses which one to eliminate. The kid now puts her hand over any two objects; all you need to do is to remember *not to pick the pencil*. After a couple of rounds the only thing left on the table is the pencil. Then ask the kid to read the paper she had tucked away into a pocket. This is a trick that has a nice impact while also being easy to perform and to teach.

CHAPTER 17

Surprising Events With Parents

The truth will set you free, but first it will piss you off.
—*Gloria Steinem*

This chapter mirrors some of the same principles and methodologies covered in Chapter 16, but with regard to parent interactions. Again, while no list of conundrums can be comprehensive, my hope is to give you enough examples so that you're equipped to reason through a range of novel situations that might arise.

► **A birth parent, who is estranged from the other birth parent, asks to not include the other birth parent in the evaluation. Assuming you believe that that person's involvement is important, what would you do?**
   The first thing you'll need to know in reflecting on this common scenario is what relevant laws apply in your state. In Pennsylvania, as I type this, most divorced parents share joint legal custody, even if one of them has primary or exclusive physical custody. If a kid is age 13 or younger, both legal custodians must approve for the child to receive an evaluation from a mental health provider, barring a court order to the contrary. This is not the case for most other kinds of health care providers (e.g., dentists), creating confusion and consternation among many parents. This can also create challenges for mental health professionals (MHPs) who have to be the bearers of this news to parents who often maintain that the other birth parent has either dropped out of the kid's life or has a toxic effect on the kid (e.g., by being drug dependent). These sorts of situations are often surmountable but, as most parents are already ambivalent about reaching out to us, it can make first contacts especially challenging.
   Leaving legal restrictions aside, and considering only clinical issues, the default, as I outline in the initial evaluation (Chapter 2), endeavors to engage both birth parents and any stepparents or live-in significant others of the birth parents. When a birth parent calls and expresses a desire to exclude the other parent, and assuming there are no legal restrictions for that parent's wishes to be granted, this is how the telephone conversation might go:

Parent: *I really don't want to involve Aiden's dad. He only sees Aiden once a month or so and I think he'd just accuse me of making a mountain out of a molehill.*

MHP: *I hear that. You don't want to be subject to unfair criticisms just because you're trying to do the right thing by your son.*

Parent: *Exactly.*

MHP: *Here's the thing, though. Your ex, as distant as he seems to have grown from Aiden, is still one of the world's leading experts on your son. So, the more I hear from such people, the more likely it is that I'll hit the bull's-eye in the formulation I develop. More-over, if there was a way to improve Aiden's relationship with his dad, that would usually only stand to help Aiden. So, I'd really like to take a crack at it, at least if you and your ex could be civil to each other during the family interview. Keep in mind, I'm only asking for him to come twice at this point: at the first interview and at the feedback session. With that said, I'll go forward without Aiden's father being involved if that's how you wish to proceed. It's just that you deserve to hear from me why I wouldn't recommend that.*

Parent: *But there are things about our family life that I really don't want Aiden's father to know about.*

MHP: *Fair enough. We could always schedule an additional appointment for you to tell me about those things.*

Parent: *Okay, then. We can try it.*

MHP: *Thanks. And if it turns out to be a bad idea to continue to include Aiden's dad, I'll be quick to bring that up for discussion.*

There are some additional wrinkles that I'll consider:

- If the parents can't be in the same room without becoming toxic with each other, I'll endeavor to schedule two family interviews, one for each side, with the kid attending both. It is remarkable, though, that sometimes the extra cost and inconvenience affiliated with scheduling two appointments can moti-vate the parents to find a way to be civil to each other in the same meeting; in these instances, the evaluation is already facilitating helpful changes for a kid.

- If the noncustodial parent is reported to have an abusive relationship with the kid, I'll ask to interview that parent alone—for example, if the other par-ent is reported to be substance dependent and is intermittingly explosive with the kid.

- If one of the parents cheated on the other parent with his or her current spouse or live-in significant other, and I have reason to believe that those wounds are still significant, I may suggest separate family interviews.

The default, however, is to involve all parent figures and to try to find ways to overcome the obstacles for doing that.

▶ **The birth parent who is calling reports that the other birth parent prefers to not be involved (they are still married and living together). Assuming you believe both parents participating is important, what would you do?**

In my experience, this happens for one of two reasons. First, the other parent feels overwhelmed by stress. Often in such households the parent who is calling is the one who takes care of health care appointments. So, the other parent just prefers to keep the arrangement that way. Mom (or Dad, but usually it's the mom) does the dentist, pediatrician, and teacher conferences. So, the family's idea is just to have Mom meet with the mental health professional (MHP) and then inform Dad what happened. Second, the mom and dad are at odds. So they are disposed to reject ideas that the other one has.

When it's the first instance, I'll say something like this: *Tanisha, it sounds like you're the parent who manages health care for your kids. So I get that Bill would just as soon not come in. However, as he's one of the world's leading experts on Aiden, I really need to hear from him. At this point I'm only asking him to come in twice: for the first family interview and for the third visit, which is the feedback session. Everything is up for negotiation after that. Do you think I could get him to come in for those two appointments?* Most of the time she'll agree. If not, I'll ask if it's okay for me to invite Bill in myself, in case the second scenario I just mentioned might be in play. It's rare for the mom to insist that he not come in. But should that happen—and I can't remember the last time it did—then I'd say something like: *Okay, we'll go forward without Bill as long as you are okay with the fact that I may need to equivocate more when I give you feedback.*

When it's the second instance, the caller will usually complain that her spouse's resistance is troubling to her. I then ask if it would be okay if I called the other parent to invite him in. Most of the time it is okay, and just about every time I call the other parent it's an easy sell. I think what happens here is that couples get so entrenched in their conflict that as soon as one of their lips starts moving the other person's head starts shaking "no." Therefore, it's much easier for each parent to evaluate the value of a proposition when it is suggested by an outside party, especially when that outside party is an MHP skilled at working with resistance.

▶ **A parent reports that the teachers are unwilling to fill out rating forms on the kid. What would you do?**

I haven't had this happen in a few years, maybe because school districts have become more accustomed to working with MHPs. But, if it does happen, usually a call to the principal fixes that. In only one instance in my career did such a call not remedy the problem, and in that case a call to the district superintendent did. Moreover, I find the very large majority of teachers value participating in our evaluations and, if anything, lament that we child MHPs don't include them enough.

▶ **Someone in the family rejects the idea of having teachers fill out rating scales. What would you do? Would your response be different depending on who was objecting (i.e., a parent versus the kid)?**

Kids without a track record of discipline problems in school often fear that their teachers will find out that they are seeing an MHP (the kids with discipline problems, I find, are less likely to care what the teachers think). Moreover, parents worry about being embarrassed by the school finding out that they have taken their kid to see an MHP, or they worry that their kid will be viewed differently by the teachers if they learn their kid is seeing an MHP. I deal with both kinds of concerns by stating that they need not mention that the forms have come from me. They can merely state that they've learned that these forms can offer them (the parents) detailed and helpful feedback about their kid's strengths and opportunities for growth and then they ask if the teacher(s) would mind filling them out.

Another concern that parents sometimes raise is to state that their kid is manifesting no problems at school and so there is no point in having the teachers fill out forms. In that case I'll also say something like this: *It may very well happen that the teacher forms come back and add nothing to what I learn. However, I can't tell you how many times parents have said that to me, but the teacher forms taught me something important that I didn't learn from any other source. In my experience your average teacher will tell you about things that either annoy the teacher or that seem to interfere with a kid's academic performance. However, they often won't bring up if a kid is struggling socially or is showing other kinds of problems. I'd rather invest a little bit more time and energy on the significant chance that I'll learn something that will help me to do a better job for you and your kid.* In the vast majority of instances, parents agree, and to me that's the main concern. On the other hand, kids may or may not end up agreeing; but the parents call the shot. Interestingly, I find that the parents who are most likely to decline my gathering teacher rating forms are parents who are employed as teachers. What those parents tell me is that they are concerned that the other teachers will gossip about their kid.

▶ **The parent asks if you are a parent. What would you do?**

This doesn't happen to me anymore because I'm older; have my office in my home, which clearly is family sized; and I often write about my parenting experiences. However, it very commonly comes up for younger MHPs and trainees. As I covered in Chapter 16, the goal here is to find out *the real question*. This is how it might go:

Parent: *Do you mind if I ask if you have kids?*
MHP: *No, I don't mind. I'll tell you in a minute if you want, but tell me first, what would it be like for you if I did versus if I didn't?*
Parent: *I don't know, I just think that if you don't have kids you might not have as much practical experience.*
MHP: *So it's important to you to know that I have the right kind of knowledge and experience to be truly helpful to Aiden.*
Parent: *Exactly.*

MHP: *Well, I'll tell you that I won't give you any feedback that isn't of a high quality and based in the best science and clinical reasoning. (If you're a trainee, this might be a place to mention that your supervisor will be involved as well.) And, if something comes up that extends beyond what I know, I would be very sure to get the consultation I need, either from the literature and/or from colleagues. Finally, if something came up that I didn't know, and I couldn't find out, then I would be very sure to make a referral to someone who could well address the concern. Does that help?*

Parent: *Yes. I didn't mean to cause offense.*

MHP: *In no way have you caused offense. Actually, I salute you for being assertive and for making sure that Aiden gets the best care.*

If the parent still wanted to know if an MHP has kids, I'd answer. That's a style thing, so others could reasonably argue for not disclosing this information. My reasoning is that to not answer risks threatening the alliance. I believe that's a greater risk than any temporary setbacks that could occur from learning that the MHP doesn't have kids. I worked clinically with kids for 10 years before I had my first kid, and I could tell that some of my parents initially doubted what I could offer them because of that. But once we got going, and they witnessed their kid improving, that concern usually faded quickly.

Childless MHPs are also challenged in these moments by their countertransference, especially trainees. Trainees normatively feel doubt about their skills. So, a parent challenging in this way can seem pretty powerful. I promise you, though, that while having kids does offer additional advantages to child MHPs, it is *hardly* essential. If the MHP's model of a kid is correct, and science based, and the treatment is delivered in an artful way, that kid will be well served.

▶ **A parent asks for a reduction in the fee. Assuming you're empowered to consider such a change—even if in consultation with a supervisor—what would you do?**

Learning to discuss money, race, sex, and sexualized transference rank among the most difficult learning tasks for trainees, though it rarely gets completely easy for anyone. Indeed, these topics tend to generate lots of discussion on professional listservs and at professional conferences.

This is another topic that doesn't lend itself to a script because there are so many permutations. These are some of the issues that I consider when a parent brings up this subject with me.

- How truthful does the parent seem? I've had some parents who drive expensive cars, and go on multiple vacations a year, ask for a fee reduction, claiming financial hardship. Such cases are less likely to witness me changing my fees.

- How much do I agree that the fee is burdensome? I've had instances in my career where parents spend more on cigarettes and alcohol than the treatment. I've had other instances when a family would take a better vacation than I could afford. I value the service I offer, have tried to price it fairly, and would need to have good evidence that (a) the parent also values it and (b) the parent is significantly burdened by the fee in a way that I can determine. Of course, sometimes families experience sudden and terrible financial hardships; in these instances, I try to treat them as I would wish to be treated.

- Is the parent's proposal for a fee reduction reasonable? When I engage in this sort of a discussion I don't suggest what the reduced fee might be, I ask the parent what he has in mind.

- How is the business side of my practice going? If it's going well, and I have the room to be flexible, and the other issues stated suggest that a fee reduction is advisable, I'll offer one. If I do, we'd also need to discuss if it's permanent or if there are circumstances that would cause it to go back to the default level (e.g., a parent transfers to a better-paying job, outgoing alimony payments stop, and so forth).

In instances when I decide not to lower my fee, I'll have a discussion with the parent regarding the pros and cons of a transfer to another clinician that might be more affordable to the family and the best methodology for arranging for that transfer.

▶ **A parent doesn't appear in time to pick up a kid after a session is complete. How would you handle this?**

Most kids carry cell phones these days. So, I'll just ask the kid to call his parent to get a status update. Otherwise, I'll have the parent's cell phone on file and I'll either have the kid call from my phone or I'll call. I generally ask the kid to wait in the waiting room until his parent appears. In the vast majority of instances, this is not a pattern. Should a pattern emerge, the parent and I would need to have a conversation about how to avoid that going forward. If that conversation didn't work and more of my time needed to be invested watching over a kid, we'd need to negotiate a fee for that. However, it has never come to that in any of the wide array of settings in which I've worked.

▶ **A parent offers you a $75 gift card. Are there any circumstances in which you'd accept the gift? If so, what are they and how would you proceed? If not, why not?**

As is the case for most of the examples of resistance and surprising events that I'm covering, this happened to me. And it has since become one of my favorite ethical vignettes to present at professional conferences. Before reading on, ask yourself what you would do if parents of a teenager indicated high satisfaction with your service and offered you such a gift. What would you do? Put this book down and think about it before reading on.

I'm imagining that you're thinking about this the way I indicated I think about gifts in the preceding chapter. The first step is to find out the client's thinking about it, offer empathy and gratitude, and then explain why it's not in the best interest of the work to accept a gift that has any significant value. *However,* you might also have thought, "Geez, I'd need to know more before answering." For those of you who had that kind of a thought, I salute you!

In this particular case I did a school staffing on the kid. I knew that the parent's insurance wouldn't cover this service. I also knew that the parents were scrapping by financially and that paying my treatment fee was a weekly stretch for them. I also liked them and their kid a lot, admiring how hard everyone was working. So when the mom asked me, after the meeting was over, in the parking lot, what she owed me, I waved my hand and said, *Nothing, this one's on me.* That was a mistake on my part, treating the moment like one at a restaurant when a bill arrives for a shared meal among friends. Had I to do it over again, I would have said, *Would it be okay with you if I did this one pro bono?* It was at the very next session that the gift card of $75 to a restaurant was offered, which was, coincidently, the sliding scale fee I had negotiated with the family. I said to the parents, smiling, *So, is this your way of saying you'd rather pay for the staffing?* To which the mom smiled and nodded "yes." I told her I got it (finally) and accepted the gift card with a thanks.

I can't think of a scenario where it would be okay to have sex with a client or to commit a crime, but for just about all other kinds of situations we usually need to know the context before we can discern the ethical and effective path. One of my favorite people to consult on ethical conundrums is ethics guru Samuel Knapp, EdD, who I think of as the Benjamin Franklin of psychology in Pennsylvania. Whenever I call him with a question, and after I explain the context as best as I can, he'll ask, "What do you think?" before sharing with me what he thinks. I think this is because Dr. Knapp knows that there are often details about the context that he may only learn once he asks me that.

▶ **A parent asks to speak to your supervisor about the work. What would you do?**

This comes up in training sites when the family knows, as they should, that the MHP-trainee is being supervised. Having been the supervisor in many of these scenarios I know how devastating *this can seem* to a trainee, probably akin to what I might feel if a client told me she was reporting me to my state's psychology regulatory board. But, most of the time, if handled well, it ends up having a neutral or a positive impact on the work and the trainee. One of the key elements is for the MHP-trainee to strive to arrive at a place of peace and calm; that may not be possible, and if it isn't, the resolution can still end up going well. But the MHP arriving at a place of peace and calm increases the odds of success, which is yet another illustration of why personal therapy can be of great benefit. A dialogue might go like this:

Parent: *Can I meet with your supervisor?*
MHP: *You certainly can. Can you tell me first, though, what good thing might happen if you did?*
Parent: *I just want to feel more confident that we're on the right path with Aiden.*

MHP: *That sounds like a great goal. Tell me, what has happened that has left you in doubt about that?*

Parent: *It's just such a fight to get him to come each time. I'm exhausted by it. So, I just want to be sure that we have a good match with you and that how you're going about things is advisable.*

MHP: *Yeah, I know he's been giving you a hard time. That's gotta be exhausting for you on some days.*

Parent: *It is.*

MHP: *Do you have any ideas regarding how I might be contributing to that, or if there are ways I could help with that, that I'm not doing yet?*

Parent: *No, not really. That's partly why I'd like to meet with your supervisor.*

MHP: *Gotcha. Let's schedule that, then. I will share, though, as a preview of coming attractions, that she and I have been talking about this issue on an ongoing basis.*

Parent: *Okay, good. Let me just join that conversation with her, then.*

MHP: *Do you have any preferences for whether I'm there also?*

Parent: *I can see advantages to you being there, but I'd like to just meet one-on-one with her. It's not like I have bad things to say about you, but I don't want to need to be concerned about weighing my words so as to not cause offense.*

MHP: *Gotcha. Okay. Let me call my supervisor and check with her. Once I do that I'll call you and we can take the next step.*

Parent: *Sounds like a plan.*

▶ **A parent sits down at a booth where you are working part-time as a waiter or waitress. What would you do?**

This is something that has happened multiple times to supervisees of mine. Related scenarios have also happened: The trainee worked as a clerk at a store where the family shopped, the trainee cut hair at a salon where a member of the family appears for a hair styling appointment, and so forth.

The first thing to keep in mind is that multiple relationships are only problematic when the client stands to be harmed or disadvantaged. There is something in our clinical culture, in my view, that gets automatically freaked out when these things happen. And, if you work in a rural setting, the odds of these things happening rise significantly. (For example, when I worked in a rural setting I once had a client of mine, who worked at the one gym in town, move his locker next to mine so that he could talk to me, which is something I only discovered after exiting the shower, with only my towel, soap, and flip-flops in tow! As is often said, comedy is pain plus time.)

The first thing to ask yourself is, "Can I avoid this multiple relationship without breaching confidentiality?" If that can happen, that's a desirable choice. It's desirable not because you're necessarily avoiding something *bad*. It's desirable because it's good to avoid potential complications when that's easy to do. So, in the vignette I've described, you might ask to switch tables or sections with another server without getting into why. If it wasn't possible, I'd suggest conducting yourself in as friendly and as typical a way as you would for that situation, trying to get yourself to a place of peace and calm. After all, it's not like you're meeting at a brothel or something! Waiting tables, or working at some other job while in graduate school, is honorable and admirable. If the family indicated a desire to start discussing the care, you could always value the question or comment, give empathy for it, and then suggest that you discuss it when they next come in so that you can give it the attention it deserves while preserving their confidentiality. Then, at the next session, if the kid or parents didn't bring up the meeting, you could cheerfully ask, "So, what was it like to see me at the restaurant the other night?" so that you can ascertain what the implications are, if any, for your work.

▶ **A parent wants to stop the work before it is finished. How might you respond to this common occurrence?**

As I indicated in Chapter 4, this is pretty common. Making the time to attend sessions and pay the fee can add significantly to a family's weekly stress load. In the early phases of the work this stress often seems well worth it to parents as the kid's symptoms are causing much more stress than the stress of attending sessions and paying the fee. But, as the kid improves, dealing with his remaining symptoms can seem less stressful than coming in for sessions. It is in these moments that a well-constructed treatment plan is like gold. This is the sequence I generally follow: (a) get a full articulation of the parent's thoughts and feelings, offering reflective listening and empathy; (b) break out the treatment plan and ask for the level of expression of each symptom indicated there (e.g., how many hours of sleep a night is Aiden currently averaging?); (c) review the goal and the distance between both where the kid was and now and where the stated goal is and now; (d) suggest your thoughts about the value of continuing, given what you know about the treatment plan goals and the course of treatment; and (e) offer that you fully support whatever the parent wants to do once you can be sure that you've successfully communicated your thoughts on the matter, including what you believe the risks might be of stopping prematurely (e.g., make sure they say back your thinking in an accurate way). It can also be helpful in these discussions to review the steps you'd like to take before stopping (e.g., complete an exposure sequence, ensure that the kid has no passive suicidal ideation for a period of one month, and so forth).

▶ **A single parent asks if it might be possible to share a coffee after the work is terminated. What would you do? Would your response be affected by whether you are attracted to the parent?**

This doesn't happen to me, probably because I wear a wedding band, am in my 50s, and look like a cross between Benjamin Franklin, Truman Capote, and Karl Rove (or so my teenager children charge whenever they want to put me on my heels). But when you're an attractive, younger clinician who doesn't wear a wedding band, this situation can certainly happen, especially if you seem kind, wise, and have been very helpful to the family.

Think about it from a single parent's perspective: You might appear to be an amazing catch. So, for that parent, who doesn't know anything about our ethical guidelines and the reasons for them, making such an offer is reasonable. For reasons like this, I think it's important to view such an offer from a place of kindness and empathy. This is a version of what you might say (as long as it's authentic): *Frank, that's a very nice offer. And I feel complimented that you've made it, not only because you're letting me know you like me, but also because I think you're also letting me know, maybe less directly, that I've been helpful to you and Aiden. A limit I have, though, is that in my field we believe that preserving our relationship as it is now is very, very important. For example, if Aiden ever needed to see me again while I work here, he could. So I can't say yes to that, but I can thank you for asking* (offering a warm smile and, hopefully, feeling warmth inside). Many clients may then react with some combination of embarrassment or apology. If so, it would be important to try to disavow the parent of those thoughts and feelings by letting him know that he has nothing to apologize for. Parents are just being human; how could they possibly know about our professional guidelines given that they haven't been trained as MHPs? (On the other hand, if a given parent seems to know that this is a no-no, but asks anyway, you could easily adapt the tail end of the dialogue to let him playfully know that he can be a bad boy in other places, but not in your office.)

▶ **A parent comes to a session noting that the kid is in the car and won't come in. What would you do?**

I've always maintained that my job begins once a parent gets her kid into my consulting room. (I tell parents not to worry if the kid promises to be difficult with me and that I have ways of dealing with that.) I've seen therapists go out to cars and try to coax kids to come in. I think that's a mistake. First, it avoids empowering a parent by providing her with more effective strategies. Second, the odds of success, for the MHP, are low; we just don't possess the power to do anything more than try to reason with a kid. And kids in these circumstances are often regressed and somewhat immune to reasoning.

So, if parents appear with this problem I bring them into my office to see if there is a unique contextual problem that I can try to help resolve (e.g., the parent told the kid, on the commute, that his phone will be taken away for a month). More likely, it's more about a general unwillingness to take part in the clinical work. In an evaluation phase, I'll suggest that a parent calmly tell her kid that something very important to him (e.g., cell phone, Xbox Live access) will be earned by coming into the consulting room (not just the waiting room). So, if he doesn't come in, he won't have earned that important thing until the time of the next appointment, and so forth. I would also be interested in instilling special time (see Chapter 9) as soon as possible. If that didn't work, the parent and I might have to meet in order to set up a behavioral program for the kid (see Chapter 13).

If this occurred during the treatment phase, and a contract or token system hasn't been set up yet, that would be the next step (see Chapter 13). The behavioral program would then include this responsibility. If a behavioral program is already in place, we may need to tweak it to solve this problem.

This child clinical work is so interesting. Just as I was editing the proof of this book a teen client of mine did, for me, a new version of this. When I greeted him in the waiting room and asked him to come in, he turned his head away and closed his eyes. I merely went into the consulting room with the door open. A few moments later his parent had convinced him to get in the room. Had I tried to deal with this kind of resistance in the waiting room I doubt it would have resolved itself so quickly.

I can't remember a time when these strategies didn't work, though watch that happen to me the week after this book is published!

▶ **A parent indicates, in the initial phone consultation, that doing a needed evaluation will depend on garnering the kid's approval. How might you advise the parent?**

As I covered in Chapter 2, most kids are neutral or opposed to coming in. If kid approval were a *sine qua non* for starting kid mental health evaluations, most of the enterprise would come to a grinding halt. Yes, it's important to get the kid's perspective. Yes, it's important for the parents to be open with their kid about their thinking about the value of a mental health evaluation. But, in this decision, I think parents should operate as a benevolent dictatorship: they lovingly insist that the kid come in should the kid object.

Sometimes parents ask for guidance about how to have the discussion with their kid. These are the three steps I suggest:

#1: Get the kid talking about the suffering he is experiencing, giving empathy for what he says. Don't rush it, as empathy may cause a deeper and wider vetting.

#2: Ask the kid, "Suppose it would be possible to get rid of this, or at least cut it down a lot, in a short period of time. Would you be interested in that?"

#3: If the kid answers the question affirmatively, the parents can share that they agree with the kid's wisdom and that they've found someone who can likely do exactly that. They then suggest that they schedule an appointment. If the kid answers "no," the parent can find out how come, in case the kid's concerns can be addressed (e.g., he has no time); if so, he might change his mind. No matter whether the kid can be brought around, the parent provides empathy for the reasons for the "no," but then shares why they look at it differently and why they are proceeding with an appointment.

▶ **You find out that someone you have been dialoguing with on a social networking site—where identities are anonymous until both parties agree to disclose—is a single parent of a kid client. What would you do? Would your response vary depending on how much you were attracted to the parent's online persona?**

Of course, this is one for which the MHP should seek out a consultation. In most instances, the ideal would probably be to stop the online relationship and determine whether a referral to another MHP is in order. The latter would probably be determined by how evolved the online relationship had become, whether that relationship would significantly interfere with the alliance or the treatment plan, and the nature of the emerging countertransference.

▶ **A parent asks if it's okay to audio record sessions, as the material is so helpful and the parent wants to be able to use it as reference material. How might you respond?**

I'm not comfortable with this request as it puts a clinical record outside of my control. I deal with it by getting a full articulation of the goal the parent is pursuing by that method, offering reflective listening and empathy as we go. I then offer an alternative method for having good resources available to the parent. In my case, most of the things that I teach parents I've included in my parenting book or on my blog. In those instances when that isn't the case, I'll use that content to develop a new blog entry. Moreover, if a parent suggests that the goal is to share the information with another treating professional, either now or in the future, I'll suggest that I'd be happy to communicate with that professional directly. Or, in other instances, I'll offer to write a report, at least if the parent expresses a desire to hire me to provide that service. Bottom line: We try to find a less potentially troubling method (e.g., a recording subsequently appears online) for reaching the parent's reasonable goal.

A PATTERN OF INTERFERING TRANSFERENCE

This isn't really a surprising event, but sometimes an MHP finds that the sort of interfering transference that she experiences across clients becomes a pattern. Most of us experience most kinds of interfering transference some of the time. But if I find that clients routinely become irritated with me, or clients routinely want to flirt with me, or clients are routinely bringing me gifts or routinely are canceling sessions, then that could be signaling a need for self-analysis, personal therapy, or consultation/supervision to get to the bottom of how I might be contributing to the pattern that is outside of my awareness.

SIDEBAR 17.1

This sidebar is adapted from two tricks in David Pogue's *Magic for Dummies*. It is a combination of the "Under the Hanky Force" and "Feel the Muscle" tricks. All you need is a deck of cards and a small towel.

You need to decide on a card and place it on top of the deck; let's say it's the king of diamonds. Tell the kid that you will shuffle the deck of cards until he says stop. You can use a standard bridge shuffle to keep the card on the top while otherwise shuffling. (As you advance in your deck manipulation skills you can shuffle the top card to the bottom and then back to the top again before you start to bridge shuffle.) Once the kid says stop, you say something like, "I'm going to do a card trick that keeps the entire deck and the card you choose out of my view. This way, you know I can't sneak a peek." Then put the deck under the towel, holding the deck with your dominant hand. This trick involves flipping the deck four times. For the first flip, rotate the deck, once under the towel, so that the face of the bottom card is now at the top while the king of diamonds is on the bottom. Ask the kid to reach in and to lift off part of the deck, while keeping it under the towel. As he lifts up part of the deck (under the towel), do the second flip so that now the king of diamonds is on the top. Have the kid reach in with his other hand and pull out the king of diamonds, saying, "Pick the top card you've cut to," then setting the king of diamonds facedown on the table. As he pulls out the king of diamonds, do your third flip so that the part of the deck you are holding is now face-up again. Ask the kid to set the deck back on top (this ensures that the cards all remain facing the same way). Now do your fourth flip and remove the towel so that the cards, when back on display, are all facedown again. Make a big show of turning around and asking your kid to look at his selected card (i.e., the king of diamonds). Tell him to make sure not to forget it and that, when he's sure he won't forget it, to put it back anywhere in the deck and to shuffle the deck as much as he'd like. Tell him you won't turn around until he's done.

Now comes the second part—the reveal. Spread the cards into four rows, all face-up (you can do more or fewer rows as you please). Tell the kid that you've worked on reading the small muscle twitches that people make when they are confronted with the truth. Give one end of your towel to the kid and you hold the other. Tell him to first visually scan the first row. Then tell him to scan the second row. Then the third, and then the fourth. Let's say the king of diamonds is in the third row. Suggest to him that his small muscle twitches you feel through the towel tell you that his card is in the third row. You can use this same method to lay out more rows of cards and repeat, or just get to the reveal as you please. You can also use this trick to augment the truth-telling tricks I described in Sidebar 10.1.

CHAPTER 18

Should You or Should You Not?

I've realized therapy is incredibly therapeutic.
—*Lisa Schroeder*

This chapter is designed especially for clinicians who are new to clinical work with kids. However, those more experienced may also find some value in reviewing these issues.

The questions I cover here are ones that trainees have often asked me when starting clinical work with kids; however, in many instances the issues apply for adult work as well. As I offer each prompt, first consider either individually, with colleagues, or in a training course, how you think about it. You'll get more from what follows if you take that step first.

▶ **Should the MHP offer a tissue to a kid or parent who is crying?**

A box of tissues is essential to have easily available for all clients. I've always put mine somewhere in view between me and the client, and always within the client's reach. So, I consider this question within that context.

I generally do not offer a tissue. My thinking is that this comes across as more paternalistic than fits my style. I figure that the tissues are there, right in front of the person. So I leave it to that person to make her own decision about whether to grab one or not. I think countertransference can cause a discomfort with client crying or a desire to appear to be a caring person. For my own part, I usually feel like we are discussing exactly what we need to be discussing and I'm glad for that. Moreover, my caring, hopefully, comes across by how I conduct myself as a clinician. Sometimes, if the person has a torrential flow of tears and isn't grabbing a tissue, I may say, adopting a kind tone: *Y'know, there's no extra charge for using the tissues.*

▶ **Should the MHP wear signs of religious affiliation (e.g., ashes on Ash Wednesday)?**

We therapists have lives, too (despite what it might seem like in graduate school). I don't think it's a good idea to sacrifice something that's important to me just because I'm a mental health professional (MHP). However, if there is a way for me to live my life and not introduce a possible complication to the work, I'll choose that path (e.g., get my ashes after my sessions are over for the day). But if that's not possible to do, I'll wear the ashes and deal with however that might affect a client, using some of the same kinds of reasoning that I have reviewed throughout this volume.

This issue has come up semi-regularly in my career, including with trainees I've supervised. For instance, I once supervised a trainee whose religious precepts indicated that he should not shake hands with women. In his case, we worked out language to include in the consent paperwork so that clients could elect to not work with him if that was problematic for them. That language included affirmations of his valuing of women and his confidence that he could serve women well.

▶ **Should the MHP display seasonal decorations (e.g., Christmas ornaments)?**

This is similar to the preceding prompt, but a little different as well. In my case, my current office is in my home. I like Christmas decorations, but I have a bunch I can choose from. *For me*, it doesn't dampen my personal agenda to have ecumenical decorations on my lawn, so that's what I put up during that time of the year. I would probably suggest a similar approach for an office setting, but also put up decorations that cover a gambit of religions. Though I've never had it happen, if a client had a concern, I'd respond with the same scripts I shared earlier in this volume.

▶ **Should the MHP avoid crossing legs and arms?**

I confess to feeling a bit annoyed by those who have suggested that MHPs need to adhere to such restrictions. The thinking appears to be that the MHP appears more open if legs and arms remain uncrossed. However, I find this suggestion to be counterproductive. In a session that is going well, the clinician adapts what Anna Freud (1992) called "even hovering attention" or what Mihaly Csikszentmihalyi (2008) called "flow." Time stops. The focus is on the important psychological events happening within the client, within the MHP, and between them. I believe it would be an interruption to that flow to break it and self-monitor about the common body positions humans adopt when in dialogue. I think it's important that an MHP feel comfortable, as long as that comfort doesn't violate a typical rule of nonverbal social engagement (e.g., not to keep one's eyes closed, not to lie down). So I'd encourage anyone reading this who is tempted to self-monitor in this way to let that go and focus on the 1,003 other important things to be attended to in a session.

▶ **Should the MHP display family pictures?**

Before I start, let me say that I don't think this is a huge deal either way. That said, I generally wouldn't, as I think the small potential disadvantages aren't worth the even smaller personal upsides. For example, pictures of the MHP's family could encourage off-the-clinical-topic discussions or provide a potential anchor for negative transference (e.g., a parent imagining that I must be a much better parent, kids feeling bad that they don't have siblings like my kids do).

Of course, in spaces where consulting rooms are shared, this usually doesn't arise as an issue.

▶ **Should the MHP link with clients on social networking sites?**

This would constitute a multiple relationship. Of course, such are not inherently ill advised. But we avoid them unless avoiding them could compromise some other very important clinical or personal agenda.

▶ **Should the MHP offer a beverage?**

This is another topic that I've seen garner a lot of discussion. For my own part, I find it hard to get my shorts in a bunch either way about it.

Most clients have no clue whether it is socially appropriate to bring a drink to meetings with an MHP. A lot of the time if I have a drink when I meet with clients, my clients appear to take that as a cue that it's fine for them to bring a beverage if they'd like. So, for that reason, I generally don't offer a drink. I figure people will choose to bring one if they want to. That said, I have offered a drink in instances where I might be doing a lengthy testing session or when a client seems to be in oral distress (e.g., coughing a lot). In these instances I wouldn't generally offer coffee to a minor, unless I have a teen that's in the habit of drinking coffee and the parents are okay with that.

All of this said, if you prefer to offer a beverage, and are prepared to make that available *all the time*, then I don't think it's a big deal. (I say "all the time" because it could introduce a needless complication, albeit probably small, if a client was counting on a beverage and the MHP had run out.)

▶ **Should the MHP go to the bathroom if feeling the urge in the middle of a session?**

I think most of us condition ourselves to go to the bathroom in between sessions, so I imagine this isn't a common challenge. For me, a key question would be, "Is this urge going to interfere with my ability to be at my best?" If no, I'd just hold it. If yes, then I might say, *Monica, please excuse me for just one moment. I'll be right back.* If I crossed paths with a parent in the waiting room I'd say, *I'll be back in just one second.* Upon return I'd just take up where we left off without comment, other than to ask if it would be okay to extend the session for the same amount of time as I was gone, a question that might have to also be asked of a parent in a waiting room. If a kid asked where I was, I'd just say *I had to take a brief break.*

▶ **Should the MHP cancel a session if sleepy?**

Clearly, it would be no good for a client to meet with a therapist who is struggling to stay awake. So, if it wasn't possible to take a 20- to 30-minute cat nap to refresh, and from just this limited perspective, I might call and see if it was possible for the client to switch to another time, preferably either that day or that same week.

This question raises the issue of the MHP's responsibility to maintain good self-care while also being professional and self-disciplined about the clinical task. Let me address each of these.

A beloved mentor of mine once said, "A professional is someone who goes on when he doesn't feel like it." For example, I once had a supervisee cancel a client, without consulting with me, because the rest of his week was busy and he had a lot to do. This supervisee argued that he would have been distracted to meet with the client and so rescheduled the client for another week. After giving him empathy for what it feels like to be overscheduled, I asked him to reflect on when he imagined he'd reach a point in his career when he didn't feel like he had a very busy week ahead of him. (This was akin to a parent stating she couldn't do special time because the week was very, very busy.) This particular supervisee ultimately realized he needed to do more to develop his professionalism.

I've learned that if my self-care goes off-line, my clinical skill set is likewise negatively impacted; from that vantage point, I owe it to both my clients and myself to maintain good self-care. In this context, there are three things I keep in mind about my professional day when I'm scheduling: I leave time to be physically active, to meditate or practice mindfulness, and to take an afternoon cat nap, with the latter having the most immediate and obvious negative impact when I've ignored it. (There are other things I make sure to do, but these are more on a one to three times a week basis.)

But, what about if the MHP tries to do the session and either falls asleep or keeps jerking in efforts to stay awake? If you were in that situation, what would you do? What would you imagine it's like for a client to experience that from her therapist? For my part, I might stand and lean against some furniture, noting that doing so will help me to focus better on the challenging topic we were covering.

▶ **Should the MHP offer a discounted fee if the client reports financial hardship?**

This is a situation where a parent has not asked for a fee reduction but brings up that it is very difficult to pay monthly bills. If a person is living paycheck to paycheck but covering her bills, I probably won't bring up the cost of treatment unless she does. But if the person appears to be in the red each month, I might say something like, *Paula, I know you said that you're finding you can't cover your bills each month. What's it like then to be coming here and paying my fee?* I've found the range of responses I receive in these moments is broad. Some will tell me that a relative is paying the fee. Some will tell me that their insurance coverage makes the cost insignificant. Some will apologize and indicate that their finances aren't really that bad and that they were just howling at the moon. However, some will indicate that the treatment fee is a significant burden (they usually don't say it that abruptly, but that's the message). Going forward, I treat the discussion like the one I covered in Chapter 17, when a parent has asked for a fee reduction. The only difference is that I'll ask: *Is there a fee reduction that would make the stress from this cost more manageable?* There are so many possible outcomes, but I generally would endeavor to make some kind of a change or accommodation in these instances, though I appreciate that this is a matter of personal style and that there are multiple, and equally acceptable, ways to think about this matter.

▶ **Should the MHP continue to see a client who inspires significant and interfering countertransference?**

The nature of this countertransference can be varied. Maybe there is sexual attraction. Maybe the therapist feels irritation shortly after a parent's lips start to move. Maybe the therapist fears a parent or has intrusive and persistent fantasies about adopting a child. I've never met an experienced kid MHP that hasn't sometimes experienced such feelings and thoughts. There are a few things I'd suggest:

- Consult with a supervisor or a colleague about the case. Regarding a peer consultation, there are a few elements I look for in determining who to consult. I want the person (a) to be experienced, (b) to be insightful, (c) to care about me, and (d) to be as likely to disagree with me as to agree.

- Consider whether a personal therapy might quickly resolve the problem. Throwing light on such thoughts and feelings can sometimes disempower them quickly.

- Consider whether a change in the treatment methodology might resolve the problem (e.g., perhaps meeting with two parents together instead of one alone, perhaps arranging for improving the quality attachments in a child's life).

- Consider whether having the family consult with another therapist might resolve underlying issues that might be fueling the countertransference. For example, an MHP might believe that an evaluation for medication is very important for a kid; however, as the parent resists this idea, the MHP becomes increasingly annoyed with the parent. It may be that arranging for the parent to get a consultation with a senior clinician would be helpful.

If these steps don't resolve the interfering countertransference, it would probably be a good idea to begin exploring whether a transfer to another—not necessarily better—MHP is advisable. I know this can feel like failing but I try not to think of it that way; I also try to help my supervisees to not think of it that way either. We all have these hitches in our personalities; it's just part of being human. Better to acknowledge that someone else, with a different personality, might be better able to promote healing for a given kid than to press on in a manner that risks sacrificing a good clinical outcome.

There is one other thought I have about this topic. In training venues it sometimes comes up that a given trainee needs to develop the psychological muscles of delivering good care to people whom that trainee might not choose to associate with personally. We all find some people attractive and others unattractive, and we vary considerably in these leanings. For example, I enjoy people who are transparent when they disagree with me, while such people can be off-putting to others. Likewise, I don't particularly care for people who habitually gravitate toward casting themselves as victims. In our personal lives we sometimes like or dislike people based on things like their hygiene, politics, socioeconomic status, and so forth. As MHPs, we are all called to rise above such personal preferences and indulgences and to see the human condition in all of those who come before us in our professional capacity. So, if I had a trainee who maintained that her countertransference about a client's hygiene was interfering too much, and that she needed to transfer the case, we'd need to have a pretty involved discussion about the things she might do to address the client's hygiene with him and the things she might do for herself to advance her professional skill set.

▶ **Should the MHP offer self-disclosure?**

I wish I knew how much time I've spent in my career discussing this issue. It feels like a lot. Here I'm going to try to distill this complex topic down to some core principles and suggestions.

Let me say, for those new to this consideration, that there are a couple of reasons why it is not a straightforward matter to self-disclose, and that this is another one of those acculturations that trainees often need to experience. In our default culture, sharing self-disclosures is the norm and, when done well, promotes friendships and bonds. In clinical work, however, self-disclosures have the potential to turn aspects of the work into meeting the therapist's personal needs and can also ratchet up the complexity of interfering transference when doing behavioral work.

In the psychodynamic traditions, self-disclosure is typically discouraged as the therapist's anonymity is thought to be promote transference analysis. Karl Menninger (1952) referred to the therapist as the "projective screen"; the argument goes that the more opaque the screen, the easier it is to discern the client's projections onto it. However, Menninger was also writing about treatments that use transference analysis as a vehicle for cure, something that is typically not true of cognitive behavioral therapy (CBT). That said, CBT therapists do well to understand and manage transference. Therefore, it's good to avoid methods that risk needlessly complicating the transference when other methods that are less fraught with risk might equally reach the same goal (e.g., promoting the therapeutic alliance).

Here are some issues to consider:

- As is often the case, so much comes down to the MHP's motivation. I've noted that some of the MHPs I've met who argue passionately about the need to regularly self-disclose are also the same colleagues who often bring conversations back to themselves when in groups. This is another illustration about how personal therapy can be so helpful. Whose needs am I pursuing when I self-disclose? Am I trying to make myself look wise or appealing? Am I bored and this is my way of snapping out of it? Am I an exhibitionistic type of person who needs to work this into my clinical work regularly? Only those who are deeply self-examined can hope to generate accurate answers to these questions.

- Is there another less complicated method available that can reach the same goal? As I've indicated throughout this volume, considering clinical issues from the context of methods and goals can be very helpful. Self-disclosure is a method that might be used to strengthen the alliance, to teach an important clinical point, or to reassure a client, to name a few goals. However, the question is, in a given moment when I'm on the precipice of a self-disclosure: Is there another method at hand, that might be less complicated, that could do this as well? If yes, I'd go there instead.

- Could changing the self-disclosure into something that someone you know experienced work as well? Most of the time when I have content from my personal life that could be useful to one of my clients, I use this technique. I believe it has most of the upside of self-disclosure with almost none of the downside.

- I would use self-disclosure only in moments when (a) a personal disclosure has value for a client when it is attached to me, (b) I've assessed that the resulting change in the transference would either be positive or neutral, and (c) I don't think it's about me being in pursuit of personal needs. These are some examples:

  − If I have a teen struggling with the notion that he is the only one who messes up on dates, I'll share one of my epic screwups that is funny. In these instances we both usually laugh as I go through it.

  − If a teen has a broken heart and seems to be feeling that she's alone, I'll share that I've been down that road as well. In this, I'll sometimes use this adapted script from an episode of *The West Wing*:

Monica, I know how terrible this is, because I've been through it also. Actually, let me tell this little story to make a point. A woman fell down a deep hole. As she settled into an awareness of how screwed she was, she hollered out for help. As a physician walked by the woman hollered up for help. The physician wrote a prescription and threw it down to her. Next, a personal trainer walked by and, upon hearing the woman's cries, threw down a regiment for increasing her strength. Finally, a therapist walked by. Upon hearing the woman's cries, the therapist jumped down into the hole. The woman turned to the therapist and asked, "What the heck are you doing? Now we're both screwed!" The therapist smiled, put his hand on the woman's shoulder, and said, no worries. I've been down here too and know the way out.

- If a kid has done something embarrassing in front of friends that he's mortified about, I'll tell a story about the time I got motion sick on a Ferris wheel and threw up all over two friends who were sitting with me.

  This is the sequence that applies in these instances. First, I sense that the transference is positive. Second, the kid feels that he is some freak from outer space living on the Earth among normal people. Third, my personal story either equals or exceeds the kid's story in terms of misfortune or error. Though not essential, I also enjoy those personal vignettes that promote sharing a laugh. I never say this directly, but the implication is, "If this can happen to this Dr. Dave, maybe I'm not such a freak."

  There can also be personal data I share in superficial exchanges. These self-disclosures are minor and incidental. I'll tell a kid if I've seen some media she's referencing or if I've been to a place she's talking about. I'll do the same thing with parents. I have this in a different category than telling stories from my life. Sometimes parents will also ask a question that, for me, is no more than a prosocial transitional question as we start and end a session: "How's your daughter doing at Cornell?" Or, "Did you have a good vacation?" Or, "I saw your son's baseball stats in the paper. Impressive." In these moments they are usually referencing material that they know from another source (I live in a relatively small community and I have a home office). I usually try to respond with an authentic, prosocial, and brief response. I can't think of a time that a parent tried to make such a moment more than transitional. If that happened, I'd just merely say something like, *Thank you for asking, and we can talk more about that if you'd like, but I have a packed agenda regarding Monica today. Would it be okay with you if we just got going with that?*

▶ **Should the MHP engage in small talk in the waiting room and on the walk to the consulting room?**

This is another question that I find it hard to get worked up about either way. I have a slight preference for just doing an introduction and suggesting which way to go as we walk together in silence. That said, if a client should start engaging in chitchat I'll follow along. But I think that when I initiate chitchat it's as if I'm saying, "Let me offer this to ease anxiety, either mine, yours, or both." As I'm usually not anxious, and wouldn't want to deal with it that way even if I were, my style is to not initiate the chatting; I also prefer to deal with client anxiety in other ways as well. Then again, my personal temperament is not to be a chitchatter. But, if that's how you like to do things, you'll get no argument from me.

▶ Should the MHP do an informal or a formal introduction?

This just about 100% comes down to a personal style. Early in my career, when I was a new doctoral clinician, I *loved* introducing myself as Dr. Palmiter or Dr. Dave to kids. I worked my tail off to earn a PhD and I'd be darned if I wasn't going to enjoy it. Of course, I also called my adult clients Mr. and Ms.

At this phase in my career, it's a matter of feel. Some clients enjoy or benefit from a formal, authoritative style at the beginning; when my intuition suggests this, I start out formally. Other clients seem to not need that at all, so I just introduce myself as David Palmiter, though I still call myself Dr. Dave to kids. If I'm in doubt, I start formal as it's always easier to relax that than to add it later. In my personal life, the only people I make call me Dr. are people who have annoyed me, medical personnel who are treating me like a four-legged member of a large herd, and my children. (Just kidding about the children, though I've been tempted!)

All this said, I think you should do whatever makes you feel comfortable, unless your supervisor or work site has a rule about this. (Even if the rule seems stupid, there are usually bigger fish that need frying, so I'd just follow along.)

▶ Should the MHP bring up lateness to sessions or extend sessions if the client has something more she wishes to discuss?

When you do this work for a while you'll discover that no matter how few structures you have, clients will express their transference through challenging them. (For example, if I had more time I'd love to do a little mini-study comparing how often clients forget their checkbooks with therapists in comparison to dentists, accountants, and so forth.) We start on time and we end on time; it's that simple and that challenging. This isn't because we are all a bunch of anal control freaks. This is because we have to practically maintain our schedules and not having this structure in place risks not being able to serve all of our clients well; moreover, acting out around start and ending times is inevitable for some clients no matter what structures we have in place, so we might as well offer an organized approach. I'll first review starting on time and then move to ending on time.

When it comes to starting on time, I've noticed, both as a professor and as a clinician, that there tend to be three personality types: those who arrive early; those who frantically arrive within a minute of the start time, on either side; and those who tend to be late. Sure, sometimes people who normally reside in one of the categories temporarily reside within another of them, but the trends are noteworthy. As a clinician and as a professor, I do interventions for those who fall in the late category, and I do them early, as I've found there is no end to them if I don't. This is the sequence I usually go through with a parent: (a) get an articulation of the obstacles she experiences, offering reflective listening and empathy; (b) affirm that we are both interested in her kid getting the full value out of sessions; (c) ask what ideas the parent has that might solve the problem; and (d) offer any tweaks or solutions that I might have. If I've also covered the problem-solving technique (see Chapter 11), this could also be used if the problem becomes a pattern. If a teen is bringing herself to individual sessions, I do the same thing with her, though I subsequently seek a parent's support if what we do on our own proves to be insufficient.

When it comes to ending on time it can be more complicated. Most of the time this is what I'll say if this happens: *I know we're right in the middle of this and I wish we could continue, but we're at the time. Would it be okay with you if we took this up first thing when we next meet?* Most of the time the client profile, and the topic under discussion, fits with that approach. Most clients have the ego strength to tolerate this and most topics are not so urgent as to need a different consideration. But there are exceptions and other issues that can come up:

- The content suggests that someone is in danger. In these instances, my first step is to rearrange whatever I was going to be doing right after the session in question. Maybe I need to be in touch with the next client to reschedule, which might happen in the waiting room and which would include my apologizing and explaining that I have an emergency I have to respond to. Or I might need to cancel a class or arrange for my wife to pick up a kid instead of me. And so forth. I then do whatever I need, evaluation or intervention wise, to stabilize the situation.

- The client is so upset that his ability to drive home, or function that night, is in question. Most of the time, experienced MHPs can see this coming. Usually the best course is to alter the topic of discussion to something less upsetting with 10 to 20 minutes left in the session so that the client's defense mechanisms can come back online. I also work with such clients on how to self-monitor going forward so that we can partner effectively in how we pace sessions. However, if I've stumbled into this with 5 minutes to go, or less, I'll ask the person what she might do to regroup. This might mean staying in session for the extra 10 minutes I have in between appointments, waiting in the waiting room for a while, calling a parent and having her bring the teen home, arranging for a fun activity, and so forth. I can't think, though, of the last time something like this required me to substantively change my plans for the next hour.

- Some kids and parents seem to morph into bringing up important content near the end of sessions. As I generally set an agenda for most sessions at the top, or at least prompt a kid or parent to tell me if there is something that he or she wants to make sure we have enough time to discuss, this doesn't happen a lot. But some people need to engage a transference that leaves them feeling cut off or unimportant to me or to see me as uncaring or controlling. In insight-oriented therapies, this is all grist for the mill and explored fully. However, in most CBT sessions this sort of transference is managed, as transference analysis is usually not on the intervention menu. So, for these folks I'd follow the same sequence I outlined for those who develop a pattern of arriving late, perhaps going a little bit more out of my way to do other things that tend to promote our alliance (e.g., pointing out strengths, using humor, teaching magic, and so forth).

- This is another area where countertransference can interfere. If I'm feeling overloaded I might welcome clients who are routinely tardy as that affords me extra time to catch up with other demands. Likewise, I might fear coming across as a mean or insensitive person if I cut off a client and end on time. The presence of this sort of countertransference signals a need to do some work through self-analysis, peer consultation, supervision, or a personal therapy.

▶ **Should the MHP text clients?**

   There is some room for style here, but security and confidentiality guidelines suggest that a conservative approach is advisable. You'll note that in my intake paperwork (Appendix A) I discourage such activity, generally. However, there are some instances when I'll text:

- If clients text about rescheduling or canceling appointments I'll usually participate.

- On occasion I've asked clients to text me after an important event to let me know how it went. One of my favorites was an adult client whose fear of heights was causing significant impairment in her professional and social functioning. Her graduating exposure was to spend 30 minutes at the top of the Empire State Building. She sent me a victory text, with a picture of her and her significant other, with beaming smiles, in that location.

- I'll sometimes ask teens to text me after they've done some task that we've agreed they'd do when I'm concerned the kid might otherwise forget to do it or avoid doing it. This is called a commitment device and I do it to create another level of support and accountability.

- I'll sometimes text an encouraging message. This is not common. However, if my relationship with a given client suggests it's okay, and doing so will help to get that person over some obstacle we've been working on, I'll do it. For instance, I recently texted a mom, who was feeling down about her efficacy, to say what an excellent parent I believe she is.

   The one thing I don't do is attempt an intervention through texting. I prefer to do that face-to-face or over the phone if it can't wait.

SIDEBAR 18.1

There are numerous calculation tricks that you can show kids or teach them to perform. An easy one is David Copperfield's "Calculation Mystery #2," which appears in his *Project Magic Handbook* that I referenced in Sidebar 16.1 in Chapter 16. For this trick all you need is a calculator (which many kids have on their cell phones), a piece of paper and pen, your mind puppet (see Sidebar 3.1 in Chapter 3), and the ability to remember three numbers: 7, 11, and 13 (take the inability to remember these three numbers as a sign that you need a vacation, preferably near a beach and with tropical beverages within reach).

Ask the kid to take out her cell phone, launch her calculator, and enter any three-digit number, telling her to be sure to not let you see her calculator at any time during the trick. Ask her also to write that number down on a piece of paper and to fold it. Now tell her to repeat the same number again. So, let's say the number is 687. After the second instruction 687,687 should appear on the calculator (you can give her an example to make sure she's done it correctly). Tell her that you will now use your mind puppet to perform three magical calculations. Tell her to think of her large number (i.e., 687,687) as you have your mind puppet read her mind. Then have the mind puppet apparently give you a number. You then say, "Please divide your number by 7. My mind puppet has told me that 7 will divide evenly into your number and that the result will not be a fraction." (It won't be a fraction.) Repeat the mind puppet sequence again, but this time choose the number 11, repeating that the result will once again be an even number. Now get a serious look on your face, stating that your mind puppet will now need to tell you a number to divide that will get the calculator to display your kid's original number. Mimic the mind reading again, then say, "My mind puppet has told me that dividing the number on your calculator by 13 will get you back to your original number." The original number will then appear. Do this a few times yourself to be sold that the math always works that way. You could also make some hay about the number 13 if you'd like, given its cultural association with things unlucky (e.g., if you wanted to challenge concepts like bad luck).

REFERENCES AND BIBLIOGRAPHY

Csikszentmihalyi, M. (2008). *Flow: The psychology of optimal experience*. New York, NY: HarperCollins.

Freud, A. (1992). *The ego and the mechanisms of defense*. London, UK: Karnac Books.

Menninger, K. (1952). *Theory of psychoanalytic technique*. New York, NY: Basic Books.

APPENDICES

APPENDIX A

Intake Forms

Parent Questionnaire
David J. Palmiter, Jr., PhD, ABPP

Name of Child: _____ Today's Date: _____

Address: _____

_____

Telephone(s): _____ May I leave messages at home?   Yes   No
          (Home)

_____ _____ Is it okay to call work #?   Yes   No
   (Work)   (Other)

                         May I leave messages at work?   Yes   No

_____ _____ May I leave messages on cell?   Yes   No
 (Cell Phone)   (Cell Phone)

E-Mail Address: _____ Phone # of Parent Not in the Home: _____

Age of Child: _____ Birth Date: _____

Describe your reason for seeking help: _____

_____

_____

Who referred you to this office? _____

When was the last time your child was examined by a physician? _____

Name of Physician: _____ Phone: _____

(continued)

Parent Questionnaire (*continued*)

List any major health problems for which your child receives treatment: _____

_____

If your child ever received a psychological evaluation or treatment for behavioral concerns, please describe such: _____

_____

List the members of your family and all others *in the primary home*:

Name	Age	Relationship to Child	Occupation/Grade

List birth parents, stepparents, siblings, or stepsiblings who are *not living in the home*:

Name	Age	Relationship to Child	Occupation/Grade

Please circle if you have any concerns about this topic in regard to your child or teen:

Nervousness	Sexual Abuse	Physical Abuse	Separation
Headaches	Stomachaches	Enuresis (Wetting)	Anger
Memory	Sleep	Encopresis (Soiling)	Alcohol
Health Problems	Concentration	Death of a Loved One	Drugs
Legal Matters	Doing Chores	Nightmares	Grades
Appetite	Food Problems	Cruelty to Animals	Energy
Loneliness	Doing Homework	Suicidal Thoughts	Depression
Divorce Issues	School Behavior	Home Behavior	Self-Control
Peer Relationships	Running Away	Tiredness	Hyperactivity

Other: _____

David J. Palmiter, Jr., PhD, ABPP
304 Royal Oaks Dr.
Clarks Summit, PA 18411

Welcome to my practice. I am delighted that you have been in touch with me for service and realize what a big step you are taking. As facilitating our relationship is important to me, I've written this handout so that you may review my policies and practices before we begin. Please ask questions, at any time, about any aspect of my policies or our work together.

I am a doctoral-level, licensed clinical psychologist with a diploma in clinical psychology from the American Board of Professional Psychology. I am also a university professor, a past president of the Pennsylvania Psychological Association, and a Fellow of the American Psychological Association, the American Academy of Clinical Psychology, and the Pennsylvania Psychological Association. I have numerous professional publications and over 25 years of clinical experience working with children, adolescents, and adults across a variety of settings. My various diplomas and license to practice are hanging in the waiting area and my complete resume is available for review at www.palmiter.com. If our work together leads to problems beyond my scope of practice, I will try to help you to find another provider who might be a better fit.

Our initial appointment begins an evaluation; at this appointment we will review your concerns and history. I have two primary goals for this evaluation. First, I will try to figure out what might be causing the problems that have brought you in. Second, I will attempt to make a plan for eliminating, controlling, or reducing the problems as fast as possible. In order for me to do a good job for you I will need to ask you questions about both current and past events and issues. I will also need to ask you questions about family members and other important people, situations, and events. Finally, I will also give you rating forms to complete at home and may request that you provide me with relevant records. A typical adult evaluation takes two sessions while a typical child or adolescent evaluation takes three sessions; in each instance, I spend considerable time on my own going through my notes, scoring and interpreting rating scales, and reviewing records. At the end of the evaluation I will share my impressions and recommendations with you. If we decide we share enough common ground to work together, I will be sure to lay out the details of any treatment, before we begin, so that you know what's involved. If one or both of us believes that it does not make sense for us to work together, I will try to help you find viable alternatives.

TREATMENT

If we enter into a treatment relationship, one of our first tasks will be to set up goals for our work. It is important that these goals be as measurable and as objective as possible. With such goals formulated we will be able to identify whether or not our work is having the desired effect(s). Once we set the goals, I will explain to you how the therapy will attempt to be helpful; it's important that you understand the principles behind what we will be doing. I hope to make our time together very worthwhile for you, as well as anyone else in your family with whom I may end up working. Counseling can be very helpful for many individuals; however, there can be some risks. The risks may include a range of unpleasant thoughts and feelings that can be associated with discovering truths. However, it is important to remember that these thoughts and feelings can be an important part of the therapy process, a process that is ultimately designed to promote healing and improvement. Other risks include not getting better, recalling unpleasant memories, and coming to perspectives that may be challenging to your current relationships and/or life circumstances. Through the course of therapy, clients sometimes make some significant changes, including decisions to realign families, to develop other relationships, to change jobs, and to change lifestyles. These decisions can be a natural outcome of healing or coming to look at life in a new way. At all points in our work I would be available to discuss any potential advantages or disadvantages to any aspect of what we do together.

APPOINTMENTS

My services are typically provided by appointment only. Therapy sessions are usually scheduled for a 50-minute slot; this does not include the time I spend preparing for the session and charting what we discussed. Evaluation and testing appointments are usually longer. When we schedule an appointment my time is reserved exclusively for you or your family member. For this reason, you will be charged for any appointments that are not canceled with at least 48 hours' notice, even when you have a good reason. Failure to provide a 48-hour notice of cancellation generally means that some other person is not able to use that appointment time and that it will go unfilled. Unlike other types of professionals, it would not be appropriate for me to double schedule hours in order to compensate for anticipated missed appointments. Charges for missed appointments cannot be submitted for health insurance reimbursement. Please initial here to indicate that you have read, understand, and agree to this policy:

_____

MESSAGES

During times that I am unavailable, or not in the office, my voice mail is available. I check for messages frequently during the daytime Monday through Friday. I am able to return a large majority of my calls the same day. However, since I am a solo practitioner in an outpatient setting, I cannot guarantee around-the-clock or weekend availability. Therefore, if you should experience a crisis, and I am not available, you should proceed to the emergency room that is closest to you. We may discuss which emergency room might be appropriate for you if we anticipate such a need. Because I am interested in maximizing the security of our communications, I generally avoid using e-mail and texting to communicate about sensitive topics; however, I am open to using these technologies to complete simple administrative tasks such as scheduling or rescheduling appointments.

OTHER PSYCHOLOGICAL SERVICES

I offer other services besides psychotherapy. These include psychological testing and facilitation, as well as problem solving, in challenging situations, including divorce, parenting conflicts, and other human relationships; I also offer consultation to individuals seeking to have questions answered about other members of their family, friends, and so on. Psychological services provided by phone are available, including communicating with those with whom we've agreed I will speak.

Sometimes the nature of a person's problems indicate that hospitalization, or the use of medication, should be considered. However, I do not prescribe medication or admit people into hospitals. In cases in which medication or hospitalization may be indicated, I would be available to work cooperatively with the physician of your choosing; I may also help you to identify an appropriate provider. (Please be advised that all consultation services are billed at the same hourly rate as my treatment services.) It would also generally be the case that clients who seek our medication treatment from a physician would do so while continuing psychological treatment with me.

RESOURCES OUTSIDE OF OUR VISITS

I have a website (www.helpingfamilies.com), a blog (www.hecticparents.com), and a Twitter page (www.twitter.com/HelpingParents). I also have a parenting book, *Working Parents, Thriving Families: 10 Strategies That Make a Difference*, and multiple online videos (please see my website for links to the latter). My clients are encouraged to use any and all of these resources.

You may find that I have a presence on social networking sites. As I take every reasonable step in my power to be of maximum service to you, I do not accept invitations from clients to network on these sites. The collective experience in my field, as well as my personal experience, is that psychologists are most likely to be of help to their clients if they do not have parallel relationships on social networking sites. If you have questions or concerns about this, please let me know.

It is not my practice to do Internet searches on my clients, as I generally rely exclusively on the information my clients have agreed to provide for me. However, in matters that could involve significant safety or risk issues (both mental and physical), or in matters that could significantly affect my clinical effectiveness, I reserve the right to use this source of information. However, this is uncommon in my practice.

PSYCHOLOGICAL TESTING

At times it may be beneficial to perform psychological testing. The decision to assess using psychological instruments would be discussed in advance. The discussion would include the nature of the tests to be utilized and what helpful goals the testing would hope to accomplish. However, professional ethics and copyright regulations mandate that the psychological tests themselves are not to be distributed to clients. It would often be necessary to schedule a four- to five-hour block of time in order to administer the tests. I would then spend additional time scoring the tests, interpreting the data, writing a report, and sharing the results. A written report for client review may also be provided depending on what was agreed to before the testing began.

TERMINATION

I work to make my services obsolete as soon as possible. That said, sometimes clients wish to stop the work before the goals have been realized. I request that if you make a decision to terminate before we have discussed it, that we schedule a termination session. If done properly, termination can be a constructive, useful process. If a referral is warranted, it would be made at that time. Of course, termination of our work may occur at any time.

CLIENT RIGHTS

At any time, any client may question and/or refuse therapeutic or diagnostic procedures or methods, or gain whatever information he or she wishes to know about the process and course of therapy. Each client is also assured of confidentiality that is protected by the professional ethics code of the American Psychological Association and Pennsylvania state law. There are, however, important exceptions to confidentiality that are legally mandated. A very large majority of my clients never have to deal with these issues. However, you need to know about the most common of these exceptions before we begin the first appointment. In general terms, the exceptions most likely to come up in my practice include the following: (1) instances that a client has an intention to harm either himself/herself and/or others; (2) instances where there is a *reasonable suspicion* of a minor being neglected or abused (i.e., physically or emotionally), whether that minor is a client of mine or not; (3) a subpoena is issued for records within the context of a legal case (e.g., the psychological functioning of the client is deemed a relevant variable); of course, in these instances the court would first have to know about our therapy relationship. Confidentiality will be respected in all cases, except as previously noted, and in those unusual cases where my clinical judgment suggests that the maintenance of confidentiality is potentially life-threatening or seriously harmful; in these rare situations, I would normally discuss all relevant matters with my client/guardian, unless I determine that doing so could be harmful. In the event that a subpoena for records or testimony is received, the policy will be that (1) I will notify the client/guardian about the subpoena; (2) the client/guardian must either provide me with a waiver of objection to the subpoena or indicate that an objection will be filed (with a copy provided to me) if it is desired that I not release records; and (3) if an objection to the subpoena is to be filed, it is the responsibility of the client/guardian to have it filed with the court. All services and expenses incurred by me for court-related issues would be charged to the client/guardian and subject to my regular payment policies (i.e., any time required for contacts with attorneys, depositions, or courtroom proceedings will be subject to the established professional fee and the regular payment policies). Please also note that my hourly fee for services attached to legal proceedings is higher than my fee for traditional clinical services.

CLIENTS WHO ARE DEPENDENTS

If you are requesting my services as the guardian or parent of a child or adult, the same policies as previously outlined still apply. However, to be an effective therapist it is important that your dependent be able to trust me and remain open. As such, I will keep confidential that which is discussed in sessions. As the parent or guardian, you have the right for general information about our work, and I'm happy to provide such; it is the specific content that your dependent shares with me that I must keep private. In general, I plan to not release specific information that your dependent provides to me; however, I will frequently initiate discussions about both your role in treatment and the progress of the work. As a parent or guardian, you clearly need to know what is going on and agree with the overall plan and progress.

CHARGES

The charges for my services are based on what I believe is fair given my qualifications and the local marketplace. Unless we arrange otherwise, all fees are due at the time that services are rendered. It is helpful if you make the check for payment out in advance of the session so that all of our time may be spent doing our work. Additional services that generate a charge:

▶ Telephone consultations that add up to more than 10 minutes a week.

▶ Time spent consulting with parties with whom we've agreed I will communicate.

▶ Commuting to and from locations at which I will be providing you a service (e.g., a school, a courtroom, etc.).

▶ Time spent providing a service at an out-of-office location.

▶ Writing a report at your request (please keep in mind that my standard evaluation fee does not include time to write a report, unless we have explicitly agreed to a fee adjustment as part of our original agreement).

- ► Completing insurance forms, or forms from other parties, at your request.

- ► Time spent reading correspondences and responding to them, whether online or by hardcopy.

Fees for telephone and out-of-office services are due at the time of the next appointment. Please initial here to indicate that you have read, understand, and agree to my policy on charges:

____

INSURANCE

I am licensed by the state of Pennsylvania to provide the services you are receiving from me. After each service is completed, I will provide you with a statement that you can submit to your health insurance company for reimbursement. This statement typically includes all of the information that most health insurance companies need from me, though they typically will ask you to attach their cover form(s) to my statement(s). Though I do not run into this often, some insurance companies may require additional information. I will release that information to them with your permission (please see the previous section about charges). If you wish, I will discuss with you the information that I am releasing to your insurance company. Please keep in mind that health insurance companies are varied, even across their own plans, in regard to what services they cover, at what rates, and from which providers. For these reasons I can make no promises regarding what a given insurance company will remit back to you. However, please let me know if I can be of any help with this.

I again welcome you to our work together. It is my hope that our time together will benefit you. Your signature below indicates that you have read, understand, and agree with all of the policies in this six-page document.

___________________________   ________________

Client Signature   Date

___________________________   ________________

Signature of Parent or Guardian   Date

___________________________   ________________

Therapist Signature   Date

APPENDIX B

Family Psychiatric History Forms

Maternal Family Psychiatric History Form
David J. Palmiter, Jr, PhD, ABPP

Please indicate with a dash mark if the person's history does not include the problem (now or in the past), a checkmark if the person has a history of difficulty in that area, and a question mark if you do not know. (Birth mother = birth mother of the person being evaluated, and so forth.)

	Birth Mother	Maternal Grandmother	Maternal Grandfather	Maternal Aunt1	Maternal Aunt2	Maternal Uncle1	Maternal Uncle2
Anger control							
Attention, hyperactivity, or impulse control							
Problems learning in school							
Disordered eating							
Rages or euphoria							
Hallucinations							
Very unusual ideas or beliefs							
Depression >2 weeks							
Anxiety >2 weeks							
Alcohol abuse							
Drug abuse							
Criminal behavior							
Perpetrator of domestic violence							
Victim of domestic violence							
Perpetrator of sex abuse							
Victim of sex abuse							

Paternal Family Psychiatric History Form
David J. Palmiter, Jr., PhD, ABPP

Please indicate with a dash mark if the person's history does not include the problem (now or in the past), a checkmark if the person has a history of difficulty in that area, and a question mark if you do not know. (Birth father = birth father of the person being evaluated, and so forth.)

	Birth Father	Paternal Grandmother	Paternal Grandfather	Paternal Aunt1	Paternal Aunt2	Paternal Uncle1	Paternal Uncle2
Anger control							
Attention, hyperactivity, or impulse control							
Problems learning in school							
Disordered eating							
Rages or euphoria							
Hallucinations							
Very unusual ideas or beliefs							
Depression >2 weeks							
Anxiety >2 weeks							
Alcohol abuse							
Drug abuse							
Criminal behavior							
Perpetrator of domestic violence							
Victim of domestic violence							
Perpetrator of sex abuse							
Victim of sex abuse							

Sibling and Cousin Psychiatric History Form
David J. Palmiter, Jr., PhD, ABPP

Please indicate with a dash mark if the person's history does not include the problem (now or in the past), a checkmark if the person has a history of difficulty in that area, and a question mark if you do not know. (Brother = birth brother of the person being evaluated, and so forth.)

	Brother	Sister	Brother	Sister	Cousin1	Cousin2	Cousin3
Anger control							
Attention, hyperactivity, or impulse control							
Problems learning in school							
Disordered eating							
Rages or euphoria							
Hallucinations							
Very unusual ideas or beliefs							
Depression >2 weeks							
Anxiety >2 weeks							
Alcohol abuse							
Drug abuse							
Criminal behavior							
Perpetrator of domestic violence							
Victim of domestic violence							
Perpetrator of sex abuse							
Victim of sex abuse							

APPENDIX C

Developmental History Form

Developmental History
David J. Palmiter, Jr., PhD, ABPP

Child's Name: _____   Person Completing _____
                                    this Form:

Child Care

Who cares for this child when s/he is not with parents (list all): _____

_____

How many hours a week is the child in the care of someone besides a parent (please list the average hours per person, per week, on average): _____

_____

Family History

Does it seem that this child is closer to one parent than the other?
Yes   No   If yes, who: _____

Is one person more responsible for discipline than the other?
Yes   No   If yes, who: _____

What discipline methods are used: _____

(continued)

Developmental History (*continued*)

Family History (*continued*)

If this child's birth parents are no longer together, how often does the child see the noncustodial parent:

Weekly or More _____   Once or Twice a Month _____

A Few Times a Year _____   Never _____

What type of residence does the child live in:

Apartment _____   Single Home _____   Other (Explain) _____

Family Rituals

Check those activities that the child does with the family just about every week, and indicate for how many hours it occurs:

☐ Meals (TV on) _____   ☐ Sports _____   ☐ Religious Services _____

☐ Meals (TV off) _____   ☐ Walks _____   ☐ Board Games _____

☐ Other (please list each weekly ritual and how many hours is spent doing it, on average, each week): _____

_____

_____

_____

List any nonholiday, special occasions that your family celebrates with traditions that have been maintained over the years that involve this child (e.g., birthdays, anniversaries, etc.): _____

_____

_____

_____

List any holidays or events that your family celebrates with traditions that have been maintained over the years that involve this child (e.g., Independence Day, Passover, Christmas, etc.): _____

_____

_____

_____

(*continued*)

Developmental History (*continued*)

Child Characteristics

What are this child's personality strengths: _____

_____

_____

_____

_____

What is good about this child's behavior: _____

_____

_____

_____

_____

List any special talents this child has (i.e., few children are as good at the thing as this child): _____

_____

_____

_____

_____

What do you find to be the most challenging thing(s) about raising this child: _____

_____

_____

_____

_____

Pregnancy

Was this pregnancy planned?   Yes   No

Was the mother under a doctor's care?   Yes   No

# of previous pregnancies/miscarriages: _____

(*continued*)

Developmental History (*continued*)

Pregnancy (*continued*)

Check if any of the following complications occurred:

☐ Difficulty Conceiving ☐ Toxemia ☐ Significant Worsening of Mood

☐ Lack of Support ☐ Anemia ☐ Vaginal Bleeding

☐ Excessive Weight Gain ☐ Measles ☐ Excessive Weight Gain

☐ Prescribed Bed Rest ☐ Flu ☐ Excessive Swelling

☐ Gestational Diabetes ☐ High Blood Pressure

☐ Other (e.g., Rh incompatibility, etc.): _____

☐ Restricted Activity (describe): _____

☐ Maternal Injury (describe): _____

_____

☐ Hospitalization During Pregnancy (describe): _____

☐ X-rays During Pregnancy (describe, including month): _____

☐ Medications Taken During Pregnancy (include months): _____

☐ Alcohol Use During Pregnancy (include amount & months): _____

☐ Smoking During Pregnancy (include amount & months): _____

Birth

Mother's age at birth: _____   Father's age at birth: _____

Mother's age at birth of the first child if this child is not the first child: _____

If this child was not born in a hospital, please describe: _____

Length of pregnancy: _____ weeks   Birth weight: _____ lbs _____ oz

Length of labor: _____ hours

Apgar score (if you don't recall, was it normal?): _____

Mother's physical and mental condition at birth and immediately afterward: _____

(*continued*)

Developmental History (*continued*)

Birth (*continued*)

Child's condition at birth and immediately afterward: _____

_____

Check if any of the following occurred during delivery and afterward:

☐ Forceps Used ☐ Induced ☐ C-section

☐ Use of Anesthesia ☐ Difficulty Breathing ☐ Breech Birth

☐ Use of Oxygen; How Long: _____ ☐ Jaundiced

☐ Bilirubin Lights; How Long: _____

☐ Incubator; How Long: _____

Please describe any birth-related complications: _____

_____

_____

_____

Length of stay in hospital for mother: _____ days; child: _____ days

Was the birth father supportive through the delivery and birth:
Yes   No;   If no, please explain: _____

_____

_____

_____

Development

Was this child breastfed?   Yes   No

If not, for what reason(s): _____

If yes, when weaned: _____

Was this child bottlefed?   Yes   No

If yes, when weaned: _____

(continued)

Developmental History (*continued*)

Development (*continued*)

At what age—year and month—did the child do each of the following on a consistent basis:

Turn Over: _____   Walk Down Stairs: _____

Sit Up Alone: _____   Respond to Sounds: _____

Crawl: _____   Understand First Words: _____

Stand Alone: _____   Speak First Words: _____

Walk Alone: _____   Speak in Sentences: _____

Walk Up Stairs: _____   Engage in Conversations: _____

Toilet-Trained Daytime: _____   Toilet-Trained Nights: _____

Play Independently: _____   Share With Other Children: _____

If you have or had any concerns about this child's developmental milestones or if there are issues that might be useful for the evaluating clinician to know about, please describe here: _____

_____

If wetting or soiling reemerged after toilet training was accomplished (including at night), please describe: _____

Were medical causes evaluated and found for any elimination problems: _____

_____

Has this child displayed consistent problems in any of the following areas? If yes, please describe:

Walking or Running No   Yes _____

Communicating   No   Yes _____

Colic   No   Yes _____

Eating   No   Yes _____

Weight   No   Yes _____

Sleeping   No   Yes _____

Riding a Bike   No   Yes _____

Skipping   No   Yes _____

Throwing   No   Yes _____

(continued)

Developmental History (*continued*)

Development (*continued*)

Catching   No   Yes _____

Separating   No   Yes _____

Excessive Crying   No   Yes _____

Excessive Anger   No   Yes _____

Excessive Sadness   No   Yes _____

Excessive Worry   No   Yes _____

Excessive Shyness   No   Yes _____

With what hand does this child . . .

. . . write or draw: Left   Right

. . . eat: Left   Right

. . . throw: Left   Right

Was this child ever required to change hand preference?   No   Yes

If yes, please explain: _____

_____

At what time does this child, on average . . .

. . . go into bed on school nights: _____   . . . go into bed on nonschool nights: _____

. . . fall asleep on school nights: _____   . . . fall asleep on nonschool nights: _____

. . . get up on school days: _____   . . . get up on nonschool days: _____

Has there been any report of this child falling asleep in school?   No   Yes
(please explain if yes): _____

_____

Does this child tend to take naps during the day?   No   Yes
(please explain if yes, including length of naps and frequency): _____

_____

Does this child complain about nightmares?   No   Yes
(please explain if yes): _____

_____

(continued)

Developmental History (*continued*)

Development (*continued*)

Does this child complain about waking in the early morning hours and not being able to fall back asleep?   No   Yes
(please explain if yes): _____

_____

How many days out of the past month would you estimate that this child sweat and breathed hard for at least 60 minutes a day: _____

_____

How many hours on **school days** does this child . . .	How many hours on **nonschool days** does this child . . .
watch TV: _____	watch TV: _____
play on the computer: _____	play on the computer: _____
read (nonhomework): _____	read (nonhomework): _____
play video games that lead to perspiration: _____	play video games that lead to perspiration: _____
play sedentary video games: _____	play sedentary video games: _____
socialize face-to-face (outside school): _____	socialize face-to-face: _____ _____

How many meals a day does this child eat: _____

What percentage of the meals that are prepared for the family does this child eat:

_____

What percentage of meals at home are prepared especially for him or her (i.e., she/he won't eat what the family is eating so a unique meal is prepared): _____

How many servings of fruit does this child consume each day: _____

How many servings of vegetables does this child consume each day: _____

How many days, in the past month, would you estimate that this child has had food from a fast-food restaurant (e.g., McDonald's, Wendy's, Burger King, etc.): _____

_____

What percentage of this child's meals are comprised primarily of processed carbohydrates (e.g., pizza, pasta, breads, french fries, etc.): _____

(*continued*)

Developmental History (*continued*)

Development (*continued*)

Does this child snack in between meals?   No   Yes
(If yes, please explain): _____

_____

At what hour does this child tend to stop eating on school nights: _____
Nonschool nights: _____

Medical History

Please indicate if this child has suffered from or experienced any of the following:

☐ German Measles	☐ Measles	☐ Rheumatic Fever
☐ Tonsillectomy	☐ Whooping Cough	☐ Mumps
☐ Swine Flu	☐ Other Surgeries	☐ Scarlet Fever
☐ Chicken Pox	☐ Encephalitis	☐ Asthma
☐ Head Injury	☐ Coma	☐ Loss of Consciousness
☐ Heart Murmur	☐ Sustained Fever	☐ High Fever (104°F or Higher)
☐ Broken Bones	☐ Sinus Problems	☐ Itchy Skin (eczema)
☐ Banging Head	☐ Accident Prone	☐ Grinds Teeth
☐ Bites Nails	☐ Tics/Twitches	☐ Rocks Back and Forth
☐ Speech Defects	☐ Vision Problem	☐ Sucks Thumb
☐ Hearing Problem	☐ Allergies	☐ Significant Constipation
☐ Chronic Cough	☐ Stuttering	☐ Ear Tubes

For any item checked in this "Medical History" section, please describe what happened and the age of the child at the time. Also use this space to describe any other significant medical problems that occurred with this child over the years or which are present now: _____

_____

_____

_____

_____

(continued)

Developmental History (*continued*)

Medical History (*continued*)

Please list any medications (i.e., name and dosage) that this child has taken for longer than 6 months and indicate the age(s) the medication was taken: _____

_____

_____

Date of last vision check: _____ Result: _____

Date of last hearing check: _____ Result: _____

Date of last physical: _____ Result: _____

Name of this child's primary doctor: _____

How often does this child see the primary doctor: _____

Social History

Does this child have any problems relating to other youth?   Yes   No
If yes, please explain: _____

_____

_____

Does this child . . .

. . . argue often with other youth?	Yes	No	. . . act bossy?	Yes	No
. . . prefer to play alone?	Yes	No	. . . act shy?	Yes	No
. . . prefer to hang out with younger kids?	Yes	No	. . . act in an eccentric way?	Yes	No
. . . prefer to hang out with older youth?	Yes	No	. . . hit other kids?	Yes	No
. . . associate with kids who get in trouble?	Yes	No	. . . act like a leader or take on leadership roles?	Yes	No

Do the child's friends . . .

. . . smoke?	Yes	No	. . . drink alcohol?	Yes	No
. . . get in trouble at school?	Yes	No	. . . use drugs?	Yes	No
. . . get in trouble with the police?	Yes	No	. . . skip school?	Yes	No

(*continued*)

Developmental History (*continued*)

Educational History

If this child attends or attended a preschool, did anyone have any concerns?   Yes   No
If yes, please explain: _____

_____

_____

If this child attends or attended kindergarten, did anyone have any concerns?   Yes   No
If yes, please explain: _____

_____

_____

Please check if your child has a history of any of the following at school:

☐ Detentions   ☐ Suspensions   ☐ Expulsions

☐ IEP   ☐ 504 Plan   ☐ Fist Fights

☐ Failing Grades   ☐ Tutoring at School   ☐ Underachieving

☐ Math Problems   ☐ Reading Problem   ☐ Regular Trips to the Nurse

☐ Grade Retention   ☐ Frequent Tardiness   ☐ >10 Days/Year Not in School

☐ Personality Conflicts With Teachers

Please explain any of the above that you have checked: _____

_____

_____

_____

_____

_____

_____

Please indicate if you have any concerns about how your child is being educated:

_____

_____

_____

_____

(*continued*)

Developmental History (*continued*)

Miscellaneous

Please indicate if any of the following have been true about this child for at least one year:

Requires too much parent attention	Yes	No	Doesn't handle change well	Yes	No
Easily overstimulated	Yes	No	Easily irritated	Yes	No
Has problems attending to academics	Yes	No	Difficult to calm down	Yes	No
Does not seem happy	Yes	No	Worries easily	Yes	No
Seems overly wound up in play	Yes	No	Impulsive	Yes	No
Uncomfortable in new situations	Yes	No	Overreacts to problems	Yes	No
Hides feelings	Yes	No	Pouts often	Yes	No

Current extracurricular involvements that this child takes part in (please indicate how many hours/week are spent in the activity): _____

_____

Past extracurricular involvements: _____

_____

_____

Are there any extracurricular involvements that your child has expressed an interest in but that have not been tried yet: _____

_____

What is this child's curfew on weeknights: _____ How about on weekend nights: _____

If this child has ever received mental health services, please indicate the following:

Name of the provider: _____

Approximate length of contact: _____

Diagnostic impression shared by the provider: _____

The goals for the work: _____

The methods used to reach the goals (i.e., type of therapy or therapies): _____

_____

(In the above space you've indicated information for the first mental health provider. If this child received additional mental health services, please use the back of this page to list the same information for each provider.)

(*continued*)

Developmental History (*continued*)

Miscellaneous (*continued*)

How many hours a month does this child do something pleasurable, *just one-on-one*, with any of the following adults (put "N/A" if the child doesn't have such a person in his or her life):

Mom _____ Dad _____   Stepmom _____   Stepdad _____

Maternal   Paternal   Maternal
Grandmother _____   Grandmother _____   Relative _____

Maternal   Paternal   Paternal
Grandfather _____   Grandfather _____   Relative _____

Other (please indicate who) _____

Please indicate if any family members use any of the following Internet resources, whether accessed through a computer, cell phone, or tablet:

Type of Site	Name of Family Member(s) (use the back page if you need more space)	Average Hours a Week (rough estimates are fine)
Facebook or similar site		
Twitter, Snapchat, or similar site		
YouTube		
Online gaming		
Online role-playing		
Doing work tasks		
Random surfing		
Other (please indicate type of site)		

Please describe the controls you use for Internet, music, and other media (just put "none" if that's the case): _____

_____

_____

_____

_____

(*continued*)

Developmental History (*continued*)

Miscellaneous (*continued*)

How would you evaluate the following (place a check in the appropriate box):

	Very Poor	Poor	A Little Poor	In Between	Barely Okay	Good	Very Good
Your self-care							
Your happiness							
Your partner's self-care							
Your partner's happiness							
Your care of your relationship with your partner							
Your partner's care of the relationship with you							
Happiness in your relationship with your partner							

Do you have concerns about the mental health of any other family members?
Yes   No. If yes, please elaborate: _____

_____

_____

Please imagine that you are in the future and that you have finished the work at this office and it has been highly successful. What will be different for your child and/or your family: _____

_____

_____

_____

What are your top goals as a parent or guardian: _____

_____

_____

(continued)

Developmental History (*continued*)

Miscellaneous (*continued*)

What are your top hopes for this child as an adult: _____

_____

_____

_____

Please indicate any other information that could be helpful to the person conducting
this evaluation: _____

_____

_____

_____

Interpersonal Inventory

Name: _____   Date: _____

Please make a list of the important people in your life (you may use the back of this sheet). Then, place these people in the various circles shown, based on how close or connected you feel to each of them, even if things are not always positive.

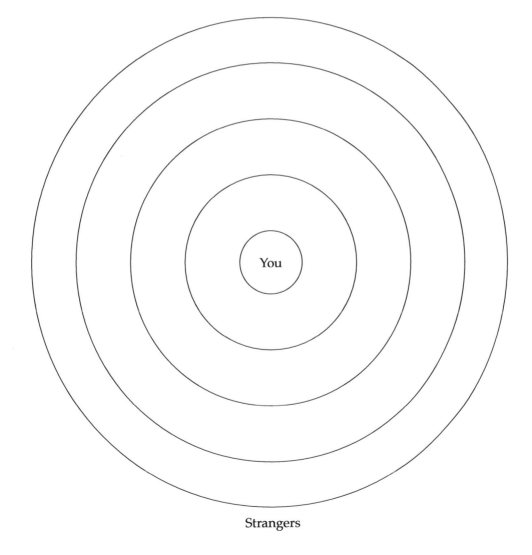

Strangers

APPENDIX E

Sentence Completion Tasks

Sentence Completion Task for Children
David J. Palmiter, Jr., PhD, ABPP

Name: _____   Date: _____

Please complete each of the following sentences (don't skip any):

I like to _____.

Most kids _____.

A teacher is _____.

I'm happy about _____.

Boys are _____.

I'm _____.

If I wasn't afraid I'd _____.

A dad is _____.

I'm sad about _____.

I'm worried about _____.

If I was sure I wouldn't get caught _____.

When I do well _____.

A mom is _____.

Girls are _____.

(continued)

Sentence Completion Task for Children (*continued*)

Grades are _____.

Brothers are _____.

I hate to _____.

School is _____.

I get mad about _____.

When I'm grown up I'll _____.

A secret I have is _____.

My friends _____.

Sisters are _____.

Sports are _____.

I think divorce _____.

Kids who take pills _____.

When my parents are together they _____.

Weekends are _____.

If I was in charge _____.

I think counseling is _____.

When it's time to do homework _____.

When I play video games _____.

College is _____.

My future is _____.

When I screw up _____.

I'm most sorry for _____.

When my friends text me _____.

The past _____.

I'm happiest about _____.

Food is _____.

I ought to be allowed to _____.

I feel guilty about _____.

I'm afraid of _____.

(*continued*)

Sentence Completion Task for Children (*continued*)

I'd never admit to _____.

Pets are _____.

Going to bed _____.

My body _____.

Grandparents are _____.

Being bullied _____.

Teen Sentence Completion Task
David J. Palmiter, Jr., PhD, ABPP

Name: _____   Date: _____

Please complete each of the following sentences (don't skip any):

I like to _____.

Most teens _____.

A teacher is _____.

I'm happy about _____.

Guys are _____.

I'm _____.

If I had no fear I'd _____.

A dad is _____.

I'm sad about _____.

I'm worried about _____.

If I was sure I wouldn't get caught _____.

When I do well _____.

A mom is _____.

Girls are _____.

Grades are _____.

Siblings are _____.

I hate to _____.

School is _____.

I get mad about _____.

When I'm an adult _____.

A secret I have is _____.

My friends _____.

Alcohol is _____.

Drugs are _____.

(continued)

Teen Sentence Completion Task (*continued*)

Divorce is _____.

Medication is _____.

My parents' relationship is _____.

Weekends are _____.

If I was in charge _____.

I think counseling is _____.

When I think about suicide _____.

Sex is _____.

College is _____.

My future is _____.

When I screw up _____.

I most regret _____.

When I go online I feel _____.

The past _____.

I'm happiest about _____.

Food is _____.

I ought to be allowed to _____.

I feel guilty about _____.

I'm afraid of _____.

I'd never admit to _____.

People who cut themselves _____.

If I could change one thing it'd be _____.

My body _____.

Grandparents are _____.

When people die _____.

APPENDIX **F**

Individual Interview With the Youth

Child/Adolescent Interview
Second Assessment Session

David J. Palmiter, Jr., PhD, ABPP

* Review confidentiality.
* Discuss the kid's reaction to the first session.

1. If you had three wishes, and could wish for anything except for money, or more wishes, what would you wish for? (If a kid says things like "world peace" congratulate him or her but then ask for a more personalized answer.)

    a.

    b.

    c.

2. If you had to be an animal instead of a person, which one would you choose? How come? (Repeat three times total.)

    a.

    b.

    c.

(continued)

Child/Adolescent Interview
Second Assessment Session (*continued*)

3. What job would you like to have when you're older? How come?

4. If you were going to be stuck on a deserted island, where there are no people, for a year, but could take one person with you, who would it be? What would you like about having that person there? If you were allowed a second person, who would you take? How come? If you were allowed a third person, but that's it, no one else for the year, who would you pick? How come?

   a.

   b.

   c.

5. What is your favorite movie? What do you like about it?

6. What is your favorite TV show? What do you like best about it?

7. Favorite recording artist or band? What's your favorite song he/she/they sing? What do you like about it?

8. What's your favorite Internet site? How come?

9. What's your favorite video game? What do you like about it?

10. If you could have a superpower, which one would you choose? How would you use it?

11. If you had the use of a time machine for one hour, how would you use it? How come?

12. If you could share a meal with a famous person, just you and him (or her), who would you choose? What's the question you'd most like answered?

13. If you could meet a famous person who is no longer living, who would it be? What would you most like to ask him or her?

14. What do you like best about your mom?

15. What is something you'd like to change about your mom? (Or, in what way is she less than perfect?)

16. What do you like best about your dad?

(*continued*)

Child/Adolescent Interview
Second Assessment Session (*continued*)

17. What is something you'd like to change about your dad? (Or, in what way is he less than perfect?)

18. What do you like best about yourself?

19. What would you most like to change about yourself? (Or, in what way are you a little less than perfect?)

Ask these questions regarding stepparents, siblings, grandparents, or other important people in the kid's life as relevant.

20. What is your best memory?

21. What is your worst memory?

22. What makes you feel:

    a. Happy

    b. Sad

    c. Mad

    d. Worried or afraid

23. Is your mom more of a happy, sad, mad, or worried person?

24. Is your dad more of a happy, sad, mad, or worried person?

25. How do your mom and dad get along?

26. All parents argue. When your parents argue, what do they argue about? How often do they argue? How do you feel when they argue? (Do this for all households the kid lives in, including how the different households get along.)

27. Do you know anyone who drinks alcohol? Tell me about it.

28. How often do your mom and dad drink? (If not covered yet.)

29. Tell me a secret that you have from your parents.

30. Has anybody ever touched you in a way that he or she was not supposed to? Tell me about it.

(*continued*)

Child/Adolescent Interview
Second Assessment Session (*continued*)

Adolescents, or younger children, if relevant:

31. How many days out of the week do you drink? Average amount? How come you don't drink (if "none")?

32. Same series of questions as #31, regarding marijuana or other relevant drugs.

33. Is there any romance in your life? Tell me about it. (Be careful to not assume heterosexuality.)

34. Have you ever had sex? How often do you have sex? Do you use birth control?

* Conclude interview with a drawing.

APPENDIX **G**

Lethality Evaluation Form

Lethality Checklist
David J. Palmiter, Jr., PhD, ABPP

Client: _____   Date: _____

Suicide Assessment Checklist

_____ Previous attempts

_____ Current suicidal feelings

_____ Current suicide plan (include access to lethal means)

_____ Feelings of hopelessness

_____ Sleep problems

_____ Appetite problems (include weight gain or weight loss)

_____ Concentration problems

_____ Current substance abuse (include smoking)

_____ Psychiatric and substance abuse history

_____ Evidence of impulsivity (e.g., sexual promiscuity, fighting, gambling)

_____ Knowledge of suicide

_____ Family history for suicide attempts

_____ Relevant family psychiatric and substance abuse history

_____ History of runaway behavior (for minors)

(continued)

Lethality Checklist (*continued*)

_____ Available support system

_____ Estimated IQ range

_____ Negative life events/stresses (including whether or not the individual has been or feels victimized or rejected and the degree of vocational satisfaction/frustration)

_____ Evidence of mania

_____ Client states willingness to comply with emergency procedures

_____ Documented consultation

_____ Documented aforementioned items and rationale for plan

Homicide Assessment Checklist

Aforementioned items from suicide checklist plus:

_____ History of violence

_____ Current homicidal feelings

_____ Current plan for violence

_____ Identified target (name, address, and phone number)

APPENDIX **H**

Treatment Plan Form

Treatment Plan
David J. Palmiter, Jr., PhD, ABPP

Problem	Goal	Method	Review Date

_____   _____
Client Signature   Date

_____   _____
Signature of Parent or Guardian   Date

APPENDIX I

Intervention Tracking Log

David J. Palmiter, Jr., PhD, ABPP

Client Name: _____

Intervention	Date	Dates of parent sessions:
☐ Treatment Plan	_____	
☐ Externalizing the Problem Name(s)	_____	Videos shared:
☐ Physiological Calming	_____	
☐ Mindfulness	_____	
☐ Behavioral Activation	_____	
☐ Coping/Happy Thoughts	_____	Magic demonstrated:
☐ Thought Testing	_____	
☐ Problem Solving	_____	
☐ Sleep Hygiene	_____	
☐ Fear Hierarchy	_____	Magic taught:
☐ Gratitude Letter	_____	
☐ Gratitude, Other	_____	
☐ Using Strengths	_____	
☐ Acts of Kindness	_____	
☐ Crisis = Pain + Opportunity	_____	

(continued)

Intervention Tracking Log (*continued*)

☐ Serenity Prayer   _____

☐ Special Time   _____

☐ Token System   _____

☐ Behavioral Contract   _____

☐ Other   _____

APPENDIX J

Recommended Resources

EVALUATION RESOURCES

▶ A nice list of screening tools available for youth can be found on the website of the School Psychiatry Program and MADI Resource Center of Massachusetts General Hospital: http://www2.massgeneral.org/schoolpsychiatry/screeningtools_table.asp.

▶ For an omnibus measure I like the *Behavioral Assessment System for Children* (available at www.pearsonclinical.com), though I sometimes also use the Achenbach system (available at http://www.aseba.org/ordering/howtoorder.html).

▶ For disruptive behavior, I like the *Disruptive Behavior Disorder Rating Scale* (available by purchasing the *Defiant Child* treatment manual from Guilford Press; this resource can be given to both parents and teachers).

▶ For anxiety disorders I like the *Multidimensional Anxiety Scale for Children* (available from several vendors).

▶ For depression I like the *Children's Depression Inventory* (available from several vendors).

▶ For bipolar disorder I like the *Young Mania Rating Scale* (available at http://dcf.psychiatry.ufl.edu/files/2011/05/Young-Mania-Rating-Scale-Measure-with-background.pdf) and the *Parent Version of the Young Mania Rating Scale* (available at http://www.healthyplace.com/images/stories/bipolar/p-ymrs.pdf).

▶ To measure a kid's strengths I like the *Resiliency Scales for Children and Adolescents* (available at www.pearsonclinical.com). See Chapter 12 for other measures designed to assess a kid's strengths (although I usually don't use those during the initial evaluation).

▶ For the screen for parental psychopathology I like the *Symptom Checklist-90–Revised* (available at www.pearsonclinical.com).

STRENGTHS ASSESSMENT

▶ The Values in Action (VIA) Youth Survey: An overview of the psychometrics can currently be found here: bit.ly/1NvgxDk. The link for the survey is currently here: http://bit.ly/1MsJ2o9.

▶ The Clifton Youth StrengthsExplorer: An overview of the psychometrics can currently be found here: bit.ly/1J5tiAc.

▶ StrengthsFinder 2.0: An overview of the psychometrics can currently be found here: bit.ly/1JXGvjZ.

INDEX

acts of kindness, 207–210
acts of kindness tracking form, 210
agitating waits, practicing mindfulness,
    121–122
American Psychological Association, 8
American Psychologist, 9
angry kids, engaging, 70–72
animal magnetism (Mesmer), 57
anxiety disorders, 52, 85
anxious kids, engaging, 72–73
anxious youth, 235–236
appointments, 318

BA. *See* behavioral activation
beauty walks, 123–124
beginning sessions, 127–128
behavioral activation (BA), 96–105, 128
    depression, 105
    explanation, 98–100
    fun activities tracking form, 104
    potentially fun activities, 100–101
biofeedback. *See* relaxation measurement
bipolar mood disorder, 52
body mindfulness, 123
booster sessions, 261–266
    in kid, 263–264
    with parents, 262–263
    See also termination and booster sessions
Breathing Under Water (Rohr), 178

case studies
    Aiden's, 5
        behavioral activation, 96–104
        coping/happy thoughts, 127–138
        engaging angry kids, 70–71
        engaging anxious kids, 73

externalizing the problem, 80–88, 92
fun activities, 101–102
happy thoughts, 130–131
initial interview, 23, 25–26, 30–31, 33
kindness, acts of, 207–208
medical and developmental history, 29
modular treatment approach, 95–96
personal history, 28
psychiatric history, 28
responding to resistance, 69–73
serenity prayer, 176–178
strengths development form, 199–200,
    204–206
substance use, 29
surprising events with parents, 288–296
termination and booster sessions,
    252–264
therapeutic alliance, 63–64
thought testing, 167–174
weekly gratitude list, 135–136
Monica's, 5
    contract, 224
    engaging kids, 235–239
    engaging parent, 241
    exposure phase, 244–246, 263
    externalizing the problem, 91
    feedback session, 40–41
    funeral exercise, 159–161
    mindfulness strategies, 121–124
    parent consultation, 152–158
    parent session, 148–151
    parents working with kids above age
        13, 223–227
    parents working with kids under age
        12, 215–223
    physiological calming, 111–117
    problem solving in family session,
        183–190

case studies (*cont.*)
    problem solving in individual session, 191–195
    surprising events, 271–284, 303, 307–308
    relaxation measurement, 119
    treatment planning, 48, 51
CBT. *See* cognitive behavioral therapy
CD. *See* conduct disorder
charges, financial, 321–322
client rights, 320–321
clients, dependents, 321
cognitive behavioral therapy (CBT), 1, 85, 132, 151, 213, 253
Complete Card Magic—Volume One: Beginner - 14 Easy to Learn Card Miracles (Griffin), 73, 179
conduct disorder (CD), 213
contracts with defiant teens, 223–228
coping thoughts, 128–133
Copperfield, David, 285, 312
countertransference, 66–67, 252, 256, 265, 278, 291, 298, 301, 305, 306, 311
Covey, Stephen, 159
crisis = pain + opportunity, 138–140
Csikszentmihalyi, Mihaly, 302

damage control treatment contracts, 53–54
defiant kids, setting a context, 213–215
developmental history form, 327–341
divorced parent session, 158–159

eating disorders, 52
Emotional Intelligence, 140
engaging
    angry kids, 70–72
    anxious kids, 72–73
establishing foundation, 17–74, 199–201
    feedback and treatment planning, 39–54
    initial evaluation, 19–33
    techniques for facilitating adherence and responding to resistance, 57–74
Ethical Principles of Psychologists and Code of Conduct, 8
ethics, positive, 8

evaluation
    framework on mental health, 19–21
    resources, 361–362
    suicidal ideation, 32
    work in between sessions, 32
Everyday Bias (Ross), 12
exposure nuances, 241–243
exposures
    engaging the kid, 235–240
    engaging the parent, 240–241
    sessions going forward, 243–247
exposure tracking form, 238
externalizing the problem, 79–92
    explanation, 81–90
    homework, 90–91

facilitating adherence
    nonspecific effects, 57–58
    therapeutic alliance, elements of, 59–66
family psychiatric history forms, 323–326
feedback session, 32
    explanation, 42–46
    medication, 46
    outline of, 39–42
form(s)
    acts of kindness tracking, 210
    developmental history, 327–341
    exposure tracking, 238
    family psychiatric history, 323–326
    fun activities tracking, 104
    happy thought tracking, 132
    intake, 315–316
    interpersonal inventory, 30, 343
    intervention tracking log, 92, 359–360
    lethality evaluation, 355–356
    maternal family psychiatric history, 324
    paternal family psychiatric history, 325
    problem solving as a family, 184
    relaxation exercise tracking, 115
    sentence completion tasks, 345–349
    sibling and cousin psychiatric history, 326
    strengths development, 202, 204–205
    strengths development tracking, 205–206
    treatment plan, 357

Franklin, Benjamin, 58
Freud, Anna, 302
fun activities
    list of, 100–101
    tracking form, 104
funeral imagery exercise, 159–162

George Washington University (GWU), 1–3
gratitude, 133–138
    letters, 137
    list, 134–136
Griffin, Gerry, 73, 179
grounding, 228, 230
GWU. *See* George Washington University

happy thought tracking form, 132

Implicit Association Test, Race, 11
individual interview, with youth, 351–354
initial evaluation
    framework of, 19–21
    office, 21–22
    preinterview work, 21
    See also initial interview
initial interview
    chief complaints, 25–26
    conclusion, 29–31
    evaluation phase, 32
    explanation, 23–25
    family history, 27–28
    family psychiatric history, 28–29
    family substance use history, 29
    goals, 31–32
    individual interview with kid, 31–32
    kid substance use, 29
    medical and developmental history, 29
    personal history, 28
    psychiatric history, 28
    psychosocial stress, 26–27
    strengths, 26
insomnia, 106–107
insurance, 322
intake forms, 315–316
interpersonal inventory, 343
intervention tracking log, 92, 359–360

Jermay, Luke, 140

kid–parent relationships, 148–151
kids
    booster sessions in, 263–264
    clinical work with, 301–311
    defiant, 213–215
    engaging anxious kids, 72–73
    engaging the, 235–240
    individual interview with, 31–32
    parent session, 148–151
    parent work, 215–228
    substance use, 29
    surprising events with, 271–285
    termination and booster sessions, 252–256
kindness, acts of, 207–210
kindness tracking form, acts of, 210
King, Martin Luther, Jr., 12

Lavoisier, Antoine, 58
lethality evaluation form, 355–356

Magic for Dummies (Pogue), 299
magic tricks, rationale for using, 5–6
    calculator trick, 312
    card force with a deck of cards, 92
    combination card trick, 299
    dime and nickels, 210
    ESP card trick, 73–74
    four fire trucks, 33
    introduction to kids, 31, 32, 33, 81
    invisible thread, 163–164
    lie detector with playing cards, 179
    magician's choice, 285
    magician's handcuffs, 248–249
    magnetic ring, PK ring, 124
    marked deck of cards, 230
    mentalism with coping/happy thoughts,
        140–141
    mind puppet introduction, 54
    needle through balloon, 141
    Project Magic Handbook (Copperfield), 285,
        312
    radar card trick, 266
    stripper card deck, 196

magic tricks, rationale for using (*cont.*)
Svengali deck of cards, 107–108
thumb tip usage, 179–180
tracking, 92, 359–360
maternal family psychiatric history form, 324
medication, 46
meditation, 123
Menninger, Karl, 306
mental health, evaluation framework on, 19–21
Mesmer, Franz Friedrich Anton, 57
messages, 318–319
mindfulness strategies
agitating waits, 121–122
beauty walks, 123–124
body mindfulness, 123
meditation, 123
mindful eating, 122
mindful photography, 122
modular treatment approach, 95–96
multiculturalism, 9–12

National Sleep Foundation (NSF), 105
nuances
obsessive-compulsive disorder, 247
single-event posttraumatic stress disorder, 247–248

obsessive-compulsive disorder, 52
oppositional defiant disorder (ODD), 213

pain and opportunity, 138–140
parent consultation, 152–159
parent-lunatics, 6–8
parent session
additional parent sessions, 162–163
common questions and concerns, 157–158
for divorced/separated parents, 158–159
preparing kid for, 148–151
timing of, 147–148
parent work with defiant kids
with kids age 13 and older, 223–228
with kids age 12 and under, 215–223
paternal family psychiatric history form, 325

PC. *See* physiological calming
Pennsylvania Psychological Association (PPA), 19
The Pennsylvania Psychologist, 8, 19
pervasive developmental disorders, 52
Phoenix Cards for Magicians (Schenk), 230
physiological calming (PC), 111–118, 128
explanation, 116–118
15-minute script, 111–115
half-hour script, 115–116
play therapy literature, 88–89
Pogue, David, 299
positive ethics, 8
positive psychology (PP), 1, 85, 133, 243, 262
posttraumatic stress disorder (PTSD), 52, 139
PP. *See* positive psychology
PPA. *See* Pennsylvania Psychological Association
problem solving, 184
example, 187
as a family, 184
in family session, 183–190
in individual session, 191–196
Project Magic Handbook (Copperfield), 285, 312
PTSD. *See* posttraumatic stress disorder
punishment
grounding, 230
response cost, 228–229
time-out, 229–230

reactive attachment disorder, 52
recommended resources, 361–362
relaxation exercise tracking form, 115
relaxation measurement, 118–121
resistance, 59–66
engaging anxious kids, 72–73
mental health professionals' response to, 66–72
resources outside of visits, 319
response cost, 228–229
Ross, Howard, 12

Schenk, Christian, 230
schizophrenia, 52

self-disclosure, 306–308
sentence completion tasks, 345–349
separated parent session, 158–159
serenity prayer, 176–178
The 7 Habits of Highly Effective People (Covey), 159
sibling and cousin psychiatric history form, 326
sleep hygiene, 105–107
social networking, 28, 278, 280–282, 298, 303, 319
special time, 147–164, 183, 189, 229, 256, 258, 262–263, 296, 304
strengths assessment, 362
strengths development form, 202, 204–205
strengths development plan, 201–206
strengths development tracking form, 205–206
substance abuse disorder, 52
suicidal ideation, 32
surprising events with kids, 271–285
surprising events with parents, 287–298

termination and booster sessions
    to kid, 252–256
    to parents first, 257–259
    to parents second, 260
termination session, 320
texting clients, 311

therapeutic alliance, elements of, 59–66
thought testing, 167–176
    standard, 172
    weighted, 173
time-out, 229–230
token system, sample, chips, 217
token system, sample, points, 222
transference, 66–67, 298, 306–311
treatment contracts, types of, 52–54
treatment plan form, 357
treatment planning, 46–48
    benefits of, 46–47
    explanation, 48–51
    externalizing the problem, 91
    with kids, 47–48
    remarks with, 51–52
    as a tool to respond to resistance, 66–74
treatment relationship, 317–318

unipolar mood disorders, 52

WAIT, teaching about, 206–207

YouTube, 140

Zeitler, William, 58